THE "OTHER" EIGHTEENTH CENTURY

THE "OTHER" EIGHTEENTH CENTURY

English Women of Letters 1660–1800

Edited by

Robert W. Uphaus and Gretchen M. Foster

EAST LANSING

COLLEAGUES PRESS

1991

ISBN 0-937191-39-6
ISBN 0-937191-40-X (pbk.)
Library of Congress Catalog Card Number 91-70494
British Library Cataloguing in Publication Data available
Copyright © 1991 Colleagues Press

Published by Colleagues Press Inc.
Post Office Box 4007
East Lansing, MI 48826

Distribution outside North America
Boydell and Brewer Ltd.
Post Office Box 9
Woodbridge, Suffolk IP12 3DF
England

Printed in the United States of America

CONTENTS

ACKNOWLEDGMENTS

The editors wish to express their gratitude for assistance received from the following libraries: the Library of Congress, the British Library, the Tonbridge School Library (Mrs. Jean Cook, Librarian), and the Michigan State University Library (Special Collections). In many ways, this textbook is the product of a close collaboration between the editors and past and present staff of Special Collections at Michigan State University — in particular, Peter Berg, Jannette Fiore, and Anne Tracy. All illustrations are reproduced by courtesy of Special Collections, Michigan State University. The editors also wish to acknowledge financial support received from the following units of Michigan State University: the Department of English (Victor Paananen, Chair), the College of Arts and Letters (John Eadie, Dean), and the Office for Research Development (John Cantlon, Vice President). Finally, the editors wish to thank our editorial intern, Kathleen McGarvey, for her meticulous work on this textbook.

INTRODUCTION

SIMPLY STATED, the purpose of this textbook is to reclaim the tradition of women's writing in England during the period 1660–1800 and to restore this tradition to its rightful place in the present-day canon of eighteenth-century literature. As we see it, *The "Other" Eighteenth Century* should enable teachers to alter significantly the way eighteenth-century literature has been customarily taught — that is, as a literature whose major contributors are almost exclusively male — and it should dramatically revise prevailing assumptions about eighteenth-century women's contributions to the canon of English literature. We fully realize that to refer to this rich tradition of women's writing as "other" may appear to be unduly provocative — indeed, may suggest that the editors have acquiesced in the marginalization of women writers.

However, our view is precisely the contrary: we choose "other" to bring this marginalization to the fore and to question conceptions of the eighteenth century that fail to represent the substantial contributions of women authors. By emphasizing "other," we wish to point out that attempting to establish the canon of British women's writing in the period 1660–1800 is not an invention of modern scholarship, but an act of historical recovery. This canon has been largely lost to modern readers, but it was well known to many eighteenth-century readers — male and female.

Put another way, this canon's "otherness" is *not* defined by its absence from eighteenth-century, as distinguished from twentieth-century, discourse. Neither does its "otherness" imply inferiority to the officially recognized, predominantly male, canon of late seventeenth- and eighteenth-century English literature. Rather, the canon's "otherness" derives, we believe, from an unsettling combination of ignorance and distortion of literary history.

If one searches the historical archive, skeptical of the apparently settled state of the traditional canon, one finds a developing and eventually flourishing tradition of women's writing during the period 1660–1800. By tradition, we mean that over time many of the women writers represented in this text demonstrate, first, an awareness that they are writing about women for women and, second, a strong sense that as women writers they belong to an ever-increasing community of women writers. This latter point in no way implies that an evolving tradition of women writers should be treated as a single monolithic construct where all women speak in one voice. To the contrary, the tradition we refer to is marked by diversity, an attribute we have emphasized throughout this

1

book. Because of this diversity of interests — thematic as well as generic — we have chosen to underscore the idea of women of letters, by which we mean that many women writers addressed a variety of issues and expressed a range of concerns that intersected with the kinds of writing produced by their male cohorts. By women of letters, we mean those numerous women writers who competed in the public arena of letters that had been traditionally occupied by men and were recognized for their substantial contributions.

While it would certainly be misleading to imply that women writers were able to sustain themselves economically by establishing a professional career of letters, recent scholarship has clearly established the extent of women's contributions to eighteenth-century literature. Such texts and series as Janet Todd's *Dictionary of British and American Women Writers 1660–1800*, Roger Lonsdale's *Eighteenth-Century Women Poets*, and the Mothers of the Novel reprint series published by Pandora Press have served as valuable historical correctives. By focusing on what we define as women of letters, *The "Other" Eighteenth Century* intends to suggest that one can now usefully speak of the development of a canon of women's literature during the period 1660–1800 and, furthermore, that this canon of women's literature needs to be fully integrated into the teaching and study of English literature from 1660–1800.

Quite significantly, we believe, many of the women of letters included in this book — including, but not limited to, Mary Astell, Aphra Behn, Anne Finch, Elizabeth Carter, Lady Mary Wortley Montagu, Mary Wollstonecraft, Hannah More, Maria Edgeworth, Anna Barbauld — interacted with, and sometimes openly resisted, their better known (that is, more frequently anthologized) male cohorts. Most non-specialist readers, for instance, would recognize only Mary Wollstonecraft's name and therefore assume, quite wrongly, that she is *sui generis*. Such an assumption would seem very strange indeed to literate eighteenth-century readers — women and men.

If we note a few facts about the publishing history of those women writers who chose to publish, we can see how much "otherness," in the sense of exclusion from the canon, is a post-eighteenth-century phenomenon. For one thing, women writers had access to major publishers (Joseph Johnson deserves particular acclaim for his commitment to women authors), as well as editors of widely-circulated magazines (Elizabeth Rowe, for example, first published in John Dunton's *Athenian Mercury* and it was he who sponsored her early poems as the "Pindarick Lady").

Moreover, the works of women writers were republished frequently during the eighteenth century, as even a cursory glance at the *British Museum Catalog of Printed Books* demonstrates.

Furthermore, by the middle of the eighteenth century the first efforts were made to formulate a canon of women's literature in England. Specifically, in 1752 George Ballard (of Magdalen College, Oxford University) published *Memoirs of Several Ladies of Great Britain Who Have Been Celebrated for their Writings or Skill in the Learned Languages, Arts and Sciences*, a modern edition of which has been published by Ruth Perry (Wayne State University Press, 1985). This volume, which includes biographies of sixty-two women writers, was subscribed to by one hundred fifty-two women and two hundred fifty-six men. Three years later, and as a direct consequence of Ballard's *Memoirs*, Bonnell Thornton and George Colman (both subscribers to Ballard's *Memoirs*) published a two-volume edition entitled *Poems By Eminent Ladies* (1755), which includes the works of eighteen women poets.

About the same time *Poems By Eminent Ladies* was published, John Duncombe released his poem *The Feminead* (1754), a celebration of the contributions of English women writers. Among the writers praised are Katherine Philips, Anne Finch, Elizabeth Rowe, and Elizabeth Carter. Twenty years later Mary Scott published a continuation of Duncombe's poem entitled *The Female Advocate* (1774), extending and updating Duncombe's list to include, among others, Anna Barbauld, Lady Mary Chudleigh, Hannah More, Lady Rachel Russell, Catherine Talbot, and Elizabeth Tollet. Finally, by the end of the eighteenth century, perhaps the most popular (and frequently republished) anthologies of English literature were Vicesimus Knox's *Elegant Extracts in Prose* (1783), *Elegant Extracts in Poetry* (1789), and *Elegant Epistles* (1790). These volumes, initially designed for school children but circulated widely to the general reading public, firmly establish—indeed, consolidate—the existence of a coherent and diverse tradition of English women of letters that includes such authors as Anna Barbauld, Elizabeth Carter, Jane Collier, Lady Mary Wortley Montagu, Lady Rachel Russell, and Elizabeth Rowe.

In light of the present-day interest in women's studies, the editors believe the time has arrived to restore this "lost" tradition of women's writing to the front and center of classroom study. Our desire is to transform what has been "other" to its rightful place as focal. In this endeavor we have organized the book in such a way as to provide the reader with the opportunity to take a sustained in-depth look at the range of women's writing from the late seventeenth until the end of the eighteenth century. Unlike typical anthologies, *The "Other" Eighteenth Century* does not adopt a "bits and pieces" approach, where the reader is at best tantalized by a short selection. Rather, *The "Other" Eighteenth Century* includes multiple selections by one writer so that the reader is able to gauge the range of a writer's concerns. Moreover, we have made every effort to use complete poems, plays, essays, letters, and chapters. In addition, this text represents the spectrum of literary modes (other than short fiction and the novel) employed by women of letters; these modes include poetry (of all kinds), literary criticism, the moral essay, the maxim, the educational essay, the epistolary essay, allegory, the sermon, songs, hymns, travel essays, and drama.

No less important, the editors have attempted to organize the collection in such a way as to display both prominent thematic concerns and major conceptual changes that occurred in the course of the growth and influence of women's writing during the period 1660–1800. Here, in brief, are some of the concerns and changes we have attempted to highlight.

The first three selections by Fell, Drake, and Astell address themselves to the ramifications of the longstanding belief in and practice of the subordination of women. Significantly, in Western culture Scripture was thought to sustain this idea of subordination, and since so many women writers were themselves Christians the doctrine of female subordination presented these women with, among other things, a major spiritual dilemma: namely, how does one faithfully practice Christianity if that very Christianity has been used to subjugate women?

Fell and Astell, for example, attack the doctrine of the subordination of women by questioning the interpretive basis of Scripture. That is, they realize that the subordination of women has been sustained by an unexamined tradition of male interpretations of the Bible. Fell demolishes the traditional admonition of women's silence, and we cannot overestimate the deep sense of inferiority such a doctrine inscribed in women. Turning the silencing of women on its head, Fell offers an alternative view of Scripture, in which she argues that "the Church of Christ is a woman, and those that speak against woman's speaking, speak against the Church of Christ." Fully realizing that Scripture does not speak itself, but rather has been spoken through *men*, Fell at once condemns the interpretive practices of men as blinded, perverse, and corrupt at the same time that she establishes a woman's voice that by its very existence defies centuries of silencing.

Astell and Drake, as well, establish voices in defiance of the phenomenon of silencing and attack the subordination of women. They do so in
ways that are both politically astute and trenchant. Both authors see that
the suppression of women's education—that is, the education of a woman's mind and the formation of her moral character, rather than the
customary emphasis on a woman's domestic skills and social graces—
derives from what Drake calls "the Usurpation of Men, and the Tyranny
of Custom (here in *England* especially)." One such custom was the Salique Law, which historically excluded women from the throne of France,
but which became symbolic of the larger doctrine of the prohibition
against women authors—in short, a literary silencing. Quite notably and
effectively, Drake challenges the validity of customary arguments based
on history, for she shrewdly notes: "To say the truth, Madam, I can't tell
how to prove all this from Ancient Records; for if any Histories were
anciently written by Women, Time, and the Malice of Men have effectually conspir'd to suppress 'em."

Drake understands history as HIS-story, but Astell launches the most
telling blow against the subordination of women by grounding her argument in the politics of her time. No person, however biased, could ignore
the force of Astell's appeal to contemporary history—specifically, her
assertion of the practical and symbolic significance of Queen Anne's reign
in England (1702–1714). The "Governor" of England, as Astell quickly
reminds her readers, is now of "the feminine Gender." From this one
observation, Astell not only interrogates the *past* subordination of
women, but she systematically dismantles the scaffolding that supported
the suppression of women. Employing both reason and ridicule, Astell
attacks the complex of assumptions—that is, the assumption of man's
natural superiority, the belief in the Salique Law, the practice of arbitrary
power, the validity of traditional scriptural interpretation, man's patriar-
chal claim to absolute sovereignty in the state and family—that had been
used by men to dominate women. Astell's argument is both destructive
and constructive: she at once reduces the notion of man's natural superiority to utter absurdity when she sarcastically observes that if this notion
were true, then "the greatest Queen [Queen Anne is foremost in her
mind] ought not to command, but to obey, her footman." Yet Astell also
builds a history of women's accomplishments, drawing primarily on
Scripture in a manner reminiscent of Margaret Fell. Moreover, she
updates her history to the present reign of Queen Anne, who serves as
both a role model for "All the great things that women might perform"

and as a compelling contradiction of all the traditional arguments used to support the subordination of women.

In a different, but no less important, manner Aphra Behn and Sarah Egerton defy the silencing of women writers, who were not only proscribed from authorship by the extended assumptions of the Salique Law, but who as writers overcame the further prohibition against women speaking of sexual desire. Both authors do much to challenge the alleged "power" — sexual as well as political — of libertine men. The whole of Behn's play *The Lucky Chance* reveals, implicitly and explicitly, the depth and degree of assumptions about sex and gender in late seventeenth-century England. But for a capsule formulation of the condition of women authors at this time, one can hardly find a more acute analysis than Behn's preface to *The Lucky Chance*.

It is clear from Behn's preface that for a woman not only to become, but to assert publicly, her status as an author was to invite being viewed not simply as a literary rival but as a sexual usurper — that is, as a woman who stakes a claim on man's traditional territory. This, of course, is another twist of the infamous Salique Law, but Behn is not an author who suffers fools silently. She realizes that the language and subject matter of her plays transgress male privilege; hence she comments that "such Masculine Strokes in me, must not be allow'd." Defiantly, she responds to her immediate accusers (and present-day literary historians would do well to consider her challenge): "That had the Plays I have writ come forth under any Mans name, and never known to have been mine; I appeal to all unbyast Judges of Sense, if they had not said that Person had made as many good Comedies, as any one Man that has writ in our Age."

Behn reveals much about the gender assumptions concerning authorship when, near the end of the preface, she pleads: "All I ask, is the Privilidge for my Masculine Part the Poet in me . . . to tread in those successful Paths my Predecessors have so long thriv'd in." The very fact that Behn must "ask" the public to accept her drama *because* she is a woman indicates the virulence of the subordination of women. No less significant and illuminating is Behn's reference to her "Masculine Part the Poet," by which she refers to the power and potency customarily ascribed to male authorship. In her drama, as well as in her many love poems and songs, Behn asserts her own potency and power as a writer and a woman. The strength of her challenge is perhaps symbolically expressed in the poem "The Disappointment," which reduces another kind of "Masculine Part" to impotence.

Sarah Egerton, too, shares Behn's sexual and authorial assertiveness. In both "The Liberty" and "The Emulation" Egerton directly attacks the suppression of women's education and authorship based on specious appeals to what she calls the "Idol Custom" and "Tyrant Custom." Referring to formal education generally and literary authorship specifically, Egerton—perhaps alluding to the reign of Queen Anne—speaks for all aspiring women when she declares, "We will our Rights in Learning's World maintain, / Wits Empire, now, shall know a Female Reign." Just as important, Egerton, like Behn, writes freely of sexual desire—both as pleasure and revulsion. "To Philaster" and "To Alexis" recollect youthful passion, while "To Orabella, marry'd to an old Man" satirically depicts the sexual mismatch between a young woman and an aged man (i.e., "What strong Persuasions made you thus to wed, / With such a Carcass scandalize your Bed?"), at the same time that it undercuts, as does Behn's *Lucky Chance*, the customary (and largely economic) basis of many arranged marriages that victimized younger women.

If Fell, Drake, Astell, Behn, and Egerton are notable for their resistance to the subordination of women, writers like Chudleigh, Philips, Finch and Russell develop, in a less overt manner, a variety of strategies by which they initially accommodate themselves to the phenomenon of subordination and yet eventually establish a unique space for women writers. When we say that these women writers "accommodate" themselves we by no means intend to imply (because we do not believe) that they acquiesced in their suppression. Rather, we wish to call attention to how these writers developed a distinctly female standpoint that enabled them to establish a critique of male assumptions.

For example, Mary Chudleigh emphasizes the distinctly female content and appeal of her poems and essays. She dedicates her *Essays Upon Several Subjects in Prose and Verse* (London, 1710) to Princess Sophia, and regarding her essays she stresses " 'Tis only to the Ladies I presume to present them." Again, in *Poems on Several Occasions* (London, 1709) Chudleigh writes that it is "the Ladies, for whom they are chiefly design'd, and to whose Service they are intirely devoted." Both statements are covert manifestos, in which Chudleigh simultaneously defines her audience of women and dismisses the need for an audience of men. Viewed in this dual context of definition and rejection, Chudleigh's apparent statement of retreat in "To Clorissa"—i.e., "When all alone in some belov'd Retreat, / Remote from Noise, from Bus'ness, and from Strife, / Those constant curst Attendants of the Great; / I freely can with my own Thoughts converse" — is, in fact, an expression of female freedom. The "Great" — whose attendants are "Noise," "Bus'ness," and "Strife" — is a shorthand reference to the world of men at court, where the integrity of self is sacrificed to public persona and ambition.

Chudleigh's idea of retreat, with its implicit critique of male values, recurs in the poetry of Philips and Finch and in the letters of Lady Russell. Despite Philips's reputation, in her time as well as ours, as a genteel writer, an alert reader ought not to miss Philips's continual commentary on the world of male ambition. Her seemingly pastoral celebration of women's retirement establishes its desirability through the repudiation of the male world of "Disguise," "Treachery," "Blood," and "Plots" ("A Retir'd Friendship"); other poems like "Content" and "Wiston Vault" mock male ambition and the desire for public distinction. Even philosophical and religious poems like "The World" and "The Soul" contain within themselves an exposé of largely male vanity, for women were hardly in a position to exercise, to full effect, the vanity of human (translate "male") wishes.

Similar to her acknowledged predecessor Katherine Philips, whom she calls "our most Vertuous Orinda," Anne Finch also employs the retirement motif both to define her own poetic voice and to question the alleged supremacy of traditional male values. The prose "Preface" we include in this book is just as important as Behn's preface to *The Lucky Chance*. Interestingly, Finch's preface was written for an unpublished collection of poems — that is, for a collection she chose not to publish. The preface helps to illuminate the barriers, social and psychological, that affected a woman's decision, first, to write and, second, to publish. To understand the development of woman's writing, we believe it is important to distinguish between women writers and women authors, for the decision by a woman to write did not necessarily mean that she wanted her writing to be published and thus for her to gain a reputation as an author.

This tension between writing (usually for a circle of friends) and publishing informs many of Finch's poems. Finch withheld from publication the prose Preface and most of the poems we include in this anthology. Finch not only assumed a distinction between writing as a private sharing among friends and publishing as a public expression to an unknown audience, but she further distinguished between those poems suitable for publication and those that were not. Unlike Philips, Finch was not as reluctant to become an author, but even as she became an author she reserved a private space for many of her most personal poems. Of the ten poems we include, just three—"To the Nightingale," "Life's Progress," and "A Nocturnal Reverie"—appeared in *Miscellany Poems* (1713). Those poems not published characteristically deal with the effects of being a woman writer in a culture dominated by male assumptions of superiority. In Finch's (private) words, "A woman that attempts the pen" is "an intruder on the rights of men." But what was traditionally perceived as a man's right either failed to recognize, or elected to ignore, a woman's need—namely, the need to write and, eventually, to publish. No other early woman poet explores as thoroughly the hostile conditions—literary, social, and psychological—for women writers as Finch does in such poems as "The Introduction," "The Apology," "On Myselfe," and "The Unequal Fetters."

Although Lady Russell, in our terminology, is a writer and not an author—the first edition of her letters was not published until 1773, fifty years after her death—she certainly became an author posthumously, for her letters went through nine editions between 1773 and 1821. Like Katherine Philips, Lady Russell is frequently depicted as a genteel, compliant woman writer—a depiction that, in our view, confuses manner with matter. The matter of Lady Russell's letters involves substantial questioning of both political and religious authority. It is true that in both cases Lady Russell comes to terms, respectively, with her husband's execution by Charles II and with her own religious doubts in response to the devastating consequences of her husband's execution. But Lady Russell's public silence—her refusal to publish her letters—is precisely the kind of accommodation that at once circumscribes a female space and implicitly establishes a critique of dominant male values. In declaring to Charles II that her dead husband was a "loyal subject," Russell questions both the evidence presented against her husband and the king's judgment in accepting that evidence. As much as Lady Russell genuinely seeks "a silent submission to this severe and terrible providence," it is our good fortune that she did "let [her] pen run too greedily upon this subject." What her pen conveys is that she, like her friend Archbishop Tillotson (then Dean of St. Paul's Cathedral, London), was one of those "few of ability and integrity" that her age produced.

In the writings of Elizabeth Tollet, Elizabeth Rowe, Elizabeth Carter, and Catherine Talbot we have emphasized (though not limited ourselves to) three principal attributes of women's writing during the mid-eighteenth century. First, as one sees in Tollet's verse, there begins to develop within women's writing a sense of predecessors. Rather than writing strictly within a male tradition of poetry, Tollet, for example, memorializes Anne Finch, concluding her poem with a reference to Finch's most famous published poem ("The Spleen"). Tollet's "The Monument" seems to allude to, and certainly invites comparison with, Katherine Philips's "Wiston Vault," and this evolving awareness of female predecessors continues in Elizabeth Carter's poem on the death of Elizabeth Rowe. Carter, in fact, wrote prefatory verses for the posthumous edition of Rowe's *Works* (1739).

A second related attribute of mid-eighteenth century women's writing is the development of a community of women writers who interacted socially and intellectually with one another. The friendship between Elizabeth Carter and Catherine Talbot — a friendship shaped to a considerable degree by common literary interests, although Talbot chose not to become an author — is representative of a developing community of women writers (later called the "Bluestockings"), a community of learned women that would enlarge for the remainder of the century. These learned women included, along with Carter and Talbot, such figures as Elizabeth Montagu, Frances Boscawen, Hannah More, and Mary Delany; and these women did interact with such well-known male counterparts as Samuel Richardson, Edmund Burke, Samuel Johnson, and Horace Walpole.

A third important attribute shared by Tollet, Rowe, Carter, and Talbot is their powerful commitment, as women writers, to use their talents (quoting Carter) "To raise the Thoughts, and moralize the Mind." Characteristically, these writers detach themselves from the stereotypical identification of women with physical beauty (as in Tollet's condemnation of "Beauty's Idol charms") and they reject the allurements of social ambition and display (as in Rowe's refusal to participate in the "busy world's detested noise, / Its wretched pleasures, and distracted joys"). Indeed, in a remarkable reversal of the traditional *carpe diem* poem, Carter urges her reader not to seize the moment of pleasure but, rather, to "seize . . . that rapid Time / That never must return" — the time, that is, for acting virtuously *now* in preparation for afterlife. Talbot, as well, stresses the moral use of time and the rejection of self-indulgent imaginings; her untitled poem beginning "Awake my Laura" summarizes the strong moral emphasis that unites Tollet, Rowe, Carter, and Talbot.

In Collier and Montagu we see two women writers whose works invite comparison with — and indeed directly address challenges to — some of the works of their male counterparts. Collier's *Art of Ingeniously Tormenting* is not simply an imitation of, but a competitive challenge to the presumed master of English satire, Jonathan Swift. Collier summons the presence of "Dean Swift's instructions" (i.e., *Directions to Servants* [1745]) as a way of inviting the reader to compare her satire with Swift's. She brilliantly mocks the eighteenth-century consumption of conduct books, offering as a replacement for propriety a new set of rules for the implementation of anti-social behavior. Furthermore, in the chapter "To Parents" Collier provides a unique twist to Swift's *Modest Proposal*, commending the parent-child relationship as an opportunity to sharpen one's skills at exercising arbitrary power—that is, the art of tormenting.

Lady Mary Wortley Montagu is no less a liberated writer than Jane Collier. Like Collier, Montagu exercises a genuine talent for satire, even at the expense of the eighteenth century's best known poet, Alexander Pope. In both "To the Imitator" (probably a collaboration with Lord Hervey) and "An Epistle from Pope" (written in 1734 but not published in her lifetime), Montagu turns the tables on two powerful male antagonists—Pope and Viscount Bolingbroke. Speaking as if she were Pope and Bolingbroke, she writes: "Mean spirits seek their villainy to hide; / We show our venom'd souls with nobler pride, / And in bold strokes have all mankind defy'd." The "venom" to which Montagu refers is not just the spite of so much satire, but Satan's venom in the Garden of Eden; about both Pope and Bolingbroke, Montagu appears to apply the following couplet from "To the Imitator": "To human Race Antipathy declare, / 'Twixt them and thee be everlasting War" (54–55). In Montagu's eyes, Pope and Bolingbroke "have all mankind defy'd" because, at bottom, their satire is misanthropic. Her response is therefore best expressed in "To the Imitator": "But as thou hate'st, be hated by Mankind."

On a less hostile note, Montagu has a wonderful penchant for indulging in what she calls "a true female spirit of contradiction." For example, the first letter we include repudiates the standard fare of "voyage-writers," who attend more to objects and locations than people and beliefs; Montagu contradicts the British view regarding the alleged "miserable confinement of the Turkish ladies," arguing that, to the contrary, they "are perhaps more free than any ladies in the universe." Repeatedly Montagu contrasts English and Turkish customs, always at the expense of England. In a similar spirit of contradiction, Montagu, who lived apart from her husband for much of her life, nevertheless rallies to the defense of marriage against La Rochefoucault's maxim. Montagu characteristically uses the "maxims of the East" to explode the "confused medley of . . . rigid maxims" typical of Western culture.

By raising the subject of marriage Montagu focuses on a central concern of many women writers. Lady Chudleigh succinctly expresses the oppressive state of many eighteenth-century marriages when she writes in "To the Ladies":

> Wife and servant are the same,
> But only differ in the name;
> For when that fatal knot is ty'd,
> Which nothing, nothing can divide;
> When she the word *obey* has said,
> And man by law supreme has made,
> Then all that's kind is laid aside,
> And nothing left but state and pride.

The "law supreme" that compels obedience from a wife is the law of coverture, where a woman places herself in the protection of her husband, giving up her legal existence as an individual to her husband. It is no exaggeration to say, therefore, that a wife becomes a servant, and the brutal consequences of coverture are precisely what lie at the heart of Sarah Pennington's *An Unfortunate Mother's Advice*.

Accused of adultery, quite possibly a trumped up charge originating with her inheriting private wealth, Pennington was expelled from her home and permanently separated from her children. Having no legal recourse, yet unwilling to be silenced, Pennington turned to writing (and authorship) to express her needs and views. The mere fact that publication was the only way she could communicate with her children underscores the oppressive consequences of a marriage based on coverture. In addition to illuminating the many dangers of marriage at this time, Pennington also vividly portrays the dangers, particularly for young women, of existing in a society well known for its mastery of duplicity, dissimulation, intrigue, and hypocrisy.

All these risks are powerfully captured by Pennington's image of society as a masquerade:

> You are just entering, my dear girl, into a World full of Deceit and Falshood, where few Persons or Things appear as they really are: Vice hides her Deformity with the borrowed garb of Virtue; and though discernable, by the unbecoming aukwardness of her Deportment under it, passes on Thousands undetected: Every present Pleasure usurps the Name of Happiness, and as such

deceives the unwary Pursuer; thus one general Mask [i.e., masquerade] disguises the Whole, and it requires a long Experience, and a penetrating Judgment to discover the Truth.

To appreciate the full import of Pennington's admonition, one need only read attentively the whole of Hannah Cowley's play *The Belle's Stratagem* which, in the words of one of the characters, Sir George Touchwood, demonstrates how much eighteenth-century society was "one universal masquerade."

Pennington's mention of the need for "penetrating Judgment" brings us to the final five authors in this anthology—Joanna Baillie, Mary Wollstonecraft, Hannah More, Maria Edgeworth, and Anna Barbauld. In our view, these five authors testify to the indisputable existence and public acknowledgment of women of letters in the late eighteenth century. However diverse their interests and ideological standpoints, these authors commanded the attention of the reading public—women and men. In diverse and divergent ways they addressed the central concerns—literary, educational, political—of their time.

Joanna Baillie, a friend of both Anna Barbauld and Maria Edgeworth, was—like Hannah Cowley—an acclaimed dramatist, though we have chosen to include an example of her dramatic criticism. Mary Wollstonecraft, certainly a controversial and pioneering figure, was a prolific author during her very abbreviated career of approximately ten years. A founding feminist, Wollstonecraft needs to be understood as an author whose contributions encompass an extraordinary array of interests.

In his essay, "My First Acquaintance with Poets," William Hazlitt recalls that Samuel Coleridge identified Wollstonecraft as a person "of imagination" as distinguished from one of "mere intellect." In so identifying Wollstonecraft, Coleridge may be alluding to her Hint 31 in which she associates genius with "a strong imagination." While it is true that Mary Wollstonecraft endorsed the imagination on aesthetic and moral grounds—she once wrote her lover, Gilbert Imlay, that "I consider those minds as the most strong and original, whose imagination acts as the stimulus to their senses"—it is not the case that she viewed the imagination as antithetical to intellect. For example, the selection from *Vindication of the Rights of Woman* displays her powerful rational critique of the oppression of women; condemning the despotism of sexual objectification, Wollstonecraft systematically implements an argument for the rights of full citizenship for women. On the other hand, in a work like *Letters Written during A Short Residence* she places greater emphasis on how the imagination awakens feelings of both love and loss. Herself educated in adversity, Wollstonecraft consistently draws on her life experiences as a woman to enforce her reasoned critique of male prejudice and to empower her own distinctive voice as a woman of letters.

Part of Wollstonecraft's critique entailed an attack on women writers (principally novelists) who promoted, knowingly or not, the fallacious "virtues" of sensibility. In a review of Elizabeth Inchbald's novel *A Simple Story*, Wollstonecraft launches a bitter attack (somewhat overstated) on women authors who weaken their female audience with sentimental pap. She complains: "Why do all female writers, even when they display their abilities, always give a sanction to the libertine reveries of men? Why do they poison the minds of their own sex, by strengthening a male prejudice that makes women systematically weak?" This critique, and others like it, should be understood as a sign of the strength and sophistication of women's writing at the end of the eighteenth century; that is, the tradition of women's writing was sufficiently established to contain within itself the exercise of self-examination and self-criticism. Wollstonecraft did not have to worry that her critique would effectively silence other women writers. Rather, she held up a standard for others to meet. In her critique of sensibility, for example, she clearly elicited responses from two other women authors—Hannah More and Maria Edgeworth— who shared her commitment to the *re-education* of women to a higher objective than that of the cultivation of sensibility.

Although More and Edgeworth are not often, if ever, associated with their contemporary, Mary Wollstonecraft, they are similarly concerned with the strengthening of "the female character." Of clearly different political persuasions from Wollstonecraft, both writers nevertheless share her commitment to raising women from the oppressed status of sexual objects of decorum and propriety to the level of moral beings capable of independently exercising, in Edgeworth's words, their "reasoning powers." Short of becoming rational beings who exercise moral choice, women were condemned to practice, as More warns, the arts by which *"little minds sometimes govern great ones."* What this practice involves Edgeworth satirically depicts in "An Essay on the Noble Science of Self-Justification," a work directly related to Collier's *Art of Ingeniously Tormenting*, including their shared use of Hamlet's line: "I will speak daggers to her, but use none" (*Hamlet* 3.2.414).

Finally, we close this anthology with a representation of the many literary interests of Anna (Aikin) Barbauld, who was recognized in her own time as an exemplary woman of letters. The March 1786 issue of *The European Magazine* wrote a lead account of Barbauld referring to her as "no less celebrated for her intellectual than her personal endowments," and observing that her works "exhibit marks of a refined and vigorous imagination, of cultivated genius, elegant manners, unbigotted religion, and unenthusiastical devotion." Belonging to a remarkably productive family (the works of the Aikin family fill thirteen pages in the *British Museum Catalog of Printed Books*), Barbauld established herself as an author, educator, literary critic, editor and pioneer in children's literature. The titles of her diverse works hint at her immense versatility: *Poems* (1773; four editions in the first year); *Miscellaneous Pieces in Prose* (1773; co-authored with her brother, John Aikin); *Lessons for Children* (1778); *Hymns in Prose for Children* (1781); *Address to the Opposers of the Repeal of Test and Corporation Acts* (1790); *Epistle to Wilberforce* (1791); *Evenings at Home* (1792; Barbauld was a contributor), *Remarks on Wakefield's Enquiry* (1792); *Correspondence of Samuel Richardson*, 6 vols. (1804); *The British Novelists*, 50 vols. (1810); *The Female Speaker* (1811).

Barbauld's status and achievement as a woman of letters are perhaps best attested to by the complaints of a male critic, William Woodfall, who felt she violated the boundaries between "male" and "female" discourse. In reviews published in 1773 and 1774 (*Monthly Review* 48 [1773]: 133, 137; 49 [1774]: 472), Woodfall—whose contention was "There is a sex in minds as well as in bodies"—comments, "We hoped the *Woman* was going to appear; and that while we admired the genius and learning of her graver compositions, we should be affected by the sensibility and passion of the softer pieces." In a subsequent review Woodfall continued, "We could never discover in Miss Aikin's [Barbauld's maiden name] compositions any peculiar touches of a feminine hand." Intended as criticism, Woodfall's remarks verify—albeit inadvertently—how completely Barbauld and her female contemporaries had conquered the traditional territory of male authorship. Shattering the stereotype of women writers who, in Woodfall's words, should engage in "the sensibility and passion of . . . softer pieces," Barbauld exemplifies the strength of woman's genius and learning.

Finally, we encourage the reader—student and scholar alike—to examine the genius and learning of the women writers presented here from a variety of points of view. In addition to the thematic and historical connections suggested by this book's organization, it would be fruitful to establish generic and thematic connections across the entire period. The reader might compare the presentation of love and marriage in the dramas of Behn and Cowley, one a typical Restoration comedy and the other a late eighteenth-century comedy of manners. Among the poets, the wide range of subjects and approaches reflects the rich variety of women's poetry during this period. From Behn's frank love lyrics to Rowe's touching verses on her husband's death and her passionate yearning for the love of God to Barbauld's mock heroic treatment of domestic chores, the reader will gain insight into the intellectual and emotional depth and breadth of this "other" tradition of writing. Studying these poems in conjunction with the poetry written by men during this period, the reader will gain a new appreciation of the contributions by women both as they parallel and contrast with the works of their male contemporaries.

The nonfiction prose also reveals these women authors exercising their talents in diverse modes. By no means confined to the "familiar letters" and tales for children often regarded as women's major literary contribution during this period, these authors' essays, serious letters, allegories, polemics, and satires show them as adept at both formal and informal prose — serious and playful, earnest and witty. Moreover, the thematic possibilities are numerous. Feminist-oriented subjects include women's education, women's friendship, marriage, sexual freedom, and the freedom to write and publish. Fell, Behn, Astell, Drake, Egerton, and Wollstonecraft are outspoken champions of women, but others such as Pennington, Russell, Philips and Carter (to name only a few) imply by their actions and the lives they led that women could be and increasingly were far more than "upper servants."

Throughout this book we have attempted to represent the impressive range of women's writing from 1660–1800. We are aware that no single anthology can do justice to the contributions of the many women who wrote and published during this period. However, this book will have fulfilled an important part of its purpose if it leads readers to explore further the works of these and other women writers. Doing so will begin the long overdue process of reintegrating into the canon of teaching and scholarship the "other" eighteenth century.

In order to preserve the sense of reading seventeenth and eighteenth-century texts, the editors have generally refrained from modernizing the selections. However, we have reduced the use of italics and capitalization of nouns.

MARGARET FELL

(1614–1702)

Religious writer, Quaker preacher, and polemicist for women's rights in the church, Fell is often called the "Mother of Quakerism." Her father was the well-to-do John Askew of Marsh Grange, whose ancestor Anne Askew was a Protestant martyr during Henry VIII's reign. At eighteen, she married Thomas Fell of Swarthmore Hall with whom she had nine children. He died in 1658. She joined the Quaker church in 1652 after meeting George Fox and became active in the cause, visiting imprisoned Quakers and petitioning for their release. During her life, she was arrested numerous times. In 1664, while in jail for the first time, she wrote the tract reprinted here, *Women's Speaking Justified*.

In 1669, she married George Fox, whose feminist ideas had strongly influenced her. Shortly after her marriage, she was again arrested, some believe by the efforts of her son who wished to gain control of her estate. Her daughter attempted to have her released, but was unsuccessful, and she remained in prison for about a year, until she was released in the spring of 1671. Fox was also frequently imprisoned for his Quakerism, and before and after their marriage Fell petitioned the Crown to have him released. In 1673, upon her petitioning Charles II for her husband's release, the king refused the release but offered to pardon him. Fell refused the pardon, insisting that Fox was innocent. After Fox's death in 1691, Fell continued her strong interest in the Quaker movement, but she appears to have become much less active in the cause. She died at her Swarthmore estate at the age of eighty-eight and is buried in the Quaker cemetery at Swarthmore. Her numerous writings are almost all centered around the Quaker religion and women's place in the church. She wrote an autobiography which included *A Brief Collection of Remarkable Passages and Occurrences* in her own life as well as *Sundry of Her Epistles, Books and Christian Testimony to Friends* (1710).

EDITION USED: *Women's Speaking Justified*, 2nd ed. (London, 1667).

WOMEN'S SPEAKING JUSTIFIED

Whereas it hath been an objection in the minds of many, and several times hath been objected by the clergy, or ministers, and others, against women's speaking in the church; and so consequently may be taken, that they are condemned [sic] for meddling in the things of God; the ground of which objection, is taken from the Apostle's words, which he writ in his First Epistle to the *Corinthians*, chap. 14 vers. 34, 35. And also that he writ to *Timothy* in the First Epistle, chap. 2. vers. 11, 12. But how far they wrong the Apostle's intentions in these Scriptures, we shall show clearly when we come to them in their course and order. But first let me lay down how God himself hath manifested his will and mind concerning women, and unto women.

And first, when *God created man in his own image: in the image of God created he them, male and female: and God blessed them, and God said unto them, be fruitful and multiply: and God said, Behold, I have given you of every herb, etc. Gen.* 1. Here God joins them together in his own image, and makes no such distinctions and differences as men do, for though they be weak, he is strong, and as he said to the Apostle, *his grace is sufficient* and *his strength is made manifest in weakness,* 2 Cor. 12.9. And such hath the Lord chosen, *even the weak things of the world to confound the things which are mighty; and things which are despised, hath God chosen to bring to nought things that are,* 1 Cor. 1. And God hath put no such difference between the male and female as men would make.

It is true, the serpent that was more subtle than any other beast of the field, came unto the woman, with his temptations, and with a lie; his subtlety discerning her to be more inclinable to hearken to him, when he said, *If ye eat, your eyes shall be opened.* And the woman saw that the fruit was good to make one wise, there the temptation got into her, and she did eat and gave to her husband, and he did eat also, and so they were both tempted into the transgression and disobedience; and therefore God said unto Adam, when that he hid himself when he heard his voice, *Hast thou eaten of the tree which I commanded thee that thou shouldest not eat?* And Adam said, *The women which thou gavest me, she gave me of the tree, and I did eat.* And the Lord said unto the woman, *What is this that thou hast done?* and the woman said, *The serpent beguiled me, and I did eat.* [Here] the woman spoke the truth unto the Lord: see what the Lord said. vers. 15. after he had pronounced sentence on the serpent; *I will put enmity between thee and the woman, and between thy seed and her seed; it shall bruise thy head, and thou shalt bruise his heel,* Gen. 3.

Let this word of the Lord which was from the beginning, stop the mouths of all that oppose women's speaking in the power of the Lord; for he hath put enmity between the woman and the serpent; and if the seed of the woman speak not, the seed of the serpent speaks; for God hath put enmity between the two seeds, and it is manifest that those that speak against the woman and her seeds' speaking speak out of the enmity of the old serpent's seed; and God hath fulfilled his word and his promise:

When the fullness of time was come, he hath sent forth his son, made of a woman, made under the Law, that we might receive the adoption of sons, Gal. 4.4,5.

Moreover, the Lord is pleased, when he mentioned his Church, to call her by the name of *Woman*, by his prophets, saying, *I have called thee as a woman forsaken, and grieved in spirit, and as a wife of youth*. Isa. 54.6.

* * *

Thus much may prove that the Church of Christ is a woman, and those that speak against the woman's speaking, speak against the Church of Christ, and the seed of the woman, which seed is Christ, that is to say, those that speak against the power of the Lord, and the spirit of the Lord speaking in a woman, simply by reason of her sex, or because she is a woman, not regarding the seed, and spirit, and power that speaks in her; such speak against Christ, and his Church, and are of the seed of the serpent, wherein lodgeth the enmity. And as God the Father made no such difference in the first creation, nor never since between the male and the female, but always out of his mercy and loving kindness, had regard unto the weak. So also, his son, Christ Jesus, confirms the same thing: when the Pharisees came to him, and asked him, if it were lawful for a man to put away his wife, he answered and said unto him, *Have you not read that he that made them in the beginning, made them male and female*, and said, *For this cause shall a man leave father and mother, and shall cleave unto his wife, and they twain shall be one flesh, wherefore they are no more than twain but one flesh; what therefore God hath joined together, let no man put asunder*, Mat. 19.4,5,6.

* * *

And now to the Apostle's words, which is the ground of the great objection against women's speaking: and first, 1 Cor. 14. Let the reader seriously read that chapter, and see the end and drift of the Apostle in speaking these words: for the Apostle is [there] exhorting the Corinthians unto charity, and to desire spiritual gifts, and not to speak in an unknown tongue, and not to be children in understanding, but to be children in malice, but in understanding to be men; and that the spirits of the prophets should be subject to the prophets, for God is not the author of confusion, but of peace: and then he saith, *Let your women keep silence in the church*, etc.

Where it doth plainly appear that the women, as well as others that were among them, were in confusion, for he saith, *How is it brethren, when ye came together, everyone of you hath a psalm, hath a doctrine, hath a tongue, hath a revelation, hath an interpretation? Let all things be done to edifying.* Here was no edifying but all was in confusion speaking together; therefore he saith, *If any man speak in an unknown tongue, let it be by two, or at most by three, and that by course, and let one interpret, but if there be no interpreter, let him keep silence in the church.* Here the man is commanded to keep silence as well as the woman, when they are in confusion and out of order.

But the Apostle saith further, *They are commanded to be in obedience, as also saith the Law; and if they will learn anything, let them ask their husbands at home, for it is a shame for a woman to speak in the church.*

Here the Apostle clearly manifests his intent; for he speaks of women that were under the Law, and in that transgression as Eve was, and such as were to learn, and not to speak publickly, but they must first ask their husbands at home, and it was a shame for such to speak in the church; and it appears clearly, that such women were speaking among the Corinthians, by the Apostle's exhorting them from malice and strife, and confusion, and he preacheth the Law unto them, and he saith, in the Law it is written, *With men of other tongues, and other lips, will I speak unto this people*, 1 Cor. 14.21.

And what is all this to women's speaking, that have the everlasting Gospel to preach, and upon whom the promise of the Lord is fulfilled, and his spirit poured upon them according to his word, Acts 2.16,17,18. And if the Apostle would have stopped such as had the spirit of the Lord poured upon them, why did he say just before, *If anything be revealed to another that sitteth by, let the first hold his peace?* and *you may all prophesie one by one?* Here he did not say that such women should not prophesy as had the revelation and spirit of God poured upon them, but their women that were under the Law, and in the transgression, and were in strife, confusion and malice in their speaking, for if he had stopped women's praying or prophesying, why doth he say: *Every man praying or prophesying having his head covered, dishonoureth his head; but every woman that prayeth or prophesieth with her head uncovered, dishonoured [sic] her head? Judge in yourselves, is it comely that a woman pray or prophesie uncovered? For the woman is not without the man, neither is the man without the woman, in the Lord,* 1 Cor. 11.3,4,13.

Also that other Scripture, in 1 Tim. 2. where he is exhorting that prayer and supplication be made every where, lifting up holy hands without wrath and doubting; he saith in the like manner also, that women must adorn themselves in modest apparel, with shamefastness and sobriety, not with broidered hair, or gold, or pearl, or costly array; he saith, *Let women learn in silence will and subjection, but I suffer not a woman to teach, nor to usurp authority over the man, but to be in silence; for Adam was first formed, then Eve; and Adam was not deceived, but the woman being deceived was in the transgression.*

Here the Apostle speaks particularly to a woman in relation to her husband, to be in subjection to him, and not to teach, nor usurp authority over him, and therefore he mentions Adam and Eve: but let it be strained to the utmost, as the opposers of women's speaking would have it, that is, that they should not preach nor speak in the church, of which there is nothing here: yet the Apostle is speaking to such as he is teaching to wear their apparel, what to wear, and what not to wear; such as were not come to wear modest apparel, and such as were not come to shamefastness and sobriety, but he was exhorting them from broidered hair, gold and pearls, and costly array; and such are not to usurp authority over the man, but to learn in silence with all subjection, as it becometh women professing godliness with good works.

And what is all this to such as have the power and spirit of the Lord Jesus poured upon them, and have the message of the Lord Jesus given unto them? Must not they speak the word of the Lord because of these undecent and unreverent women that the Apostle speaks of, and to, in these two Scriptures? And how are the men of this generation blinded, that bring these scriptures, and pervert the Apostle's words, and corrupt this intent in speaking of them, and by these scriptures, endeavour to stop the message and word of the Lord God in women, by condemning and despising of them. If the Apostle would have had women's speaking stopped, and did not allow of them, why did he entreat his true yokefellow to help those women, who laboured with him in the gospel? Phil. 4.3 And why did the Apostles join together in prayer and supplication with the women and Mary the mother of Jesus, and with his Brethren, Acts 1.14 if they had not allowed, and had union and fellowship with the spirit of God, wherever it was revealed in women as well as others? But all this opposing and gainsaying of women's speaking hath risen out of the bottomless pit, and spirit of darkness that hath spoken for these many hundred years together in this night of apostacy, since the revelations have ceased and been hid, and so that spirit hath limited and bound all up within its bond and compass, and so would suffer none to speak but such as that spirit of darkness approved of, man or woman.

*   *   *

But blessed be the Lord, his time is over, which was above twelve hundred Years, and the darkness is past, and the night of Apostacy draws to an end, and the true light now shines, the morning-Light the bright morning Star, the Root and Off-spring of *David*, he is risen, he is risen, glory to the highest for evermore; and the joy of the morning is come, and the Bride, the Lambs Wife, is making her self ready, as a Bride that is adorning for her Husband, and to her is granted that she shall be arrayed in fine linnen, clean and white, and the fine linnen is the Righteousness of the Saints: The *Holy Jerusalem* is descending out of Heaven from God, having the Glory of God, and her light is like a Jasper stone, clear as Christal.

And this is that free Woman that all the Children of the Promise are born of; not the Children of the bond-woman, which is *Hagar*, which genders to strife and to bondage, and which answers to *Jerusalem* which is in bondage with her Children: but this is *the Jerusalem which is free, which is the Mother of us all*; And so this bond-woman and her children, that are born after the flesh, have persecuted them that are born after the Spirit, even untill now; but now the bond-woman and her Seed is to be cast out, that hath kept so long in bondage and in slavery, and under limits; this bond-woman and her brood is to be cast out, and our Holy City, the *New Jerusalem*, is coming down from Heaven, and her Light will shine throughout the whole earth, even as a *Jasper stone, clear as Christal*, which brings freedom and liberty, and perfect Redemption to her whole Seed; and this is that woman and Image of the Eternal God, that God hath owned, and doth own, and will own for evermore.

JUDITH DRAKE

(fl. 1696)

Little is known about Judith Drake. She is believed to have been the sister of James Drake, who was born in Cambridge in 1667, and who wrote the poem which prefaces the *Essay in Defence of the Female Sex* (1696), attributed to Judith Drake by Ruth Perry in her book *The Celebrated Mary Astell* (1986). James Drake was a physician, a Tory activist, and political pamphleteer. His father gave him a liberal education, and if Judith was indeed his sister, she may also have received a better than usual education. Moreover, Judith Drake apparently practiced medicine, which she could have learned from James. Ruth Perry notes that, in 1723, she was charged with medical malpractice. In her spirited defense, Drake asserted that she had been successfully practicing for years.

Drake's *Essay* was originally attributed to Mary Astell. Florence Smith noted in her biography *Mary Astell* (1916) that it shows a "difference in point of view" from Astell's usual writing (176). Smith notes that an eighteenth-century book catalogue attributed the *Essay* to "Mrs. Drake," and this is confirmed by a pencilled note on the British Museum's copy of the work. More recently, Ruth Perry has concluded that Drake wrote the *Essay* and that it was the "first imitation" of Astell's *Serious Proposal to the Ladies*. Perry supports her attribution by noting that Drake says the company of women could benefit men, "a question that would never have occurred to Astell, who did not concern herself with what was good or bad for men" (106).

EDITION USED: *An Essay In Defence of The Female Sex* (London, 1696).

FROM AN ESSAY IN DEFENCE OF THE FEMALE SEX

THE CONVERSATION we had 'tother day, makes me, Dear *Madam*, but more sensible of the unreasonableness of your desire; which obliges me to inform you further upon a Subject, wherein I have more need of your instruction. The strength of Judgment, sprightly Fancy, and admirable Address, you shew'd upon that Occasion, speak you so perfect a Mistress of that Argument (as I doubt not but you are of any other that you please to engage in) that whoever, would speak or write well on it, ought first to be your Schollar. Yet to let you see how absolutely you may command me, I had rather be your *Eccho*, than be silent when You bid me speak, and beg your excuse rather for my Failures, than want of Complacence. I know You will not accuse me for a Plagiary if I return You nothing, but

23

what I have glean'd from You, when You consider, that I pretend not to make a Present, but to pay the Interest only of a Debt. Nor can You tax me with Vanity, since no Importunity of a Person less lov'd, or valu'd by me than your self could have extorted thus much from me. This Consideration leaves me no room to doubt but that you will with your usual Candour pardon those Defects, and correct those Errors, which proceed only from an over forward Zeal to oblige You, though to my own Disadvantage.

The defence of our Sex against so many and so great Wits as have so strongly attack'd it, may justly seem a Task too difficult for a Woman to attempt. Not that I can, or ought to yield, that we are by Nature less enabled for such an Enterprize, than Men are; which I hope at least to shew plausible Reasons for, before I have done: But because through the Usurpation of Men, and the Tyranny of Custom (here in *England* especially) there are at most but few, who are by Education, and acquir'd Wit, or Letters sufficiently quallified for such an Undertaking. For my own part I shall readily own, that as few as there are, there may be and are abundance, who in their daily Conversations approve themselves much more able, and sufficient Assertors of our Cause, than thy self; and I am sorry that either their Business, their other Diversions, or too great Indulgence of their Ease, hinder them from doing publick Justice to their Sex. The Men by Interest or Inclination are so generally engag'd against us, that it is not to be expected, that any one Man of Wit should arise so generous as to engage in our Quarrel, and be the Champion of our Sex against the Injuries and Oppressions of his own. Those Romantick days are over, and there is not so much as a *Don Quixot* of the Quill left to succour the distressed Damsels. 'Tis true, a Feint of something of this Nature was made three or four Years since by one; but how much soever his Eugenia may be oblig'd to him, I am of Opinion the rest of her Sex are but little beholding to him. For as you rightly observ'd, *Madam*, he has taken more care to give an Edge to his Satyr, than force to his Apology; he has play'd a sham Prize, and receives more thrusts than he makes; and like a false Renegade fights under our Colours only for a fairer Opportunity of betraying us. But what could be expected else from a Beau? An Annimal that can no more commend in earnest a Womans Wit, than a Man's Person, and that compliments ours, only to shew his own good Breeding and Parts. He levels his Scandal at the whole Sex, and thinks us sufficiently fortified, if out of the Story of Two Thousand Years he has been able to pick up a few Examples of Women illustrious for their Wit,

Learning or Vertue, and Men infamous for the contrary; though I think the most inveterate of our Enemies would have spar'd him that labour, by granting that all Ages have produc'd Persons famous or infamous of both Sexes; or they must throw up all pretence to Modesty, or Reason.

I have neither Learning, nor Inclination to make a Precedent, or indeed any use of Mr. W's. labour'd Common Place Book; and shall leave Pedants and School-Boys to rake and tumble the Rubbish of Antiquity, and muster all the *Heroes* and *Heroins* they can find to furnish matter for some wretched Harangue, or stuff a miserable Declamation with instead of Sense or Argument.

I shall not enter into any dispute, whether Men, or Women be generally more ingenious, or learned; that Point must be given up to the advantages Men have over us by their Education, Freedom of Converse, and variety of Business and Company. But when any Comparison is made between 'em, great allowances must be made for the disparity of those Circumstances. Neither shall I contest about the preheminence of our Virtues; I know there are too many Vicious, and I hope there are a great many Virtuous of both Sexes. Yet this I may say, that whatever Vices are found amongst us, have in general both their source, and encouragement from them.

The Question I shall at present handle is, whether the time an ingenious Gentleman spends in the Company of Women, may justly be said to be misemploy'd or not? I put the question in general terms; because whoever holds the affirmative must maintain it so, or the Sex is no way concern'd to oppose him. On the other side I shall not maintain the Negative, but with some Restrictions and Limitations; because I will not be bound to justifie those Women, whose Vices and ill Conduct expose them deservedly to the Censure of the other Sex, as well as of their own. The Question being thus stated, let us consider the end and purposes, for which Conversation was at first instituted, and is yet desirable; and then we shall see, whether they may not all be found in the Company of Women. These Ends, I take it, are the same with those we aim at in all our other Actions, in general only two, Profit or Pleasure. These are divided into those of the Mind, and those of the Body. Of the latter I shall take no further Notice, as having no Relation to the present Subject; but shall confine my self wholly to the Mind, the Profit of which is the Improvement of the Understanding, and the Pleasure is the Diversion, and Relaxation of its Cares and Passions. Now if either of these Ends be attainable by the Society of Women, I have gain'd my Point. However, I hope to make it appear, that they are not only both to be met with in the Conversation of Women, but one of them more generally, and in greater measure than in Mens.

Our Company is generally by our Adversaries represented as unprofitable and irksome to Men of Sense, and by some of the more vehement Sticklers against us, as Criminal. These Imputations as they are unjust, especially the latter, so they savour strongly of the Malice, Arrogance and Sottishness of those, that most frequently urge 'em; who are commonly either conceited Fops, whose success in their Pretences to the favour of our Sex has been no greater than their Merit, and fallen very far short of their Vanity and Presumption, or a sort of morose, ill-bred, unthinking Fellows, who appear to be Men only by their Habit and Beards, and are scarce distinguishable from Brutes but by their Figure and Risibility. But I shall wave these Reflections at present, however just, and come closer to our Argument. If Women are not quallified for the Conversation of ingenious Men, or, to go yet further, their friendship, it must be because they want some one condition, or more, necessarily requisite to either. The necessary Conditions of these are Sense, and good nature, to which must be added, for Friendship, Fidelity and Integrity. Now if any of these be wanting to our Sex, it must be either because Nature has not been so liberal as to bestow 'em upon us; or because due care has not been taken to cultivate those Gifts to a competent measure in us.

The first of these Causes is that, which is most generally urg'd against us, whether it be in Raillery, or Spight. I might easily cut this part of the Controversy short by an irrefragable Argument, which is, that the express intent, and reason for which Woman was created, was to be a Companion, and help meet to Man; and that consequently those, that deny 'em to be so must argue a Mistake in Providence, and think themselves wiser than their Creator. But these Gentlemen are generally such passionate Admirers of themselves, and have such a profound value and reverence for their own Parts, that they are ready at any time to sacrifice their Religion to the Reputation of their Wit, and rather than lose their point, deny the truth of the History. There are others, that though they allow the Story yet affirm, that the propagation, and continuance of Mankind, was the only Reason for which we were made; as if the Wisdom that first made Man, cou'd not without trouble have continu'd that Species by the same or any other Method, had not this been most conducive to his happiness, which was the gracious and only end of his Creation. But these superficial Gentlemen wear their Understandings like their Clothes, always set and formal, and wou'd no more Talk than Dress out of Fashion; Beau's that, rather than any part of their outward Figure shou'd be damag'd, wou'd wipe the dirt of their shoes with their Handkercher, and that value themselves infinitely more upon modish Nonsense, than upon the best Sense against the Fashion. But since I do not intend to make this a religious Argument, I shall leave all further Considerations of this Nature to the Divines, whose more immediate Business and Study it is to assert the Wisdom of Providence in the Order, and distribution of this World, against all that shall oppose it.

To proceed therefore if we be naturally defective, the Defect must be either in Soul or Body. In the Soul it can't be, if what I have hear'd some learned Men maintain, be true, that all Souls are equal, and alike, and that consequently there is no such distinction, as Male and Female Souls; that there are no innate *Ideas*, but that all the Notions we have, are deriv'd from our External Senses, either immediately, or by Reflection. These Metaphysical Speculations, I must own Madam, require much more Learning and a stronger Head, than I can pretend to be Mistress of, to be consider'd as they ought: Yet so bold I may be, as to undertake the defence of these Opinions, when any of our jingling Opponents think fit to refute 'em.

Neither can it be in the Body, (if I may credit the Report of learned Physicians) for there is no difference in the Organization of those Parts, which have any relation to, or influence over the Minds; but the Brain, and all other Parts (which I am not Anatomist enough to name) are contriv'd as well for the plentiful conveyance of Spirits, which are held to be the immediate Instruments of Sensation, in Women, as Men. I see therefore no natural Impediment in the structure of our Bodies; nor does Experience, or Observation argue any: We use all our Natural Faculties, as well as Men, nay and our Rational too, deducting only for the advantages before mention'd.

Let us appeal yet further to Experience, and observe those Creatures that deviate least from simple Nature, and see if we can find any difference in Sense, or understanding between Males and Females. In these we may see Nature plainest, who lie under no constraint of Custom or Laws, but those of Passion or Appetite, which are Natures, and know no difference of Education, nor receive any Byass by prejudice. We fee great distance in Degrees of Understanding, Wit, Cunning and Docility (call them what you please) between the several Species of Brutes. An Ape, a Dog, a Fox, are by daily Observation found to be more Docile, and more

Subtle than an Ox, a Swine, or a Sheep. But a She Ape is as full of, and as ready at Imitation as a He; a Bitch will learn as many Tricks in as short a time as a Dog, a Female Fox has as many Wiles as a Male. A thousand instances of this kind might be produc'd; but I think these are so plain, that to instance more were a superfluous labour; I shall only once more take notice, that in Brutes and other Animals there is no difference bewixt Male and Female in point of Sagacity, notwithstanding there is the fame distinction of Sexes, that is between Men and Women. I have read, that some Philosophers have held Brutes to be no more than meer Machines, a sort of Divine Clock-work, that Act only by the force of nice unseen Springs without Sensation, and cry out without feeling Pain, Eat without Hunger, Drink without Thirst, fawn upon their Keepers without seeing 'em, hunt Hares without Smelling, &c. Here Madam is cover for our Antagonists against the last Argument so thick, that there is no beating 'em out. For my part, I shall not envy 'em their refuge, let 'em lie like the wild *Irish* secure within their Boggs; the field is at least ours, so long as they keep to their Fastnesses. But to quit this Topick, I shall only add, that if the learnedest He of 'em all can convince me of the truth of this Opinion, He will very much stagger my Faith; for hitherto I have been able to observe no difference between our Knowledge and theirs, but a gradual one; and depend upon Revelation alone, that our Souls are Immortal, and theirs not.

But if an Argument from Brutes and other Animals shall not be allow'd as conclusive, (though I can't see, why such an Inference should not be valid, since the parity of Reason is the same on both sides in this Case.) I shall desire those, that hold against us to observe the Country People, I mean the inferiour sort of them, such as not having Stocks to follow Husbandry upon their own Score, subsist upon their daily Labour. For amongst these, though not so equal as that of Brutes, yet the Condition of the two Sexes is more level, than amongst Gentlemen, City Traders, or rich Yeomen. Examine them in their several Businesses, and their Capacities will appear equal; but talk to them of things indifferent, and out of the Road of their constant Employment, and the Ballance will fall on our side, the Women will be found the more ready and polite. Let us look a little further, and view our Sex in a state of more improvement, amongst our Neighbours the *Dutch*. There we shall find them managing not only the Domestick Affairs of the Family, but making, and receiving all Payments as well great as small, keeping the Books, ballancing the Accounts, and doing all the Business, even the nicest of Merchants, with as much Dexterity and Exactness as their, or our Men can do. And I have often hear'd some of our considerable Merchants blame the conduct of our Country-Men in this point; that they breed our Women so ignorant of Business; whereas were they taught Arithmetick, and other Arts which require not much bodily strength, they might supply the places of abundance of lusty Men now employ'd in sedentary Business; which would be a mighty profit to the Nation by sending those Men to Employments, where hands and Strength are more requir'd, especially at this time when we are in such want of People. Beside that it might prevent the ruine of many Families, which is often occasion'd by the Death of Merchants in full Business, and leaving their Accounts perplex'd, and embroil'd to a Widdow and Orphans, who understanding nothing of the Husband or Father's Business occasions the Rending, and oftentimes the utter Confounding a fair Estate; which might be prevented, did the Wife but understand Merchants Accounts, and were made acquainted with the Books.

I have yet another Argument from Nature, which is, that the very Make and Temper of our Bodies shew that we were never design'd for Fatigue; and the Vivacity of our Wits, and Readiness of our Invention (which are confess'd even by our Adversaries) demonstrate that we were chiefly intended for Thought and the Exercise of the Mind. Whereas on the contrary it is apparent from the strength and size of their Limbs, the Vigour and Hardiness of their Constitutions, that Men were purposely fram'd and contriv'd for Action, and Labour. And herein the Wisdom and Contrivance of Providence is abundantly manifested; for as the one Sex is fortified with Courage and Ability to undergo the necessary Drudgery of providing Materials for the sustenance of Life in both; so the other is furnish'd with Ingenuity and Prudence for the orderly management and distribution of it, for the Relief and Comfort of a Family; and is over and above enrich'd with a peculiar Tenderness and Care requisite to the Cherishing their poor helpless Off-fpring. I know our Opposers usually miscall our quickness of Thought, Fancy and Flash, and christen their own heaviness by the specious Names of Judgment and Solidity; but it is easie to retort upon 'em the reproachful Ones of Dullness and Stupidity with more Justice. I shall pursue this Point no further, but continue firm in my Persuasion, that Nature has not been so Niggardly to us, as our Adversaries would insinuate, till I see better cause to the contrary, then I have hitherto at any time done. Yet I am ready to yield to Conviction, whoever offers it; which I don't suddenly expect.

It remains then for us to enquire, whether the Bounty of Nature be wholly neglected, or stifled by us, or so far as to make us unworthy the Company of Men? Or whether our Education (as bad as it is) be not sufficient to make us a useful, nay a necessary part of Society for the greatest part of Mankind. This cause is seldom indeed urg'd against us by the Men, though it be the only one, that gives 'em any advantage over us in understanding. But it does not serve their Pride, there is no Honour to be gain'd by it: For a Man ought no more to value himself upon being Wiser than a Woman, if he owe his Advantage to a better Education, and greater means of Information, then he ought to boast of his Courage, for beating a Man, when his Hands were bound. Nay it would be so far from Honourable to contend for preference upon this Score, that they would thereby at once argue themselves guilty both of Tyranny, and of Fear: I think I need not have mention'd the latter; for none can be Tyrants but Cowards. For nothing makes one Party slavishly depress another, but their fear that they may at one time or other become Strong or Couragious enough to make themselves equal to, if not superiour to their Masters. This is our Case; for Men being sensible as well of the Abilities of Mind in our Sex, as of the strength of Body in their own, began to grow Jealous, that we, who in the Infancy of the World were their Equals and Partners in Dominion, might in process of Time, by Subtlety and Stratagem, become their Superiours; and therefore began in good time to make use of Force (the Origine of Power) to compell us to a Subjection, Nature never meant; and made use of Natures liberality to them to take the benefit of her kindness from us. From that time they have endeavour'd to train us up altogether to Ease and Ignorance; as Conquerors use to do to those, they reduce by Force, that so they may disarm 'em, both of Courage and Wit; and consequently make them tamely give up their Liberty, and abjectly submit their Necks to a slavish Yoke. As the World grew more Populous, and Mens Necessities whetted their Inventions, so it increas'd their Jealousy, and sharpen'd their Tyranny over us, till by degrees, it came to that height of Severity, I may say Cruelty, it is now at in all the Eastern parts of the World, where the Women, like our Negroes in our Western Plantations, are born slaves, and live Prisoners all their Lives. Nay, so far has this barbarous Humour prevail'd, and spread it self, that in some parts of *Europe*, which pretend to be most refin'd and civiliz'd, in spite of Christianity, and the Zeal for Religion which they so much affect, our Condition is not very much better. And even in *France*, a Country that treats our Sex with more Respect than most do, We are by the *Salique Law* excluded from Soveraign Power. The *French* are an ingenious People, and the Contrivers of that Law knew well enough, that We were no less capable of Reigning, and Governing well, than themselves; but they were suspicious, that if the Regal Power shou'd fall often into the hands of Women, they would favour their own Sex, and might in time restore 'em to their Primitive Liberty and Equality with the Men, and so break the neck of that unreasonable Authority they so much affect over us; and therefore made this Law to prevent it. The Historians indeed tell us other Reasons, but they can't agree among themselves, and as Men are Parties against us, and therefore their Evidence may justly be rejected. To say the truth Madam, I can't tell how to prove all this from Ancient Records; for if any Histories were anciently written by Women, Time, and the Malice of Men have effectually conspir'd to suppress 'em; and it is not reasonable to think that Men shou'd transmit, or suffer to be transmitted to Posterity, any thing that might shew the weakness and illegallity of their Title to a Power they still exercise so arbitrarily, and are so fond of. But since daily Experience shews, and their own Histories tell us, how earnestly they endeavour, and what they act, and suffer to put the same Trick upon one another, 'tis natural to suppose they took the same measures with us at first, which now they have effected, like the Rebels in our last Civil Wars, when they had brought the Royal Party under, they fall together by the Ears about the Dividend. The Sacred History takes no notice of any such Authority they had before the Flood, and their Own confess that whole Nations have rejected it since, and not suffer'd a Man to live amongst them, which cou'd be for no other Reason, than their Tyranny. For upon less provocation the Women wou'd never have been so foolish, as to deprive themselves of the benefit of that Ease and Security, which a good agreement with their Men might have afforded 'em. 'Tis true the same Histories tell us, that there were whole Countries where were none but Men, which border'd upon 'em. But this makes still for us; for it shews that the Conditions of their Society were not so easie, as to engage their Woman to stay amongst 'em; but as liberty presented it self, they withdrew and retired to the *Amazons*. But since our Sex can hardly boast of so great Privileges, and so easie a Servitude any where as in *England*, I cut this ungrateful Digression short in acknowledgement; tho' Fetters of Gold are still Fetters, and the softest Lining can never make 'em so easy, as Liberty.

MARY ASTELL

(1666–1731)

Author of feminist polemics and religious tracts, Mary Astell was born in Newcastle in 1666, the daughter of a coal merchant. Her clergyman uncle, encouraged by his niece's keen and eager mind, gave her an education. Her mother died when she was about twenty, and Astell left Newcastle to settle permanently in London. The first work Astell published is still her best known: *A Serious Proposal to the Ladies* (1694). It contains her radical proposal for establishing retreats for women where they could study, meditate, and become "wise and good" without the interference or jeers of English society. The influential Bishop Burnet misunderstood Astell's *Proposal* as an attempt to organize Catholic nunneries and violently opposed it, thus killing the idea for the time being. A continuation of her *Proposal* published in 1697 attempted to instruct uneducated women in the rules of rationality. In 1700, Astell published her tradition defying *Reflections on Marriage*. Astell was a devout Anglican; she published a number of religious tracts as well as an epistolary debate with Reverend John Norris (1695) about religious issues. She remained unmarried, and her high-minded manner caused her to be considered haughty by some of her contemporaries.

Although Astell published her writings anonymously, her identity as their author was widely known. Despite her strong feminist stance, she escaped public censure because of her political and religious conservatism, her exemplary life, and her influential friends. At sixty-five, Astell submitted to a mastectomy, which in the eighteenth century was a ghastly ordeal without anesthetic or antibiotic. She died of surgical complications.

EDITION USED: *Some Reflections Upon Marriage*, 4th ed. (London, 1730).

APPENDIX TO
SOME REFLECTIONS UPON MARRIAGE

THE REFLECTOR, who hopes Reflector is not bad English, (now Governor is happily of the feminine gender) guarded against curiosity in vain: For a certain ingenuous gentleman, as she is inform'd, had the good-nature to own these Reflections, so far, as to affirm that he had the original MS, in his closet, a proof she is not able to produce; and so to make himself responsible for all their faults, for which,' she returns him all due acknowledgment. However, the generality being of opinion, that a man would have had more prudence and manners than to have publish'd such unseasonable truths, or to have betray'd the *Arcana imperii* [imperial secrets] of his sex; she humbly confesses, that the contrivance and execution of this design, which is unfortunately accus'd of being so destructive to the government, (of the men, I mean) is intirely her own. She neither advis'd with Friends, nor turn'd over antient or modern authors, nor prudently submitted to the correction of such as are, or such as think they are good judges, but with an English spirit and genius, set out upon the forlorn hope, meaning no hurt to any body, nor designing any thing but the publick good, and to retrieve, if possible, the native liberty, the rights and privileges of the subject.

Far be it from her to stir up sedition of any sort: none can abhor it more; and she heartily wishes, that our Masters would pay their civil and ecclesiastical governors the same submission, which they themselves exact from their domestick subjects. Nor can she imagine how she any way undermines the masculine empire or blows the trumpet of rebellion to the moiety of mankind. Is it by exhorting women, not to expect to have their own will in any thing, but to be intirely submissive, when once they have made choice of a Lord and Master, though he happen not to be so wise, so kind, or even so just a governor as was expected? She did not, indeed, advise them to think his folly wisdom, nor his brutality, that love and worship he promised in his matrimonial oath; for this required a flight of wit and sense much above her poor ability, and proper only to masculine understandings. However, she did not in any manner prompt them to resist, or to abdicate the perjur'd spouse, though the Laws of God, and the land, make special provision for it, in a case, wherein, as is to be fear'd, few Men can truly plead not guilty.

'Tis true, through want of learning, and of that superior genius which men, as men, lay claim to, she was ignorant of the natural inferiority of our sex, which our masters lay down as a self-evident and fundamental truth. She saw nothing in the reason of things, to make this either a principle or a conclusion, but much to the contrary; it being sedition at least, if not treason, to assert it in this reign. For if by the natural superiority of their sex, they mean, that every man is by nature superior to every woman, which is the obvious meaning, and that which must be stuck to if they would speak sense, it would be a sin in any woman, to have dominion over any man, and the greatest queen ought not to command, but to obey, her footman: because no municipal laws can supersede or change the law of nature: So that if the dominion of the men be such, the Salique Law, as unjust as English men have ever thought it, ought to take place over all the earth, and the most glorious reigns in the English, Danish, Castilian, and other annals, were wicked violations of the law of nature!

If they mean that some Men are superior to some women, this is no great discovery; had they turn'd the tables, they might have seen that some women are superior to some men. Or had they been pleased to remember their oaths of allegiance and supremacy, they might have known, that one woman is superior to all the men in these nations, or else they have sworn to very little purpose. And it must not be suppos'd, that their reason and religion would suffer them to take oaths, contrary to the law of nature and reason of things.

By all which it appears, that our Reflector's ignorance is very pitiable; it may be her misfortune, but not her crime, especially since she is willing to be better inform'd, and hopes she shall never be so obstinate as to shut her eyes against the light of truth, which is not to be charg'd with novelty, how late soever we may be bless'd with the discovery. Nor can error, be it as antient as it may, ever plead prescription against truth. And since the only way to remove all doubts, to answer all objections, and to give the mind entire satisfaction, is not by affirming, but by proving, so that every one may see with their own eyes, and judge according to the best of their own understandings; she hopes it is no presumption to insist on this natural right of judging for her self, and the rather, because by quitting it, we give up all the means of rational conviction. Allow us then as many glasses as you please to help our sight, and as many good arguments as you can afford to convince our understandings: but don't exact of us, we beseech you, to affirm that we see such things as are only the discovery of men who have quicker senses; or, that we understand, and know what we have by hearsay only; for to be so excessively complaisant, is neither to see nor to understand.

That the custom of the world, has put women, generally speaking, into a state of subjection, is not denied; but the right can no more be prov'd from the fact, than the predominancy of vice can justify it. A certain great man, has endeavour'd to prove, by reasons not contemptible, that in the original state of things the woman was the superior, and that her subjection to the man is an effect of the fall, and the punishment of her sin: and, that ingenious theorist Mr. Whiston asserts, that before the fall there was a greater equality between the two sexes. However this be, 'tis certainly no arrogance in a woman to conclude, that she was made for the service of God, and that this is her end. Because God made all things for Himself, and a rational mind is too noble a being to be made for the sake of service of any creature. The service she at any time becomes oblig'd to pay to man, is only a business by the bye, just as it may be any man's business and duty to keep hogs; he was not made for this, but if he hires himself out to such an employment, he ought conscientiously to perform it. Nor can any thing be concluded to the contrary from St. Paul's Argument, I Cor. xi. for he argues only for decency and order, according to the present custom and state of things: Taking his words strictly and literally, they prove too much, in that praying and prophecying in the Church are allow'd the women, provided they do it with their head cover'd as well as the men; and no inequality can be inferr'd from hence, neither from the gradation the Apostle there uses, that *the head of every man is Christ, and that the head of the woman is the man, and the head of Christ is God;* it being evident from the form of Baptism, that there is no natural inferiority among the divine persons, but that they are in all things coequal. The Apostle, indeed, adds, that *the man is the Glory of God, and the woman the Glory of Man,* etc. But what does he infer from hence? He says not a word of inequality, or natural inferiority; but concludes, that a woman ought to cover her head, and a man ought not to cover his, and that even nature itself teaches us, that if a man have long hair it is a shame unto him. Whatever the Apostle's argument proves in this place, nothing can be plainer, than that there is much more said against the present fashion of men wearing long hair, than for that supremacy they lay claim to. For by all that appears in the text, it is not so much a law of nature, that women should obey men, as that men should not wear long hair. Now how can a Christian Nation allow fashions contrary to the law of nature, forbidden by an Apostle, and declared by him to be a shame to men? Or if custom may make an alteration in one case, it may in another, but what then becomes of the nature of reason of things? Besides, the conclusion the Apostle draws from his argument concerning women, viz. that they *should have power on their heads because of the angels,* is so very obscure a text, that that ingenious paraphrast, who pleads so much for the natural subjection of women, ingeniously confesses, that he does not understand it. Probably it refers to some custom among the Corinthians, which being well known to them, the Apostle only hints at it, but which we are ignorant of, and therefore apt to mistake him. 'Tis like, that the false Apostle whom St. Paul writes against, had led captive some of their rich and powerful, but silly women, who having as mean an opinion of the reason God had given them, as any deceiver could desire, did not, like the noble minded Bereans, *search the scriptures whether those things were so,* but lazily took up with having mens persons in admiration, and follow'd their leaders blindfold, the certain rout to destruction. And it is also probable, that the same cunning seducer imploy'd these women to carry on his own designs, and putting them upon what he might not think fit to appear in himself, made them guilty of indecent behaviour in the Church of Corinth. And therefore St. Paul thought it necessary to reprove them so severely, in order to humble them; but this being done, he takes care in the conclusion to set the matter on a right foot, placing the two sexes on a level, to keep men, as much as might be, from taking those advantages which people who have strength in their hands, are apt to assume over those who can't contend with them. For, says he, nevertheless, or notwithstanding the former argument, *the man is not without the woman, nor the woman without the man, but all things of God.* The relation between the two sexes is mutual, and the dependence reciprocal, both of them depending intirely upon God, and upon Him only; which one would think, is no great argument of the natural inferiority of either sex.

Our Reflector is of opinion, that disputes of this kind, extending to human nature in general, and not peculiar to those to whom the Word of God has been revealed, ought to be decided by natural reason only. And, that the Holy Scripture should not be interested in the present controversy, in which it determines nothing, any more than it does between the Copernican and Ptolomean systems. The design of those Holy Books being to make us excellent moralists and perfect Christians, not great philosophers, and being writ for the vulgar as well as for the learned, they are accommodated to the common way of speech and the usage of the world, in which we have but a short probation, so that it matters not much what part we act, whether of governing or obeying, provided we perform it well with respect to the world to come.

One does not wonder, indeed, that when an adversary is drove to a non-plus, and reason declares against him, he flies to authority, especially to divine, which is infallible, and therefore ought not to be disputed. But Scripture is not always on their side who make parade of it, and through their skill in languages, and the tricks of the schools, wrest it from its genuine sense to their own inventions. And supposing, not granting, that it were apparently to the womens disadvantage, no fair and generous adversary but would be asham'd to urge this advantage: because women, without their own fault, are kept in ignorance of the original, wanting languages and other helps to criticise on the sacred text, of which, they know no more, than men are pleas'd to impart in their translations. In short, they shew their desire to maintain their hypotheses, but by no means their reverence to the Sacred Oracles, who engage them in such disputes. And therefore, the blame be theirs, who have unnecessarily introduc'd them in the present subject, and who, by saying, that the reflections were not agreeable to scripture, oblige the reflector to shew, that those who affirm it must either mistake her meaning, or the sense of Holy Scripture, or both, if they think what they say, and do not find fault meerly because they resolve to do so. For, had she ever writ any thing contrary to those sacred Truths, she would be the first in pronouncing its condemnation.

But what says the Holy Scripture? It speaks of women as in a state of subjection, and so it does of the Jews and Christians, when under the dominion of the Chaldeans and Romans, requiring of the one as well as of the other, a quiet submission to them under whose power they liv'd. But will any one say, that these had a natural superiority and right to dominion? that they had a superior understanding, of any pre-eminence, except what their greater strength acquir'd? Or, that the other were subjected to their adversaries for any other reason but the punishment of their sins, and, in order to their reformation? Or for the exercise of their vertue, and because the order of the world and the good of society requir'd it?

If mankind had never sin'd, reason would always have been obeyed, there would have been no struggle for dominion, and brutal power would not have prevail'd. But in the lapsed state of mankind, and now, that men will not be guided by their reason but by their appetites, and do not what they *ought* but what they *can,* the reason, or that which stands for it, the will and pleasure of the governor, is to be the reason of those who will not be guided by their own, and must take place for order's sake, although it should not be conformable to right reason. Nor can there be any society great or little, from empires down to private families, without a last resort, to determine the affairs of that society by an irresistible sentence. Now unless this supremacy be fix'd somewhere, there will be a perpetual contention about it, such is the love of dominion, and let the reason of things be what it may, those who have least force or cunning to supply it, will have the disadvantage. So that since women are acknowledged to have least bodily strength, their being commanded to obey is in pure kindness to them, and for their quiet security, as well as for the exercise of their vertue. But does it follow, that domestick governors have more sense than their subjects, any more than that other governors have? We do not find that any man thinks the worse of his own understanding, because another has superior power; or concludes himself less capable of a post of honour and authority, because he is not prefer'd to it. How much time would lie on mens hands, how empty would the places of concourse be, and how silent most companies, did men forbear to censure their governors, that is, in effect, to think themselves wiser. Indeed, government would be much more desirable than it is, did it invest the possessor with a superior understanding as well as power. And if meer power gives a right to rule, there can be no such thing as usurpation; but a highwayman, so long as he has strength to force, has also a right to require our obedience.

Again, if absolute sovereignty be not necessary in a state, how comes it to be so in a family? Or if in a family why not in a state; since no reason can be alledged for the one that will not hold more strongly for the other? If the authority of the husband, so far as it extends, is sacred and inalienable, why not that of the Prince? The domestick sovereign is without dispute elected, and the stipulations and contract are mutual; is it not then partial in man to the last degree, to contend for, and practise that arbitrary dominion in their families, which they abhor and exclaim against in the state? For if arbitrary power is evil in it self, and an improper method of governing rational and free agents, it ought not to be practis'd any where; nor is it less, but rather more mischievous in families than in kingdoms, by how much 100,000 tyrants are worse than one. What though a husband can't deprive a wife of life without being responsible to the law, he may, however, do what is much more grievous to a generous mind, render life miserable, for which she has no redress, scarce pity, which is afforded to every other complainant, it being thought a wife's duty to suffer every thing without complaint. If all men are born free, how is it that all women are born slaves? As they must be, if the being subjected to the inconstant, uncertain, unknown, arbitrary will of men, be the perfect condition of slavery? And, if the essence of freedom consists, as our masters say it does, in having a standing rule to live by? And why is slavery so much condemn'd and strove against in one case, and so highly applauded, and held so necessary and so sacred in another?

'Tis true, that God told Eve after the Fall, that her husband should rule over her: And so it is, that he told Esau by the mouth of Isaac his father, that he should serve his younger brother, and should in time, when he was strong enough to do it, break the yoke from off his neck. Now, why one text should be a command anymore than the other, and not both of them be predictions only; or why the former should prove Adam's natural right to rule, and much less every man's any more than the latter is a proof of Jacob's right to rule, and of Esau's to rebel, one is yet to learn? The text in both cases foretelling what would be; but neither of them determining what *ought* to be.

But the Scripture commands *Wives to submit themselves to their own Husbands.* True; for which St. Paul gives a mystical reason (Eph. v. 22, etc.) and St. Peter, a prudential and charitable one (I Pet. iii.) but neither of them derive that subjection from the law of nature. Nay, St. Paul, as if he foresaw and meant to prevent this plea, giving directions for their conduct to women in general, I Tim. ii. when he comes to speak of subjection, he changes his phrase from women, which denotes the whole sex, to woman, which in the New Testament is appropriated to a wife.

As for his not suffering women to speak in the Church, no sober person that I know of pretends to it. That learned paraphrast, indeed, who lays so much stress on the natural subjection, provided this prerogative be secur'd, is willing to give up the other. For he endeavours to prove, that inspir'd women, as well as men, us'd to speak in the Church, and that St. Paul does not forbid it, but only takes care that the women should signify their subjection by wearing a veil. But the Apostle is his own best expositor, let us therefore compare his precepts with his practice, for he was all of a piece, and did not contradict himself. Now by this comparison we find, that though he forbids Women to teach in the Church, and this for several prudential reasons, like those he introduces with an *I give my opinion, and now speak I, not the Lord,* and not because of any law of nature, or positive divine precept, for that the words they are commanded (I Cor. xiv. 24.) are not in the original, appears from the italick character, yet he did not found this prohibition on any suppos'd want of understanding in woman, or of ability to teach; neither does he confine them at all times to learn in silence. For the eloquent Apollos, who was himself a teacher, was instructed by Priscilla, as well as by her husband Aquila, and was improv'd by them both in the Christian faith. Nor does St. Paul blame her for this, or suppose that she usurp'd authority over that great man; so far from this, that as she is always honourably mention'd in Holy Scripture, so our Apostle, in his salutations, Rom. xvi. places her in the front, even before her husband, giving to her, as well as to him, the noble title of, his helper in Christ Jesus, and of one to whom all the churches of the Gentiles had great obligations.

But it will be said perhaps, that in I Tim. ii. 13, etc. St. Paul argues for the woman's subjection from the reason of things. To this I answer, that it must be confess'd, that this (according to the vulgar interpretation) is a very obscure place, and I should be glad to see a natural, and not a forc'd interpretation given of it by those who take it literally: whereas if it be taken allegorically, with respect to the mystical union between Christ and his Church, to which St. Paul frequently accommodates the matrimonial relation, the difficulties vanish. For the earthly Adam's being form'd before Eve, seems as little to prove her natural subjection to him, as the living creatures, fishes, birds and beasts being form'd before them both proves that mankind must be subject to these animals. Nor can the Apostle mean that Eve only sinned, or that she only was deceiv'd, for if Adam sinn'd wilfully and knowingly, he became the greater transgressor. But it is very true, that the second Adam, the man Christ Jesus, was first form'd, and then his spouse the Church. He was not in any respect deceiv'd, nor does she pretend to infallibility. And from this second Adam, promis'd to Eve in the day of our first parents transgression, and from Him only, do all their race, men as well as women, derive their hopes of salvation. Nor is it promis'd to either sex on any other terms besides perseverance in faith, charity, holiness and sobriety.

If the learned will not admit of this interpretation, I know not how to contend with them. For sense is a portion that God Himself has been pleased to distribute to both sexes with an impartial hand, but learning is what men have engross'd to themselves, and one can't but admire their great improvements! For, after doubting whether there is such a thing as truth, and after many hundred years disputes about it, in the last century an extraordinary genius arose, (whom yet some are pleased to call a visionary) enquir'd after it, and laid down the best method of finding it. Not to the general liking of the Men of Letters, perhaps, because it was wrote in a vulgar language, and was so natural and easy as to debase truth to common understandings, shewing too plainly, that learning and true knowledge are two different things.

For it often happens (says that Author) that women and children acknowledge the falsehood of those prejudices we contend with, because they do not dare to judge without examination, and they bring all the attention they are capable of to what they read. Whereas on the contrary, the learned continue wedded to their own opinions, because they will not take the trouble of examining what is contrary to their receiv'd doctrines.

Sciences, indeed, have been invented and taught long ago, and as men grew better advis'd, new modelled. So that it is become a considerable piece of learning to give an account of the rise and progress of the sciences, and of the various opinions of men concerning them. But certainty and demonstration are much pretended to in this present age, and being obtain'd in many things, 'tis hoped men will never dispute them away in that which is of greatest importance, the way of salvation. And because there is not any thing more certain than what is delivered in the Oracles of God, we come now to consider what they offer in favour of our sex.

Let it be promis'd, (according to the reasoning of a very ingenious person in a like case) that one text for us, is more to be regarded than many against us. Because the one being different from what custom has established, ought to be taken with philosophical strictness; whereas the many being express'd according to the vulgar mode of speech, ought to have no greater stress laid on them, than that evident condescension will bear. One place then were sufficient, but we have many instances wherein Holy Scripture considers women very differently from what they appear in the common prejudices of mankind.

The world will hardly allow a woman to say any thing well, unless, as she borrows it from men, or as assisted by them. But God Himself allows that the daughters of *Zelophehad spake right,* and passes their request into a law. Considering how much the tyranny, shall I say, or the superior force of men, keeps women from acting in the world, or doing any thing considerable, and remembring withal the conciseness of the sacred story, no small part of it is bestow'd in transmitting the history of women, famous in their generations: Two of the canonical books, bearing the names of those great women whose vertues and actions are there recorded. *Ruth* being call'd from among the Gentiles to be an ancestor of the Messiah, and *Esther* being rais'd up by God to be the great instrument of the deliverance of prosperity of the Jewish church.

The character of Isaac, though one of the most blameless men taken notice of in the Old Testament, must give place to *Rebecca's,* whose affections are more reasonably plac'd than his, her favourite son being the same who was God's favourite. Nor was the blessing bestow'd according to his, but to her desire; so that if you will not allow, that her command to Jacob superseded Isaac's to Esau, his desire to give the blessing to this son, being evidently an effect of partiality; you must at least grant, that she paid greater deference to the divine revelation, and for this reason, at least, had a right to oppose her husband's design; which, it seems, Isaac was sensible of, when upon his disappointment, he trembled so exceedingly. And so much notice is taken even of Rebecca's nurse, that we have an account where she died, and where she was buried.

God is pleased to record it among His favours to the ingrateful Jews, that He sent before them His servants Moses, Aaron, and *Miriam;* who was also a prophetess, and instructed the Women how to bear their part with Moses in his triumphal hymn. Is she to be blam'd for her ambition? And is not the High Priest Aaron also, who has his share in the reproof as well as in the crime? nor could she have mov'd sedition if she had not been a considerable person, which appears also by the respect the people paid her, in deferring their journey till she was ready.

Where shall we find a nobler piece of poetry than *Deborah's* Song? Or a better and greater ruler than that renowned woman, whose government so much excelled that of the former judges? And though she had a husband, she herself judged Israel, and consequently was the sovereign, of whom we know no more than the name. Which instance, as I humbly suppose, overthrows the presence of natural inferiority. For it is not the bare relation of a fact, by which none ought to be concluded, unless it is conformable to a rule, and to the reason of things: But *Deborah's* government was conferr'd on her by God Himself. Consequently the sovereignty of a woman is not contrary to the law of nature; for the law of nature is the law of God, who cannot contradict Himself; and yet it was God who inspir'd and approv'd that great Woman, raising her up to judge and to deliver His people Israel.

Not to insist on the courage of that valiant woman, who deliver'd Thebez by slaying the assailant; nor upon the preference which God thought fit to give to Sampson's mother, in sending the Angel to her, and not to her husband, whose vulgar fear she so prudently answer'd, as plainly shews her superior understanding: to pass over *Abigail's* wise conduct, whereby she preserv'd her family and deserved David's acknowledgments, for restraining him from doing a rash and unjustifiable action; the holy penman giving her the character of a woman of good understanding, whilst her husband has that of a churlish and foolish person, and a son of Belial: to say nothing of the *wise Woman* (as the text calls her) of *Tekoah;* or of her of Abel, who has the same epithet, and who by her prudence delivered the city and appeas'd a dangerous rebellion: nor of the Queen of Sheba, whose journey to hear the wisdom of Solomon, shews her own good judgment and great share in that excellent endowment. Solomon does not think himself too wise to be instructed by his mother, nor too great to record her lessons, which, if he had followed, he might have spared the trouble of repentance, and been delivered from a great deal of that vanity he so deeply regrets.

What reason can be assign'd why the mothers of the Kings of Judah, are so frequently noted in those very short accounts that are given of their reigns, but the great respect paid them, or perhaps their influence on the government, and share in the administration? This is not improbable, since the wicked Athaliah had power to carry on her intrigues so far as to get possession of the throne, and to keep it for some years. Neither was there any necessity for Asa's removing his mother (or grandmother) from being Queen, if this were merely titular, and did not carry power and authority along with it. And we find what influence *Jezabel* had in Israel, indeed to her husband's and her own destruction.

It was a widow-woman whom God made choice of to sustain his prophet Elijah at Zarephah. And the history of the Shunamite is a noble instance of the account that is made of women in Holy Scripture. For whether it was not the custom in Shunem for the husband to dictate, or whether her's was conscious of her superior vertue, or whatever was the reason, we find it is she who governs, dwelling with great honour and satisfaction among her own people. Which happiness she understood so well, and was so far from a troublesome ambition, that she desires no recommendation to the King or Captain of the Host, when the prophet offer'd it, being already greater than they could make her. The text calls her a great woman, whilst her husband is hardly taken notice of, and this, no otherwise than as performing the office of a Bailiff. It is her piety and hospitality that are recorded. She invites the prophet to her house; who converses with, and is entertained by her. She gives her husband no account of her affairs any further, than to tell him her designs, that he may see them executed. And when he desires to know the reason of her conduct, all the answer she affords is, well, or, as the margin has it from the Hebrew, Peace. Nor can this be thought assuming, since it is no more than what the prophet encourages, for all his addresses are to her, he takes no notice of her husband. His benefits are conferr'd on her, 'tis she and her household whom he warns of a famine, and 'tis she who appeals to the King for the restitution of her house and land. I would not infer from hence that women, generally speaking, ought to govern in their families when they have a husband; but I think this instance and example is a sufficient proof, that if by custom or contract, or the laws of the country, or birth-right, (as in the case of sovereign princesses) they have the supreme authority, it is no usurpation, nor do they act contrary to Holy Scripture, nor consequently to the law of nature. For they are no where, that I know of, forbidden to claim their just right: the Apostle, 'tis true, would not have them usurp authority, where custom and the law of the strongest had brought them into subjection, as it has in these parts of the world. Though in remoter regions, if travellers rightly inform us, the succession to the crown is intail'd on the female line.

God Himself, who is no respecter of persons, with whom there is neither bond nor free, male nor female, but they are all one in Christ Jesus, did not deny women that divine gift the spirit of prophecy, neither under the Jewish nor Christian Dispensation. We have nam'd two great Prophetesses already, *Miriam* and *Deborah;* and besides other instances, *Huldah* the prophetess was such an Oracle, that the good King Josiah, that great pattern of vertue, sends even the High Priest himself to consult her, and to receive directions from her in the most arduous affairs. *It shall come to pass,* saith the Lord, *that I will pour out my Spirit upon all flesh, and your sons and your daughters shall prophesy,* which was accordingly fulfill'd by the mission of the Holy Ghost on the Day of Pentecost, as St. Peter tells us. And, besides others, there is mention of four daughters of Philip, virgins, who did prophesy. For as in the Old, so in the New Testament, women make a considerable figure, the Holy Virgin receiving the greatest honour that human nature is capable of, when the Son of God vouchsafed to be her son, and to derive his humanity from her only. And if it is a greater blessing to hear the Word of God and keep it, who are more considerable for their assiduity in this, than the female disciples of our Lord? *Mary* being exemplary, and receiving a noble Encomium from Him, for her choice of the better part.

It would be thought tedious to enumerate all the excellent women mentioned in the New Testament, whose humble penitence and ardent love, as *Magdalen's;* their lively faith and holy importunity, as the Syrophenician's, extraordinary piety and uprightness, as *Elizabeth's;* hospitality, charity and diligence, as *Martha's, Tabitha's,* etc. (see St. Luke viii); frequent and assiduous devotions and austerities, as *Anna's;* constancy and courage, perseverance, and ardent zeal, as that of the holy women who attended our Lord to His Cross, when His disciples generally forsook, and the most courageous had denied Him; are recorded for our example. Their love was stronger than death, it followed our Saviour into the grave. And, as a reward, both the Angel, and even the Lord Himself, appears first to them, and sends them to preach the great article of the resurrection to the very Apostles, who being, as yet, under the power of prejudices of their sex, esteem'd the holy womens *words as idle tales, and believed them not.*

Some men will have it, that the reason of our Lord's appearing first to the women, was, their being least able to keep a secret; a witty and masculine remark, and wonderfully reverent! But not to dispute whether those women were blabs or no, there are many instances in Holy Scripture, of women who did not betray the confidence repos'd in them. Thus *Rahab,* though formerly an ill woman, being converted by the report of those miracles, which though the *Israelites saw,* yet they *believed not in God, nor put their trust in his word,* she acknowledges the God of Heaven, and, as a reward of her faithful service in concealing Joshua's spies, is, with her family, exempted from the ruin of her country, and also has the honour of being named in the Messiah's genealogy. *Michal,* to save David's life, exposes her self to the fury of a jealous and tyrannical prince. A girl was trusted by David's grave counsellors to convey him intelligence in his Son's rebellion; and when a lad had found it out, and blab'd it to Absalom, the king's friends confiding in the prudence and fidelity of a woman, were secur'd by her. When our Lord escaped from the Jews, he trusted himself in the hands of *Martha* and *Mary.* So does St. Peter with another *Mary,* when the angel deliver'd him from Herod, the damsel *Rhoda* too, was acquainted with the secret. More might be said, but one would think here is enough to shew, that whatever other great and wise reasons men may have for despising women, and keeping them in ignorance and slavery, it can't be from their having learnt to do so in Holy Scripture. The Bible is for, and not against us, and cannot without great violence done to it, be urg'd to our prejudice.

However, there are strong and prevalent reasons which demonstrate the superiority and pre-eminence of the men. For in the first place, boys have much time and pains, care and cost bestow'd on their education, girls have little or none. The former are early initiated in the sciences, are made acquainted with antient and modern discoveries, they study books and men, have all imaginable encouragement; not only fame, a dry reward now a-days, but also title, authority, power, and riches themselves, which purchase all things, are the reward of their improvement. The latter are restrain'd, frown'd upon, and beat, nor for, but from the muses; laughter and ridicule, that never-failing scare-crow, is set up to drive them from the tree of knowledge. But if, in spite of all difficulties nature prevails, and they can't be kept so ignorant as their masters would have them, they are star'd upon as monsters, censur'd, envied, and every way discouraged, or, at the best, they have the fate the proverb assigns them, *vertue is prais'd and starv'd*. And therefore, since the coarsest materials need the most curing, as every workman can inform you, and the worst ground the most elaborate culture, it undeniably follows, that mens understandings are superior to womens, for, after many years study and experience, they become wise and learned, and women are not born so!

Again, men are possessed of all places of power, trust and profit, they make laws and exercise the magistracy, not only the sharpest sword, but even all the swords and blunderbusses are theirs, which by the strongest logick in the world, gives them the best title to every thing they please to claim as their prerogative: who shall contend with them? Immemorial prescription is on their side in these parts of the world, antient tradition and modern usage! Our fathers, have all along, both taught and practised superiority over the weaker sex, and consequently women are by nature inferior to men, as was to be demonstrated. An argument which must be acknowledged unanswerable; for, as well as I love my sex, I will not pretend a reply to such demonstration!

Only let me beg to be inform'd, to whom we poor fatherless maids, and widows who have lost their masters, owe subjection? It can't be to all men in general, unless all men were agreed to give the same commands; do we then fall as strays, to the first who finds us? By the maxims of some men, and the conduct of some women one would think so. But whoever he be that thus happens to become our master, if he allows us to be reasonable creatures, and does not meerly compliment us with that title, since no man denies our readiness to use our tongues, it would tend, I should think, to our master's advantage, and therefore he may please to be advis'd to teach us to improve our reason. But if reason is only allow'd us by way of raillery, and the secret maxim is, that we have none, or little more than brutes, 'tis the best way to confine us with chain and block to the chimney-corner, which probably, might save the estates of some families and the honour of others.

I do not propose this to prevent a rebellion, for women are not so well united as to form an insurrection. They are for the most part wise enough to love their chains, and to discern how very becomingly they fit. They think as humbly of themselves as their masters can wish, with respect to the other sex, but in regard to their own, they have a spice of masculine ambition, every one would lead, and none would follow. Both sexes being too apt to envy, and too backward in emulating, and take more delight in detracting from their neighbour's vertue, than in improving their own. And therefore, as to those women who find themselves born for slavery, and are so sensible of their own meanness, as to conclude it impossible to attain to any thing excellent, since they are, or ought to be best acquainted with their own strength and genius, she's a fool who would attempt their deliverance or improvement. No, let them enjoy the great honour and felicity of their tame, submissive and depending temper! Let the men applaud, and let them glory in this wonderful humility! Let them receive the flatteries and grimaces of the other sex, live unenvied by their own, and be as much belov'd as one such woman can afford to love another! Let them enjoy the glory of treading in the footsteps of their predecessors, and of having prudence to avoid that audacious attempt of soaring beyond their sphere! Let them huswife or play, dress, and be pretty entertaining company! Or, which is better, relieve the poor to ease their own compassions, read pious books, say their prayers, and go to church, because they have been taught and us'd to do so, without being able to give a better reason for their faith and practice! Let them not by any means aspire at being women of understanding, because no man can endure a woman of superior sense, or would treat a reasonable woman civilly, but that he thinks he stands on higher ground, and, that she is so wise as to make exceptions in his favour, and to take her measures by his directions; they may pretend to sense, indeed, since meer pretences only render one the more ridiculous! Let them, in short, be what is call'd very women, for this is most acceptable to all sorts of men; or let them aim at the title of good devout women, since some men can bear with this; but let them not judge of the sex by their own scantling: for the great author of nature and fountain of all perfection, never design'd that the mean and imperfect, but that the most compleat and excellent of His creatures in every kind, should be the standard to the rest.

To conclude; if that Great Queen who has subdued the proud, and made the pretended invincible more than once fly before her; who has rescued an empire, reduced a kingdom, conquer'd provinces in as little time almost as one can travel them, and seems to have chain'd victory to her standard; who disposes of crowns, gives laws and liberty to Europe, and is the chief instrument in the hand of the Almighty, to pull down and to set up the great men of the earth; who conquers every where for others, and no where for her self but in the hearts of the conquer'd, who are of the number of those who reap the benefit of her triumphs; whilst she only reaps for her self the lawrels of disinterested glory, and the royal pleasure of doing heroically; if this glory of her own sex, and envy of the other, will not think we need, or does not hold us worthy of, the protection of her ever victorious arms, and men have not the gratitude, for her sake at least, to do justice to her sex, who has been such a universal benefactress to theirs: adieu to the liberties, not of this or that nation or reign only, but of the Moiety of Mankind! To all the great things that women might perform, inspir'd by her example, encouraged by her smiles, and supported by her power! To their discovery of new worlds for the exercise of her goodness, new sciences to publish her fame, and reducing nature it self to a subjection to her empire! To their destroying those worst of Tyrants impiety and immorality, which dare to stalk about even in her own dominions, and to devour souls almost within view of her throne, leaving a stench behind them scarce to be corrected even by the incense of her devotions! To the women's tracing a new path to honor, in which none shall walk but such as scorn to cringe in order to rise, and who are proof both against giving and receiving flattery! In a word, to those halcyon, or, if you will, *Millennium* days, in which the wolf and the lamb shall feed together, and a tyrannous domination, which nature never meant, shall no longer render useless, if not hurtful, the industry and understandings of half mankind!

APHRA BEHN
(1640–1689)

Poet, playwright, novelist, and translator, Aphra Behn was probably the first English woman to earn her living solely through writing. Her early life is unclear. Her first biographer, identified only as "one of the Fair Sex," wrote in the "Life and Memoirs" that prefaces Behn's *Works*, "She was a Gentlewoman by Birth, of a good Family in the City of Canterbury in Kent; her Father's name was Johnson." Her father seems to have been appointed to a government post in Surinam, West Indies. He died on the voyage out, but Aphra arrived at the island, stayed at Sir Robert Harley's plantation, probably had an affair with a political exile named William Scot, and is believed to have taken part in a slave rebellion. At some point, she returned to London where she is believed to have married a tradesman of Dutch ancestry named Behn. He died of the plague in 1664. In 1666, she was sent to Antwerp, Holland, as a British spy, although it appears the government officials did not believe the reports she sent them. On her return to England, she was briefly imprisoned for debt.

At thirty years old, alone and impoverished but undaunted, Behn began writing plays. From about 1670 until her death nineteen years later, she wrote sixteen plays, most of which were successful and some of which are still performed today. One of these is *The Lucky Chance*, first produced in 1687. Her first smash hit was *The Rovers* (1677), which she brought out anonymously. It is a free-wheeling ribald comedy that most people assumed must have been written by a man. It is still her most popular play and is produced today more often than any of her others.

In addition to a highly successful career as a playwright, Behn was an accomplished poet, especially in her shorter lyrics, which celebrate the joys of sex as well as the trials of love. These show her acquaintance with the classic and contemporary poetry. Her songs, many of which are contained in her plays, display her ability to combine traditional poetic devices, especially the pastoral conventions, with her characteristic directness of expression. Her collected *Poems* were published in 1684.

Behn is also one of the founders of the English novel. Her *Love Letters between a Nobleman and His Sister* (1684–87) was very popular and is available in print today. It is based on a real scandal in which an English nobleman eloped with his sister-in-law. She also wrote *Oroonoko* (1688), a novel based on her experiences in Surinam, which depicts the rebel slave leader as an African prince. It, too, is still in print. She translated several works from French, including the romantic story *Agnes de Castro* (1688) which was made into a play by Catherine Trotter.

Behn is known for her sexual freedom, her frank (even coarse) language, and her criticism of the double standard that gave men sexual freedom, but insisted that women remain chaste. She identified woman's eternal dilemma in "Poems Appended to Lycidus":

> They fly if Honour take our part,
> Our Virtue drives 'em o're the field.
> We lose 'em by too much desert,
> And Oh! they fly us if we yeild [sic].

In the preface to *The Lucky Chance*, Behn, in typically direct language, defends herself against charges of scandalous writing and attacks the double standard for authors. If she writes of cuckolds and prostitutes, she sees "nothing unnatural or obscene: 'tis proper for the Characters." She further observes: "had the Plays I have writ come forth under any Mans Name, and never known to have been mine; I appeal to all unbyast Judges of Sense, if they had not said that Person had made as many good Comedies, as any one Man that has writ in our Age; but a Devil on't the Woman damns the Poet." Determined to think and act with the freedom of a man, she delights in turning the sexual tables, as in "The Disappointment," in which the man rather than the woman falls victim to sexual desire.

Behn was a remarkable woman, who flouted the conventions of her time. Recently, scholars have rediscovered her works and are justly asserting the importance of her contributions to English literature.

EDITION USED: *The Works of Aphra Behn,* ed. Montague Summers (London, 1915).

The Invitation

Damon I cannot blame your will,
'Twas Chance and not Design did kill;
For whilst you did prepare your Charmes,
On purpose *Silvia* to subdue:
I met the Arrows as they flew,   5
And sav'd her from their harms.

Alas she cannot make returnes,
Who for a Swaine already Burnes;
A Shepherd whom she does Caress:
With all the softest marks of Love,   10
And 'tis in vaine thou seek'st to move
The cruel Shepherdess.

Content thee with this Victory,
Think me as faire and young as she:

I'le make thee *Garlands* all the day,   15
And in the Groves we'l sit and sing;
I'le Crown thee with the pride o'th' Spring,
When thou art Lord of *May*.

The Disappointment

1

One day the Amorous *Lysander*,
By an impatient Passion sway'd,
Surpriz'd fair *Cloris*, that lov'd Maid,
Who could defend her self no longer.
All things did with his Love conspire;   5
The gilded Planet of the Day,
In his gay Chariot drawn by Fire,
Was now descending to the Sea,
And left no Light to guide the World,
But what from *Cloris* Brighter Eyes was hurld.   10

2

In a lone Thicket made for Love,
Silent as yielding Maids Consent,
She with a Charming Languishment,
Permits his Force, yet gently strove;
Her Hands his Bosom softly meet,   15
But not to put him back design'd,
Rather to draw 'em on inclin'd:
Whilst he lay trembling at her Feet,
Resistance 'tis in vain to show;
She wants the pow'r to say — *Ah! What d'ye do?*   20

3

Her Bright Eyes sweet, and yet severe,
Where Love and Shame confus'dly strive,
Fresh Vigor to *Lysander* give;
And breathing faintly in his Ear,

She cry'd—*Cease, Cease—your vain Desire,*   25
Or I'll call out—What would you do?
My Dearer Honour ev'n to You
I cannot, must not give—Retire,
Or take this Life, whose chiefest part
I gave you with the Conquest of my Heart.   30

4

But he as much unus'd to Fear,
As he was capable of Love,
The blessed minutes to improve,
Kisses her Mouth, her Neck, her Hair;
Each Touch her new Desire Alarms,   35
His burning trembling Hand he prest
Upon her swelling Snowy Brest,
While she lay panting in his Arms.
All her Unguarded Beauties lie
The Spoils and Trophies of the Enemy.   40

5

And now without Respect or Fear,
He seeks the Object of his Vows,
(His Love no Modesty allows)
By swift degrees advancing—where
His daring Hand that Altar seiz'd,   45
Where Gods of Love do sacrifice:
That Awful Throne, that Paradice
Where Rage is calm'd, and Anger pleas'd;
That Fountain where Delight still flows,
And gives the Universal World Repose.   50

6

Her Balmy Lips incountring his,
Their Bodies, as their Souls; are joyn'd;
Where both in Transports Unconfin'd
Extend themselves upon the Moss.
Cloris half dead and breathless lay;   55

Her soft Eyes cast a Humid Light,
Such as divides the Day and Night;
Or falling Stars, whose Fires decay:
And now no signs of Life she shows,
But what in short-breath'd Sighs returns and goes.   60

7

He saw how at her Length she lay;
He saw her rising Bosom bare;
Her loose thin *Robes*, through which appear
A Shape design'd for Love and Play;
Abandon'd by her Pride and Shame.   65
She does her softest Joys dispence,
Off'ring her Virgin-Innocence
A Victim to Loves Sacred Flame;
While the o'er-Ravish'd Shepherd lies
Unable to perform the Sacrifice.   70

8

Ready to taste a thousand Joys,
The too transported hapless Swain
Found the vast Pleasure turn'd to Pain;
Pleasure which too much Love destroys:
The willing Garments by he laid,   75
And Heaven all open'd to his view,
Mad to possess, himself he threw
On the Defenceless Lovely Maid.
But Oh what envying God conspires
To snatch his Power, yet leave him the Desire!   80

9

Nature's Support (without whose Aid
She can no Humane Being give)
It self now wants the Art to live;
Faintness its slack'ned Nerves invade:
In vain th' inraged Youth essay'd   85
To call its fleeting Vigor back,
No motion 'twill from Motion take;
Excess of Love his Love betray'd:

In vain he Toils, in vain Commands;
The Insensible fell weeping in his Hand.   90

10

In this so Amorous Cruel Strife,
Where Love and Fate were too severe,
The poor *Lysander* in despair
Renounc'd his Reason with his Life:
Now all the brisk and active Fire   95
That should the Nobler Part inflame,
Serv'd to increase his Rage and Shame,
And left no Spark for New Desire:
Not all her Naked Charms cou'd move
Or calm that Rage that had debauch'd his Love.   100

11

Cloris returning from the Trance
Which Love and soft Desire had bred,
Her timerous Hand she gently laid
(Or guided by Design or Chance)
Upon that Fabulous *Priapus*,   105
That Potent God, as Poets feign;
But never did young *Shepherdess*,
Gath'ring of Fern upon the Plain,
More nimbly draw her Fingers back,
Finding beneath the verdant Leaves a Snake: 110

12

Than *Cloris* her fair Hand withdrew,
Finding that God of her Desires
Disarm'd of all his Awful Fires,
And Cold as Flow'rs bath'd in the Morning Dew.
Who can the *Nymph's* Confusion guess?   115
The Blood forsook the hinder Place,
And strew'd with Blushes all her Face,
Which both Disdain and Shame exprest:

And from *Lysander's* Arms she fled,
Leaving him fainting on the Gloomy Bed.   120

13

Like Lightning through the Grove she hies,
Or *Daphne* from the *Delphick God*,
No Print upon the grassey Road
She leaves, t' instruct Pursuing Eyes.
The Wind that wanton'd in her Hair,   125
And with her Ruffled Garments plaid,
Discover'd in the Flying Maid
All that the Gods e'er made, if Fair.
So *Venus*, when her *Love* was slain,
With Fear and Haste flew o'er the Fatal Plain.   130

14

The *Nymph's* Resentments none but I
Can well Imagine or Condole:
But none can guess *Lysander's* Soul,
But those who sway'd his Destiny.
His silent Griefs swell up to Storms,   135
And not one God his Fury spares;
He curs'd his Birth, his Fate, his Stars;
But more the *Shepherdess's* Charms,
Whose soft bewitching Influence
Had Damn'd him to the *Hell* of Impotence.   140

To Alexis in Answer to his Poem
against Fruition

Ah hapless sex! who bear no charms,
But what like lightning flash and are no more,
    False fires sent down for baneful harms,
Fires which the fleeting Lover feebly warms
    And given like past Beboches o're,   5

Like Songs that please (thô bad,) when new,
But learn'd by heart neglected grew.

In vain did Heav'n adorn the shape and face
With Beautyes which by Angels forms it drew:
In vain the mind with brighter Glories Grace,   10
While all our joys are stinted to the space
     Of one betraying enterview,
With one surrender to the eager will
We're short-liv'd nothing, or a real ill.

Since Man with that inconstancy was born,   15
To love the absent, and the present scorn,
     Why do we deck, why do we dress
     For such a short-liv'd happiness?
     Why do we put Attraction on,
Since either way tis we must be undon?   20

     They fly if Honour take our part,
     Our Virtue drives 'em o're the field.
     We lose 'em by too much desert,
     And Oh! they fly us if we yeild.
Ye Gods! is there no charm in all the fair   25
To fix this wild, this faithless, wanderer?

     Man! our great business and our aim,
     For whom we spread our fruitless snares,
No sooner kindles the designing flame,
     But to the next bright object bears   30
The Trophies of his conquest and our shame:
     Inconstancy's the good supream
The rest is airy Notion, empty Dream!

     Then, heedless Nymph, be rul'd by me
     If e're your Swain the bliss desire;   35
     Think like *Alexis* he may be
     Whose wisht Possession damps his fire;
     The roving youth in every shade
Has left some sighing and abandon'd Maid,

For tis a fatal lesson he has learn'd,   40
After fruition ne're to be concern'd.

Song

Love in fantastick Triumph sat,
    Whilst bleeding Hearts around him flow'd,
For whom fresh Pains he did create,
    And strange Tyrannick Pow'r he shew'd;
From thy bright Eyes he took his Fires,   5
    Which round about in sport he hurl'd;
But 'twas from mine he took Desires,
    Enough t'undo the amorous World.

From me he took his Sighs and Tears,
    From thee his Pride and Cruelty;   10
From me his Languishments and Fears,
    And ev'ry killing Dart from thee:
Thus thou, and I, the God have arm'd,
    And set him up a Deity;
But my poor Heart alone is harm'd,   15
    Whilst thine the Victor is, and free.

The Willing Mistriss

Amyntas led me to a Grove,
    Where all the Trees did shade us;
The Sun it self, though it had Strove,
    It could not have betray'd us:
The place secur'd from humane Eyes,   5
    No other fear allows,
    But when the Winds that gently rise,
Doe Kiss the yeilding Boughs.

Down there we satt upon the Moss,
    And did begin to play   10

A Thousand Amorous Tricks, to pass
    The heat of all the day.
A many Kisses he did give:
    And I return'd the same
Which made me willing to receive   15
    That which I dare not name.

His Charming Eyes no Aid requir'd
    To tell their softning Tale;
On her that was already fir'd,
    'Twas Easy to prevaile.   20
He did but Kiss and Clasp me round,
    Whilst those his thoughts Exprest:
And lay'd me gently on the Ground;
    Ah who can guess the rest?

To Lysander

1

Take back that Heart, you with such Caution give,
Take the fond valu'd Trifle back;
I hate Love-Merchants that a Trade wou'd drive;
And meanly cunning Bargains make.

2

I care not how the busy Market goes,   5
And scorn to chaffer for a price:
Love does one Staple Rate on all impose,
Nor leaves it to the Traders choice.

3

A Heart requires a Heart unfeign'd and True,
Though Subt'ly you advance the Price,   10
And ask a Rate that Simple Love ne'er knew:
And the free Trade Monopolize.

4

An humble *Slave* the Buyer must become,
She must not bate a Look or Glance,
You will have all, or you'll have none;   15
See how Loves Market you inhaunce.

5

Is't not enough, I gave you Heart for Heart,
But I must add my Lips and Eies;
I must no friendly Smile or Kiss impart;
But you must *Dress* me with Advice.   20

6

And every Hour still more unjust you grow,
Those Freedoms you my life deny,
You to *Adraste* are oblig'd to show,
And give her all my Rifled Joy.

7

Without Controul she gazes on that Face,   25
And all the happy Envyed Night,
In the pleas'd circle of your fond imbrace:
She takes away the Lovers Right.

8

From me she ravishes those silent hours,
That are by Sacred Love my due;   30
Whilst I in vain accuse the Angry Powers,
That makes me hopeless Love pursue.

9

Adrastes Ears with that dear Voice are blest,
That Charms my Soul at every Sound,
And with those *Love-Inchanting* Touches prest: 35
Which I ne'er felt without a Wound.

10

She has thee all: whilst I with silent Grief
The Fragments of thy Softness feel,
Yet dare not blame the happy licenc'd Theif:
That does my Dear-bought Pleasures steal.   40

11

Whilst like a glimering Taper still I burn,
And waste my self in my own flame,
Adraste takes the welcome rich Return:
And leaves me all the hopeless Pain.

12

Be just, my lovely *Swain*, and do not take   45
Freedoms you'll not to me allow;
Or give *Amynta* so much Freedom back:
That she may rove as well as you.

13

Let us then love upon the honest Square,
Since Interest neither have design'd,   50
For the sly Gamester, who ne'er plays me fair,
Must Trick for Trick expect to find.

THE LUCKY CHANCE

Preface

THE LITTLE Obligation I have to some of the witty Sparks and Poets of the
Town, has put me on a Vindication of this Comedy from those Censures
that Malice, and ill Nature have thrown upon it, tho in vain: The Poets I
heartily excuse, since there is a sort of Self-Interest in their Malice, which I
shou'd rather call a witty Way they have in this Age, of Railing at every
thing they find with pain successful, and never to shew good Nature and
speak well of any thing; but when they are sure 'tis damn'd, then they

afford it that worse Scandal, their Pity. And nothing makes them so thorough-stitcht an Enemy as a full Third Day, that's Crime enough to load it with all manner of Infamy; and when they can no other way prevail with the Town, they charge it with the old never failing Scandal— That 'tis not fit for the Ladys: As if (if it were as they falsly give it out) the Ladys were oblig'd to hear Indecencys only from their Pens and Plays and some of them have ventur'd to treat 'em as Coursely as 'twas possible, without the least Reproach from them; and in some of their most Celebrated Plays have entertained 'em with things, that if I should here strip from their Wit and Occasion that conducts 'em in and makes them proper, their fair Cheeks would perhaps wear a natural Colour at the reading them: yet are never taken Notice of, because a Man writ them, and they may hear that from them they blush at from a Woman—But I make a Challenge to any Person of common Sense and Reason—that is not wilfully bent on ill Nature, and will in spight of Sense wrest a double *Entendre* from every thing, lying upon the Catch for a Jest or a Quibble, like a Rook for a Cully; but any unprejudic'd Person that knows not the Author, to read any of my Comedys and compare 'em with others of this Age, and if they find one Word that can offend the chastest Ear, I will submit to all their peevish Cavills; but Right or Wrong they must be Criminal because a Woman's; condemning them without having the Christian Charity, to examine whether it be guilty or not, with reading, comparing, or thinking; the Ladies taking up any Scandal on Trust from some conceited Sparks, who will in spight of Nature be Wits and *Beaus*; then scatter it for Authentick all over the Town and Court, poysoning of others Judgments with their false Notions, condemning it to worse than Death, Loss of Fame. And to fortifie their Detraction, charge me with all the Plays that have ever been offensive; though I wish with all their Faults I had been the Author of some of those they have honour'd me with.

For the farther Justification of this Play; it being a Comedy of Intrigue Dr. *Davenant* out of Respect to the Commands he had from Court, to take great Care that no Indecency should be in Plays, sent for it and nicely look't it over, putting out anything he but imagin'd the Criticks would play with. After that, Sir *Roger L'Estrange* read it and licens'd it, and found no such Faults as 'tis charg'd with: Then Mr. *Killigrew*, who more severe than any, from the strict Order he had, perus'd it with great Circumspection; and lastly the Master Players, who you will I hope in some Measure esteem Judges of Decency and their own Interest, having been so many Years Prentice to the Trade of Judging.

I say, after all these Supervisors the Ladys may be convinc'd, they left nothing that could offend, and the Men of their unjust Reflections on so many Judges of Wit and Decencys. When it happens that I challenge any one, to point me out the least Expression of what some have made their Discourse, they cry, *That Mr.* Leigh *opens his Night Gown, when he comes into the Bride-chamber*; if he do, which is a Jest of his own making, and which I never saw, I hope he has his Cloaths on underneath? And if so, where is the Indecency? I have seen in that admirable Play of *Oedipus*, the Gown open'd wide, and the Man shown in his Drawers and Waist coat, and never thought it an Offence before. Another crys, *Why we know not what they mean, when the Man takes a Woman off the Stage, and another is thereby cuckolded*; is that any more than you see in the most Celebrated of your Plays? as the *City Politicks*, the *Lady Mayoress*, and the *Old Lawyers Wife*, who goes with a Man she never saw before, and comes out again the joyfull'st Woman alive, for having made her Husband a Cuckold with such Dexterity, and yet I see nothing unnatural nor obscene: 'tis proper for the Characters. So in that lucky Play of the *London Cuckolds*, not to recite Particulars. And in that good Comedy of *Sir Courtly Nice*, the *Taylor to the young Lady*—in the fam'd Sir *Fopling Dorimont* and *Bellinda*, see the very Words—in *Valentinian*, see the Scene between the *Court Bawds*. And *Valentinian* all loose and ruffld a Moment after the Rape, and all this you see without Scandal, and a thousand others The *Moor of Venice* in many places. The *Maids Tragedy*—see the Scene of undressing the Bride, and between the *King* and *Amintor*, and after between the *King* and *Evadne*—All these I Name as some of the best Plays I know; If I should repeat the Words exprest in these Scenes I mention, I might justly be charg'd with course ill Manners, and very little Modesty, and yet they so naturally fall into the places they are designed for, and so are proper for the Business, that there is not the least Fault to be found with them; though I say those things in any of mine wou'd damn the whole Peice, and alarm the Town. Had I a Day or two's time, as I have scarce so many Hours to write this in (the Play, being all printed off and the Press waiting,) I would sum up all your Beloved Plays, and all the Things in them that are past with such Silence by; because written by Men: such Masculine Strokes in me, must not be allow'd. I must conclude those Women (if there be any such) greater Critics in that sort of Conversation than my self, who find any of that sort in mine, or any thing that can justly be reproach't. But 'tis in vain by dint of Reason or Comparison to convince the obstinate Criticks, whose Business is to find Fault, if not by a loose and gross Imagination to create them, for they must either find the Jest, or make it; and those of this sort fall to my share, they find Faults of another kind for the Men Writers. And this one thing I will venture to say, though against my Nature, because it has a Vanity in it: That had the Plays I have writ come forth under any Mans Name, and never known to have been mine; I appeal to all unbyast Judges of Sense, if they had not said that Person had made as many good Comedies, as any one Man that has writ in our Age; but a Devil on't the Woman damns the Poet.

Ladies, for its further Justification to you, be pleas'd to know, that the first Copy of this Play was read by several Ladys of very great Quality, and unquestioned Fame, and received their most favourable Opinion, not one charging it with the Crime, that some have been pleas'd to find in the Acting. Other Ladys who saw it more than once, whose Quality and Vertue can sufficiently justifie any thing they design to favour, were pleas'd to say, they found an Entertainment in it very far from scandalous; and for the Generality of the Town, I found by my Receipts it was not thought so Criminal. However, that shall not be an Incouragement to me to trouble the Criticks with new Occasion of affronting me, for endeavouring at least to divert; and at this rate, both the few Poets that are left, and the Players who toil in vain will be weary of their Trade.

I cannot omit to tell you, that a Wit of the Town, a Friend of mine at *Wills* Coffee House, the first Night of the Play, cry'd it down as much as in him lay, who before had read it and assured me he never saw a prettier Comedy. So complaisant one pestilent Wit will be to another, and in the full Cry make his Noise too; but since 'tis to the witty Few I speak, I hope the better Judges will take no Offence, to whom I am oblig'd for better Judgments; and those I hope will be so kind to me, knowing my Conversation not at all addicted to the Indecencys alledged, that I would much less practice it in a Play, that must stand the Test of the censoring World. And I must want common Sense, and all the Degrees of good Manners, renouncing my Fame, all Modesty and Interest for a silly Sawcy fruitless Jest, to make Fools laugh, and Women blush, and wise Men asham'd; My self all the while, if I had been guilty of this Crime charg'd to me, remaining the only stupid, insensible. Is this likely, is this reasonable to be believ'd by any body, but the wilfully blind? All I ask, is the Priviledge for my Masculine Part the Poet in me, (if any such you will allow me) to tread in those successful Paths my Predecessors have so long thriv'd in, to take those Measures that both the Ancient and Modern Writers have set me, and by which they have pleas'd the World so well: If I must not, because of my Sex, have this Freedom, but that you will usurp all to your selves; I lay down my Quill, and you shall hear no more of me, no not so much as to make Comparisons, because I will be kinder to my Brothers of the Pen, than they have been to a defenceless Woman; for I am not content to write for a Third day only. I value Fame as much as if I had been born a *Hero*; and if you rob me of that, I can retire from the ungrateful World, and scorn its fickle Favours.

Dramatis Personæ

SIR FEEBLE FAINWOU'D, an old Alderman to be married to LETICIA
SIR CAUTIOUS FULBANK, an old Banker married to JULIA
MR. GAYMAN, a Spark of the Town, Lover of JULIA
MR. BELLMOUR, contracted to LETICIA, disguis'd, and passes for SIR FEEBLE'S Nephew
MR. BEARJEST, Nephew to SIR CAUTIOUS, a Fop
CAPT. NOISEY, his Companion
MR. BREDWEL, Prentice to SIR CAUTIOUS, and Brother to LETICIA, in love with DIANA
RAG, Footman to GAYMAN
RALPH, Footman to SIR FEEBLE
DICK, Footman to SIR CAUTIOUS
GINGLE, a Music Master
A POST-MAN
Two PORTERS
A SERVANT

LADY FULBANK, in love with GAYMAN, honest and generous
LETICIA, contracted to BELLMOUR, married to SIR FEEBLE, young and virtuous
DIANA, Daughter to SIR FEEBLE, in love with BREDWEL; virtuous
PERT, LADY FULBANK'S Woman
GAMMER GRIME, Landlady to GAYMAN, a Smith's Wife in Alsatia
SUSAN, Servant to SIR FEEBLE
PHILLIS, LETICIA'S Woman

A PARSON, FIDLERS, DANCERS and SINGERS

Prologue

Since with old Plays you have so long been cloy'd,
As with a Mistress many years enjoy'd,
How briskly dear Variety you pursue;
Nay, though for worse ye change, ye will have New.
Widows take heed some of you in fresh Youth   5
Have been the unpitied Martyrs of this Youth.
When for a drunken Sot, that had kind hours,
And taking their own freedoms, left you yours;
'Twas your delib'rate choice your days to pass
With a damn'd, sober, self-admiring Ass,   10
Who thinks good usage for the Sex unfit,
And slights ye out of Sparkishness and Wit.
But you can fit him — Let a worse Fool come,
If he neglect, to officiate in his room.
Vain amorous Coxcombs every where are found,   15
Fops for all uses, but the Stage abound.
Though you shou'd change them oftener than your Fashions,
There still wou'd be enough for your Occasions:
But ours are not so easily supplied,
All that cou'd e'er quit cost, we have already tried.   20
Nay, dear sometimes have bought the Frippery stuff. ⎫
This, Widows, you — I mean the old and tough —   ⎬
Will never think, be they but Fool enough.   ⎭

    Such will with any kind of Puppies play; ⎫
But we must better know for what we pay: ⎬   25
We must not purchase such dull Fools as they. ⎭
Shou'd we shew each her own partic'lar Dear,
What they admire at home, they wou'd loath here.
Thus, though the Mall, the Ring, the Pit is full,
And every Coffee-House still swarms with Fool;   30
Though still by Fools all other Callings live,
Nay our own Women by fresh Cullies thrive,
Though your Intrigues which no Lampoon can cure,
Promise a long Succession to ensure;
And all your Matches plenty do presage: 35
Dire is the Dearth and Famine on the Stage.
Our Store's quite wasted, and our Credit's small,
Not a Fool left to bless our selves withal.

We're forc't at last to rob, (which is great pity,
Though 'tis a never-failing Bank) the City.   40
   We show you one to day intirely new,
And of all Jests, none relish like the true.
Let that the value of our Play inhance,
Then it may prove indeed the Lucky Chance.

Act I.

SCENE I. *The Street, at break of Day.*

   [*Enter* BELLMOUR *disguis'd in a travelling Habit.*]
BEL. Sure 'tis the day that gleams in yonder East,
   The day that all but Lovers blest by Shade
   Pay chearful Homage to:
   Lovers! and those pursu'd like guilty me
   By rigid Laws, which put no difference
   'Twixt fairly killing in my own Defence,
   And Murders bred by drunken Arguments,
   Whores, or the mean Revenges of a Coward.
   —This is *Leticia's* Father's House— [*looking about.*]
      And that the dear Balcony
      That has so oft been conscious of our Loves;
      From whence she has sent me down a thousand Sighs,
      A thousand looks of Love, a thousand Vows.
      O thou dear witness of those charming Hours,
      How do I bless thee, how am I pleas'd to view thee
      After a tedious Age of Six Months Banishment.
         [*Enter* MR. GINGLE *and several with Musick.*]
FID. But hark ye, Mr. *Gingle*, is it proper to play before the Wedding?
GIN. Ever while you live, for many a time in playing after the first night,
   the Bride's sleepy, the Bridegroom tir'd, and both so out of humour,
   that perhaps they hate any thing that puts 'em in mind they are
   married. [*They play and sing.*]
         [*Enter* PHILLIS *in the Balcony, throws 'em Money.*]
      RISE, Cloris, charming Maid, arise!
         And baffle breaking Day,
      Shew the adoring World thy Eyes
         Are more surprizing gay;
      The Gods of Love are smiling round,
         And lead the Bridegroom on,

And Hymen has the Altar crown'd.
While all thy sighing Lovers are undone.

To see thee pass they throng the Plain;
  The Groves with Flowers are strown,
And every young and envying Swain
  Wishes the hour his own.
Rise then, and let the God of Day,
  When thou dost to the Lover yield,
Behold more Treasure given away
  Than he in his vast Circle e'er beheld.

BEL. Hah, *Phillis, Leticia's* Woman!

GING. Fie, Mrs. *Phillis,* do you take us for Fiddlers that play for Hire? I came to compliment Mrs. *Leticia* on her Wedding-Morning because she is my Scholar.

PHIL. She sends it only to drink her Health.

GING. Come, Lads, let's to the Tavern then— [*Ex. Musick.*]

BEL. Hah! said he *Leticia?*

Sure, I shall turn to Marble at this News:
I harden, and cold Damps pass through my senseless Pores.
—Hah, who's here?

[*Enter* GAYMAN *wrapt in his Cloke.*]

GAY. 'Tis yet too early, but my Soul's impatient, And I must see *Leticia.* [*Goes to the door.*]

BEL. Death and the Devil—the Bridegroom! Stay, Sir, by Heaven, you pass not this way.

[*Goes to the door as he is knocking, pushes him away, and draws.*]

GAY. Hah! what art thou that durst forbid me Entrance?—Stand off.

[*They fight a little, and closing view each other.*]

BEL. *Gayman!*

GAY. My dearest *Bellmour!*

BEL. Oh thou false Friend, thou treacherous base Deceiver!

GAY. Hah, this to me, dear *Harry?*

BEL. Whither is Honour, Truth and Friendship fled?

GAY. Why, there ne'er was such a Virtue, 'Tis all a Poet's Dream.

BEL. I thank you, Sir.

GAY. I'm sorry for't, or that ever I did any thing that could deserve it: put up your Sword—an honest man wou'd say how he's offended, before he rashly draws.

BEL. Are not you going to be married, Sir?

GAY. No, Sir, as long as any Man in *London* is so, that has but a handsom Wife, Sir.

BEL. Are you not in love, Sir?

GAY. Most damnably, — and wou'd fain lie with the dear jilting Gipsy.

BEL. Hah, who would you lie with, Sir?

GAY. You catechise me roundly — 'tis not fair to name, but I am no Starter, *Harry*; just as you left me, you find me. I am for the faithless *Julia* still, the old Alderman's Wife. — 'Twas high time the City should lose their Charter, when their Wives turn honest: But pray, Sir, answer me a Question or two.

BEL. Answer me first, what makes you here this Morning?

GAY. Faith, to do you service. Your damn'd little Jade of a Mistress has learned of her Neighbours the Art of Swearing and Lying in abundance, and is —

BEL. To be married! [*Sighing.*]

GAY. Even so, God save the Mark; and she'll be a fair one for many an Arrow besides her Husband's, though he an old *Finsbury* Hero this threescore Years.

BEL. Who mean you?

GAY. Why, thy Cuckold that shall be, if thou be'st wise.

BEL. Away;
Who is this Man? thou dalliest with me.

GAY. Why, an old Knight, and Alderman here o'th' City, Sir *Feeble Fainwou'd*, a jolly old Fellow, whose Activity is all got into his Tongue, a very excellent Teazer; but neither Youth nor Beauty can grind his Dudgeon to an Edge.

BEL. Fie, what Stuff's here!

GAY. Very excellent Stuff, if you have but the Grace to improve it.

BEL. You banter me — but in plain *English*, tell me,
What made you here thus early,
Entring yon House with such Authority?

GAY. Why, your Mistress *Leticia*, your contracted Wife, is this Morning to be married to old Sir *Feeble Fainwou'd*, induc'd to't I suppose by the great Jointure he makes her, and the improbability of your ever gaining your Pardon for your high Duel — Do I speak *English* now, Sir?

BEL. Too well, would I had never heard thee.

GAY. Now I being the Confident in your Amours, the Jack-go-be-tween — the civil Pimp, or so — you left her in charge with me at your

Departure.

BEL. I did so.

GAY. I saw her every day; and every day she paid the Tribute of a shower of
Tears, to the dear Lord of all her Vows, young *Bellmour*:
Till faith at last, for Reasons manifold,
I slackt my daily Visits.

BEL. And left her to Temptation—was that well done?

GAY. Now must I afflict you and my self with a long tale of Causes why;
Or be charg'd with want of Friendship.

BEL. You will do well to clear that Point to me.

GAY. I see you're peevish, and you shall be humour'd.—You know my
Julia play'd me e'en such another Prank as your false one is going to
play you, and married old Sir *Cautious Fulbank* here i'th' City; at
which you know I storm'd, and rav'd, and swore, as thou wo't now,
and to as little purpose. There was but one way left, and that was
cuckolding him.

BEL. Well, that Design I left thee hot upon.

GAY. And hotly have pursu'd it: Swore, wept, vow'd, wrote, upbraided,
prayed and railed; then treated lavishly, and presented high—till,
between you and I, *Harry*, I have presented the best part of Eight
hundred a year into her Husband's hands, in Mortgage.

BEL. This is the Course you'd have me steer, I thank you.

GAY. No, no, Pox on't, all Women are not Jilts. Some are honest, and will
give as well as take; or else there would not be so many broke i'th' City.
In fine, Sir, I have been in Tribulation, that is to say, Moneyless, for six
tedious Weeks, without either Clothes, or Equipage to appear withal;
and so not only my own Love-affair lay neglected—but thine
too—and I am forced to pretend to my Lady, that I am i'th' Country
with a dying Uncle—from whom, if he were indeed dead, I expect two
thousand a Year.

BEL. But what's all this to being here this Morning?

GAY. Thus have I lain conceal'd like a Winter-Fly, hoping for some blest
Sunshine to warm me into life again, and make me hover my flagging
Wings; till the News of this Marriage (which fills the Town) made me
crawl out this silent Hour, to upbraid the fickle Maid.

BEL. Didst thou?—pursue thy kind Design. Get me to see her; and sure
no Woman, even possest with a new Passion, grown confident even to
Prostitution, but when she sees the Man to whom she's sworn so
very—very much, will find Remorse and Shame.

GAY. For your sake, though the day be broke upon us, And I'm undone, if seen—I'll venture in— [*Throws his Cloke over.*]

    [*Enter* SIR FEEBLE FAINWOU'D, SIR CAUTIOUS FULBANK, BEARJEST *and* NOISEY. *Pass over the Stage, and go in.*]

Hah—see the Bridegroom!

And with him my destin'd Cuckold, old Sir *Cautious Fulbank*.

—Hah, what ail'st thou, Man?

BEL. The Bridegroom!

Like *Gorgon's* Head he'as turned me into Stone.

GAY. *Gorgon's* Head—a Cuckold's Head—'twas made to graft upon.

BEL. By Heaven, I'll seize her even at the Altar, and bear her thence in Triumph.

GAY. Ay, and be borne to *Newgate* in Triumph, and be hanged in Triumph—'twill be cold Comfort, celebrating your Nuptials in the Press-Yard, and be wak'd next Morning, like Mr. *Barnardine* in the Play—Will you please to rise and be hanged a little, Sir?

BEL. What wouldst thou have me do?

GAY. As many an honest Man has done before thee—Cuckold him—cuckold him.

BEL. What—and let him marry her! She that's mine by sacred Vows already! By Heaven, it would be flat Adultery in her!

GAY. She'll learn the trick, and practise it the better with thee.

BEL. Oh Heavens! *Leticia* marry him! and lie with him!—

Here will I stand and see this shameful Woman,

See if she dares pass by me to this Wickedness.

GAY. Hark ye, *Harry*—in earnest have a care of betraying your self; and do not venture sweet Life for a fickle Woman, who perhaps hates you.

BEL. You counsel well—but yet to see her married!

How every thought of that shocks all my Resolutions!—

But hang it, I'll be resolute and saucy,

Despise a Woman who can use me ill,

And think my self above her.

GAY. Why, now thou art thy self—a Man again. But see, they're coming forth, now stand your ground.

    [*Enter* SIR FEEBLE, SIR CAUTIOUS, BEARJEST, NOISEY, LETICIA *sad,* DIANA, PHILLIS. *Pass over the Stage.*]

BEL. 'Tis she; support me; *Charles*, or I shall sink to Earth,

—Methought in passing by she cast a scornful glance at me;

Such charming Pride I've seen upon her Eyes,
When our Love-Quarrels arm'd 'em with Disdain—
—I'll after 'em, if I live she shall not 'scape me.
  [*Offers to go,* GAY. *holds him.*]
GAY. Hold, remember you're proscribed,
And die if you are taken.
BEL. I've done, and I will live, but he shall ne'er enjoy her.
  —Who's yonder, *Ralph*, my trusty Confident?
    [*Enter* RALPH.]
Now though I perish I must speak to him.
  —Friend, what Wedding's this?
RAL. One that was never made in Heaven, Sir;
'Tis Alderman *Fainwou'd*, and Mrs. *Leticia Bredwel.*
BEL. *Bredwel*—I have heard of her,—she was Mistress—
RAL. To fine Mr. *Bellmour*, Sir,—ay, there was a Gentlemen
  —But rest his Soul—he's hang'd, Sir. [*Weeps.*]
BEL. How! hang'd?
RAL. Hang'd, Sir, hang'd—at the *Hague* in *Holland.*
GAY. I heard some such News, but did not credit it.
BEL. For what, said they, was he hang'd?
RAL. Why, e'en for High Treason, Sir, he killed one of their Kings.
GAY. *Holland's* a Commonwealth, and is not rul'd by Kings.
RAL. Not by one, Sir, but by a great many; this was a Cheesemonger—they
  fell out over a Bottle of Brandy, went to Snicker Snee; Mr. *Bellmour* cut
  his Throat, and was hang'd for't, that's all, Sir.
BEL. And did the young Lady believe this?
RAL. Yes, and took on most heavily—the Doctors gave her over—and
  there was the Devil to do to get her to consent to this Marriage—but
  her Fortune was small, and the hope of a Ladyship, and a Gold Chain
  at the Spittal Sermon, did the Business—and so your Servant, Sir [*Ex.*
  RALPH.]
BEL. So, here's a hopeful Account of my sweet self now.
    [*Enter* POST-MAN *with Letters.*]
POST. Pray, Sir, which is Sir *Feeble Fainwou'd's?*
BEL. What wou'd you with him, Friend?
POST. I have a Letter here from the *Hague* for him.
BEL. From the *Hague*! Now have I a curiosity to see it—I am his
  Servant—give it me—[*Gives it him, and Exit.*]—Perhaps here may be
  the second part of my Tragedy, I'm full of Mischief, *Charles*—and

have a mind to see this Fellow's Secrets. For from this hour I'll be his evil Genius, haunt him at Bed and Board; he shall not sleep nor eat; disturb him at his Prayers, in his Embraces; and teaze him into Madness.

Help me, Invention, Malice, Love, and Wit: [*Opening the Letter.*]
Ye Gods, and little Fiends, instruct my Mischief. [*Reads.*]
Dear Brother,

> ACCORDING to your desire I have sent for my Son from St. Omer's, whom I have sent to wait on you in England; he is a very good Accountant, and fit for Business, and much pleas'd he shall see that Uncle to whom he's so obliged, and which is so gratefully acknowledged by—Dear Brother, your affectionate Brother,
>
> Francis Fainwou'd.

—Hum—hark ye, *Charles*, do you know who I am now?

GAY. Why, I hope a very honest Friend of mine, *Harry Bellmour*.

BEL. No, Sir, you are mistaken in your Man.

GAY. It may be so.

BEL. I am, d'ye see, *Charles*, this very individual, numerical young Mr.—*what ye call'um Fainwou'd*, just come from *St. Omers* into *England*—to my Uncle the Alderman. I am, *Charles*, this very Man.

GAY. I know you are, and will swear't upon occasion.

BEL. This lucky Thought has almost calm'd my mind.

And if I don't fit you, my dear Uncle,

May I never lie with my Aunt.

GAY. Ah, Rogue—but prithee what care have you taken about your Pardon? 'twere good you should secure that.

BEL. There's the Devil, *Charles*,—had I but that—but I have had a very good Friend at work, a thousand Guyneys, that seldom fails; but yet in vain, I being the first Transgressor since the Act against Duelling.

But I impatient to see this dear delight of my Soul, and hearing from none of you this six weeks, came from *Brussels* in this disguise—for the *Hague* I have not seen, though hang'd there—but come—let's away, and compleat me a right *St. Omer's* Spark, that I may present my self as soon as they come from Church. [*Exeunt.*]

SCENE II. *Sir Cautious Fulbank's* House.

[*Enter* LADY FULBANK, PERT *and* BREDWEL. BREDWEL *gives her a Letter.* LADY FULBANK *reads.*]

DID my Julia know how I languish in this cruel Separation, she would afford me her pity, and write oftner. If only the Expectation of two thousand a year kept me from you, ah! Julia, how easily would I abandon that Trifle for your more valued sight; but that I know a Fortune will render me more agreeable to the charming Julia, I should quit all my Interest here, to throw my self at her Feet, to make her sensible how I am intirely her Adorer.

Charles Gayman.

—Faith, *Charles*, you lie—you are as welcome to me now, Now when I doubt thy Fortune is declining.
As if the Universe were thine.

PERT. That, Madam, is a noble Gratitude. For if his Fortune be declining, 'tis sacrificed to his Passion for your Lady ship.

—'Tis all laid out on Love.

L. FUL. I prize my Honour more than Life,
Yet I had rather have given him all he wish'd of me,
Than be guilty of his Undoing.

PERT. And I think the Sin were less.

L. FUL. I must confess, such Jewels, Rings and Presents as he made me, must needs decay his Fortune.

BRED. Ay, Madam, his very Coach at last was turned into a Jewel for your Ladyship. Then, Madam, what Expences his Despair have run him on—
As Drinking and Gaming, to divert the Thought of your marrying my old Master.

L. FUL. And put in Wenching too.—

BRED. No, assure your self, Madam—

L. FUL. Of that I would be better satisfied—and you too must assist me, as e'er you hope I should be kind to you in gaining you *Diana*. [*To* BREDWEL.]

BRED. Madam, I'll die to serve you.

PERT. Nor will I be behind in my Duty.

L. FUL. Oh, how fatal are forc'd Marriages!
How many Ruins one such Match pulls on!
Had I but kept my Sacred Vows to *Gayman*,
How happy had I been—how prosperous he!
Whilst now I languish in a loath'd embrace,
Pine out my Life with Age—Consumptions, Coughs.
—But dost thou fear that *Gayman* is declining?

BRED. You are my Lady, and the best of Mistresses —
Therefore I would not grieve you, for I know
You love this best — but most unhappy Man.

L. FUL. You shall not grieve me — prithee on.

BRED. My Master sent me yesterday to Mr. *Crap*, his Scrivener, to send to one Mr. *Wasteall*, to tell him his first Mortgage was out, which is two hundred pounds a Year — and who has since ingaged five or six hundred more to my Master; but if this first be not redeem'd, he'll take the Forfeit on't, as he says a wise Man ought.

L. FUL. That is to say, a Knave, according to his Notion of a wise Man.

BRED. Mr. *Crap*, being busy with a borrowing Lord, sent me to Mr. *Wasteall*, whose Lodging is in a nasty Place called *Alsatia*, at a Black-Smith's.

L. FUL. But what's all this to *Gayman?*

BRED. Madam, this *Wasteall* was Mr. *Gayman*.

L. FUL. *Gayman!* Saw'st thou *Gayman?*

BRED. Madam, Mr. *Gayman*, yesterday.

L. FUL. When came he to Town?

BRED. Madam, he has not been out of it.

L. FUL. Not at his Uncle's in *Northamptonshire?*

BRED. Your Ladyship was wont to credit me.

L. FUL. Forgive me — you went to a Black-Smith's —

BRED. Yes, Madam; and at the door encountred the beastly thing he calls a Landlady; who lookt as if she had been of her own Husband's making, compos'd of moulded Smith's Dust. I ask'd for Mr. *Wasteall*, and she began to open — and did so rail at him, that what with her *Billinsgate*, and her Husband's hammers, I was both deaf and dumb — at last the hammers ceas'd, and she grew weary, and call'd down Mr. *Wasteall*; but he not answering — I was sent up a Ladder rather than a pair of Stairs; at last I scal'd the top, and enter'd the inchanted Castle; there did I find him, spite of the noise below, drowning his Cares in Sleep.

L. FUL. Whom foundst thou? *Gayman?*

BRED. He, Madam, whom I waked — and seeing me, Heavens, what Confusion seiz'd him! which nothing but my own Surprize could equal. Asham'd — he wou'd have turn'd away; but when he saw, by my dejected Eyes, I knew him, He sigh'd, and blusht, and heard me tell my Business: Then beg'd I wou'd be secret; for he vow'd his whole Repose and Life depended on my silence. Nor had I told it now, but that your Ladyship may find some speedy means to draw him from this desperate Condition.

L. FUL. Heavens, is't possible?

BRED. He's driven to the last degree of Poverty—Had you but seen his Lodgings, Madam!

L. FUL. What were they?

BRED. 'Tis a pretty convenient Tub, Madam. He may lie a long in't, there's just room for an old join'd Stool besides the Bed, which one cannot call a Cabin, about the largeness of a Pantry Bin, or a Usurer's Trunk; there had been Dornex Curtains to't in the days of Yore; but they were now annihilated, and nothing left to save his Eyes from the Light, but my Landlady's Blue Apron, ty'd by the strings before the Window, in which stood a broken six-penny Looking-Glass, that shew'd as many Faces as the Scene in *Henry* the Eighth, which could but just stand upright, and then the Comb-Case fill'd it.

L. FUL. What a leud Description hast thou made of his Chamber?

BRED. Then for his Equipage, 'tis banist to one small Monsieur, who (saucy with his Master's Poverty) is rather a Companion than a Footman.

L. FUL. But what said he to the Forfeiture of his Land?

BRED. He sigh'd and cry'd, Why, farewel dirty Acres; It shall not trouble me, since 'twas all but for Love!

L. FUL. How much redeems it?

BRED. Madam, five hundred Pounds.

L. FUL. Enough—you shall in some disguise convey this Money to him, as from an unknown hand: I wou'd not have him think it comes from me, for all the World: That Nicety and Virtue I've profest, I am resolved to keep.

PERT. If I were your Ladyship, I wou'd make use of Sir *Cautious's* Cash: pay him in his own Coin.

BRED. Your Ladyship wou'd make no Scruple of it, if you knew how this poor Gentleman has been us'd by my unmerciful Master.

L. FUL. I have a Key already to his Counting-House; it being lost, he had another made, and this I found and kept.

BRED. Madam, this is an excellent time for't, my Master being gone to give my Sister *Leticia* at Church.

L. FUL. 'Tis so, I'll go and commit the Theft, whilst you prepare to carry it, and then we'll to dinner with your Sister the Bride. [*Exeunt.*]

SCENE III. *The House of* SIR FEEBLE.

[*Enter* SIR FEEBLE, LETICIA, SIR CAUTIOUS, BEARJEST, DIANA, NOISEY.
SIR FEEBLE *sings and salutes 'em.*]

SIR FEEB. Welcome, *Joan Sanderson*, welcome, welcome. [*Kisses the Bride.*]
Ods bobs, and so thou art, Sweet-heart. [*So to the rest.*]

BEAR. Methinks my Lady Bride is very melancholy.

SIR CAU. Ay, ay, Women that are discreet, are always thus upon their Wedding-day.

SIR FEEB. Always by day-light, Sir *Cautious.*
But when bright Phœbus does retire,
To Thetis' Bed to quench his fire,
And do the thing we need not name,
We Mortals by his influence do the same.
Then then the blushing Maid lays by
Her simpering, and her Modesty;
And round the Lover clasps and twines
Like Ivy, or the circling Vines.

SIR FEEB. Here, *Ralph*, the Bottle, Rogue, of Sack, ye Rascal; hadst thou been a Butler worth hanging, thou wou'dst have met us at the door with it. — Ods bods, Sweet-heart, thy health.

BEAR. Away with it, to the Bride's *Haunce in Kelder.*

SIR FEEB. Gots so, go to, Rogue, go to, that shall be, Knave, that shall be the morrow morning; he — ods bobs, we'll do't, Sweet heart; here's to't. [*Drinks again.*]

LET. I die but to imagine it, wou'd I were dead indeed.

SIR FEEB. Hah — hum — how's this? Tears upon the Wedding day? Why, why — you Baggage, you, ye little Ting, Fools-face — away, you Rogue, you're naughty, you're naughty. [*Patting and playing, and following her.*] Look — look — look now, — buss it — buss it — buss it — and Friends; did'ums, did'ums beat its none silly Baby — away, you little Hussey, away, and pledge me — [*She drinks a little.*]

SIR CAU. A wise discreet Lady, I'll warrant her; my Lady would prodigally have took it off all.

SIR FEEB. Dear's its nown dear Fubs; buss again, buss again, away, away — ods bobs, I long for Night — look, look, Sir *Cautious*, what an Eye's there!

SIR CAU. Ay, so there is, Brother, and a modest Eye too.

SIR FEEB. Adad, I love her more and more, *Ralph* — call old *Susan* hither—come, Mr. *Bearjest*, put the Glass about. Ods bobs, when I was a young Fellow, I wou'd not let the young Wenches look pale and wan—but would rouse 'em, and touse 'em, and blowze 'em, till I put a colour in their Cheeks, like an Apple *John*, affacks—Nay, I can make a shift still, and Pupsey shall not be jealous.

[*Enter* SUSAN, SIR FEEBLE *whispers her, she goes out.*]

LET. Indeed, not I; Sir. I shall be all Obedience.

SIR CAU. A most judicious Lady; would my *Julia* had a little of her Modesty; but my Lady's a Wit.

[*Enter* SUSAN *with a Box.*]

SIR FEEB. Look here, my little Puskin, here's fine Playthings for its nown little Coxcomb—go—get you gone—get you gone, and off with this St. *Martin's* Trumpery, these Play-house Glass Baubles, this Necklace, and these Pendants, and all this false Ware; ods bobs, I'll have no Counterfeit Geer about thee, not I. See—these are right as the Blushes on thy Cheeks, and these as true as my Heart, my Girl. Go, put 'em on, and be fine. [*Gives 'em her.*]

LET. Believe me, Sir, I shall not merit this kindness.

SIR FEEB. Go to—More of your Love, and less of your Ceremony—give the old Fool a hearty buss, and pay him that way—he, ye little wanton Tit, I'll steal up—and catch ye and love ye—adod, I will—get ye gone—get ye gone.

LET. Heavens, what a nauseous thing is an old Man turn'd Lover! [*Ex.* LETICIA *and* DIANA.]

SIR CAU. How, steal up, Sir *Feeble*—I hope not so; I hold it most indecent before the lawful hour.

SIR FEEB. Lawful hour! Why, I hope all hours are lawful with a Man's own Wife.

SIR CAU. But wise Men have respect to Times and Seasons.

SIR FEEB. Wise young Men, Sir *Cautious*; but wise old Men must nick their Inclinations; for it is not as 'twas wont to be, for it is not as 'twas wont to be— [*Singing and Dancing.*]

[*Enter* RALPH.]

RAL. Sir, here's a young Gentleman without wou'd speak with you.

SIR FEEB. Hum—I hope it is not that same *Bellmour* come to forbid the Banes—if it be, he comes too late—therefore bring me first my long Sword, and then the Gentleman. [*Exit* RALPH.]

BEA. Pray, Sir, use mine, it is a travell'd Blade I can assure you, Sir.

SIR FEEB. I thank you, Sir.

[*Enter* RALPH and BELLMOUR disguis'd, gives him a Letter, he reads.]

How—my Nephew!

Francis Fainwou'd! [*Embraces him.*]

BEL. I am glad he has told me my Christian name.

SIR FEEB. Sir *Cautious*, know my Nephew—'tis a young *St. Omers* Scholar—but none of the Witnesses.

SIR CAU. Marry, Sir, and the wiser he; for they got nothing by't.

BEA. Sir, I love and honour you, because you are a Traveller.

SIR FEEB. A very proper young Fellow, and as like old *Frank Fainwou'd* as the Devil to the Collier; but, *Francis*, you are come into a very leud Town, *Francis*, for Whoring, and Plotting, and Roaring, and Drinking; but you must go to Church, *Francis*, and avoid ill Company, or you may make damnable Havock in my Cash, *Francis*,—what, you can keep Merchants Books?

BEL. That's been my study, Sir.

SIR FEEB. And you will not be proud, but will be commanded by me, *Francis?*

BEL. I desire not to be favour'd as a Kinsman, Sir, but as your humblest Servant.

SIR FEEB. Why, thou'rt an honest Fellow, *Francis*,—and thou'rt heartily welcome—and I'll make thee fortunate. But come, Sir *Cautious*, let you and I take a turn i'th' Garden, and get a right understanding between your Nephew Mr. *Bearjest*, and my Daughter *Dye*.

SIR CAU. Prudently thought on, Sir, I'll wait on you.—

[*Ex.* SIR FEEBLE, *and* SIR CAUTIOUS.]

BEA. You are a Traveller, I understand.

BEL. I have seen a little part of the World, Sir.

BEA. So have I, Sir, I thank my Stars, and have performed most of my Travels on Foot, Sir.

BEL. You did not travel far then, I presume, Sir?

BEA. No, Sir, it was for my diversion indeed; but I assure you, I travell'd into *Ireland* a-foot, Sir.

BEL. Sure, Sir, you go by shipping into *Ireland?*

BEA. That's all one, Sir, I was still a-foot, ever walking on the Deck.

BEL. Was that your farthest Travel, Sir?

BEA. Farthest—why, that's the End of the World—and sure a Man can go no farther.

BEL. Sure, there can be nothing worth a Man's Curiosity?

BEA. No, Sir, I'll assure you, there are the Wonders of the World, Sir: I'll hint you this one. There is a Harbour which since the Creation was never capable of receiving a Lighter, yet by another Miracle the King of *France* was to ride there with a vast Fleet of Ships, and to land a hundred thousand Men.

BEL. This is a swinging Wonder—but are there store of Mad-men there, Sir?

BEA. That's another Rarity to see a Man run out of his Wits.

NOI. Marry, Sir, the wiser they I say.

BEA. Pray, Sir, what store of Miracles have you at *St. Omers?*

BEL. None, Sir, since that of the wonderful *Salamanca* Doctor, who was both here and there at the same Instant of time.

BEA. How, Sir? why, that's impossible.

BEL. That was the Wonder, Sir, because 'twas impossible.

NOI. But 'twas a greater, Sir, that 'twas believed.

[*Enter* L FULB. *and* PERT, SIR CAU. *and* SIR FEEB.]

SIR FEEB. Enough, enough, Sir *Cautious*, we apprehend one another. Mr. *Bearjest*, your Uncle here and I have struck the Bargain, the Wench is yours with three thousand Pound present, and something more after Death, which your Uncle likes well.

BEA. Does he so, Sir? I'm beholding to him; then 'tis not a Pin matter whether I like or not, Sir.

SIR FEEB. How, Sir, not like my Daughter *Dye?*

BEA. Oh, Lord, Sir,—die or live, 'tis all one for that, Sir—I'll stand to the Bargain my Uncle makes.

PERT. Will you so, Sir? you'll have very good luck if you do. [*Aside.*]

BEA. Prithee hold thy Peace, my Lady's Woman.

L. FUL. Sir, I beg your pardon for not waiting on you to Church—I knew you wou'd be private.

[*Enter* LET. fine in Jewels.]

SIR FEEB. You honour us too highly now, Madam. [*Presents his Wife, who salutes her.*]

L. FUL. Give you Joy, my dear *Leticia!* I find, Sir, you were resolved for Youth, Sit and Beauty.

SIR FEEB. Ay, ay, Madam, to the Comfort of many a hoping Coxcomb: but *Lette*,—Rogue *Lette*—thou wo't not make me free o'th' City a second time, wo't thou entice the Rogues with the Twire and the wanton Leer—the amorous Simper that cries, come, kiss me—then the pretty round Lips are pouted out—he, Rogue, how I long to be at 'em! — well, she shall never go to Church more, that she shall not.

L. FUL. How, Sir, not to Church, the chiefest Recreation of a City Lady?

SIR FEEB. That's all one, Madam, that tricking and dressing, and prinking and patching, is not your Devotion to Heaven, but to the young Knaves that are lick'd and comb'd and are minding you more than the Parson — ods bobs, there are more Cuckolds destin'd in the Church, than are made out of it.

SIR CAU. Hah, ha, ha, he tickles ye, i'faith, Ladies. [*To his Lady.*]

BEL. Not one chance look this way — and yet I can forgive her lovely Eyes,
Because they look not pleas'd with all this Ceremony;
And yet methinks some sympathy in Love
Might this way glance their Beams — I cannot hold —
— Sir, is this fair Lady my Aunt?

SIR FEEB. Oh, *Francis!* Come hither, *Francis. Lette*, here's a young Rogue has a mind to kiss thee. [*Puts them together, she starts back.*]
— Nay, start not, he's my own Flesh and Blood,
My Nephew — Baby — look, look how the young
Rogues stare at one another; like will to like, I see that.

LET. There's something in his Face so like my *Bellmour*, it calls my Blushes up, and leaves my Heart defenceless.
     [*Enter* RALPH.]

RALPH. Sir, Dinner's on the Table.

SIR FEEB. Come, come — let's in then — Gentlemen and Ladies,
And share to day my Pleasures and Delight,
But —
Adds bobs, they must be all mine own at Night. [*Exeunt.*]

Act II.

SCENE I. *Gayman's* Lodging.

[*Enter* GAYMAN *in a Night-Cap, and an old Campaign Coat tied about him, very melancholy.*]

GAY. Curse on my Birth! Curse on my faithless Fortune!
Curse on my Stars, and curst be all — but Love!
That dear, that charming Sin, though t'have pull'd
Innumerable Mischiefs on my head,
I have not, nor I cannot find Repentance for.
Nor let me die despis'd, upbraided, poor:
Let Fortune, Friends and all abandon me —
But let me hold thee, thou soft smiling God,

Close to my heart while Life continues there.
Till the last pantings of my vital Blood,
Nay, the last spark of Life and Fire be Love's!
    [*Enter* RAG.]
— How now, *Rag*, what's a Clock?

RAG. My Belly can inform you better than my Tongue.

GAY. Why, you gormandizing Vermin you, what have you done with the Three pence I gave you a fortnight ago.

RAG. Alas, Sir, that's all gone long since.

GAY. You gutling Rascal, you are enough to breed a Famine in a Land. I have known some industrious Footmen, that have not only gotten their own Livings, but a pretty Livelihood for their Masters too.

RAG. Ay, till they came to the Gallows, Sir.

GAY. Very well, Sirrah, they died in an honourable Calling — but hark ye, *Rag*, — I have business, very earnest business abroad this Evening; now were you a Rascal of Docity, you wou'd invent a way to get home my last Suit that was laid in Lavender — with the Appurtenances thereunto belonging, as Perriwig, Cravat, and so forth.

RAG. Faith, Master, I must deal in the black Art then, for no human means will do't — and now I talk of the black Art, Master, try your Power once more with my Landlady.

GAY. Oh! name her not, the thought on't turns my Stomach — a sight of her is a Vomit; but he's a bold Hero that dares venture on her for a kiss, and all beyond that sure is Hell it self — yet there's my last, last Refuge — and I must to this Wedding — I know not what, — but something whispers me, — this Night I shall be happy — and without *Julia* 'tis impossible!

RAG. *Julia*, who's that? my Lady *Fulbank*, Sir?

GAY. Peace, Sirrah — and call — a — no — Pox on't, come back — and yet — yes — call my fulsome Landlady. [*Exit* RAG.]
Sir *Cautious* knows me not by Name or Person.
And I will to this Wedding, I'm sure of seeing *Julia* there.
And what may come of that — but here's old Nasty coming.
I smell her up — hah, my dear Landlady.
    [*Enter* RAG *and* LANDLADY.]
Quite out of breath — a Chair there for my Landlady.

RAG. Here's ne'er a one, Sir.

LAND. More of your Money and less of your Civility, good Mr. *Wasteall*.

GAY. Dear Landlady —

LAND. Dear me no Dears, Sir, but let me have my Money—Eight Weeks Rent last Friday; besides Taverns, Ale-houses, Chandlers, Landresses' Scores, and ready Money out of my Purse; you know it, Sir.

GAY. Ay, but your Husband don't; speak softly.

LAND. My Husband! what, do you think to fright me with my Husband?—I'd have you to know I'm an honest Woman, and care not this—for my Husband. Is this all the thanks I have for my kindness, for patching, borrowing and shifting for you; 'twas but last Week I pawn'd my best Petticoat, as I hope to wear it again, it cost me six and twenty shillings besides Making; then this Morning my new *Norwich* Mantua followed, and two postle Spoons, I had the whole dozen when you came first; but they dropt, and dropt, till I had only *Judas* left for my Husband.

GAY. Hear me, good Landlady.

LAND. Then I've past my word at the *George Tavern*, for forty Shillings for you, ten Shillings at my Neighbour *Squabs* for Ale, besides seven Shillings to Mother *Suds* for Washing; and do you fob me off with my Husband?

GAY. Here, *Rag*, run and fetch her a Pint of Sack—there's no other way of quenching the Fire in her flabber Chops. [*Exit* RAG.]

—But, my dear Landlady, have a little Patience.

LAND. Patience! I scorn your Words, Sir—is this a place to trust in? tell me of Patience, that us'd to have my money before hand; come, come, pay me quickly—or old *Gregory Grimes* house shall be too hot to hold you.

GAY. Is't come to this, can I not be heard?

LAND. No, Sir, you had good Clothes when you came first, but they dwindled daily, till they dwindled to this old Campaign—with tan'd coloured Lining—once red—but now all Colours of the Rain-bow, a Cloke to sculk in a Nights, and a pair of piss-burn'd shammy Breeches. Nay, your very Badge of Manhood's gone too.

GAY. How, Landlady! nay then, i'faith, no wonder if you rail so.

LAND. Your Silver Sword I mean—transmogrified to this two-handed Basket Hilt—this old Sir *Guy of Warwick*—which will sell for nothing but old Iron. In fine, I'll have my money, Sir, or i'faith, *Alsatia* shall not shelter you.

[*Enter* RAG.]

GAY. Well, Landlady—if we must part—let's drink at parting; here, Landlady, here's to the Fool—that shall love you better than I have done. [*Sighing, drinks.*]

LAND. Rot your Wine—dy'e think to pacify me with Wine, Sir?
[*She refusing to drink, he holds open her Jaws,* RAG *throws a Glass of Wine into her Mouth.*]

—What, will you force me?—no—give me another Glass, I scorn to be so uncivil to be forced, my service to you, Sir—this shan't do, Sir.
[*She drinks, he, embracing her, sings.*]
Ah, Cloris, 'tis in vain you scold,
Whilst your Eyes kindle such a Fire.
Your Railing cannot make me cold,
So fast as they a Warmth inspire.

LAND. Well, Sir, you have no reason to complain of my Eyes nor my Tongue neither, if rightly understood. [*Weeps.*]

GAY. I know you are the best of Landladies,
As such I drink your Health—
But to upbraid a Man in Tribulation—fie—'tis not done like a Woman of Honour, a Man that loves you too. [*She drinks.*]

LAND. I am a little hasty sometimes, but you know my good Nature.

GAY. I do, and therefore trust my little wants with you. I shall be rich again—and then, my dearest Landlady—

LAND. Wou'd this Wine might ne'er go through me, if I wou'd not go, as they say, through Fire and Water—by Night or by Day for you. [*She drinks.*]

GAY. And as this is Wine I do believe thee. [*He drinks.*]

LAND. Well—you have no money in your Pocket now, I'll warrant you—here—her's ten Shillings for you old *Greg'ry* knows not of. [*Opens a great greasy purse.*]

GAY. I cannot in Conscience take it, good Faith, I cannot—besides, the next Quarrel you'll hit me in the Teeth with it.

LAND. Nay, pray no more of that; forget it, forget it. I own I was to blame—here, Sir, you shall take it.

GAY. Ay,—but what shou'd I do with Money in these damn'd Breeches?—No, put it up—I can't appear abroad thus—no, I'll stay at home, and lose my business.

LAND. Why, is there no way to redeem one of your Suits?

GAY. None—none—I'll e'en lay me down and die.

LAND. Die—marry, Heavens forbid—I would not for the World—let me see—hum—what does it lie for?

GAY. Alas! dear Landlady, a Sum—a Sum.

LAND. Well, say no more, I'll lay about me.

GAY. By this kiss but you shall not—*Assafetida*, by this Light.

LAND. Shall not? that's a good one, i'faith: shall you rule, or I?

GAY. But shou'd your Husband know it? —

LAND. Husband—marry come up, Husbands know Wives secrets? No, sure, the World's not so bad yet—where do your things lie? and for what?

GAY. Five Pounds equips me—*Rag* can conduct you—but I say you shall not go, I've sworn.

LAND. Meddle with your matters—let me see, the Caudle Cup that *Molly's* Grandmother left her, will pawn for about that sum—I'll sneak it out—well, Sir, you shall have your things presently—trouble not your head, but expect me. [*Ex.* LANDLADY *and* RAG.]

GAY. Was ever man put to such beastly shifts? 'Sdeath, how she stunk— my senses are most luxuriously regal'd—there's my perpetual Musick too—[*Knocking of Hammers on a Anvil.*]
    The ringing of Bells is an Ass to't.
        [*Enter* RAG.]

RAG. Sir, there's one in a Coach below wou'd speak to you.

GAY. With me, and in a Coach! who can it be?

RAG. The Devil, I think, for he has a strange Countenance.

GAY. The Devil! shew your self a Rascal of Parts, Sirrah, and wait on him up with Ceremony.

RAG. Who, the Devil, Sir?

GAY. Ay, the Devil, Sir, if you mean to thrive. [*Exit* RAG.]
    Who can this be—but see he comes to inform me—withdraw.
        [*Enter* BREDWEL *drest like a Devil.*]

BRED. I come to bring you this—[*Gives him a Letter.*]
        [GAYMAN reads.]
    RECEIVE what Love and Fortune present you with, be grateful and be silent, or 'twill vanish like a dream, and leave you more wretched that it found You.

                                                    Adieu.

    —hah—[*Gives him a bag of Money.*]

BRED. Nay, view it, Sir, 'tis all substantial Gold.

GAY. Now dare not I ask one civil question for fear it vanish all—[*Aside.*]
    But I may ask, how 'tis I ought to pay for this great Bounty.

BRED. Sir, all the Pay is Secrecy—

GAY. And is this all that is required, Sir?

BRED. No, you're invited to the Shades below.

GAY. Hum, Shades below! — I am not prepared for such a Journey, Sir.

BRED. If you have Courage, Youth or Love, you'll follow me:
When Night's black Curtain's drawn around the World,
And mortal Eyes are safely lockt in sleep, [*In feign'd Heroick Tone.*]
And no bold Spy dares view when Gods caress,
Then I'll conduct thee to the Banks of Bliss.
— *Durst thou not trust me?*

GAY. Yes, sure, on such substantial security. [*Hugs the Bag.*]

BRED. Just when the Day is vanish'd into Night,
And only twinkling Stars inform the World,
Near to the Corner of the silent Wall,
In Fields of *Lincoln's-Inn*, thy Spirit shall meet thee.
— Farewell. [*Goes out.*]

GAY. Hum — I am awake sure, and this is Gold I grasp.
I could not see this Devil's cloven Foot;
Nor am I such a Coxcomb to believe,
But he was as substantial as his Gold.
Spirits, Ghosts, Hobgoblins, Furies, Fiends and Devils,
I've often heard old Wives fright Fools and Children with,
Which, once arriv'd to common Sense, they laugh at.
— No, I am for things possible and Natural:
Some Female Devil, old and damn'd to Ugliness,
And past all Hopes of Courtship and Address,
Full of another Devil called Desire,
Has seen this Face — this Shape — this Youth,
And thinks it's worth her Hire. It must be so:
I must moil on in the damn'd dirty Road,
And sure such Pay will make the Journey easy:
And for the Price of the dull drudging Night,
All Day I'll purchase new and fresh Delight. [*Exit.*]

SCENE II. *Sir* FEEBLE'S *House.*

[*Enter* LETICIA, *pursu'd by* PHILLIS.]

PHIL. Why, Madam, do you leave the Garden,
For this retreat to Melancholy?

LET. Because it suits my Fortune and my Humour;
And even thy Presence wou'd afflict me now.

PHIL. Madam, I was sent after you; my Lady *Fulbank* has challeng'd Sir
Feeble at Bowls, and stakes a Ring of fifty Pound against his new

Chariot.

LET. Tell him I wish him Luck in every thing,
But in his Love to me—
Go tell him I am viewing of the Garden. [*Ex.* PHILLIS.]
    [*Enter* BELLMOUR *at a distance behind her.*]
—Blest be this kind Retreat, this 'lone Occasion,
That lends a short Cessation to My Torments,
And gives me leave to vent my Sighs and Tears. [*Weeps.*]

BEL. And doubly blest be all the Powers of Love,
That give me this dear Opportunity.

LET. Where were you, all ye pitying Gods of Love?
That once seem'd pleas'd at *Bellmour's* Flame and mine,
And smiling join'd our Hearts, our sacred Vows,
And spread your Wings, and held your Torches high.

BEL. Oh—[*She starts, and pauses.*]

LET. Where were you now? When this unequal Marriage
Gave me from all my Joys, gave me from *Bellmour*;
Your Wings were flag'd, your Torches bent to Earth,
And all your little Bonnets veil'd your Eyes;
You saw not, or were deaf and pitiless.

BEL. Oh, my *Leticia!*

LET. Hah, 'tis there again; that very voice was *Bellmour's*:
Where art thou, Oh thou lovely charming Shade?
For sure thou canst not take a Shape to fright me.
—What art thou?—speak! [*Not looking behind her yet for fear.*]

BEL. Thy constant true Adorer,
Who all this fatal Day has haunted thee
To ease his tortur'd Soul. [*Approaching nearer.*]

LET. My Heart is well acquainted with that Voice,
But Oh, my Eyes dare not encounter thee. [*Speaking with signs of
fear.*]

BEL. Is it because thou'st broken all thy Vows?
—Take to thee Courage, and behold thy Slaughters.

LET. Yes, though the Sight wou'd blast me, I wou'd view it. [*Turns.*]
—'Tis he—'tis very *Bellmour!* or so like—
I cannot doubt but thou deserv'st this Welcome.
    [*Embraces him.*]

BEL. Oh my *Leticia!*

LET. I'm sure I grasp not Air; thou art no Fantom:

Thy Arms return not empty to my Bosom,
But meet a solid Treasure.

BEL. A Treasure thou so easily threw'st away;
A Riddle simple Love ne'er understood.

LET. Alas, I heard, my *Bellmour*, thou wert dead.

BEL. And was it thus you mourn'd my Funeral?

LET. I will not justify my hated Crime:
But Oh! remember I was poor and helpless,
And much reduc'd, and much impos'd upon. [BELLMOUR *weeps*.]

BEL. And Want compell'd thee to this wretched Marriage—did it?

LET. 'Tis not a Marriage, since my *Bellmour* lives;
The Consummation were Adultery.
I was thy Wife before, wo't thou deny me?

BEL. No, by those Powers that heard our mutual Vows,
Those Vows that tie us faster than dull Priests.

LET. But oh, my *Bellmour*, thy sad Circumstances
Permit thee not to make a publick Claim:
Thou art proscribed, and diest if thou art seen.

BEL. Alas!

LET. Yet I wou'd wander with thee o'er the World,
And share thy humblest Fortune with thy Love.

BEL. Is't possible, *Leticia*, thou wou'dst fly
To foreign Shores with me?

LET. Can *Bellmour* doubt the Soul he knows so well?

BEL. Perhaps in time the King may find my Innocence,
and may extend his Mercy:
Mean time I'll make provision for our Flight.

LET. But how 'twixt this and that can I defend
My self from the loath'd Arms of an impatient Dotard,
That I may come a spotless Maid to thee?

BEL. Thy native Modesty and my Industry
Shall well enough secure us.
Feign your nice Virgin-Cautions all the day;
Then trust at night to my Conduct to preserve thee.
—And wilt thou yet be mine? Oh, swear a-new,
Give me again thy Faith, thy Vows, thy Soul;
For mine's so sick with this Day's fatal Business,
It needs a Cordial of that mighty strength;
Swear—swear, so as if thou break'st—

Thou mayst be — any thing — but damn'd, *Leticia.*

LET. Thus then, and hear me, Heaven! [*Kneels.*]

BEL. And thus — I'll listen to thee. [*Kneels.*]

    [*Enter* SIR FEEBLE, L. FULBANK, SIR CAUTIOUS.]

SIR FEEB. *Lette, Lette, Lette,* where are you, little Rogue, *Lette?*

    — Hah — hum — what's here — [BEL. *snatches her to his Bosom, as if she fainted.*]

BEL. Oh Heavens, she's gone, she's gone!

SIR FEEB. Gone — whither is she gone? — it seems she had the Wit to take good Company with her — [*The Women go to her, take her up.*]

BEL. She's gone to Heaven, Sir, for ought I know.

SIR CAU. She was resolv'd to go in a young Fellow's Arms, I see.

SIR FEEB. Go to, *Francis* — go to.

L. FUL. Stand back, Sir, she recovers.

BEL. Alas, I found her dead upon the Floor,

    — Shou'd I have left her so — if I had known your mind —

SIR FEEB. Was it so — was it so? — Got so, by no means, *Francis.* —

LET. Pardon him, Sir, for surely I had died,

But for his timely coming.

SIR FEEB. Alas, poor Pupsey — was it sick — look here — here's a fine thing to make it well again. Come, buss, and it shall have it — oh, how I long for Night. *Ralph,* are the Fidlers ready?

RAL. They are tuning in the Hall, Sir.

SIR FEEB. That's well, they know my mind. I hate that same twang, twang, twang, fum, fum, fum, tweedle, tweedle, tweedle, then scrue go the Pins, till a man's Teeth are on an edge; then snap, says a small Gut, and there we are at a loss again. I long to be in bed with a — hey tredodle, tredodle, tredodle, — with a hay tredool, tredodle, tredo — [*Dancing and playing on his Stick like a Flute.*]

SIR CAU. A prudent Man would reserve himself — Good-facks, I danc'd so on my Wedding-day, that when I came to Bed, to my Shame be it spoken, I fell fast asleep, and slept till morning.

L. FUL. Where was your Wisdom then, Sir *Cautious?* But I know what a wise Woman ought to have done.

SIR FEEB. Odsbobs, that's Wormwood, that's Wormwood — I shall have my young Hussey set a-gog too; she'll hear there are better things in the World than she has at home, and then odsbobs, and then they'll ha't, adod, they will, Sir *Cautious.* Ever while you live, keep a Wife ignorant, unless a Man be as brisk as his Neighbours.

SIR CAU. A wise Man will keep 'em from baudy Christnings then, and Gossipings.

SIR FEEB. Christnings and Gossipings! why, they are the very Schools that debauch our Wives, as Dancing-Schools do our Daughters.

SIR CAU. Ay, when the overjoy'd good Man invites 'em all against that time Twelve-month: Oh, he's a dear Man, cries one — I must marry, cries another, here's a Man indeed — my Husband — God help him —

SIR FEEB. Then he falls to telling of her Grievance, till (half maudlin) she weeps again: Just my Condition, cries a third: so the Frolick goes round, and we poor Cuckolds are anatomiz'd, and turn'd the right side outwards; adsbobs, we are, Sir *Cautious*.

SIR CAU. Ay, ay, this Grievance ought to be redrest, Sir *Feeble*; and grave and sober part o'th' Nation are hereby ridicul'd, —
Ay, and cuckolded too for ought I know.

L. FUL. Wise Men knowing this, should not expose their Infirmities, by marrying us young Wenches; who, without Instruction, find how we are impos'd upon.

[*Enter Fiddles playing,* MR. BEARJEST *and* DIANA *dancing;*
BREDWEL, NOISEY, &c.]

L. FUL. So, Cousin, I see you have found the way to Mrs. *Dy's* Heart.

BEA. Who, I, my dear Lady Aunt? I never knew but one way to a Woman's Heart, and that road I have not yet travelled; for my Uncle, who is a wise Man, says Matrimony is a sort of a — kind of a — as it were, d'ye see, of a Voyage, which every Man of Fortune is bound to make one time or other: and Madam — I am, as it were — a bold Adventurer.

DIA. And are you sure, Sir, you will venture on me?

BEA. Sure! — I thank you for that — as if I could not believe my Uncle; For in this case a young Heir has no more to do, but to come and see, settle, marry, and use you scurvily.

DIA. How, Sir, scurvily?

BEA. Very scurvily, that is to say, be always fashionably drunk, despise the Tyranny of your Bed, and reign absolutely — keep a Seraglio of Women, and let my Bastard Issue inherit; be seen once a Quarter, or so, with you in the Park for Countenance, where we loll two several ways in the gilt Coach like *Janus*, or a Spread-Eagle.

DIA. And do you expect I shou'd be honest the while?

BEA. Heaven forbid, not I, I have not met with that Wonder in all my Travels.

L. FUL. How, Sir, not an honest Woman?

BEA. Except my Lady Aunt—Nay, as I am a Gentleman and the first of my Family—you shall pardon me, here—cuff me, cuff me soundly. [*Kneels to her.*]
   [*Enter* GAYMAN *richly drest.*]
GAY. This Love's a damn'd bewitching thing—Now though I should lose my Assignation with my Devil, I cannot hold from seeing *Julia* to night: hah—there, and with a Fop at her Feet.—Oh Vanity of Woman! [*Softly pulls her.*]
L. FUL. Oh, Sir, you're welcome from *Northamptonshire*.
GAY. Hum—surely she knows the Cheat. [*Aside.*]
L. FUL. You are so gay, you save me, Sir, the labour of asking if your Uncle be alive.
GAY. Pray heaven she have not found my Circumstances! [*Aside.*]
   But if she have, Confidence must assist me—
   —And, Madam, you're too gay for me to inquire
   Whether you are that *Julia* which I left you?
L. FUL. Oh, doubtless, Sir—
GAY. But why the Devil do I ask—Yes, you are still the same; one of those hoiting Ladies, that love nothing like Fool and Fiddle; Crouds of Fops; had rather be publickly, though dully, flatter'd, than privately ador'd: you love to pass for the Wit of the Company, by talking all and loud.
L. FUL. Rail on, till you have made me think my Virtue at so low Ebb, it should submit to you.
GAY. What—I'm not discreet enough;
   I'll babble all in my next high Debauch,
   Boast of your Favours, and describe your Charms
   To every wishing Fool.
L. FUL. Or make most filthy Verses of me—
   Under the name of *Cloris*—you *Philander*,
   Who in leud Rhimes confess the dear Appointment;
   What Hour, and where, how silent was the Night,
   How full of Love your Eyes, and wishing mine.
   Faith, no; if you can afford me a Lease of your Love,
   Till the old Gentleman my Husband depart this wicked World,
   I'm for the Bargain.
SIR CAU. Hum—what's here, a young Spark at my Wife? [*Goes about 'em.*]
GAY. Unreasonable *Julia*, is that all,
   My Love, my Sufferings, and my Vows must hope?

Set me an Age—say when you will be kind,
And I will languish out in starving Wish:
But thus to gape for Legacies of Love,
Till Youth be past Enjoyment,
The Devil I will as soon—farewel. [*Offers to go.*]

L. FUL. Stay, I conjure you stay.

GAY. And lose my Assignation with my Devil. [*Aside.*]

SIR CAU. 'Tis so, ay, ay, 'tis so—and wise Men will perceive it; 'tis here—here in my forehead, it more than buds; it sprouts, it flourishes.

SIR FEEB. So, that young Gentleman has nettled him, stung him to the quick: I hope he'll chain her up—the Gad-Bee's in his Quonundrum—in Charity I'll relieve him—Come, my Lady *Fulbank*, the Night grows old upon our hands; to dancing, to jiggiting—Come, shall I lead your Ladyship?

L. FUL. No, Sir, you see I am better provided—
[*Takes* GAYMAN'S *hand.*]

SIR CAU. Ay, no doubt on't, a Pox on him for a young handsome Dog. [*They dance all.*]

SIR FEEB. Very well, very well, now the Posset; and then—ods bobs, and then—

DIA. And then we'll have t'other Dance.

SIR FEEB. Away, Girls, away, and steal the Bride to Bed; they have a deal to do upon their Wedding-nights; and what with the tedious Ceremonies of dressing and undressing, the smutty Lectures of the Women, by way of Instruction, and the little Stratagems of the young Wenches—odds bobs, a Man's cozen'd of half his Night: Come, Gentlemen, one Bottle, and then—we'll toss the Stocking.
[*Exeunt all but* L. FUL. BRED. *who are talking, and* GAYMAN.]

L. FUL. But dost thou think he'll come?

BRED. I do believe so, Madam—

L. FUL. Be sure you contrive it so, he may not know whither, or to whom he comes.

BRED. I warrant you, Madam, for our Parts.
[*Exit* BREDWEL, *stealing out* GAYMAN.]

L. FUL. How now, what, departing?

GAY. You are going to the Bride-Chamber.

L. FUL. No matter, you shall stay—

GAY. I hate to have you in a Croud.

L. FUL. Can you deny me—will you not give me one lone hour i'th' Garden?

GAY. Where we shall only tantalize each other with dull kissing, and part with the same Appetite we met—No, Madam; besides, I have business—

L. FUL. Some Assignation—is it so indeed?

GAY. Away, you cannot think me such a Traitor; 'tis more important business—

L. FUL. Oh, 'tis too late for business—let to morrow serve.

GAY. By no means—the Gentleman is to go out of Town.

L. FUL. Rise the earlier then—

GAY. —But, Madam, the Gentleman lies dangerously—sick—and should he die—

L. FUL. 'Tis not a dying Uncle, I hope, Sir?

GAY. Hum—

L. FUL. The Gentleman a dying, and to go out of Town to morrow?

GAY. Ay—a—he goes—in a Litter—'tis his Fancy, Madam—Change of Air may recover him.

L. FUL. So may your change of Mistress do me, Sir—farewel. [*Goes out.*]

GAY. Stay, *Julia*—Devil, be damn'd—for you shall tempt no more, I'll love and be undone—but she is gone—
And if I stay, the most that I shall gain
Is but a reconciling Look, or Kiss.
No, my kind Goblin—
    I'll keep my Word with thee, as the least Evil;
    A tantalizing Woman's worse than Devil. [*Exit.*]

Act III.

SCENE I. Sir Feeble's *House.*

[A SONG *made by* MR. CHEEK.]
NO more, Lucinda, ah! expose no more
    To the admiring World those conquering Charms:
In vain all day unhappy Men adore,
    What the kind Night gives to my longing Arms.
Their vain Attempts can ne'er successful prove,
    Whilst I so well maintain the Fort of Love.

Yet to the World with so bewitching Arts,
    Your dazling Beauty you around display,

And triumph in the Spoils of broken Hearts,
　That sink beneath your feet, and croud your Way.
Ah! suffer now your Cruelty to cease,
　And to a fruitless War prefer a Peace.
[*Enter* RALPH *with Light*, SIR FEEBLE, *and* BELLMOUR *sad.*]

SIR FEEB. So, so, they're gone — Come, *Francis*, you shall have the Honour of undressing me for the Encounter; but 'twill be a sweet one, *Francis*.

BEL. Hell take him, how he teazes me! [*Undressing all the while.*]

SIR FEEB. But is the young Rogue laid, *Francis* — is she stoln to Bed? What Tricks the young Baggages have to whet a man's Appetite?

BEL. Ay, Sir — Pox on him — he will raise my Anger up to Madness, and I shall kill him to prevent his going to Bed to her. [*Aside.*]

SIR FEEB. A pise of those Bandstrings — the more haste the less speed.

BEL. Be it so in all things, I beseech thee, *Venus.*

SIR FEEB. Thy aid a little, *Francis* — oh, oh — thou choakest me, 'sbobs, what dost mean? [*Pinches him by the Throat.*]

BEL. You had so hamper'd 'em, Sir — the Devil's very mischievous in me. [*Aside.*]

SIR FEEB. Come, come, quick, good *Francis*, adod, I'm as yare as a Hawk at the young Wanton — nimbly, good *Francis*, untruss, untruss.

BEL. Cramps seize ye — what shall I do? the near Approach distracts me. [*Aside.*]

SIR FEEB. So, so, my Breeches, good *Francis*. But well, *Francis*, how dost think I got the young Jade my Wife?

BEL. With five hundred pounds a year Jointure, Sir.

SIR FEEB. No, that wou'd not do, the Baggage was damnably in love with a young Fellow they call *Bellmour*, a handsome young Rascal he was, they say, that's truth on't; and a pretty Estate: but happening to kill a Man he was forced to fly.

BEL. That was great pity, Sir.

SIR FEEB. Pity! hang him, Rogue, 'sbobs, and all the young Fellows in the Town deserve it; we can never keep our Wives and Daughters honest for rampant young Dogs; and an old Fellow cannot put in amongst 'em, under being undone, with Presenting, and the Devil and all. But what dost think I did? being damnably in love — I feign'd a Letter as from the *Hague*, wherein was a Relation of this same *Bellmour's* being hang'd.

BEL. Is't possible, Sir, you cou'd devise such News?

SIR FEEB. Possible, Man! I did it, I did it; she swooned at the News, shut her self up a whole Month in her Chamber; but I presented high: she sigh'd and wept, and swore she'd never marry: still I presented; she hated, loathed, spit upon me; still, adod, I presented, till I presented my self effectually in Church to her; for she at last wisely considered her Vows were cancell'd, since *Bellmour* was hang'd.

BEL. Faith, Sir, this was very cruel, to take away his Fame, and then his Mistress.

SIR FEEB. Cruel! thou'rt an Ass, we are but even with the brisk Rogues, for they take away our Fame, cuckold us, and take away our Wives: so, so, my Cap, *Francis*.

BEL. And do you think this Marriage lawful, Sir?

SIR FEEB. Lawful! it shall be when I've had Livery and Seisin of her Body—and that shall be presently Rogue,—quick—besides, this *Bellmour* dares as well be hang'd as come into *England*.

BEL. If he gets his Pardon, Sir—

SIR FEEB. Pardon! no, no, I have took care for that, for I have, you must know, got his Pardon already.

BEL. How, Sir! got his Pardon, that's some amends for robbing him of his Wife.

SIR FEEB. Hold, honest *Francis*: What, dost think 'twas in kindness to him! No, you Fool, I got his Pardon my self, that no body else should have it, so that if he gets any body to speak to his Majesty for it, his Majesty cries he has granted it; but for want of my appearance, he's defunct, trust up, hang'd, *Francis*.

BEL. This is the most excellent Revenge I ever heard of.

SIR FEEB. Ay, I learnt it of a great Politician of our Times.

BEL. But have you got his Pardon?—

SIR FEEB. I've done't, I've done't; Pox on him, it cost me five hundred pounds though: Here 'tis, my Solicitor brought it me this Evening. [*Gives it him.*]

BEL. This was a lucky hit—and if it scape me, let me be hang'd by a Trick indeed.[*Aside.*]

SIR FEEB. So, put it into my Cabinet,—safe, *Francis*, safe.

BEL. Safe, I'll warrant you, Sir.

SIR FEEB. My Gown, quick, quick,—t'other Sleeve, Man—so now my Night-cap; well, I'll in, throw open my Gown to fright away the Women, and jump into her Arms.[*Exit* SIR FEEBLE.]

BEL. He's gone, quickly, oh Love inspire me!

[*Enter a* FOOTMAN.]

FOOT. Sir, my Master, Sir *Cautious Fulbank*, left his Watch on the little Parlor-Table to night, and bid me call for't.

BEL. Hah—the Bridegroom has it, Sir, who is just gone to Bed, it shall be sent him in the Morning.

FOOT. 'Tis very well, Sir—your Servant— [*Exit* FOOTMAN.]

BEL. Let me see—here is the Watch, I took it up to keep for him—but his sending has inspir'd me with a sudden Stratagem, that will do better than Force, to secure the poor trembling *Leticia*—who, I am sure, is dying with her Fears. [*Exit* BELLMOUR.]

SCENE II. *Changes to the Bed-chamber;*
LETICIA *in an undressing by the Women at the Table.*

[*Enter to them* SIR FEEBLE FAINWOU'D.]

SIR FEEB. What's here? what's here? the prating Women still. Ods bobs, what, not in Bed yet? for shame of Love, *Leticia*.

LET. For shame of Modesty, Sir; you wou'd not have me go to Bed before all this Company.

SIR FEEB. What, the Women! why, they must see you laid, 'tis the fashion.

LET. What, with a Man? I wou'd not for the World. Oh, *Bellmour*, where art thou with all thy promised aid? [*Aside.*]

DIA. Nay, Madam, we shou'd see you laid indeed.

LET. First in my Grave, *Diana*.

SIR FEEB. Ods bobs, here's a Compact amongst the Women—High Treason against the Bridegroom—therefore, Ladies, withdraw, or, adod, I'll lock you all in.

[*Throws open his Gown, they run all away, he locks the door.*]

So, so, now we're alone, *Leticia*—off with this foolish Modesty, and Night Gown, and slide into my Arms. [*She runs from him.*]

H'e', my little Puskin—what, fly me, my coy *Daphne*, [*He pursues her. Knocking.*]

Hah—who's that knocks—who's there?—

BEL. [*Within.*] 'Tis I, Sir, 'tis I, open the door presently.

SIR FEEB. Why, what's the matter, is the House a-fire?

BEL. [*Within.*] Worse, Sir, worse— [*He opens the door,* BELLMOUR *enters with the Watch in his hand.*]

LET. 'Tis *Bellmour's* Voice!

BEL. Oh, Sir, do you know this Watch?

SIR FEEB. This Watch!

BEL. Ay, Sir, this Watch?

SIR FEEB. This Watch!—why, prithee, why dost tell me of a Watch? 'tis Sir

Cautious Fulbank's Watch; what then, what a Pox dost trouble me with Watches? [*Offers to put him out, he returns.*]

BEL. 'Tis indeed his Watch, Sir, and by this Token he has sent for you, to come immediately to his House, Sir.

SIR FEEB. What a Devil, art mad, *Francis?* or is his Worship mad, or does he think me mad? — go, prithee tell him I'll come to him to morrow. [*Goes to put him out.*]

BEL. To morrow, Sir! why all our Throats may be cut before to morrow.

SIR FEEB. What sayst thou, Throat cut?

BEL. Why, the City's up in Arms, Sir, and all the Aldermen are met at *Guild-Hall*; some damnable Plot, Sir.

SIR FEEB. Hah — Plot — the Alderman met at *Guild-Hall!* — hum — why, let 'em meet, I'll not lose this Night to save the Nation.

LET. Wou'd you to bed, Sir, when the weighty Affairs of State require your Presence?

SIR FEEB. — Hum — met at *Guild-Hall;* — my Clothes, my Gown again *Francis*, I'll out — out! what, upon my Wedding-night? No — I'll in. [*Putting on his Gown pausing, pulls it off again.*]

LET. For shame, Sir, shall the Reverend Council of the City debate without you?

SIR FEEB. Ay, that's true, that's true; come truss again, *Francis*, truss again — yet now I think on't, *Francis* prithee run thee to the Hall, and tell 'em 'tis my Wedding-night, d'ye see, *Francis*; and let some body give my Voice for —

BEL. What, Sir?

SIR FEEB. Adod, I cannot tell; up in Arms, say you! why, let 'em fight Dog, fight Bear; mun, I'll to Bed — go —

LET. And shall his Majesty's Service and his Safety lie unregarded for a slight Woman, Sir?

SIR FEEB. Hum, his Majesty! — come, haste, *Francis*, I'll away, and call *Ralph*, and the Footmen, and bid 'em arm; each Man shoulder his Musket, and advance his Pike — and bring my Artillery Implements quick — and let's away: Pupsey — b'u'y, Pupsey, I'll bring it a fine thing yet before Morning, it may be — let's away: I shall grow fond, and forget the business of the Nation — Come, follow me, *Francis*. — [*Exit* SIR FEEBLE, BELLMOUR *runs to* LETICIA.]

BEL. Now, my *Leticia*, if thou e'er didst Love,
If ever thou design'st to make me blest —
Without delay fly this adulterous Bed.

SIR FEEB. Why, *Francis*, where are you, Knave? [SIR FEEB. *within.*]

BEL. I must be gone, lest he suspect us — I'll lose him, and return to thee immediately — get thy self ready. —

LET. I will not fail, my Love. [*Exit* BELLMOUR.]

Old Man forgive me — thou the Aggressor art,

Who rudely forc'd the Hand without the Heart.

She cannot from the Paths of Honour rove,

Whose Guide's Religion, and whose End is Love. [*Exit.*]

SCENE III. *Changes to a Wash-house, or Out-House.*

[*Enter with a Dark-lanthorn* BREDWEL *disguis'd like a Devil, leading* GAYMAN.]

BRED. Stay here till I give notice of your coming.

[*Exit* BREDWEL, *leaves his Dark-Lantern.*]

GAY. Kind Light, a little of your aid — now must I be peeping, though my Curiosity should lose me all — hah — Zouns, what here — a Hovel or a Hog-sty? hum, see the Wickedness of Man, that I should find no time to swear in, but just when I'm in the Devil's Clutches.

[*Enter* PERT, *as an old Woman, with a Staff.*]

OLD W. Good Even to you, fair Sir.

GAY. Ha — defend me; if this be she, I must rival the Devil, that's certain.

OLD W. Come, young Gentleman, dare not you venture?

GAY. He must be as hot as *Vesuvius* that does — I shall never earn my Morning's Present.

OLD W. What, do you fear a longing Woman, Sir?

GAY. The Devil I do — this is a damn'd Preparation to Love.

OLD W. Why stand you gazing, Sir? A Woman's Passion is like the Tide, it stays for no man when the hour is come —

GAY. I'm sorry I have took it at its Turning;

I'm sure mine's ebbing out as fast.

OLD W. Will you not speak, Sir — will you not on?

GAY. I wou'd fain ask — a civil Question or two first.

OLD W. You know too much Curiosity lost Paradise.

GAY. Why, there's it now.

OLD W. Fortune and Love invite you, if you dare follow me.

GAY. This is the first thing in Petticoats that ever dar'd me in vain. Were I but sure she were but human now — for sundry Considerations she might down — but I will on — [*She goes, he follows; both go out.*]

SCENE IV. *A Chamber in the Apartments of* L. FULBANK.

[*Enter* OLD WOMAN *follow'd by* GAYMAN *in the dark.*]

[*Soft Musick plays, she leaves him.*]
GAY. —Hah, Musick—and Excellent!

Song.

OH! Love, that stronger art than Wine,
Pleasing Delusion, Witchery divine,
Want to be priz'd above all Wealth,
Disease that has more Joys than Health;
Though we blaspheme thee in our Pain,
And of thy Tyranny complain,
We all are better'd by thy Reign.

What Reason never can bestow,
We to this useful Passion owe.
Love wakes the dull from sluggish Ease,
And learns a Clown the Art to please:
Humbles the Vain, kindles the Cold,
Makes Misers free, and Cowards bold.
'Tis he reforms the Sot from Drink,
And teaches airy Fops to think.
When full brute Appetite is fed,
And choak'd the Glutton lies, and dead;
Thou new Spirits dost dispense,
And fine'st the gross Delights of Sense.
Virtue's unconquerable Aid,
That against Nature can persuade;
And makes a roving Mind retire
Within the Bounds of just Desire.
Chearer of Age, Youth's kind Unrest,
And half the Heaven of the blest.

GAY. Ah, *Julia, Julia!* if this soft Preparation
   Were but to bring me to thy dear Embraces;
   What different Motions wou'd surround my Soul,
   From what perplex it now.
      [*Enter Nymphs and Shepherds, and dance.*]
      [*Then two dance alone. All go out but* PERT *and a Shepherd.*]
   —If these be Devils, they are obliging ones:
   I did not care if I ventur'd on that last Female Fiend.

[*Man sings.*]
> Cease your Wonder, cease your Guess,
> Whence arrives your happiness.
> Cease your Wonder, cease your Pain,
> Human Fancy is in vain.

Chorus. 'Tis enough, you once shall find,
> Fortune may to Worth be kind; [*gives him Gold.*]
> And Love can leave off being blind.

[PERT *sings.*]
> You, before you enter here
> On this sacred Ring must swear, [*Puts it on his Finger, holds his Hand.*]
> By the Figure which is round,
> Your Passion constant and profound;
> By the Adamantine Stone,
> To be fixt to one alone:
> By the Lustre, which is true,
> Ne'er to break your sacred Vow.
> Lastly, by the Gold that's try'd,
> For Love all Dangers to abide.

[*They all dance about him, while those same two sing.*]

Man. Once about him let us move,
> To confirm him true to Love.

Pert. Twice with mystick turning Feet,
> Make him silent and discreet.

Man. Thrice about him let us tread,
> To keep him ever young in Bed.

[*Gives him another part.*]

Man. Forget Aminta's *proud Disdain;*
> Haste here, and sigh no more in vain,
> The Joy of Love without the Pain.

Pert. That God repents his former Slights,
> And Fortune thus your Faith requites.

Both. Forget Aminta's *proud Disdain;*
> Then taste, and sigh no more in vain,
> The Joy of Love without the Pain,
> The Joy of Love without the Pain.

[*Exeunt all* DANCERS. *Looks on himself, and feels about him.*]

GAY. What the Devil can all this mean? If there be a Woman in the

Case—sure I have not liv'd so bad a Life, to gain the dull Reputation of so modest a Coxcomb, but that a Female might down with me, without all this Ceremony. Is it care of her Honour?—that cannot be—this Age affords none so nice: Nor Fiend nor Goddess can she be, for these I saw were Mortal. No—'tis a Woman—I am positive. Not young nor handsom, for then Vanity had made her glory to have been seen. No—since 'tis resolved, a Woman—she must be old and ugly, and will not balk my Fancy with her sight, but baits me more with this essential Beauty.

Well—be she young or old, Woman or Devil,
She pays, and I'll endeavour to be civil. [Exit.]

SCENE V. *In the same House. The flat Scene of the Hall.*

[*After a Knocking, enter* BREDWEL *in his masking Habit, with his Vizard in the one Hand, and a Light in t'other, in haste.*]

BRED. Hah, knocking so late at our Gate—

[*Opens the door.*]

[*Enter* SIR FEEBLE *drest, and arm'd Cap-a-pee, with a broad Waste-Belt stuck round with Pistols, a Helmet, Scarf, Buff-coat and half Pike.*]

SIR FEEB. How now, how now, what's the matter here?

BRED. Matter, what, is my Lady's innocent Intrigue found out?—Heavens, Sir, what makes you here in this warlike Equipage?

SIR FEEB. What makes you in this showing Equipage, Sir?

BRED. I have been dancing among some of my Friends.

SIR FEEB. And I thought to have been fighting with some of my Friends. Where's Sir *Cautious*, where's Sir *Cautious?*

BRED. Sir *Cautious*—Sir, in Bed.

SIR FEEB. Call him, call him—quickly, good *Edward*.

BRED. Sure my Lady's Frolick is betray'd, and he comes to make Mischief. However, I'll go and secure Mr. *Gayman*. [*Exit* BREDWEL.]

[*Enter* SIR CAUTIOUS *and* DICK *his Boy with Light.*]

DICK. Pray, Sir, go to Bed, here's no Thieves; all's still and well.

SIR CAU. This last Night's misfortune of mine, *Dick*, has kept me waking, and methought all night, I heard a kind of a silent Noise. I am still afraid of Thieves; mercy upon me, to lose five hundred Guineas at one clap, *Dick*.—Hah—bless me! what's yonder? Blow the great Horn, *Dick*—Thieves—Murder, Murder!

SIR FEEB. Why, what a Pox, are you mad? 'Tis I, 'tis I, man.

SIR CAU. I, who am I? Speak—declare—pronounce.

SIR FEEB. Your Friend, old *Feeble Fainwou'd.*

SIR CAU. How, Sir *Feeble!* At this late hour, and on his Wedding-Night—why, what's the matter, Sir—is it Peace or War with you?

SIR FEEB. A Mistake, a Mistake, proceed to the business, good Brother, for time you know is precious.

SIR CAU. Some strange Catastrophe has happened between him and his Wife to Night, and makes him disturb me thus—[*Aside.*]

—Come, sit, good Brother, and to the business as you say— [*They sit one at one end of the Table, the other at the other;* DICK *sets down the Light and goes out—both sit gaping and staring, and expecting when either should speak.*]

SIR FEEB. As soon as you please, Sir. Lord, how wildly he stares! He's much disturb'd in's mind—Well, Sir, let us be brief—

SIR CAU. As brief as you please, Sir—Well, Brother— [*Pausing still.*]

SIR FEEB. So, Sir.

SIR CAU. How strangely he stares and gapes—some deep concern.

SIR FEEB. Hum—hum—

SIR CAU. I listen to you, advance—

SIR FEEB. Sir?

SIR CAU. A very distracted Countenance—pray Heaven he be not mad, and a young Wife is able to make an old Fellow mad, that's the Truth on't. [*Aside.*]

SIR FEEB. Sure 'tis something of his Lady—he's so loth to bring it out—I am sorry you are thus disturb'd, Sir.

SIR CAU. No disturbance to serve a Friend—

SIR FEEB. I think I am your Friend indeed, Sir *Cautious*, or I wou'd not have been here upon my Wedding-Night.

SIR CAU. His Wedding-Night—there lies his Grief, poor Heart! Perhaps she has cuckolded him already—[*Aside.*]—Well, come, Brother—many such things are done—

SIR FEEB. Done—hum—come, out with it; Brother—what troubles you to Night?

SIR CAU. Troubles me—why, knows he I am robb'd? [*Aside.*]

SIR FEEB. I may perhaps restore you to the Rest you've lost.

SIR CAU. The Rest; why, have I lost more since? Why, know you then who did it?—Oh, how I'd be reveng'd upon the Rascal!

SIR FEEB. 'Tis—Jealousy, the old Worm that bites— [*Aside.*] Who is it you suspect?

SIR CAU. Alas, I know not whom to suspect, I wou'd I did; but if you cou'd discover him—I wou'd so swinge him—

SIR FEEB. I know him—what, do you take me for a Pimp, Sir? I know him—there's your Watch again, Sir; I'm your Friend, but no Pimp, Sir—[*Rises in Rage.*]

SIR CAU. My Watch; I thank you, Sir—but why Pimp, Sir?

SIR FEEB. Oh, a very thriving Calling, Sir,—and I have a young Wife to practise with. I know your Rogues.

SIR CAU. A young Wife!—'tis so, his Gentlewoman has been at Hot-Cockles without her Husband, and he's Horn-mad upon't. I suspected her being so close in with his Nephew—in a Fit with a Pox—[*Aside.*] Come, come, Sir *Feeble*, 'tis many an honest Man's Fortune.

SIR FEEB. I grant it, Sir—but to the business, Sir, I came for.

SIR CAU. With all my Soul—

> [*They sit gaping, and expecting when either should speak.*
> *Enter* BREDWEL *and* GAYMAN *at the door.* BREDWEL *sees them,*
> *and puts* GAYMAN *back again.*]

BRED. Hah—Sir *Feeble*, and Sir *Cautious* there—what shall I do? For this way we must pass, and to carry him back wou'd discover my Lady to him, betray all, and spoil the Jest—retire, Sir, your Life depends upon your being unseen. [*Go out.*]

SIR FEEB. Well, Sir, do you not know that I am married, Sir? and this my Wedding Night?

SIR CAU. Very good, Sir.

SIR FEEB. And that I long to be in bed?

SIR CAU. Very well, Sir.

SIR FEEB. Very good, Sir, and very well, Sir—why then what the Devil do I make here, Sir? [*Rises in a rage.*]

SIR CAU. Patience, Brother—and forward.

SIR FEEB. Forward! lend me your hand, good Brother; let's feel your Pulse; how has this Night gone with you?

SIR CAU. Ha, ha, ha—this is the oddest Conundrum—sure he's mad—and yet now I think on't, I have not slept to night, nor shall I ever sleep again, till I have found the Villain that robb'd me. [*Weeps.*]

SIR FEEB. So, now he weeps—far gone—this Laughing and Weeping is a very bad sign! [*Aside.*] Come, let me lead you to your Bed.

SIR CAU. Mad, stark mad—no, now I'm up 'tis no matter—pray ease your troubled Mind—I am your Friend—out with it—what, was it acted? or but designed?

SIR FEEB. How, Sir?

SIR CAU. Be not asham'd, I'm under the same Predicament I doubt, little better than a—but let that pass.

SIR FEEB. Have you any Proof?

SIR CAU. Proof of what, good Sir?

SIR FEEB. Of what! why, that you're a Cuckold; Sir, Cuckold, if you'll ha't.

SIR CAU. Cuckold! Sir, do ye know what ye say?

SIR FEEB. What I say?

SIR CAU. Ay, what you say, can you make this out?

SIR FEEB. I make it out!

SIR CAU. Ay, Sir—if you say it, and cannot make it out, you're a—

SIR FEEB. What am I, Sir? What am I?

SIR CAU. A Cuckold as well as my self, Sir; and I'll sue you for *Scandalum Magnatum*; I shall recover swinging Damages with a City-Jury.

SIR FEEB. I know of no such thing, Sir.

SIR CAU. No, Sir?

SIR FEEB. No, Sir.

SIR CAU. Then what wou'd you be at, Sir?

SIR FEEB. I be at, Sir! what wou'd you be at, Sir?

SIR CAU. Ha, ha, ha—why this is the strangest thing—to see an old Fellow, a Magistrate of the City, the first Night he's married, forsake his Bride and Bed, and come arm'd Cap-a-pee, like *Gargantua*, to disturb another old Fellow, and banter him with a Tale of a Tub; and all to be-cuckold him here—in plain *English*, what's your Business?

SIR FEEB. Why, what the Devil's your Business, and you go to that?

SIR CAU. My Business, with whom?

SIR FEEB. With me, Sir, with me; what a Pox do you think I do here?

SIR CAU. 'Tis that I wou'd be glad to know, Sir.

[*Enter* DICK.]

SIR FEEB. Here, *Dick*, remember I've brought back your Master's Watch; next time he sends for me o'er Night, I'll come to him in the Morning.

SIR CAU. Ha, ha, ha, I send for you! Go home and sleep, Sir—Ad, and ye keep your Wife waking to so little purpose, you'll go near to be haunted with a Vision of Horns. [*Exit* DICK.]

SIR FEEB. Roguery, Knavery, to keep me from my Wife—Look ye, this was the Message I receiv'd. [*Tells him seemingly.*]

[*Enter* BREDWEL *to the Door in a white Sheet like a Ghost, speaking to* GAYMAN *who stands within.*]

BRED. Now, Sir, we are two to two, for this way you must pass or be taken
in the Lady's Lodgings—I'll first adventure out to make you pass the
safer, and that he may not, if possible, see Sir *Cautious*, whom I shall
fright into a Trance, I am sure.

And Sir *Feeble*, the Devil's in't if he know him. [*Aside.*]

GAY. A brave kind Fellow this.

[*Enter* BREDWEL *stalking on as a Ghost by them.*]

SIR CAU. Oh—undone,—undone; help, help;—I'm dead, I'm dead. [*Falls
down on his Face;* SIR FEEBLE *stares,—and stands still.*]

BRED. As I could wish. [*Aside, turns.*]

Come on, thou ghastly thing, and follow me.

[*Enter* GAYMAN *like a Ghost, with a Torch.*]

SIR CAU. Oh Lord, oh Lord!

GAY. Hah!—old Sir *Feeble Fainwou'd*—why, where the Devil am I?—'Tis
he:—and be it where it will, I'll fright the old Dotard for cozening my
Friend of his Mistress. [*Stalks on.*]

SIR FEEB. Oh, guard me,—guard me—all ye Pow'rs! [*Trembling.*]

GAY. Thou call'st in vain, fond Wretch—for I am *Bellmour*,

Whom first thou robb'st of Fame and Life,

And then what dearer was,—his Wife.

[*Goes out, shaking his Torch at him.*]

SIR CAU. Oh Lord—oh Lord!

[*Enter* L. FULBANK *in an undress, and* PERT *undrest.*]

L. FUL. Heavens, what noise is this?—So he's got safe out I see—hah, what
thing art thou? [*Sees* SIR FEEBLE *arm'd.*]

SIR FEEB. Stay, Madam, stay—'tis I, a poor trembling Mortal.

L. FUL. Sir *Feeble Fainwou'd!*—rise,—are you both mad?

SIR CAU. No, no,—Madam, we have seen the Devil.

SIR FEEB. Ay, and he was as tall as the Monument.

SIR CAU. With Eyes like a Beacon—and a Mouth,—Heaven bless us, like
London Bridge at a full Tide.

SIR FEEB. Ay, and roar'd as loud.

L. FUL. Idle Francies, what makes you from your Bed? and you, Sir, from
your Bride?

[*Enter* DICK *with Sack.*]

SIR FEEB. Oh! that's the business of another day, a mistake only, Madam.

L. FUL. Away, I'm asham'd to see wise Men so weak; the Fantoms of the
Night, or your own Shadows, the Whimseys of the Brain for want of

Rest, or perhaps *Bredwel*, your Man — who being wiser than his
Master, play'd you this Trick to fright you both to Bed.

SIR FEEB. Hum — adod, and that may be, for the young Knave when he let
me in to Night, was drest up for some Waggery —

SIR CAU. Ha, ha, ha 'twas even so, sure enough, Brother —

SIR FEEB. Ads bobs, but they frighted me at first basely — but I'll home to
Pupsey, there may be Roguery, as well as here — Madam, I ask your
Pardon, I see we're all mistaken.

L. FUL. Ay, Sir *Feeble*, go home to your Wife. [*Ex. severally.*]

SCENE VI. *The Street.*

[*Enter* BELLMOUR *at the door, knocks, and enter to him from the
House,* PHILLIS.]

PHIL. Oh, are you come, Sir? I'll call my Lady down.

BEL. Oh, haste, the Minutes fly — leave all behind.
And bring *Leticia* only to my Arms. [*A noise of People.*]
— Hah, what noise is that? 'Tis coming this way,
I tremble with my fears — hah, Death and the Devil,
'Tis he —

[*Enter* SIR FEEBLE *and his Men arm'd, goes to the door, knocks.*]
Ay, 'tis he, and I'm undone — what shall I do to kill him now? besides,
the Sin wou'd put me past all Hopes of pardoning.

SIR FEEB. A damn'd Rogue to deceive me thus. —

BEL. Hah — see, by Heaven *Leticia*, Oh, we are ruin'd!

SIR FEEB. Hum — what's here, two Women? — [*Stands a little off.*]

[*Enter* LETICIA *and* PHILLIS *softly, undrest, with a Box.*]

LET. Where are you, my best Wishes? Lord of my Vows — and Charmer of
my Soul? Where are you?

BEL. Oh, Heavens! — [*Draws his Sword half-way.*]

SIR FEEB. Hum, who's here? My Gentlewoman — she's monstrous kind of
the sudden. But whom is't meant to? [*Aside.*]

LET. Give me your hand, my Love, my Life, my All — Alas! where are
you?

SIR FEEB. Hum — no, no, this is not to me — I am jilted, cozen'd,
cuckolded, and so forth. — [*Groping, she takes hold of* SIR FEEB.]

LET. Oh, are you here? indeed you frighted me with your Silence — here,
take these Jewels, and let us haste away.

SIR FEEB. Hum — are you thereabouts, Mistress? was I sent away with a
Sham-Plot for this! — She cannot mean it to me. [*Aside.*]

LET. Will you not speak? — will you not answer me? — do you repent already? — before Enjoyment are you cold and false?

SIR FEEB. Hum, before Enjoyment — that must be me. Before Enjoyment — Ay, ay, 'tis I — I see a little Prolonging a Woman's Joy, sets an Edge upon her Appetite. [*Merrily.*]

LET. What means my Dear? shall we not haste away?

SIR FEEB. Haste away! there 'tis again — No — 'tis not me she means: what, at your Tricks and Intrigues already? — Yes, yes, I am destin'd a Cuckold —

LET. Say, am I not your Wife? can you deny me?

SIR FEEB. Wife! adod, 'tis I she means — 'tis I she means — [*Merrily.*]

LET. Oh *Bellmour, Bellmour.* [SIR FEEB. *starts back from her hands.*]

SIR FEEB. Hum — what's that — *Bellmour!*

LET. Hah! Sir *Feeble!* — he would not, Sir, have us'd me thus unkindly.

SIR FEEB. Oh — I'm glad 'tis no worse — *Bellmour*, quoth a! I thought the Ghost was come again.

PHIL. Why did you not speak, Sir, all this while? — my Lady weeps with your Unkindness.

SIR FEEB. I did but hold my peace, to hear how prettily she prattled Love: But, fags, you are naught to think of a young Fellow — ads bobs, you are now.

LET. I only say — he wou'd not have been so unkind to me.

SIR FEEB. But what makes ye out at this Hour, and with these Jewels?

PHIL. Alas, Sir, we thought the City was in Arms, and packt up our things to secure 'em, if there had been a necessity for Flight. For had they come to plundering once, they wou'd have begun with the rich Aldermen's Wives, you know, Sir.

SIR FEEB. Ads bobs, and so they would — but there was no Arms, nor Mutiny — where's *Francis?*

BEL. Here, Sir.

SIR FEEB. Here, Sir — why, what a story you made of a Meeting in the Hall, and — Arms, and — a — the Devil of any thing was stirring, but a couple of old Fools, that sat gaping and waiting for one another's business —

BEL. Such a Message was brought me, Sir.

SIR FEEB. Brought! thou'rt an Ass, *Francis* — but no more — come, come, let's to bed —

LET. To Bed, Sir! what, by Day-light? — for that's hasting on — I wou'd not for the World — the Night wou'd hide my Blushes — but the Day — wou'd let me see my self in your Embraces.

SIR FEEB. Embraces, in a Fiddlestick; why, are we not married?

LET. 'Tis true, Sir, and Time will make me more familiar with you, but yet
my Virgin Modesty forbids it. I'll to *Diana's* Chamber, the Night will
come again.

SIR FEEB. For once you shall prevail; and this damn'd Jant has pretty well
mortified me: — a Pox of your Mutiny, *Francis*. — Come, I'll conduct
thee to *Diana*, and lock thee in, that I may have thee safe, Rogue. —
We'll give young Wenches leave to whine and blush,
And fly those Blessings which — ads bobs, they wish. [*Exeunt.*]

Act IV.

SCENE I. SIR FEEBLE'S *House.*

[*Enter* LADY FULBANK, GAYMAN *fine, gently pulling her back by
the hand; and* RALPH *meets 'em.*]

L. FUL. How now, *Ralph* — Let your Lady know I am come to wait on her.
[*Exit* RALPH.]

GAY. Oh, why this needless Visit —
Your Husband's safe, at least till Evening safe.
Why will you not go back,
And give me one soft hour, though to torment me?

L. FUL. You are at leisure now, I thank you, Sir.
Last Night when I with all Love's Rhetorick pleaded,
And Heaven knows what last Night might have produced,
You were engag'd! False Man, I do believe it,
And I am satisfied you love me not. [*Walks away in scorn.*]

GAY. Not love you!
Why do I waste my Youth in vain pursuit,
Neglecting Interest, and despising Power?
Unheeding and despising other Beauties.
Why at your feet are all my Fortunes laid,
And why does all my Fate depend on you?

L. FUL. I'll not consider why you play the Fool,
Present me Rings and Bracelets; why pursue me;
Why watch whole Nights before my senseless Door,
And take such Pains to shew your self a Coxcomb.

GAY. Oh! why all this?
By all the Powers above, by this dear Hand,
And by this Ring, which on this Hand I place,
On which I've sworn Fidelity to Love;
I never had a Wish or soft Desire

To any other Woman,
Since *Julia* sway'd the Empire of my Soul.
L. FUL. Hah, my own Ring I gave him last night. [*Aside.*]
    —Your Jewel, Sir, is rich:
    Why do you part with things of so much value,
    So easily, and so frequently?
GAY. To strengthen the weak Arguments of Love.
L. FUL. And leave your self undone?
GAY. Impossible, if I am blest with *Julia*.
L. FUL. Love's a thin Diet, nor will keep out Cold.
    You cannot satisfy your Dunning Taylor,
    To cry—I am in Love!
    Though possible you may your Seamstress.
GAY. Does ought about me speak such Poverty?
L. FUL. I am sorry that it does not, since to maintain
    This Gallantry, 'tis said you use base means,
    Below a Gentleman.
GAY. Who dares but to imagine it's a Rascal,
    A Slave, below a beating—what means my *Julia?*
L. FUL. No more dissembling, I know your Land is gone
    —I know each Circumstance of all your Wants;
    Therefore—as e'er you hope that I should love you ever—
    Tell me—where 'twas you got this Jewel, Sir.
GAY. Hah—I hope 'tis no stol'n Goods; [*Aside.*]
    Why on the sudden all this nice examining?
L. FUL. You trifle with me, and I'll plead no more.
GAY. Stay—why—I bought it, Madam—
L. FUL. Where had you Money, Sir? You see I am No Stranger to your
    Poverty.
GAY. This is strange—perhaps it is a secret.
L. FUL. So is my Love, which shall be kept from you. [*Offers to go.*]
GAY. Stay, *Julia*—your Will shall be obey'd, [*Sighing.*]
    Though I had rather die than be obedient,
    Because I know you'll hate me when 'tis told.
L. FUL. By all my Vows, let it be what it will,
    It ne'er shall alter me from loving you.
GAY. I have—of late—been tempted—
    With Presents, Jewels, and large Sums of Gold.
L. FUL. Tempted! by whom?

GAY. The Devil, for ought I know.

L. FUL. Defend me, Heaven! the Devil?

I hope you have not made a Contract with him.

GAY. No, though in the Shape of Woman it appear'd.

L. FUL. Where met you with it?

GAY. By Magick Art I was conducted—I know not how,
To an inchanted Palace in the Clouds,
Where I was so attended—
Young dancing, singing Fiends innumerable.

L. FUL. Imagination all!

GAY. But for the amorous Devil, the old *Proserpine.* —

L. FUL. Ay, she—what said she? —

GAY. Not a word: Heaven be prais'd, she was a silent Devil—but she was laid in a Pavilion, all form'd of gilded Clouds, which hung by Geometry, whither I was conveyed, after much Ceremony, and laid in Bed with her; where with much ado, and trembling with my Fears—I forc'd my Arms about her.

L. FUL. And sure that undeceiv'd him. [*Aside.*]

GAY. But such a Carcase 'twas—deliver me—so rivell'd, lean and rough—a Canvas Bag of wooden Ladles were a better Bed-fellow.

L. FUL. Now though I know that nothing is more distant than I from such a Monster—yet this angers me.

Death! cou'd you love me and submit to this?

GAY. 'Twas that first drew me in—
The tempting Hope of Means to conquer you,
Wou'd put me upon any dangerous Enterprize:
Were I the Lord of all the Universe,
I am so lost in Love,
For one dear Night to clasp you in my Arms,
I'd lavish all that World—then die with Joy.

L. FUL. 'Slife, after all to seem deform'd, old, ugly— [*Walking in a fret.*]

GAY. I knew you would be angry when you heard it. [*He pursues her in a submissive posture.*]

[*Enter* SIR CAUTIOUS, BEARJEST, NOISEY *and* BREDWEL.]

SIR CAU. How, what's here? —my Lady with the Spark that courted her last Night? —hum—with her again so soon? —Well, this Impudence and Importunity undoes more City-Wives than all their unmerciful Finery.

GAY. But, Madam—

L. FUL. Oh, here's my Husband—you'd best tell him your Story—what makes him here so soon?—[*Angry.*]

SIR CAU. Me his Story! I hope he will not tell me he'as a mind to cuckold me.

GAY. A Devil on him, what shall I say to him?

L. FUL. What, so excellent at Intrigues, and so dull at an Excuse? [*Aside.*]

GAY. Yes, Madam, I shall tell him—
    [*Enter* BELLMOUR.]

L. FUL. —Is my Lady at leisure for a Visit, Sir?

BEL. Always to receive your Lady ship. [*She goes out.*]

SIR CAU. With me, Sir, wou'd you speak?

GAY. With you, Sir, if your name be *Fulbank*.

SIR CAU. Plain *Fulbank!* methinks you might have had a Sirreverence under your Girdle, Sir; I am honoured with another Title, Sir—[*Goes talking to the rest.*]

GAY. With many, Sir, that very well become you— [*Pulls him a little aside.*]
    I've something to deliver to your Ear.

SIR CAU. So, I'll be hang'd if he do not tell me, I'm a Cuckold now: I see it in his Eyes. My Ear, Sir! I'd have you to know I scorn any man's secrets, Sir;—for ought I know you may whisper Treason to me, Sir. Pox on him, how handsom he is, I hate the sight of the young Stallion. [*Aside.*]

GAY. I wou'd not be so uncivil, Sir, before all this Company.

SIR CAU. Uncivil! Ay, ay, 'tis so, he cannot be content to cuckold, but he must tell me so too.

GAY. But since you will have it, Sir—you are—a Rascal—a most notorious Villain, Sir, d'ye hear—

SIR CAU. Yes, yes, I do hear—and am glad 'tis no worse. [*Laughing.*]

GAY. Griping as Hell—and as insatiable—worse than a Brokering Jew, not all the Twelve Tribes harbour such a damn'd Extortioner.

SIR CAU. Pray, under favour, Sir, who are you? [*Pulling off his Hat.*]

GAY. One whom thou hast undone—

SIR CAU. Hum—I'm glad of that however. [*Aside smiling.*]

GAY. Racking me up to a starving Want and Misery, Then took advantages to ruin me.

SIR CAU. So, and he'd revenge it on my Wife— [*Aside smiling.*]

GAY. Do not you know one *Wasteall*, Sir?
    [*Enter* RALPH *with Wine, sets it on a Table.*]

SIR CAU. *Wasteall*—ha, ha, ha,—if you are any Friend to that poor Fellow—you may return and tell him, Sir—d'ye hear—that the Mortgage of two hundred pound a Year is this day out, and I'll not bait him an hour, Sir—ha, ha, ha,—what, do you think to hector civil Magistrates?

GAY. Very well, Sir, and is this your Conscience?

SIR CAU. Conscience! what do you tell me of Conscience? Why, what a noise is here—as if the undoing a young Heir were such a Wonder; ods so I've undone a hundred without half this ado.

GAY. I do believe thee—and am come to tell you—I'll be none of that Number—for this Minute I'll go and redeem it—and free myself from the Hell of your Indentures.

SIR CAU. How, redeem it! sure the Devil must help him then.—Stay, Sir—stay—Lord, Sir, what need you put your self to that trouble? your Land is in safe hands, Sir; come, come, sit down—and let us take a Glass of Wine together, Sir—

BEL. Sir, my service to you. [*Drinks to him.*]

GAY. Your Servant, Sir. Wou'd I cou'd come to speak to *Bellmour*, which I dare not do in publick, lest I betray him. I long to be resolv'd where 'twas Sir *Feeble* was last night—if it were he—by which I might find out my invisible Mistress.

NOI. Noble Mr. *Wasteall*—[*Salutes him, so does* BEARJEST.]

BEL. Will you please to sit, Sir?

GAY. I have a little business, Sir—but anon I'll wait on you—your Servant, Gentlemen—I'll to *Crap* the Scrivener's. [*Goes out.*]

SIR CAU. Do you know this *Wasteall*, Sir?—[*To* NOISEY.]

NOI. Know him, Sir! ay, too well—

BEA. The World's well amended with him, Captain, since I lost my Money to him and you at the *George* in *White-Fryers*.

NOI. Ay, poor Fellow—he's sometimes up, and sometimes down, as the Dice favour him—

BEA. Faith, and that's pity; but how came he so fine o'th' sudden? 'Twas but last week he borrowed eighteen pence of me on his Waste-Belt to pay his Dinner in an Ordinary.

BEL. Were you so cruel, Sir, to take it?

NOI. We are not all one Man's Children; faith, Sir, we are here to Day, and gone to Morrow—

SIR CAU. I say 'twas done like a wise Man, Sir; but under favour, Gentlemen, this *Wasteall* is a Rascal—

NOI. A very Rascal, Sir, and a most dangerous Fellow—he cullies in your Prentices and Cashiers to play—which ruins so many o'th' young Fry i'th' City—

SIR CAU. Hum—does he so—d'ye hear that, *Edward?*

NOI. Then he keeps a private Press, and prints your *Amsterdam* and *Leyden* Libels.

SIR CAU. Ay, and makes 'em too, I'll warrant him; a dangerous Fellow—

NOI. Sometimes he begs for a lame Soldier with a wooden Leg.

BEA. Sometimes as a blind Man, sells Switches in *New-Market* Road.

NOI. At other times he runs the Country like a Gipsey—tells Fortunes and robs Hedges, when he's out of Linen.

SIR CAU. Tells Fortunes too!—nay, I thought he dealt with the Devil—Well, Gentlemen, you are all wide o' this Matter—for to tell you the Truth—he deals with the Devil, Gentlemen—otherwise he could never have redeem'd his Land. [*Aside.*]

BEL. How, Sir, the Devil!

SIR CAU. I say the Devil; Heaven bless every wise Man from the Devil.

BEA. The Devil, sha! there's no such Animal in Nature; I rather think he pads.

NOI. Oh, Sir, he has not Courage for that—but he's an admirable Fellow at your Lock.

SIR CAU. Lock! My Study-Lock was pickt—I begin to suspect him—

BEA. I saw him once open a Lock with the Bone of a Breast of Mutton, and break an Iron Bar asunder with the Eye of a Needle.

SIR CAU. Prodigious!—well, I say the Devil still.

   [*Enter* SIR FEEBLE.]

SIR FEEB. Who's this talks of the Devil?—a Pox of the Devil, I say, this last night's Devil has so haunted me—

SIR CAU. Why, have you seen it since, Brother?

SIR FEEB. In Imagination, Sir.

BEL. How, Sir, a Devil?

SIR FEEB. Ay, or a Ghost.

BEL. Where, good Sir?

BEA. Ay, where? I'd travel a hundred Mile to see a Ghost—

BEL. Sure, Sir, 'twas Fancy.

SIR FEEB. If 'twere a Fancy, 'twas a strong one; and Ghosts and Fancy are all one if they can deceive. I tell you—if ever I thought in my Life—I thought I saw a Ghost—Ay, and a damnable impudent Ghost too; he said he was a—a Fellow here—they call *Bellmour.*

BEL. How, Sir!

BEA. Well, I wou'd give the world to see the Devil, provided he were a civil affable Devil, such as one as *Wasteall's* Acquaintance is—

SIR CAU. He can show him too soon, it may be. I'm sure as civil as he is, he helps him to steal my Gold, I doubt—and to be sure—Gentlemen, you say he's a Gamester—I desire when he comes anon, that you wou'd propose to sport a Dye, or so—and we'll fall to play for a Teaster, or the like—and if he sets any money, I shall go near to know my own Gold, by some remarkable Pieces amongst it; and if he have it, I'll hang him, and then all his six hundred a Year will be my own, which I have in Mortgage.

BEA. Let the Captain and I alone to top upon him—mean time, Sir, I have brought my Musick, to entertain my Mistress with a Song.

SIR FEEB. Take your own methods, Sir—they are at leisure—while we go drink their Healths within. Adod, I long for night, we are not half in kelter, this damn'd Ghost will not out of my Head yet.

    [*Exeunt all but* BELLMOUR.]

BEL. Hah—a Ghost! what can he mean? A Ghost, and *Bellmour's!*

  —Sure my good Angel, or my Genius,

In pity of my Love, and of *Leticia*—

But see *Leticia* comes, but still attended—

    [*Enter* LETICIA, LADY FULBANK, DIANA.]

  —Remember—oh, remember to be true? [*Aside to her, passing by goes out.*]

L. FUL. I was sick to know with what Christian

Patience you bore the Martyrdom of this Night.

LET. As those condemn'd bear the last Hour of Life.

A short Reprieve I had—and by a kind Mistake,

Diana only was my Bedfellow—[*Weeps.*]

DIA. And I wish for your Repose you ne'er had seen my Father. [*Weeps.*]

LET. And so do I, I fear he has undone me—

DIA. And me, in breaking of his word with *Bredwel*—

L. FUL. —So—as *Trincolo* says, wou'd you were both hang'd for me, for putting me in mind of my Husband.

For I have e'en no better luck than either of you—

  —Let our two Fates warn your approaching one:

I love young *Bredwel* and must plead for him.

DIA. I know his Virtue justifies my Choice:

But Pride and Modesty forbids I shou'd unlov'd pursue him.

LET. Wrong not my Brother so, who dies for you —

DIA. Cou'd he so easily see me given away,
    Without a Sigh at parting?
    For all the day a Calm was in his Eyes,
    And unconcern'd he look'd and talk'd to me;
    In dancing never prest my willing Hand,
    Nor with a scornful Glance reproach'd my Falshood.

LET. Believe me, that Dissembling was his Master-piece.

DIA. Why should he fear, did not my Father promise him?

LET. Ay, that was in his wooing time to me:
    But now 'tis all forgotten — [*Musick at the door.*]
        [*After which enter* BEARJEST *and* BREDWEL.]

L. FUL. How now, Cousin! Is this high piece of Gallantry from you?

BEA. Ay, Madam, I have not travel'd for nothing —

L. FUL. I find my Cousin is resolv'd to conquer, he assails with all his
    Artillery of Charms; we'll leave him to his success, Madam. — [*Ex.*
    LETICIA *and* L. FULBANK.]

BEA. Oh Lord, Madam, you oblige me — look *Ned*, you had a mind to
    have a full view of my Mistress, Sir, and — here she is. [*He stands
    gazing.*]
    Go, salute her — look how he stands now; what a sneaking thing is a
    Fellow who has never travel'd and seen the World! — Madam — this is a
    very honest Friend of mine, for all he looks so simply.

DIA. Come, he speaks for you, Sir.

BEA. He, Madam! though he be but a Banker's Prentice, Madam, he's as
    pretty a Fellow of his Inches as any i'th' City — he has made love in
    Dancing-Schools, and to Ladies of Quality in the middle Gallery, and
    shall joke ye — and repartee with any Fore-man within the Walls —
    prithee to her — and commend me, I'll give thee a new Point Crevat.

DIA. He looks as if he cou'd not speak to me.

BEA. Not speak to you! yes, Gad, Madam, and do any thing to you too.

DIA. Are you his Advocate, Sir? [*In scorn.*]

BEA. For want of a better — [*Stands behind him, pushing him on.*]

BRED. An Advocate for Love I am,
    And bring you such a Message from a Heart —

BEA. Meaning mine, dear Madam.

BRED. That when you hear it, you will pity it.

BEA. Or the Devil's in her —

DIA. Sir, I have many Reasons to believe,

It is my Fortune you pursue, not Person.

BEA. There is something in that, I must confess. [*Behind him.*]
But say what you will, *Ned.*

BRED. May all the Mischiefs of despairing Love
Fall on me if it be.

BEA. That's well enough —

BRED. No, were you born an humble Village-Maid,
That fed a Flock upon the neighbouring Plain;
With all that shining Vertue in your Soul,
By Heaven, I wou'd adore you — love you — wed you —
Though the gay World were lost by such a Nuptial. [BEAR. *looks on him.*]
— This — I wou'd do, were I my Friend the Squire. [*Recollecting.*]

BEA. Ay, if you were me — you might do what you pleas'd; but I'm of another mind.

DIA. Shou'd I consent, my Father is a Man whom Interest sways, not Honour; and whatsoever Promises he'as made you, he means to break 'em all, and I am destin'd to another.

BEA. How, another — his Name, his Name, Madam — here's *Ned* and I fear ne'er a single Man i'th' Nation, What is he — what is he? —

DIA. A Fop, a Fool, a beaten Ass — a Blockhead.

BEA. What a damn'd Shame's this, that Women shou'd be sacrificed to Fools, and Fops must run away with Heiresses — whilst we Men of Wit and Parts dress and dance, and cook and travel for nothing but to be tame Keepers.

DIA. But I, by Heaven, will never be that Victim:
But where my Soul is vow'd, 'tis fix'd for ever.

BRED. Are you resolv'd, are you confirm'd in this?
Oh my *Diana*, speak it o'er again. [*Runs to her, and embraces her.*]
Bless me, and make me happier than a Monarch.

BEA. Hold, hold, dear *Ned* — that's my part, I take it.

BRED. Your Pardon, Sir, I had forgot my self.
— But this is short — what's to be done in this?

BEA. Done! I'll enter the House with Fire and Sword, d'ye see, not that I care this — but I'll not be fob'd off — what, do they take me for a Fool — an Ass?

BRED. Madam, dare you run the risk of your Father's Displeasure, and run away with the Man you love?

DIA. With all my Soul —

BEA. That's hearty—and we'll do it—*Ned* and I here—and I love an Amour with an Adventure in't like *Amadis de Gaul*—Harkye, *Ned*, get a Coach and six ready to night when 'tis dark, at the back Gate—

BRED. And I'll get a Parson ready in my Lodging, to which I have a Key through the Garden, by which we may pass unseen.

BEA. Good—Mun, here's Company—

[*Enter* GAYMAN *with his Hat and Money in't,* SIR CAUTIOUS *in a rage,* SIR FEEBLE, LADY FULBANK, LETICIA, CAPTAIN NOISEY, BELLMOUR.]

SIR CAU. A hundred Pound lost already! Oh Coxcomb, old Coxcomb, and a wise Coxcomb—to turn Prodigal at my Years, why, I was bewitcht!

SIR FEEB. Shaw, 'twas a Frolick, Sir, I have lost a hundred Pound as well as you. My Lady has lost, and your Lady has lost, and the rest—what, old Cows will kick sometimes, what's a hundred Pound?

SIR CAU. A hundred Pound! why, 'tis a sum, Sir—a sum—why, what the Devil did I do with a Box and Dice!

L. FUL. Why, you made a shift to lose, Sir? And where's the harm of that? We have lost, and he has won; anon it may be your Fortune.

SIR CAU. Ay, but he could never do it fairly, that's certain. Three hundred Pound! why, who came you to win so unmercifully, Sir?

GAY. Oh, the Devil will not lose a Gamester of me, you see, Sir.

SIR CAU. The Devil!—mark that, Gentlemen—

BEA. The Rogue has damn'd luck sure, he has got a Fly—

SIR CAU. And can you have the Conscience to carry away all our Money, Sir?

GAY. Most assuredly, unless you have the courage to retrieve it. I'll set it at a Throw, or any way: what say you, Gentlemen?

SIR FEEB. Ods bobs, you young Fellows are too hard for us every way, and I'm engag'd at an old Game with a new Gamester here, who will require all an old Man's stock.

L. FUL. Come, Cousin, will you venture a Guinea? Come, Mr. *Bredwel.*

GAY. Well, if no body dare venture on me, I'll send away my Cash—[*They all go to play at the Table, but* SIR CAU. SIR FEEB. *and* GAY.]

SIR CAU. Hum—must it all go?—a rare sum, if a Man were but sure the Devil wou'd but stand Neuter now—[*Aside.*]—Sir, I wish I had any thing but ready Money to stake: three hundred Pound—a fine Sum!

GAY. You have Moveables, Sir, Goods—Commodities—

SIR CAU. That's all one, Sir; that's Money's worth, Sir: but if I had any thing that were worth nothing—

GAY. You wou'd venture it,—I thank you, Sir,—I wou'd your Lady were worth nothing—

SIR CAU. Why, so, Sir?

GAY. Then I wou'd set all this against that Nothing.

SIR CAU. What, set it against my Wife?

GAY. Wife, Sir! ay, your Wife—

SIR CAU. Hum, my Wife against three hundred Pounds! What, all my Wife, Sir?

GAY. All your Wife! Why, Sir, some part of her wou'd serve my turn.

SIR CAU. Hum—my Wife—why, if I shou'd lose, he cou'd not have the Impudence to take her. [*Aside.*]

GAY. Well, I find you are not for the Bargain, and so I put up—

SIR CAU. Hold, Sir—why so hasty—my Wife? no—put up your Money, Sir—what, lose my Wife for three hundred Pounds!—

GAY. Lose her, Sir!—why, she shall be never the worse for my wearing, Sir—the old covetous Rogue is considering on't, I think—What say you to a Night? I'll set it to a Night—there's none need know it, Sir.

SIR CAU. Hum—a Night!—three hundred Pounds for a Night! why, what a lavish Whore-master's this! We take Money to marry our Wives, but very seldom part with 'em, and by the Bargain get Money—For a Night, say you?—Gad, if I shou'd take the Rogue at his word, 'twou'd be a pure Jest. [*Aside.*]

SIR FEEB. You are not mad, Brother.

SIR CAU. No, but I'm wise—and that's as good; let me consider.—

SIR FEEB. What, whether you shall be a Cuckold or not?

SIR CAU. Or lose three hundred Pounds—consider that. A Cuckold!—why, 'tis a word—an empty sound—'tis Breath—'tis Air—'tis nothing:—but three hundred Pounds—Lord, what will not three hundred Pounds do? You may chance to be a Cuckold for nothing, Sir—

SIR FEEB. It may be so—but she shall do't discretly then.

SIR CAU. Under favour, you're an Ass, Brother; this is the discreetest way of doing it, I take it.

SIR FEEB. But wou'd a wise man expose his Wife?

SIR CAU. Why, *Cato* was a wiser Man than I, and he lent his Wife to a young Fellow they call'd *Hortensius*, as Story says; and can a wise Man have a better Precedent than *Cato?*

SIR FEEB. I say, *Cato* was an Ass, Sir, for obliging any young Rogue of 'em all.

SIR CAU. But I am of *Cato's* mind. Well, a single Night you say.

GAY. A single Night—to have—to hold—possess—and so forth, at discretion.

SIR CAU. A Night—I shall have her safe and sound i'th' Morning.

SIR FEEB. Safe, no doubt on't—but how sound. —

GAY. And for Non-performance, you shall pay me three hundred Pounds, I'll forfeit as much if I tell—

SIR CAU. Tell?—why, make your three hundred pounds six hundred, and let it be put into the *Gazet*, if you will, Man.—But it's a Bargain?

GAY. Done—*Sir Feeble* shall be witness—and there stands my Hat.
    [*Puts down his Hat of Money, and each of 'em take a Box and Dice, and kneel on the Stage, the rest come about 'em.*]

SIR CAU. He that comes first to One and thirty wins— [*They throw and count.*]

L. FUL. What are you playing for?

SIR FEEB. Nothing, nothing—but a Trial of Skill between an old Man and a Young—and your Ladyship is to be Judge.

L. FUL. I shall be partial, Sir.

SIR CAU. Six and five's Eleven— [*Throws, and pulls the Hat towards him.*]

GAY. Cater Tray—Pox of the Dice—

SIR CAU. Two fives—one and twenty— [*Sets up, pulls the Hat nearer.*]

GAY. Now, Luck—Doublets of sixes—nineteen.

SIR CAU. Five and four—thirty— [*Draws the Hat to him.*]

SIR FEEB. Now if he wins it, I'll swear he has a Fly indeed—'tis impossible without Doublets of sixes—

GAY. Now Fortune smile—and for the future frown. [*Throws.*]

SIR CAU. —Hum—two sixes— [*Rises and looks dolefully round.*]

L. FUL. How now? what's the matter you look so like an Ass, what have you lost?

SIR CAU. A Bauble—a Bauble—'tis not for what I've lost—but because I have not won—

SIR FEEB. You look very simple, Sir—what think you of *Cato* now?

SIR CAU. A wise Man may have his failings—

L. FUL. What has my Husband lost?—

SIR CAU. Only a small parcel of Ware that lay dead upon my hands, Sweetheart.

GAY. But I shall improve 'em, Madam, I'll warrant you.

L. FUL. Well, since 'tis no worse, bring in your fine Dancer, Cousin, you say you brought to entertain your Mistress with. [BEARJEST *goes out.*]

GAY. Sir, you'll take care to see me paid to Night?

SIR CAU. Well, Sir—but my Lady, you must know, Sir, has the common frailties of her Sex, and will refuse what she even longs for, if persuaded to't by me.

GAY. 'Tis not in my Bargain to sollicit her, Sir, you are to procure her—or three hundred pounds, Sir; chuse you whether.

SIR CAU. Procure her! with all my soul, Sir; alas, you mistake my honest meaning, I scorn to be so unjust as not to see you a-bed together; and then agree as well as you can, I have done my part—In order to this, Sir—get but your self conveyed in a Chest to my house, with a Direction upon't for me; and for the rest—

GAY. I understand you.

SIR FEEB. *Ralph*, get supper ready.

[*Enter* BEA. *with Dancers; all go out but* SIR CAUTIOUS.]

SIR CAU. Well, I must break my Mind, if possible, to my Lady—but if she shou'd be refractory now—and make me pay Three hundred Pounds—why, sure she won't have so little Grace—Three hundred Pounds sav'd, is three hundred pounds got—by our account—Cou'd All—

Who of this City-Privilege are free,
Hope to be paid for Cuckoldom like me;
Th' unthriving Merchant, whom gray Hair adorns,
Before all Ventures wou'd ensure his Horns;
For thus, while he but lets spare Rooms to hire,
His Wife's crack'd Credit keeps his own entire. [*Exit.*]

Act V.

SCENE I. SIR CAUTIOUS *his House.*

[*Enter* BELLMOUR *alone, sad.*]

BEL. The Night is come, oh my *Leticia!*
The longing Bridegroom hastens to his Bed;
Whilst she with all the languishment of Love,
And sad Despair, casts her fair Eyes on me,
Which silently implore, I would deliver her.
But how! ay, there's the Question—hah—[*Pausing.*]
I'll get my self hid in her Bed-chamber—
And something I will do—may serve us yet—
If all my Arts should fail—I'll have recourse [*Draws a dagger.*]
To this—and bear *Leticia* off by force.
—But see she comes—

[*Enter* LADY FULBANK, SIR CAUTIOUS, SIR FEEBLE, LETICIA, BEARJEST,
NOISEY, GAYMAN. *Exit* BELLMOUR.]

SIR FEEB. Lights there, *Ralph*.

And my Lady's Coach there—[BEARJEST *goes to* GAYMAN.]

BEA. Well, Sir, remember you have promised to grant me my diabolical
Request, in shewing me the Devil—

GAY. I will not fail you, Sir.

L. FUL. Madam, your Servant; I hope you'll see no more Ghosts, *Sir
Feeble*.

SIR FEEB. No more of that, I beseech you, Madam: Prithee, *Sir Cautious*,
take away your Wife—Madam, your Servant—[*All go out after the
Light.*]

—Come, *Lette, Lette*; hasten, Rogue, hasten to thy Chamber; away,
here be the young Wenches coming— [*Puts her out, he goes out.*]

[*Enter* DIANA, *puts on her Hood and Scarf.*]

DIA. So—they are gone to Bed; and now for *Bredwel*—the Coach waits,
and I'll take this opportunity.

Father, farewell—if you dislike my course,

Blame the old rigid Customs of your Force. [*Goes out.*]

SCENE II. *A Bed-chamber.*

[*Enter* SIR FEEBLE, LETICIA, *and* PHILLIS.]

LET. Ah, *Phillis!* I am fainting with my Fears,

Hast thou no comfort for me? [*He undresses to his Gown.*]

SIR FEEB. Why, what art doing there—fiddle fading—adod, you young
Wenches are so loth to come to—but when your hands in, you have no
mercy upon us poor Husbands.

LET. Why do you talk so, Sir?

SIR FEEB. Was it anger'd at the Fool's Prattle? tum a-me, tum a-me, I'll
undress it, effags, I will—Roguy.

LET. You are so wanton, Sir, you make me blush—

I will not go to bed, unless you'll promise me—

SIR FEEB. No bargaining, my little Hussey—what, you'll tie my hands
behind me, will you? [*She goes to the Table.*]

LET. —What shall I do?—assist me, gentle Maid,

Thy Eyes methinks put on a little hope.

PHIL. Take Courage, Madam—you guess right—be confident.

SIR FEEB. No whispering, Gentlewoman—and putting Tricks into her
head; that shall not cheat me of another Night—Look on that silly
little round Chitty-face—look on those smiling roguish loving Eyes

there—look—look how they laugh, twire, and tempt—he, Rogue—I'll buss 'em there, and here, and every where—ods bods—away, this is fooling and spoiling of a Man's Stomach, with a bit here, and a bit there—to Bed—to Bed—

[*As she is at the Toilet, he looks over her shoulder, and sees her Face in the Glass.*]

LET. Go you first, Sir, I will but stay to say my Prayers, which are that Heaven wou'd deliver me. [*Aside.*]

SIR FEEB. Say thy Prayers!—What, art thou mad! Prayers upon thy Wedding-night! a short Thanksgiving or so—but Prayers quoth a—'Sbobs, you'll have time enough for that, I doubt—

LE. I am asham'd to undress before you, Sir; go to Bed—

SIR FEEB. What, was it asham'd to shew its little white Foots, and its little round Bubbies—well, I'll go, I'll go—I cannot think on't, no I cannot—

[*Going towards the Bed,* BELLMOUR *comes forth from between the Curtains, his Coat off, his Shirt bloody, a Dagger in his hand, and his Disguise off.*]

BEL. Stand—

SIR FEEB. Ah—

LET. and PHIL. [*squeak*]—Oh, Heavens!—why, is it *Bellmour?* [*Aside to* PHIL.]

BEL. Go not to Bed, I guard this sacred Place,
And the Adulterer dies that enters here.

SIR FEEB. Oh—why do I shake?—sure I'm a Man, what art thou?

BEL. I am the wrong'd, the lost and murder'd *Bellmour.*

SIR FEEB. O Lord! it is the same I saw last night—Oh!—hold thy dread Vengeance—pity me, and hear me—Oh! a Parson—a Parson—what shall I do—Oh! where shall I hide my self?

BEL. I'th' utmost Borders of the Earth I'll find thee—
Seas shall not hide thee, nor vast Mountains guard thee:
Even in the depth of Hell I'll find thee out,
And lash thy filthy and adulterous Soul.

SIR FEEB. Oh! I am dead, I'm dead; will no Repentence save me? 'twas that young Eye that tempted me to sin; Oh!—

BEL. See, fair Seducer, what thou'st made me do;
Look on this bleeding Wound, it reach'd my Heart,
To pluck my dear tormenting Image thence,
When News arriv'd that thou hadst broke thy Vow.

SIR FEEB. Oh Lord! oh! I'm glad he's dead though.

LET. Oh, hide that fatal Wound, my tender Heart faints with a Sight so horrid! [*Seems to Weep.*]

SIR FEEB. So, she'll clear her self, and leave me in the Devil's Clutches.

BEL. You've both offended Heaven, and must repent or die.

SIR FEEB. Ah, — I do confess I was an old Fool, — bewitcht with Beauty, besotted with Love, and do repent most heartily.

BEL. No, you had rather yet go on in Sin:
Thou wou'dst live on, and be a baffled Cuckold.

SIR FEEB. Oh, not for the World, Sir! I am convinc'd and mortifi'd.

BEL. Maintain her fine, undo thy Peace to please her, and still be Cuckol'd on, — believe her, — trust her, and be Cuckol'd still.

SIR FEEB. I see my Folly — and my Age's Dotage — and find the Devil was in me — yet spare my Age — ah! spare me to repent.

BEL. If thou repent'st, renounce her, fly her sight; —
Shun her bewitching Charms, as thou wou'dst Hell,
Those dark eternal Mansions of the dead —
Whither I must descend.

SIR FEEB. Oh — wou'd he were gone! —

BEL. Fly — be gone — depart, vanish for ever from her to some more safe and innocent Apartment.

SIR FEEB. Oh, that's very hard! —

[*He goes back trembling,* BELLMOUR *follows in with his Dagger up; both go out.*]

LET. Blest be this kind Release, and yet methinks it grieves me to consider how the poor old Man is frighted. [BELLMOUR re-enters, puts on his Coat.]

BEL. — He's gone, and lock'd himself into his Chamber —
And now, my dear *Leticia,* let us fly —
Despair till now did my wild Heart invade,
But pitying Love has the rough Storm allay'd. [*Exeunt.*]

SCENE III. SIR CAUTIOUS *his Garden.*

[*Enter two* PORTERS *and* RAG, *bearing* GAYMAN *in a Chest; set it down, he comes forth with a Dark-lanthorn.*]

GAY. Set down the Chest behind yon hedge of Roses — and then put on those Shapes I have appointed you — and be sure you well-favour'dly bang both *Bearjest* and *Noisey,* since they have a mind to see the Devil.

RAG. Oh, Sir, leave 'em to us for that; and if we dò not play the Devil with 'em, we deserve they shou'd beat us. But, Sir, we are in *Sir Cautious* his Garden, will he not sue us for a Trespass?

GAY. I'll bear you out; be ready at my Call. [*Exeunt.*]

—Let me see—I have got no ready stuff to banter with—but no matter, any Gibberish will serve the Fools—'tis now about the hour of Ten—but Twelve is my appointed lucky Minute, when all the Blessings that my Soul could wish, shall be resign'd to me.

[*Enter* BREDWEL.]

—Hah! who's there? *Bredwel?*

BRED. Oh, are you come, Sir—and can you be so kind to a poor Youth, to favour his Designs, and bless his Days?

GAY. Yes, I am ready here with all my Devils, both to secure you your Mistress, and to cudgel your Captain and Squire, for abusing me behind my Back so basely.

BRED. 'Twas most unmanly, Sir, and they deserve it—I wonder that they come not.

GAY. How durst you trust her with him?

BRED. Because 'tis dangerous to steal a City-Heiress, and let the Theft be his—so the dear Maid be mine—Hark—sure they come—

[*Enter* BEARJEST *runs against* BREDWEL.]

—Who's there? Mr. *Bearjest?*

BEA. Who's that? *Ned?* Well, I have brought my Mistress, hast thou got a Parson ready, and a License?

BRED. Ay, ay, but where's the Lady?

BEA. In the Coach, with the Captain at the Gate. I came before, to see if the Coast be clear.

BRED. Ay, Sir; but what shall we do? here's Mr. *Gayman* come on purpose to shew you the Devil, as you desir'd.

BEA. Sho! a Pox of the Devil, Man—I can't attend to speak with him now.

GAY. How, Sir! D'ye think my Devil of so little Quality, to suffer an Affront unrevenged?

BEA. Sir, I cry his Devilship's Pardon: I did not know his Quality. I protest, Sir, I love and honour him, but I am now just going to be married, Sir; and when that Ceremony's past, I'm ready to go to the Devil as soon as you please.

GAY. I have told him your Desire of seeing him, and shou'd you baffle him?

BEA. Who, I, Sir! Pray, let his Worship know, I shall be proud of the

Honour of his Acquaintance; but, Sir, my Mistress and the Parson wait
in *Ned's* Chamber.

GAY. If all the World wait, Sir, the Prince of Hell will stay for no Man.

BRED. Oh, Sir, rather than the Prince of the Infernals shall be affronted,
I'll conduct the Lady up, and entertain her till you come, Sir.

BEA. Nay, I have a great mind to kiss his—Paw, Sir; but I cou'd wish you'd
shew him me by day-light, Sir.

GAY. The Prince of Darkness does abhor the Light. But, Sir, I will for once
allow your Friend the Captain to keep you company.

[*Enter* NOISEY *and* DIANA.]

BEA. I'm much oblig'd to you, Sir; oh, Captain— [*Talks to him.*]

BRED. Haste, Dear; the Parson waits,
To finish what the Powers design'd above.

DIA. Sure nothing is so bold as Maids in Love! [*They go out.*]

NOI. Psho! he conjure—he can flie as soon.

GAY. Gentlemen, you must be sure to confine your selves to this Circle,
and have a care you neither swear, nor pray.

BEA. Pray, Sir! I dare say neither of us were ever that way gifted.

[*A horrid Noise.*]

GAY. Cease your Horror, cease your Haste.
And calmly as I saw you last,
Appear! Appear!
By thy Pearls and Diamond Rocks,
By thy heavy Money-Box,
By thy shining Petticoat,
That hid thy cloven Feet from Note;
By the Veil that hid thy Face,
Which else had frighten'd humane Race: [*Soft Musick ceases.*]
Appear, that I thy Love may see,
Appear, kind Fiends, appear to me.
A Pox of these Rascals, why come they not?

[*Four enter from the four corners of the Stage, to Musick that
plays; they dance, and in the Dance, dance round 'em, and
kick, pinch, and beat 'em.*]

BEA. Oh, enough, enough! Good Sir, lay 'em, and I'll pay the Musick—

GAY. I wonder at it—these Spirits are in their Nature kind, and
peaceable—but you have basely injur'd some body—confess, and they
will be satisfied—

BEA. Oh, good Sir, take your *Cerberuses* off—I do confess, the Captain here, and I have violated your Fame.

NOI. Abus'd you, — and traduc'd you, — and thus we beg your pardon —

GAY. Abus'd me! 'Tis more than I know, Gentlemen.

BEA. But it seems your Friend the Devil does.

GAY. By this time *Bredwel's* married.

— Great *Pantamogan*, hold, for I am satisfied, [*Ex. Devils.*]
And thus undo my Charm — [*Takes away the Circle, they run out.*]
So, the Fools are going, and now to *Julia's* Arms. [*Going.*]

SCENE IV. LADY FULBANK'S *Anti-chamber.*

[*She discover'd undrest at her Glass;* SIR CAUTIOUS *undrest.*]

L. FUL. But why to Night? indeed you're wondrous kind methinks.

SIR CAU. Why, I don't know — a Wedding is a sort of an Alarm to Love; it calls up every Man's courage.

L. FUL. Ay, but will it come when 'tis call'd?

SIR CAU. I doubt you'll find it to my Grief — [*Aside.*]
— But I think 'tis all one to thee, thou car'st not for my Complement; no, thou'dst rather have a young Fellow.

L. FUL. I am not us'd to flatter much; if forty Years were taken from your Age, 'twou'd render you something more agreeable to my Bed, I must confess.

SIR CAU. Ay, ay, no doubt on't.

L. FUL. Yet you may take my word without an Oath,
Were you as old as Time, and I were young and gay
As *April* Flowers, which all are fond to gather;
My Beauties all should wither in the Shade,
E'er I'd be worn in a dishonest Bosom.

SIR CAU. Ay, but you're wondrous free methinks, sometimes, which gives shreud suspicions.

L. FUL. What, because I cannot simper, look demure,
and justify my Honour, when none questions it?
— Cry fie, and out upon the naughty Women,
Because they please themselves — and so wou'd I.

SIR CAU. How, wou'd, what cuckold me?

L. FUL. Yes, if it pleas'd me better than Vertue, Sir.
But I'll not change my Freedom and my Humour,
To purchase the dull Fame of being honest.

SIR CAU. Ay, but the World, the World —

L. FUL. I value not the Censures of the Croud.

SIR CAU. But I am old.

L. FUL. That's your fault, Sir, not mine.

SIR CAU. But being so, if I shou'd be good-natur'd, and give thee leave to love discreetly —

L. FUL. I'd do't without your leave, Sir.

SIR CAU. Do't — what, cuckold me?

L. FUL. No, love discreetly, Sir, love as I ought, love honestly.

SIR CAU. What, in love with any body, but your own Husband?

L. FUL. Yes.

SIR CAU. Yes, quoth a — is that your loving as you ought?

L. FUL. We cannot help our Inclinations, Sir,
No more than Time, or Light from coming on —
But I can keep my Virtue, Sir, intire.

SIR CAU. What, I'll warrant, this is your first Love, *Gayman?*

L. FUL. I'll not deny that Truth, though even to you.

SIR CAU. Why, in consideration of my Age, and your Youth, I'd bear a Conscience — provided you do things wisely.

L. FUL. Do what thing, Sir?

SIR CAU. You know what I mean —

L. FUL. Hah — I hope you wou'd not be a Cuckold, Sir.

SIR CAU. Why — truly in a civil way — or so.

L. FUL. There is but one way, Sir, to make me hate you;
And that wou'd be tame suffering.

SIR CAU. Nay, and she be thereabouts, there's no discovering.

L. FUL. But leave this fond discourse, and, if you must,
Let us to Bed.

SIR CAU. Ay, ay, I did but try your Virtue, mun — dost think I was in earnest?

[*Enter* SERVANT.]

SERV. Sir, here's a Chest directed to your Worship.

SIR CAU. Hum, 'tis *Wasteall* — now does my heart fail me — A Chest say you — to me — so late; — I'll warrant it comes from Sir *Nicholas Smuggle* — some prohibited Goods that he has stoln the Custom of, and cheated his Majesty — Well, he's an honest Man, bring it in — [*Exit* SERVANT.]

L. FUL. What, into my Apartment, Sir, a nasty Chest!

SIR CAU. By all means — for if the Searchers come, they'll never be so uncivil to ransack thy Lodgings; and we are bound in Christian Charity to do for one another — Some rich Commodities, I am sure — and some fine Knick-knack will fall to thy share, I'll warrant thee — Pox on him for a young Rogue, how punctual he is! [*Aside.*]

[*Enter with the Chest.*]

—Go, my Dear, go to Bed—I'll send Sir *Nicholas* a Receit for the Chest, and be with thee presently—[*Ex. severally.* GAYMAN *peeps out of the Chest, and looks round him wondring.*]

GAY. Hah, where am I? By Heaven, my last Night's Vision—'Tis that inchanted Room, and yonder's the Alcove! Sure 'twas indeed some Witch, who knowing of my Infidelity—has by Inchantment brought me hither—'tis so—I am betray'd—[*Pauses.*]

Hah! or was it *Julia*, that last night gave me that lone Opportunity?—but hark, I hear some coming— [*Shuts himself in.*]

[*Enter* SIR CAUTIOUS.]

SIR CAU. [*Lifting up the Chest-lid.*] So, you are come, I see—[*Goes, and locks the door.*]

GAY. Hah—he here! nay then, I was deceiv'd, and it was *Julia* that last night gave me the dear Assignation. [*Aside.*] [SIR CAUTIOUS *peeps into the Bed-chamber.*]

L. FUL. [*Within.*] Come, Sir *Cautious*, I shall fall asleep, and then you'll waken me.

SIR CAU. Ay, my Dear, I'm coming—she's in Bed—I'll go put out the Candle, and then—

GAY. Ay, I'll warrant you for my part—

SIR CAU. Ay, but you may over-act your part, and spoil all—But, Sir, I hope you'll use a Christian Conscience in this business.

GAY. Oh, doubt not, Sir, but I shall do you Reason.

SIR CAU. Ay, Sir, but—

GAY. Good Sir, no more Cautions; you, unlike a fair Gamester, will rook me out of half my Night—I am impatient—

SIR CAU. Good Lord, are you so hasty? if I please, you shan't go at all.

GAY. With all my soul, Sir; pay me three hundred Pound, Sir—

SIR CAU. Lord, Sir, you mistake my candid meaning still. I am content to be a Cuckold, Sir—but I wou'd have things done decently, d'ye mind me?

GAY. As decently as a Cuckold can be made, Sir.

—But no more disputes, I pray, Sir.

SIR CAU. I'm gone—I'm gone—but harkye, Sir, you'll rise before day? [*Going out, returns.*]

GAY. Yet again—

SIR CAU. I vanish, Sir—but harkye—you'll not speak a word, but let her think 'tis I?

GAY. Be gone, I say, Sir—[*He runs out.*]

I am convinc'd last night I was with *Julia*.

Oh Sot, insensible and dull!

[*Enter softly* SIR CAUTIOUS.]

SIR CAU. So, the Candle's out—give me your hand. [*Leads him softly in.*]

SCENE V. *Changes to a Bed-chamber.*

[LADY FULBANK *suppos'd in Bed. Enter* SIR CAUTIOUS *and* GAYMAN *by dark.*]

SIR CAU. Where are you, my Dear? [*Leads him to the bed.*]

L. FUL. Where shou'd I be—in Bed; what, are you by dark?

SIR CAU. Ay, the Candle went out by Chance.

[GAYMAN *signs to him to be gone; he makes grimaces as loath to go, and Exit.*]

SCENE VI. *Draws over, and represents another Room in the same House.*]

[*Enter* PARSON, DIANA, *and* PERT *drest in* DIANA'S *Clothes.*]

DIA. I'll swear, Mrs. *Pert*, you look very prettily in my Clothes; and since you, Sir, have convinc'd me that this innocent Deceit is not unlawful, I am glad to be the Instrument of advancing Mrs. *Pert* to a Husband, she already has so just a Claim to.

PAR. Since she has so firm a Contract, I pronounce it a lawful Marriage—but hark, they are coming sure—

DIA. Pull your Hoods down, and keep your Face from the Light. [DIANA *runs out.*]

[*Enter* BEARJEST *and* NOISEY *disorder'd.*]

BEA. Madam, I beg your Pardon—I met with a most devilish Adventure;—your Pardon too, Mr. Doctor, for making you wait.—But the business is this, Sir—I have a great mind to lie with this young Gentlewoman to Night, but she swears if I do, the Parson of the Parish shall know it.

PAR. If I do, Sir, I shall keep Counsel.

BEA. And that's civil, Sir—Come, lead the way,

With such a Guide, the Devil's in't if we can go astray. [*Exeunt.*]

SCENE VII. *Changes to the Anti-chamber.*

[*Enter* SIR CAUTIOUS.]

SIR CAU. Now cannot I sleep, but am as restless as a Merchant in stormy

Weather, that has ventur'd all his Wealth in one Bottom. — Woman is a leaky Vessel. — if she should like the young Rogue now, and they should come to a right understanding — why, then I am a — Wittal — that's all, and shall be put in Print at *Snow-hill*, with my Effigies o'th' top, like the sign of Cuckolds Haven. — Hum — they're damnable silent — pray Heaven he have not murdered her, and robbed her — hum — hark, what's that? — a noise! — he has broke his Covenant with me, and shall forfeit the Money — How loud they are? Ay, ay, the Plot's discovered, what shall I do? — Why, the Devil is not in her sure, to be refractory now, and peevish; if she be, I must pay my Money yet — and that would be a damn'd thing. — sure they're coming out — I'll retire and hearken how 'tis with them. [*Retires.*]

[*Enter* LADY FULBANK *undrest*, GAYMAN, *half undrest upon his Knees, following her, holding her Gown.*]

L. FUL. Oh! You unkind — what have you made me do? Unhand me, false Deceiver — let me loose —

SIR CAU. Made her do? — so, so — 'tis done — I'm glad of that — [*Aside peeping.*]

GAY. Can you be angry, *Julia?*
Because I only seiz'd my Right of Love.

L. FUL. And must my Honour be the Price of it?
Could nothing but my Fame reward your Passion?
— What, make me a base Prostitute, a foul Adulteress?
Oh — be gone, be gone — dear Robber of my Quiet. [*Weeping.*]

SIR CAU. Oh, fearful! —

GAY. Oh! Calm your rage, and hear me; if you are so,
You are an innocent Adulteress.
It was the feeble Husband you enjoy'd
In cold imagination, and no more;
Shily you turn'd away — faintly resign'd.

SIR CAU. Hum, did she so? —

GAY. Till my Excess of Love betray'd the Cheat.

SIR CAU. Ay, ay, that was my Fear.

L. FUL. Away, be gone — I'll never see you more —

GAY. You may as well forbid the Sun to shine.
Not see you more! — Heavens! I before ador'd you,
But now I rave! And with my impatient Love,
A thousand mad and wild Desires are burning!
I have discover'd now new Worlds of Charms,

And can no longer tamely love and suffer.

SIR CAU. So—I have brought an old House upon my Head,
Intail'd Cuckoldom upon my self.

L. FUL. I'll hear no more—Sir *Cautious*,—where's my Husband?
Why have you left my Honour thus unguarded?

SIR CAU. Ay, ay, she's well enough pleas'd, I fear, for all.

GAY. Base as he is, 'twas he expos'd this Treasure;
Like silly *Indians* barter'd thee for Trifles.

SIR CAU. O treacherous Villain!—

L. FUL. Hah—my Husband do this?

GAY. He, by Love, he was the kind Procurer,
Contriv'd the means, and brought me to thy Bed.

L. FUL. My Husband! My wise Husband!
What fondness in my Conduct had he seen,
To take so shameful and so base Revenge?

GAY. None—'twas filthy Avarice seduc'd him to't.

L. FUL. If he cou'd be so barbarous to expose me,
Cou'd you who lov'd me—be so cruel too?

GAY. What—to possess thee when the Bliss was offer'd?
Possess thee too without a Crime to thee?
Charge not my Soul with so remiss a flame,
So dull a sense of Virtue to refuse it.

L. FUL. I am convinc'd the fault was all my Husband's—
And here I vow—by all things just and sacred,
To separate for ever from his Bed. [*Kneels.*]

SIR CAU. Oh, I am not able to indure it—
Hold—oh, hold, my Dear—[*He kneels as she rises.*]

L. FUL. Stand off—I do abhor thee—

SIR CAU. With all my Soul—but do not make rash Vows.
They break my very Heart—regard my Reputation.

L. FUL. Which you have had such care of, Sir, already—
Rise, 'tis in vain you kneel.

SIR CAU. No—I'll never rise again—Alas! Madam, I was merely drawn in; I
only thought to sport a Dye or so: I had only an innocent design to
have discover'd whether this Gentleman had stoln my Gold, that so I
might have hang'd him—

GAY. A very innocent Design indeed!

SIR CAU. Ay, Sir, that's all, as I'm an honest man.—

L. FUL. I've sworn, nor are the Stars more fix'd than I.

[*Enter* SERVANT.]

SERV. How! my Lady and his Worship up?

—Madam, a Gentleman and a Lady below in a Coach knockt me up, and say they must speak with your Ladyship.

L. FUL. This is strange!—bring them up—

[*Exit* SERVANT.]

Who can it be, at this odd time of neither Night nor Day?

[*Enter* LETICIA, BELLMOUR, *and* PHILLIS.]

LET. Madam, your Virtue, Charity and Friendship to me, has made me trespass on you for my Life's security, and beg you will protect me, and my Husband— [*Points at* BELLMOUR.]

SIR CAU. So, here's another sad Catastrophe!

L. FUL. Hah—does *Bellmour* live? is't possible?

Believe me, Sir, you ever had my Wishes;

And shall not fail of my Protection now.

BEL. I humbly thank your Ladyship.

GAY. I'm glad thou hast her, *Harry*; but doubt thou durst not own her; nay dar'st not own thy self.

BEL. Yes, Friend, I have my Pardon—

But hark, I think we are pursu'd already—

But now I fear no force. [*A noise of some body coming in.*]

L. FUL. However, step into my Bed-chamber.

[*Exeunt* LETICIA, GAYMAN *and* PHILLIS.]

[*Enter* SIR FEEBLE *in an Antick manner.*]

SIR FEEB. Hell shall not hold thee—nor vast Mountains cover thee, but I will find thee out—and lash thy filthy and Adulterous Carcase. [*Coming up in a menacing manner to* SIR CAU.]

SIR CAU. How—lash my filthy Carcase?—I defy thee, Satan—

SIR FEEB. 'Twas thus he said.

SIR CAU. Let who's will say it, he lies in's Throat.

SIR FEEB. How, the Ghostly—hush—have a care—for 'twas the Ghost of *Bellmour*—Oh! hide that bleeding Wound, it chills my Soul!—[*Runs to the* LADY FULBANK.]

L. FUL. What bleeding Wound?—Heaven, are you frantick, Sir?

SIR FEEB. No—but for want of rest, I shall e'er Morning. [*Weeps.*]

—She's gone—she's gone—she's gone—

SIR CAU. Ay, ay, she's gone, she's gone indeed. [SIR CAU. *weeps.*]

SIR FEEB. But let her go, so I may never see that dreadful Vision—harkye, Sir—a word in your Ear—have a care of marrying a young Wife.

SIR CAU. Ay, but I have married one already. [*Weeping.*]

SIR FEEB. Hast thou? Divorce her—flie her, quick—depart—be gone, she'll cuckold thee—and still she'll cuckold thee.

SIR CAU. Ay, Brother, but whose fault was that?—Why, are not you married?

SIR FEEB. Mum—no words on't, unless you'll have the Ghost about your Ears; part with your Wife, I say, or else the Devil will part ye.

L. FUL. Pray go to Bed, Sir.

SIR FEEB. Yes, for I shall sleep now, I shall lie alone; [*Weeps.*] Ah, Fool, old dull besotted Fool—to think she'd love me—'twas by base means I gain'd her—cozen'd an honest Gentleman of Fame and Life—

L. FUL. You did so, Sir but 'tis not past Redress—you may make that honest Gentleman amends.

SIR FEEB. Oh, wou'd I could, so I gave half my Estate—

L. FUL. That Penitence atones with him and Heaven.—Come forth, *Leticia*, and your injur'd Ghost.

          [*Enter* LETICIA, BELLMOUR, *and* PHILLIS.]

SIR FEEB. Hah, Ghost—another Sight would make me mad indeed.

BEL. Behold me, Sir, I have no Terror now.

SIR FEEB. Hah—who's that, *Francis!*—my Nephew *Francis*

BEL. *Bellmour*, or *Francis*, chuse you which you like, and I am either.

SIR FEEB. Hah, *Bellmour!* and no Ghost?

BEL. *Bellmour*—and not your Nephew, Sir.

SIR FEEB. But art alive? Ods bobs, I'm glad on't, Sirrah;—But are you real, *Bellmour?*

BEL. As sure as I'm no Ghost.

GAY. We all can witness for him, Sir.

SIR FEEB. Where be the Minstrels, we'll have a Dance—adod, we will—Ah—art thou there, thou cozening little Chits-face?—a Vengeance on thee—thou madest me an old doting loving Coxcomb—but I forgive thee—and give thee all thy Jewels, and you your Pardon, Sir, so you'll give me mine; for I find you young Knaves will be too hard for us.

BEL. You are so generous, Sir, that 'tis almost with grief I receive the Blessing of *Leticia*.

SIR FEEB. No, no, thou deservest her; she would have made an old fond Blockhead of me, and one way or other you wou'd have had her—ods bobs, you wou'd—

[*Enter* BEARJEST, DIANA, PERT, BREDWEL, *and* NOISEY.]

BEA. Justice, Sir, Justice — I have been cheated — abused — assassinated and ravisht!

SIR CAU. How, my Nephew ravisht! —

PERT. No, Sir, I am his Wife.

SIR CAU. Hum — my Heir marry a Chamber-maid!

BEA. Sir, you must know I stole away Mrs. *Dy*, and brought her to *Ned's* Chamber here — to marry her.

SIR FEEB. My Daughter *Dy* stoln —

BEA. But I being to go to the Devil a little, Sir, whip — what does he, but marries her himself, Sir; and fob'd me off here with my Lady's cast Petticoat —

NOI. Sir, she's a Gentlewoman, and my Sister, Sir.

PERT. Madam, 'twas a pious Fraud, if it were one; for I was contracted to him before — see, here it is — [*Gives it 'em.*]

ALL. A plain Case, a plain Case.

SIR FEEB. Harkye, Sir, have you had the Impudence to marry my Daughter Sir? [*To* BREDWEL, *who with* DIANA *kneels.*]

BRED. Yes, Sir, and humbly ask your Pardon, and your Blessing —

SIR FEEB. You will ha't, whether I will or not — rise, you are still too hard for us: Come, Sir, forgive your Nephew —

SIR CAU. Well, Sir, I will — but all this while you little think the Tribulation I am in, my Lady has forsworn my Bed.

SIR FEEB. Indeed, Sir, the wiser she.

SIR CAU. For only performing my Promise to this Gentleman.

SIR FEEB. Ay, you showed her the Difference, Sir; you're a wise man. Come, dry your Eyes — and rest your self contented, we are a couple of old Coxcombs; d'ye hear, Sir, Coxcombs.

SIR CAU. I grant it, Sir; and if I die, Sir, I bequeath my Lady to you — with my whole Estate — my Nephew has too much already for a Fool [*To* GAYMAN.]

GAY. I thank you, Sir — do you consent, my *Julia?*

L. FUL. No, Sir — you do not like me — a canvas Bag of wooden Ladles were a better Bed-fellow.

GAY. Cruel Tormenter! Oh, I could kill myself with shame and anger!

L. FUL. Come hither, *Bredwel* — witness for my Honour — that I had no design upon his Person, but that of trying his Constancy.

BRED. Believe me, Sir, 'tis true — I feigned a danger near — just as you got to bed — and I was the kind Devil, Sir, that brought the Gold to you.

BEA. And you were one of the Devils that beat me, and the Captain here, Sir?

GAY. No truly, Sir, those were some I hired — to beat you for abusing me to day.

NOI. To make you 'mends, Sir, I bring you the certain News of the death of Sir *Thomas Gayman*, your Uncle, who has left you Two thousand pounds a year —

GAY. I thank you, Sir — I heard the news before.

SIR CAU. How's this; Mr. *Gayman*, my Lady's first Lover? I find, Sir *Feeble*, we were a couple of old Fools indeed, to think at our Age to cozen two lusty young Fellows of their Mistresses; 'tis no wonder that both the Men and the Women have been too hard for us; we are not fit Matches for either, that's the truth on't.

> The Warrior needs must to his Rival yield,
> Who comes with blunted Weapons to the Field.

Epilogue

Long have we turn'd the point of our just Rage
On the half Wits, and Criticks of the Age.
Oft has the soft, insipid Sonneteer
In *Nice* and *Flutter*, seen his Fop-face here.
Well was the ignorant lampooning Pack   5
Of shatterhead Rhymers whip'd on *Craffey's* back;
But such a trouble Weed is Poetaster,
The lower 'tis cut down, it grows the faster.
Though Satir then had such a plenteous crop,
An After Math of Coxcombs is come up;   10
Who not content false Poetry to renew,
By sottish Censures wou'd condemn the true.
Let writing like a Gentleman — fine appear,
But must you needs judge too en *Cavalier*?
These whiffling Criticks, 'tis our Auth'ress fears,   15
And humbly begs a Trial by her Peers:
Or let a Pole of Fools her fate pronounce,
There's no great harm in a good quiet Dunce.
But shield her, Heaven! from the left-handed blow
Of airy Blockheads who pretend to know.   20

On downright Dulness let her rather split,
Than be Fop-mangled under colour of Wit.
    Hear me, ye Scribling Beaus,—
Why will you in sheer Rhyme, without one stroke ⎞
Of Poetry, Ladies just Disdain provoke,   ⎬   25
And address Songs to whom you never spoke? ⎠
In doleful Hymns for dying Felons fit,
Why do you tax their Eyes, and blame their Wit?
Unjustly of the Innocent you complain,
'Tis Bulkers give, and Tubs must cure your pain.   30
Why in Lampoons will you your selves revile?
'Tis true, none else will think it worth their while:
But thus you're hid! oh, 'tis a politick Fetch;
So some have hang'd themselves to ease *Jack Ketch*.
Justly your Friends and Mistresses you blame, ⎞   35
For being so they well deserve the shame,   ⎬
'Tis the worst scandal to have borne that name. ⎠
    At Poetry of late, and such whose Skill ⎞
Excels your own, you dart a feeble Quill;   ⎬
Well may you rail at what you ape so ill. ⎠   40
With virtuous Women, and all Men of Worth,
You're in a state of mortal War by Birth.
Nature in all her Atom-Fights ne'er knew
Two things so opposite as Them and You.
On such your Muse her utmost fury spends,   45
They're slander'd worse than any but your Friends.
More years may teach you better; the mean while,
If you can't mend your Morals, mend your Style.

SARAH FYGE EGERTON

(1670–1723)

Sarah Egerton, a poet, was born one of six daughters of Thomas Fyge and his wife, Mary Beacham. Fyge, a London physician, came from a landed family and was himself a reasonably skilled poet. He banished his daughter from home when she was only sixteen because she had published a poem, *The Female Advocate* (1686), which was a satirical response to Robert Gould's misogynistic *Love Given O'er: Or, A Satyr Against the Pride, Lust and Inconstancy of Women* (1683). Sarah lived with relatives in the country, a circumstance she complains of in her early poems, and sometime later she married Edward Field, an attorney, who died before 1700. While married to Field, she wrote an ode and three elegies on the late John Dryden, whom she may have known. She contributed the elegies to *The Nine Muses* (1700), a volume of verse on Dryden written by women and edited by Delarivière Manley.

Sometime before 1703, she married the Reverend Thomas Egerton, who was her second cousin and twenty years her senior. His own children were already adults, and they had no others. The marriage was apparently unhappy almost from the start, at least partly because Sarah fell in love with Henry Pierce, a friend of her first husband and the "Alexis" of her poems. Sarah Egerton's divorce petition in 1703 charged her husband with cruelty; he countered by submitting evidence of his own cuckoldry. Evidence indicates that the divorce was never granted. That same year Egerton published *Poems on Several Occasions* (1703). She died at the age of fifty-three, having outlived her husband by only three years.

EDITION USED: *Poems on Several Occasions* (London, 1703).

The Liberty

Shall I be one, of those obsequious Fools,
That square there lives, by Customs scanty Rules;
Condemn'd for ever, to the puny Curse,
Of Precepts taught, at Boarding-school, or Nurse,
That all the business of my Life must be,
Foolish, dull Trifling, Formality.
Confin'd to a strict Magick complaisance,
And round a Circle, of nice visits Dance,
Nor for my Life beyond the Chalk advance:
The Devil Censure, stands to guard the same,   10

One step awry, he tears my ventrous Fame.
So when my Friends, in a facetious Vein,
With Mirth and Wit, a while can entertain;
Tho' ne'er so pleasant, yet I must not stay,
If a commanding Clock, bids me away: 15
But with a sudden start, as in a Fright,
I must be gone indeed, 'tis after Eight.
Sure these restraints, with such regret we bear, ⎫
That dreaded Censure, can't be more severe,   ⎬
Which has no Terror, if we did not fear;   ⎭   20
But let the Bug-bear, timerous Infants fright,
I'll not be scar'd, from Innocent delight:
Whatever is not vicious, I dare do,   ⎫
I'll never to the Idol Custom bow,   ⎬
Unless it suits with my own Humour too.   ⎭   25
Some boast their Fetters, of Formality,   ⎫
Fancy they ornamental Bracelets be,   ⎬
I'm sure their Gyves, and Manacles to me.   ⎭
To their dull fulsome Rules, I'd not be ty'd,
For all the Flattery that exalts their Pride: 30
My Sexs forbids, I should my Silence break,
I lose my Jest, cause Women must not speak.
Mysteries must not be, with my search Prophan'd,
My Closet not with books, but Sweat-meats cram'd
A little China, to advance the Show,   35
My Prayer Book, and seven Champions, or so.
My Pen if ever us'd imploy'd must be,   ⎫
In lofty Themes of useful Houswifery,   ⎬
Transcribing old Receipts of Cookery: ⎭
And what is necessary 'mongst the rest,   ⎫   40
Good Cures for Agues, and a cancer'd Breast, ⎬
But I can't here, write my *Probatum est.** ⎭
My daring Pen, will bolder Sallies make,
And like my self, an uncheck'd freedom take;
Not chain'd to the nice Order of my Sex,   45

---

*It has been proved.

And with restraints my wishing Soul perplex:
I'll blush at Sin, and not what some call Shame,
Secure my Virtue, slight precarious Fame.
This Courage speaks me, Brave, 'tis surely worse,
To keep those Rules, which privately we Curse: 50
And I'll appeal, to all the formal Saints,
With what reluctance they indure restraints.

The Emulation

Say Tyrant Custom, why must we obey,
The impositions of thy haughty Sway;
From the first dawn of Life, unto the Grave,
Poor Womankind's in every State, a Slave.
The Nurse, the Mistress, Parent and the Swain,   5
For Love she must, there's none escape that Pain;
Then comes the last, the fatal Slavery,
The Husband with insulting Tyranny
Can have ill Manners justify'd by Law;
For Men all join to keep the Wife in awe.   10
Moses who first our Freedom did rebuke,
Was Marry'd when he writ the Pentateuch;
They're Wise to keep us Slaves, for well they know,
If we were loose, we soon should make them, so.
We yeild like vanquish'd Kings whom Fetters bind,   15
When chance of War is to Usurpers kind;
Submit in Form; but they'd our Thoughts controul,
And lay restraints on the impassive Soul:
They fear we should excel their sluggish Parts,
Should we attempt the Sciences and Arts.   20
Pretend they were design'd for them alone,
So keep us Fools to raise their own Renown;
Thus Priests of old their Grandeur to maintain,
Cry'd vulgar Eyes would sacred Laws Prophane.
So kept the Mysteries behind a Screen,   25
There Homage and the Name were lost had they been seen:
But in this blessed Age, such Freedom's given,

That every Man explains the Will of Heaven;
And shall we Women now sit tamely by,
Make no excursions in Philosophy,   30
Or grace our Thoughts in tuneful Poetry?
We will our Rights in Learning's World maintain,
Wits Empire, now, shall know a Female Reign;
Come all ye Fair, the great Attempt improve,
Divinely imitate the Realms above;   35
There's ten celestial Females govern Wit,
And but two Gods that dare pretend to it;
And shall these finite Males reverse their Rules,
No, we'll be Wits, and then Men must be Fools.

To Philaster

Go perjur'd youth and count what Nymph you please,
Your passion now is but a dull Disease,
With worn-out Sighs deceive some list'ning Ear,
Who longs to know how 'tis and what men swear,
She'l think they'r new from you; cause so to her   5
Poor cousin'd Fool, she ne'er can know the Charms
Of being first encircled in thy Arms,
When all Love's Joys were innocent and gay,
As fresh and blooming as the new-born day.
Your Charms did then with native Sweetness flow,   10
The forc'd-kind Complaisance you now bestow,
Is but a false agreeable Design,
But you had Innocence when you were mine,
And all your Words, and Smiles, and Looks Divine.
How proud, methinks, thy Mistress does appear   15
In sully'd Cloths, which I'd no longer wear;
Her Bosom too with wither'd Flowers drest
Which lost their Sweets in my first chosen Breast;
Perjur'd imposing Youth, cheat who you will,
Supply defect of Truth with amorous Skill;   20
Yet thy Address must needs insipid be,
For the first Ardour of thy Soul was all possess'd by me.

To Orabella, marry'd to an old Man

Tell me fair Nymph who justly had design'd,
A charming Youth to suit your equal Mind;
What did seduce you thus to match with one,
Whom if by Nature made she'll scarcely own?
For form'd so many Centuries ago,   5
She has forgot if he's her Work or no;
I think the way to do his Reverence right,
Is to suppose him a Pre-Adamite.
Your blooming youth his Age beyond decay,   ⎫
Will teach censorious Malice what to say,   ⎬   10
Who spite of Virtue will your Fame betray.   ⎭
What strong Persuasions made you thus to wed,
With such a Carcass scandalize your Bed?
Sure 'twas no earthly Gain that charm'd you to't,
Nothing but hopes of Heaven should make me do't: 15
But since there's other ways to gain that Bliss, ⎫
Dispatching Martyrdom I wou'd not miss,   ⎬
To be secur'd, could I but 'scape from this.   ⎭
The Monster Twin whose Brother grew from's Side,
With all the Stench he suffer'd when he dy'd,   20
Is a just Emblem of so yok'd a Bride.
But Ptisick, Gout and Palsie have their Charms,
And did intice you to his trembling Arms:
Kind amorous Glances from his hollow Eyes,
Did your gay Breast with rapturous Joys surprize.   25
Ah! who can blame to see a Yielding Maid,
By all these blooming charms to Love betray'd.
Oh! for a vestal's Coldness to resist
The tempting Softness in such Beauties drest.
The bright Idea soon dissolves in Air,   30
And in it's room the Picture of Despair.
A moving Skeleton he seems to be,
Nature's antienest Anatomy.
Worth Observation, hang him up therefore
In *Gresham* College, and I'll ask no more.   35

To Alexis, on his absence

Say, lovely Youth, why all this niceness shown,
Is modest Passion, so offensive grown?
I'll not oblige too far, nor force my Charms,
To tempt your Coyness to my slighted Arms:
Give me but leave, with secret sighs to Gaze,   5
And silent Joys, view that dear fatal Face.
I never dress'd, nor smil'd, us'd no soft Art,   ⎫
No little Amorous cheat to win your Heart,   ⎬
Nor knew in mine you had so great a Part;   ⎭
Till from my Sight you cautiously remov'd,   10
Then, not till then, I knew how well I lov'd:
'Twas my Advice, you should awhile absent,
I ne'er design'd it for a Banishment.
But wisely you, as if you fear'd your Fate,
Shun what you would not Love, and cannot hate;   15
Yet spite of all your Vanity and Care,
Know my *Alexis*, that I have you here:
Here in my Breast, your dearest Image glows,
Warms every Wish, and softens all my Vows,
Inspires my Muse, to wanton in your charms,   20
And feast on Joys, which are deny'd my Arms:
In melting strains, she shall my passion tell,
Describe those lovely Eyes, and smiles so well.
Till every Nymph who my soft Lines shall see,
Sighs and Adores, and owns she loves like me.   25
That Shape, that Mein, that dear undoing Tongue,   ⎫
With thousand unknown charms shall fill my Song,   ⎬
To glad the listening World and make it last as long. ⎭
With an Eternal blast the trump of Fame,   ⎫
Will sound *Alexis* and *Clarinda*'s Name,   ⎬   30
Your matchless Graces, my unequall'd Flame.   ⎭
You shall this fondness on my Muse forgive,
And tho' not in my Arms, in my soft numbers live:
While warlike Heroes who are half Divine,
Shall have their Glories sung, in meaner Lays than thine.   35

LADY MARY CHUDLEIGH

(1656–1710)

An essayist and poet, Lady Chudleigh was born Mary Lee, the daughter of Richard Lee, Esq., of Winslade, Devon. Nothing is known of her mother or her own early life, but her writings show she must have read widely in the Greek and Roman classics, English literature, and philosophy. At seventeen she married thirty-year-old Sir George Chudleigh of Ashton, Devon, by whom she had three children. The marriage was unhappy and no doubt provided much of the material for her dismal assessment of "that wretched state" in her poem "To the Ladies." Additional sorrow came with the untimely death of her only daughter, Eliza Maria.

Inspired by the work of Mary Astell, Chudleigh sought to follow her lead as an advocate for women. Her chance came when, in 1699, she heard the Reverend John Sprint preach a wedding sermon endorsing the total subjugation of wives to their husbands. In a stinging rebuttal, Chudleigh published her poem in dialogue, *The Ladies Defence: or, The Bride Woman's Counsellor Answer'd* (1700/ 1701). She published it anonymously, but her initials were attached to the "Epistle Dedicatory." She stigmatized marriage as "slavery" and attacked the notion that women should be kept ignorant. The poem raised a public stir, and Chudleigh was encouraged to publish *Poems on Several Occasions* (1703) under her own name. She republished the poems and the *Defense* in 1709 and the next year fully established her reputation with *Essays Upon Several Subjects in Prose and Verse* (1710). She died the same year, at fifty-four, after having been crippled by rheumatism and bed-ridden for some time. She left behind a number of unpublished works, including some translations of Lucian, two operas, and a masque. Her grave at Ashton, Devon, is marked with neither a monument nor an inscription.

EDITION USED: *Poems on Several Occasions* (London, 1703).

To The Ladies

Wife and servant are the same,
But only differ in the name:
For when that fatal knot is ty'd,
Which nothing, nothing can divide:
When she the word *obey* has said,
And man by law supreme has made,
Then all that's kind is laid aside,
And nothing left but state and pride:

145

Fierce as an eastern prince he grows
And all his innate rigor shows: 10
Then but to look, to laugh, or speak,
Will the nuptual contract break.
Like mutes, she signs alone must make,
And never any freedom take:
But still be govern'd by a nod,   15
And fear her husband as a God:
Him still must serve, him still obey,
And nothing act, and nothing say,
But what her haughty lord thinks fit,
Who with the power, has all the wit.   20
Then shun, oh! shun that wretched state,
And all the fawning flatt'rers hate:
Value yourselves, and Men despise:
You must be proud, if you'll be wise.

To Clorissa

1

To your lov'd Bosom pleas'd *Marissa* flies;
That place where sacred Friendship gives a Right,
And where ten thousand Charms invite.
Let others Pow'r and awful Greatness prize;
Let them exchange their Innocence and Fame   5
For the dear Purchase of a mighty Name:
Let greedy Wretches hug their darling Store,
The tempting Product of their Toils adore,
And still with anxious Souls, desire and grasp at more:
While I disdain to have my Bliss confin'd   10
To things which Fortune can bestow, or take,
To things so foreign to the Mind,
And which no part of solid Pleasure make:
Those Joys of which I am possesst,
Are safely lodg'd within my Breast,   15

Where like deep Waters, undisturb'd they flow,
And as they pass, a glassy smoothness show:
Unmov'd by Storms, or by the Attacks of Fate,
I envy none, nor wish a happier State.

                          2

When all alone in some belov'd Retreat,   20
Remote from Noise, from Bus'ness, and from Strife,
Those constant curst Attendants of the Great;
I freely can with my own Thoughts converse,
And clothe them in ignoble Verse,
'Tis then I tast the most delicious Feast of Life: 25
There, uncontroul'd I can my self survey,
And from Observers free,
My intellectual Pow'rs display,
And all th' opening Scenes of beauteous Nature see:
Form bright Ideas, and enrich my Mind,   30
Enlarge my Knowledge, and each Error find;
Inspect each Action, ev'ry Word dissect,
And on the Failures of my Life reflect:
Then from my Self, to Books, I turn my Sight,
And there, with silent Wonder and Delight,   35
Gaze on th' instructive venerable Dead,
Those that in Virtue's School were early bred,
And since by Rules of Honour always led;
Who its strict Laws with nicest care obey'd,
And were by calm unbyass'd Reason sway'd: 40
Their great Examples elevate my Mind,
And I the force of all their Precepts find;
By them inspir'd, above dull Earth I soar,
And scorn those Trifles which I priz'd before.

                          3

Next these Delights Love claims the chiefest Part,   45
That gentle Passion governs in my Heart:
Its sacred Flames dilate themselves around,
And like pure Aether no Confinement know:
Where ever true Desert is found,
I pay my Love and Wonder too: 50

Wit, when alone, has Pow'r to please,
And Virtue's charms 'resistless prove;
But when they both combine,
When both together shine,
Who coldly can behold a Glory so Divine?   55
Since you, *Clorissa*, have a Right to these,
And since you both possess,
You've, sure, a double Title to my Love,
And I my Fate shall bless,
For giving me a Friend, in whom I find   60
United, all the Graces of the Female kind.

4

Accept that Heart your Merit makes your own,
And let the Kindness for the Gift attone:
Love, Constancy, and spotless Truth I bring,
These give a Value to the meanest Thing.   65
O! let our Thoughts, our Interests be but one,
Our Griefs and Joys, be to each other known:
In all Concerns we'll have an equal share,
Enlarge each Pleasure, lessen ev'ry Care:
Thus, of a thousand Sweets possest,   70
We'll live in one another's Breast:
When present, talk the flying Hours away,
When absent, thus, our tender Thoughts convey:
And, when by the decrees of Fate
We're summon'd to a higher State,
We'll meet again in the blest Realms of Light,
And in each other there eternally delight.

The Elevation

1

O How ambitious is my Soul,
    How high she now aspires!
There's nothing can on Earth controul,
    Or limit her Desires.

2

Upon the Wings of Thought she flies   5
    Above the reach of Sight,
And finds a way thro' pathless Skies
    To everlasting Light:

3

From whence with blameless Scorn she views
    The Follies of mankind;   10
And smiles to see how each pursues
    Joys fleeting as the Wind.

4

Yonder's the little Ball of Earth,
    It lessens as I rise;
That Stage of transitory Mirth,   15
    Of lasting Miseries:

5

My Scorn does into Pity turn,
    And I lament the Fate
Of Souls, that still in Bodies mourn,
    For Faults which they create: 20

6

Souls without Spot, till Flesh they wear,
    Which their pure Substance stains:
While they th' uneasie Burthen bear,
    They're never free from Pains.

KATHERINE PHILIPS

(1631–1664)

A poet and playwright known to her admirers as the "Matchless Orinda," Philips was born in London to Presbyterian parents, John Fowler, a merchant, and Katherine, a doctor's daughter. She was educated at a fashionable boarding school in Hackney, where she distinguished herself as a bright pupil. Her father died when she was eleven, and four years later her mother married Sir Richard Philips, who moved the family to his home in Cardigan, Wales. At sixteen, Katherine married James Philips, her stepfather's son by a previous marriage, who was considerably older than she. Katherine spent her early married years in Wales, where she bore a son, who died in infancy, and a daughter. In her secluded country home, Katherine Philips wrote her first poetry, much of which celebrated her passionate, platonic friendships with women. Her husband, a follower of Oliver Cromwell, rose to prominence in the Puritan government, and Katherine began to spend some of her time in London.

With the restoration of the monarchy in 1660, Philips's husband experienced political difficulties, but Katherine was still able to participate in the cultural revival occurring in the court of Charles II. She became friends with some of the most influential figures. The poets John Dryden and Abraham Cowley admired her verse. She corresponded with the strong-minded and ambitious Margaret Cavendish, Duchess of Newcastle. The Earl of Orrery was her patron, and Sir Charles Cotterell, Charles II's Master of Ceremonies, was her confidential correspondent and editor. Her drama *Pompey*, a translation into heroic couplets of the French tragedian Corneille's *La Morte de Pompée*, was produced in London during 1662–63 and established her reputation. Its initial fame may have come because the author was a woman, but Philips's *Pompey* continued to be produced for the next sixteen years and was judged a much more faithful rendering of Corneille than that produced by Edmund Waller and other seventeenth-century wits.

Earlier in her career, Philips had refused to publish poetry, declaring she "never writ any line in my life with an intention to have it printed." However, a pirated edition of rough copies of her poems, entitled *Poems by the Incomparable Mrs K.P.* (1664), shocked her into a "sharp fit of sickness." In self defense, she authorized Cotterell to publish a correct edition, which appeared in 1667 after her death. While engaged in translating Corneille's *Horace*, Philips contracted smallpox and died at thirty-two, at the height of her immense popularity. Despite her fame, she escaped the kind of censure that Aphra Behn incurred. Philips's exemplary life and modesty kept her safe from slander.

EDITION USED: *Poems on Several Occasions* (London, 1710).

Upon the double Murther of King CHARLES I

I think not on the State, nor am concern'd
Which way soever the great Helm is turn'd:
But as that Son, whose Father's Danger nigh,
Did force his Native Dumbness, and untie
The fetter'd Organs; so this is a Cause   5
That will excuse the Breach of Nature's Laws.
Silence were now a Sin, nay Passion now
Wise Men themselves for Merit would allow.
What noble Eye could see (and careless pass)
The dying Lion kick'd by ev'ry Ass?   10
Has *Charles* so *broke God's Laws*, he must not have
A quiet Crown, nor yet a quiet grave?
Tombs have been Sanctuaries; Thieves lye there
Secure from all their Penalty and Fear.
Great *Charles* his double Misery was *this*,   15
Unfaithful Friends, ignoble Enemies.
Had any Heathen been this Prince's Foe,
He would have wept to see him injur'd so.
His Title was his Crime, they'd Reason good
To quarrel at the Right they had withstood.   20
He broke God's Laws, and therefore he must die;
And what shall then become of thee and I?
Slander must follow Treason; but yet stay,
Take not our Reason with our King away.
Tho' you have seiz'd upon all our Defence,   25
Yet do not sequester our common Sense.
Christ will be King, but I n'er understood
His Subjects built his Kingdom up with Blood,
Except their own; or that he would dispence
With his Commands, tho' for his own Defence.   30
Oh! to what height of horrour are they come
Who dare pull down a Crown, tear up a Tomb?

Friendship's Mystery: To my dearest Lucasia

1

Come, my *Lucasia*, since we see
    That Miracles Mens Faith do move,
By Wonder and by Prodigy
    To the dull angry World let's prove
    There's a Religion in our Love.   5

2

For though we were design'd t'agree,
    That Fate no Liberty destroys,
But our Election is as free
    As Angels, who with greedy choice
    Are yet determin'd to their Joys.   10

3

Our Hearts are doubled by the loss,
    Here Mixture is Addition grown;
We both diffuse, and both ingross:
    And we whose Minds are so much one,
    Never, yet ever are alone.   15

4

We court our own Captivity
    Than Thrones more great and innocent:
'Twere Banishment to be set free,
    Since we wear Fetters whose intent
    Not Bondage is, but Ornament.   20

5

Divided Joys are tedious found,
    And Griefs united easier grow:
We are our selves but by rebound,
    And all our Titles shuffled so,
    Both Princes, and both Subjects too.   25

6

Our Hearts are mutual Victims laid,
　　While they (such Pow'r in Friendship lies)
Are Altars, Priests, and Off'rings made:
　　And each Heart which thus kindly dies,
　　Grows deathless by the Sacrifice.　　　　　　　　　　30

A retir'd Friendship: To Ardelia

1

Come, my *Ardelia*, to this Bow'r,
　　Where kindly mingling Souls awhile
Let's innocently spend an Hour,
　　And at all serious Follies smile.

2

Here is no quarrelling for Crowns,　　　　　　　　　5
　　Nor fear of changes in our Fate;
No trembling at the great ones Frowns,
　　Nor any Slavery of State.

3

Here's no Disguise nor Treachery,
　　Nor any deep-conceal'd Design;　　　　　　　　10
From Blood and Plots this Place is free,
　　And calm as are those Looks of thine.

4

Here let us sit and bless our Stars,
　　Who did such happy Quiet give,
As that remov'd from Noise of Wars　　　　　　　15
　　In one anothers Hearts we live.

5

Why should we entertain a Fear?
　　Love cares not how the World is turn'd:

If crouds of Dangers shou'd appear,
   Yet Friendship can be unconcern'd. 20

6

We wear about us such a Charm,
   No Horror can be our Offence;
For Mischief's self can do no harm
   To Friendship, or to Innocence.

7

Let's mark how soon *Apollo's* Beams 25
   Command the Flocks to quit their Meat,
And not entreat the neighb'ring Streams
   To quench their Thirst, but cool their Heat.

8

In such a scorching Age as this
   Who would not ever seek a Shade, 30
Deserve their Happiness to miss,
   As having their own Peace betray'd.

9

But we (of one another's Mind
   Assur'd) the boist'rous World disdain;
With quiet Souls, and unconfin'd, 35
   Enjoy what Princes wish in vain.

Content: To My dearest Lucasia

1

   Content, the false World's best Disguise,
   The Search and Faction of the Wise,
     Is so abstruse and hid in Night,
     That, like that Fairy Red-cross Knight,
Who treach'rous Falshood for clear Truth had got, 5
Men think they have it when they have it not.

2

For Courts Content would gladly own,
But she ne'er dwelt about a Throne:
And to be flatter'd, Rich, and Great,
Are Things which do Mens Senses cheat.   10
But grave Experience long since this did see,
Ambition and Content would ne'er agree.

3

Some vainer would Content expect
From what their bright Outsides reflect:
But sure Content is more Divine   15
Than to be digg'd from Rock or Mine:
And they that know her Beauties will confess,
She needs no Lustre from a glitt'ring Dress.

4

In Mirth some place her, but she scorns
Th'Assistance of such crackling Thorns,   20
Nor owes her self to such thin Sport,
That is so sharp and yet so short:
And Painters tell us they the same Strokes place,
To make a laughing and a weeping Face.

5

Others there are that place Content   25
In Liberty from Government:
But whomsoe'er Passions deprave,
Though free from Shackles, he's a Slave.
Content and Bondage differ only then,
When we are chain'd by Vices, not by Men.   30

6

Some think the Camp Content does know,
And that she sits o'th' Victor's Brow:
But in his Laurel there is seen
Often a Cypress-bow between.
Nor will Content her self in that place give,   35
Where Noise and Tumult and Destruction live.

7

But yet the most Discreet believe,
The Schools this Jewel do receive,
And thus far's true without dispute,
Knowledge is still the sweetest Fruit.   40
But whilst Men seek for Truth they lose their Peace;
And who heaps Knowledge, Sorrow doth increase.

8

But now some sullen Hermit smiles,
And thinks he all the World beguiles,
And that his Cell and Dish contain   45
What all Mankind wish for in vain.
But yet his Pleasure's follow'd with a Groan,
For Man was never born to be alone.

9

Content her self best comprehends
Betwixt two Souls, and they two Friends,   50
Whose either Joys in both are fix'd
And multiply'd by being mix'd:
Whose Minds and Interests are so the same;
Their Griefs, when once imparted, lose that Name.

10

These far remov'd from all bold Noise,   55
And (what is worse) all hollow Joys,
Who never had a mean design,
Whose Flame is serious and divine,
And calm, and even, must contented be,
For they've both Union and Society.   60

11

Then, my *Lucasia*, we who have
Whatever Love can give or crave;
Who can with pitying Scorn survey
The Trifles which the most betray;
With Innocence and perfect Friendship fir'd,   65
By Virtue join'd, and by our Choice retir'd.

12

Whose Mirrors are the crystal Brooks,
Or else each others Hearts and Looks;
Who cannot wish for other things
Than Privacy and Friendship brings: 70
Whose Thoughts and Persons chang'd and mixt as one,
Enjoy content or else the World hath none.

Wiston Vault

And why this Vault and Tomb? alike we must
Put off Distinction, and put on our Dust.
Nor can the stateliest Fabrick help to save
From the Corruptions of a common Grave;
Nor for the Resurrection more prepare,   5
Than if the Dust were scatter'd into Air.
What then? Th' Ambition's just, say some, that we
May thus perpetuate our Memory.
Ah false vain Task of Art! ah poor weak Man!
Whose Monument does more than's Merit can;   10
Who by his Friends best Care and Love's abus'd,
And in his very Epitaph accus'd:
For did they not suspect his Name would fall,
There would not need an Epitaph at all.
But after Death too I would be alive,   15
And shall, if my *Lucasia* do, survive.
I quit these Pomps of Death, and am content,
Having her Heart to be my Monument:
Though ne'er Stone to me, 'twill Stone for me prove,
By the peculiar Miracles of Love.   20
There I'll Inscription have which no Tomb gives,
Not, *Here* Orinda *lies*, but, *Here she lives*.

The World

We falsly think it due our Friends,
That we should grieve for their untimely Ends.

He that surveys the World with serious Eyes,
And stirs her from her gross and weak Disguise,
Shall find 'tis Injury to mourn their Fate;   5
He only dies untimely who dies late.
For if 'twere told to Children in the Womb,
To what a Stage of Mischiefs they must come;
Could they foresee with how much Toil and Sweat
Men court that gilded Nothing, being Great;   10
What Pains they take not to be what they seem,
Rating their Bliss by others false Esteem,
And sacrificing their Content, to be
Guilty of grave and serious Vanity;
How each Condition hath its proper Thorns,   15
And what one Man admires, another scorns;
How frequently their Happiness they miss,
So far even from agreeing what it is,
That the same Person we can hardly find,
Who is an Hour together in one Mind: 20
Sure they would beg a Period of their Breath,
And what we call their Birth would count their Death.
Mankind is mad; for none can live alone,
Because their Joys stand by Comparison:
And yet they quarrel at Society,   25
And strive to kill they know not whom, nor why.
We all live by mistake, delight in Dreams,
Lost to our selves, and dwelling in Extreams;
Rejecting what we have, tho' ne'er so good,
And prizing what we never Understood.   30
Compared t' our boisterous Inconstancy
Tempests are calm, and Discords Harmony.
Hence we reverse the World, and yet to find
The God that made can hardly please our Mind.
We live by chance, and slip into Events;   35
Have all of Beasts except their Innocence.
The Soul, which no Man's Pow'r can reach, a Thing
That makes each Woman Man, each Man a King,
Doth so much lose, and from its height so fall,
That some contend to have no soul at all.   40

'Tis either not observ'd, or at the best
By Passion sought withal, by Sin deprest.
Freedom of Will (God's image) is forgot;
And if we know it, we improve it not.
Our thoughts, tho' nothing can be more our own,   45
Are still unguided, very seldom known.
Time 'scapes our Hands as Water in a Sieve,
We come to die e'er we begin to live.
Truth, the most suitable and noble Prize,
Food of our Spirits, yet neglected lies.   50
Error and Shadows are our choice, and we
Owe our Perdition to our own Decree.
If we search Truth, we make it more obscure;
And when it shines, cannot the Light endure.
For most Men now, who plod, and eat, and drink,   55
Have nothing less their Bus'ness than to think
And those few that enquire, how small a share
Of truth they find, how dark their Notions are!
That serious Evenness that calms the Breast,
And in a Tempest can bestow a Rest,   60
We either not attempt, or else decline,
By ev'ry Trifle snatch'd from our Design.
(Others he must in his Deceits involve,
Who is not true unto his own Resolve.)
We govern not our selves, but loose the Reins,   65
Counting our Bondage to a thousand chains;
And with as many Slaveries content,
As there are Tyrants ready to torment,
We live upon a Rack extended still
To one Extream or both, but always ill.   70
For since our Fortune is not understood,
We suffer less from bad than from the good.
The Sting is better drest and longer lasts,
As surfeits are more dangerous than Fasts.
And to compleat the Misery to us,   75
We see Extreams are still contiguous.
And as we run so fast from what we hate,
Like Squibs on Ropes, to know no middle state;
So outward Storms strengthned by us, we find

Our Fortune as disorder'd as our Mind.   80
But that's excused by this, it doth its part;
A treach'rous World befits a treach'rous Heart.
All Ill's our own; the outward Storms we loath
Receive from us their Birth, their Sting, or both
And that our Vanity be past a doubt,   85
'Tis one new Vanity to find it out.
Happy are they to whom God gives a Grave,
And from themselves as from his Wrath doth save,
'Tis good not to be born; but if we must,
The next good is, soon to return to Dust.   90
When th' uncag'd Soul, fled to Eternity,
Shall rest, and live, and sing, and love, and see.
Here we but crawl and grovel, play and cry;
Are first our own, then others, Enemy:
But there shall be defac'd both stain and score,   95
For Time, and Death, and Sin shall be no more.

The Soul

1

How vain a Thing is Man, whose noblest Part,
    That Soul which thro' the World doth rome,
Traverses Heav'n, finds out the Depth of Art,
    Yet is so ignorant at home.

2

In ev'ry Brook or Mirrour we can find   5
    Reflections of our Face to be;
But a true Optick to present our Mind
    We hardly get, and darkly see.

3

Yet in the Search after our selves we run,
    Actions and Causes we survey;   10

And when the weary Chase is almost done,
    Then from our Quest we slip away.

4

'Tis strange and sad, that since we do believe
    We have a Soul must never die,
There are so few that can a Reason give   15
    How it obtains that Life, or why.

5

I wonder not to find those that know most,
    Profess so much their Ignorance;
Since in their own Souls greatest Wits are lost,
    And of themselves have scarce a glance.   20

6

But somewhat sure doth here obscurely lye,
    That above Dross would fain advance,
And pants and catches at Eternity,
    As 'twere its own Inheritance.

7

A Soul self-mov'd which can dilate, contract,   25
    Pierces and judges Things unseen:
But this gross Heap of Matter cannot act,
    Unless impulsed from within.

8

Distance and Quantity, to Bodies due,
    The state of Souls cannot admit;   30
And all the Contraries which Nature knew
    Meet there, nor hurt themselves, nor it.

9

God never Body made so bright and clean,
    Which Good and Evil could discern:

What these Words Honesty and Honour mean,   35
    The Soul alone knows how to learn.

10

And tho' tis true she is imprison'd here,
    Yet hath the Notions of her own,
Which Sense doth only jog, awake, and clear,
    But cannot the first make known.   40

11

The Soul her own Felicity hath laid,
    And independent on the Sense,
Sees the weak Terrors which the World invade
    With Pity or with Negligence.

12

So unconcern'd she lives, so much above   45
    The Rubbish of a sordid Jail,
That nothing doth her Energy improve
    So much as when those Structures fail.

13

She's then a Substance subtile, strong and pure,
    So immaterial and refin'd,   50
As speaks her from the Body's Fate secure,
    And wholly of a diff'rent kind.

14

Religion for Reward in vain would look,
    Virtue were doom'd to Misery,
All Actions were like Bubbles in a Brook,   55
    Were't not for Immortality.

15

But as that Conqueror who Millions spent
    Thought it too mean to give a Mite;
So the World's Judge can never be content
    To bestow less than Infinite.   60

16

Treason against Eternal Majesty
　　Must have Eternal Justice too;
And since unbounded Love did satisfie,
　　He will unbounded Mercy shew.

17

It is our narrow Thoughts shorten these Things,　　65
　　By their Companion Flesh inclin'd;
Which feeling its own Weakness, gladly brings
　　The same Opinion to the Mind.

18

We stifle our own Sun, and live in Shade;
　　But where its Beams do once appear,　　70
They make that Person of himself afraid,
　　And to his own Acts most severe.

19

For ways to sin close, and our Breasts disguise
　　From outward Search, we soon may find:
But who can his own Soul bribe or surprise,　　75
　　Or Sin without a Sting behind?

20

He that Commands himself, is more a Prince,
　　Than he who Nations keeps in Awe,
Who yield to all that does their Souls convince,
　　Shall never need another Law.　　80

ANNE FINCH, COUNTESS OF WINCHILSEA

(1661–1720)

Poet, dramatist and fable writer, Anne, Countess of Winchilsea, was born to Sir William Kingsmill and his wife, Anne Haslewood, in Sydmonton, near Southampton. Orphaned by the age of three, she and her half sister Dorothy were probably raised by her uncle, Sir William Haslewood. In 1683, Anne became an attendant of Mary of Modena, wife to James, Duke of York, and soon to be King James II. At court she met Heneage Finch, one of the Duke's Gentlemen of the Bedchamber. Despite her initial resistance Finch finally succeeded in his suit "To win a stubborn and ungrateful heart," as she phrased it. Also at court she met the poet Anne Killigrew. In 1688, James II resigned the throne, and Heneage Finch was arrested when he tried to follow the king to France. After his release, the Finches left London and by the early 1690s were settled at Eastwell Park in Kent, the Finch ancestral home. Heneage Finch inherited the estate in 1712, and he and Anne became Count and Countess of Winchilsea.

In the peaceful environment of Eastwell, Anne pursued the poetry writing she had begun while at court, and her husband enthusiastically supported her efforts. In his prefatory poem to Charles Gildon's *New Collection of Poems on Several Occasions* (1701), Nicholas Rowe saluted her as "Ardelia," destined to redeem poetry from the "wretched Bards" of the past generation: "The Empire, which she saves, shall own her sway, / And all *Parnassus* her blest Laws obey." She circulated her poetry in manuscript and contributed to miscellanies. Some of her poems were even included in Delarivière Manley's scandalous *Secret Memoirs . . . from the New Atlantis* (1709). She published only one volume of her own, *Miscellany Poems on Several Occasions* (1713), but left behind two unpublished manuscripts containing many of her more personal poems.

Her friends included many well-known literary figures, such as Elizabeth Rowe, Jonathan Swift, Matthew Prior, and Alexander Pope. Although Pope greatly admired "The Spleen," his admiration seems to have cooled. In the comedy *Three Hours after Marriage*, on which Pope collaborated with John Gay and John Arbuthnot, the character of "Phoebe Clinket" was popularly believed to be a portrait of Anne Finch. An ink-stained would-be author desperate to publish, Phoebe keeps a servant at hand with a desk strapped to her back in case inspiration should strike her mistress. Other writers have held her in much higher esteem: among them Matthew Prior, William Wordsworth, and Virginia Woolf. Wordsworth especially admired her poem, "A Nocturnal Reverie." He included seventeen of her poems in an anthology entitled *Poems and Extracts from The Works of Anne, Countess of Winchilsea and Others* that he presented to a friend, Lady Mary Lowther, in 1819.

EDITION USED: *Poems of Anne Countess of Winchilsea,* ed. Myra Reynolds (Chicago, 1903).

THE PREFACE

BEAUMONT IN the beginni[n]g of a Coppy of Verses to his freind Fletcher (upon the ill successe of his Faithfull Shepheardesse) tells him,

> I know too well! that no more, then the man
> That travells throo' the burning Deserts, can
> When he is beaten with the raging Sun,
> Half smother'd in the dust, have power to run
> From a cool River, which himself doth find,
> E're he be slack'd; no more can he, whose mind
> Joys in the Muses, hold from that delight,
> When Nature, and his full thoughts, bid him write.

And this indeed, I not only find true by my own experience, but have also too many wittnesses of itt against me, under my own hand in the following Poems; which tho' never meritting more then to be once read, and then carlessly scatter'd or consum'd; are grown by the partiality of some of my freinds, to the formidable appearance of a Volume; tho' but in Manuscript, and have been solicited to a more daring manefestation, which I shall ever resist, both from the knowledge of their incapassity, of bearing a publick tryal; and also, upon recalling to my memory, some of the first lines I ever writt, which were part of an invocation of Apollo, whose wise and limitted answer to me, I did there suppose to be

> I grant thee no pretence to Bays,
>   Nor in bold print do thou appear;
> Nor shalt thou reatch Orinda's prayse,
>   Tho' all thy aim, be fixt on Her.

And tho' I have still avoided the confident producing anything of mine in thatt manner, yett have I come too neer itt, and been like those imperfect penitents, who are ever relenting, and yett ever returning to the same offences. For I have writt, and expos'd my uncorrect Rimes, and immediatly repented; and yett have writt again, and again suffer'd them to be seen; tho' att the expence of more uneasy reflections, till at last (like them) wearied with uncertainty, and irresolution, I rather chuse to be harden'd in an errour, then to be still att the trouble of endeavering to over come itt: and now, neither deny myself the pleasure of writing, or any longer make a mistery of that to my freinds and acquaintance, which does so little deserve itt; tho' itt is still a great satisfaction to me, that I was not so far abandon'd by my prudence, as out of a mistaken vanity, to lett any attempts of mine in Poetry, shew themselves whilst I liv'd in such a publick place as the Court, where every one wou'd have made their remarks upon a Versifying Maid of Honour; and far the greater number with prejudice, if not contempt. And indeed, the apprehension of this, had so much wean'd me from the practice and inclination to itt; that had nott an utter change in my Condition, and Circumstances, remov'd me into the solitude, & security of the Country, and the generous kindnesse of one that possest the most delightfull seat in itt; envited him, from whom I was inseperable, to partake of the pleasures of itt, I think I might have stopp'd ere it was too late, and suffer'd those few compositions I had then by me, to have sunk into that oblivion, which I ought to wish might be the lott of all that have succeeded them. But when I came to Eastwell, and cou'd fix my eyes only upon objects naturally inspiring soft and Poeticall immaginations, and found the Owner of itt, so indulgent to that Art, so knowing in all the rules of itt, and att his pleasure, so capable of putting them in practice; and also most obligingly favorable to some lines of mine, that had fall'n under his Lordship's perusal, I cou'd no longer keep within the limmitts I had prescrib'd myself, nor be wisely reserv'd, in spite of inclination, and such powerfull temptations to the contrary. Again I engage my self in the service of the Muses, as eagerly as if

> From their new Worlds, I know not where,
> There golden Indies in the air—

they cou'd have supply'd the material losses, which I had lately sustain'd in this. And now, whenever I contemplate all the several beautys of this Park, allow'd to be (if not of the Universal yett) of our British World infinitely the finest,

> A pleasing wonder throo' my fancy moves,
> Smooth as her lawnes, and lofty as her Groves.
> Boundlesse my Genius seems, when my free sight,
> Finds only distant skys to stop her flight.
> Like mighty Denhams, then, methinks my hand,
> Might bid the Landskip, in strong numbers stand,
> Fix all itts charms, with a Poetick skill,
> And raise itts Fame, above his Cooper's hill.

This, I confesse, is whatt in itts self itt deserves, but the unhappy difference is, that he by being a real Poet, cou'd make that place (as he sais) a

Parnassus to him; whilst I, that behold a real Parnassus here, in that
lovely Hill, which in this Park bears that name, find in my self, so little of
the Poet, that I am still restrain'd from attempting a description of itt in
verse, tho' the agreeablenesse of the subject, has often prompted me most
strongly to itt.

But now, having pleaded an irresistable impulse, as my excuse for
writing, which was the cheif design of this Preface, I must also expresse
my hopes of excaping all suspition of vanity, or affectation of applause
from itt; since I have in my introduction, deliver'd my sincere opinion
that when a Woman meddles with things of this nature,

So strong, th' opposing faction still appears,
The hopes to thrive, can ne're outweigh the fears.

And, I am besides sensible, that Poetry has been of late so explain'd, the
laws of itt being putt into familiar languages, that even those of my sex,
(if they will be so presumptuous as to write) are very accountable for their
transgressions against them. For what rule of Aristotle, or Horace is there,
that has not been given us by Rapin, Despreaux, D'acier, my Lord Rosco-
mon, etc.? What has Mr. Dryden omitted, that may lay open the very
misteries of this Art? and can there any where be found a more delight-
some, or more usefull piece of Poetry, then that,

correct Essay,
Which so repairs, our old Horatian way.

If then, after the perusal of these, we fail, we cannott plead any want, but
that of capacity, or care, in both of which I own myself so very defective,
y^t whenever any things of mine, escape a censure, I allways attribute itt,
to the good nature or civility of the Reader; and not to any meritt in the
Poems, which I am satisfy'd are so very imperfect, and uncorrect, that I
shall not attempt their justifycation.

For the subjects, I hope they are att least innofensive; tho' sometimes
of Love; for keeping within those limmitts which I have observ'd, I know
not why itt shou'd be more faulty, to treat of that passion, then of any
other violent excursion, or transport of the mind. Tho' I must confesse,
the great reservednesse of Mrs. Philips in this particular, and the prayses I
have heard given her upon that account, together with my desire not to
give scandal to the most severe, has often discourag'd me from making
use of itt, and given me some regrett for what I had writt of that kind,
and wholy prevented me from putting the Aminta of Tasso into English

verse, from the verbal translation that I procured out of the Italian, after I had finish'd the first act extreamly to my satisfaction; and was convinc'd, that in the original, itt must be as soft and full of beautys, as ever anything of that nature was; but there being nothing mixt with itt, of a serious morality, or usefullnesse, I sacrafis'd the pleasure I took in itt, to the more sollid reasonings of my own mind; and hope by so doing to have made an attonement, to my gravest readers, for the two short pieces of that Pastoral, taken from the French, the Songs, and other few lighter things which yett remain in the following sheetts.

As to Lampoons, and all sorts of abusive verses, I ever so much detested, both the underhand dealing and uncharitablenesse which accompanys them, that I never suffer'd my small talent, to be that way employ'd; tho' the facility of doing itt, is too well known to many, who can but make two words rime; and there wants not some provocation often, either from one's own resentments, or those of others, to put such upon itt, as are any way capable of that mean sort of revenge. The only coppy of mine that tends towards this, is the letter to Ephelia, in answer to an invitation to the Town; but, as that appears to have been long written, by the mention made of my Lord Roscommon, under the name of Piso, given to him first, in a Panegerick, of Mr. Wallers, before his Art of Poetry; so I do declare, that att the time of composing itt, there was no particular person meant by any of the disadvantageous Caracters; and the whole intention of itt, was in general to expose the Censorious humour, foppishnesse and coquetterie that then prevail'd. And I am so far from thinking there is any ill in this, that I wish itt oftener done, by such hands as might sufficiently ridicule, and wean us from those mistakes in our manners, and conversation.

Plays, were translated by our most vertuous Orinda; and mine, tho' originals, I hope are not lesse reserv'd. The Queen of Cyprus, I once thought to have call'd the Triumphs of Love and Innocence; and doubted not but the latter part of the Title, wou'd have been as aptly apply'd as the former. Aristomenes is wholy Tragicall, and, if itt answer my intention, moral and inciting to Vertue. What they are as to the performance, I leave to the judgment of those who shall read them; and if any one can find more faults then I think to be in y^m; I am much mistaken. I will only add, that when they were compos'd, itt was far from my intention ever to own them, the first was for my own private satisfaction, only an Essay wheither I cou'd go throo' with such a peice of Poetry. The other, I was led to, by the strong impressions, which some wonderfull circumstances in the life of Aristomenes, made upon my fancy; and cheifly the sweetnesse of his temper, observable in itt, wrought upon me; for which reason tho' itt may be I did not so Poetically, I chose rather to represent him Good, then Great; and pitch'd upon such parts of the relation, and introduc'd such additional circumstances of my own, as might most illustrate that, and shew him to be (as declared by the Oracle) the best of Men. I know not what effect they will have upon others, but I must acknowledge, that the giving some interruption to those melancholy thoughts, which posesst me, not only for my own, but much more for the misfortunes of those to whom I owe all immaginable duty, and gratitude, was so great a benefitt; that I have reason to be satisfy'd with the undertaking, be the performance never so inconsiderable. And indeed, an absolute solitude (which often was my lott) under such dejection of mind, cou'd not have been supported, had I indulg'd myself (as was too natural to me) only in the contemplation of present and real afflictions, which I hope will plead my excuse, for turning them for relief, upon such as were immaginary, & relating to Persons no more in being. I had my end in the writing, and if they please not those who will take the pains to peruse them, itt will be a just accusation to my weaknesse, for letting them escape out of their concealment; but if attended with a better successe, the satisfaction any freind of mine, may take in them, will make me think my time past, not so unprofitably bestowed, as otherwise I might; and which I shall now endeavour to redeem, by applying myself to better employments, and when I do write to chuse, my subjects generally out of Devinity, or from moral and serious occasions; which made me place them last, as capable of addition; For when we have run throo' all the amusements of life, itt will be found, that there is but one thing necessary; and they only Wise, who chuse the better part. But since there must be also, some relaxation, some entertaining of the spiritts,

> Whilst Life by Fate is lent to me,
> Whilst here below, I stay,
> Religion, my sole businesse be,
> And Poetry, my play.

The Introduction

Did I, my lines intend for publick view,
How many censures, wou'd their faults persue,

Some wou'd, because such words they do affect,
Cry they're insipid, empty, uncorrect.
And many, have attain'd, dull and untaught   5
The name of Witt, only by finding fault.
True judges, might condemn their want of wirt,
And all might say, they're by a Woman writt.
Alas! a woman that attempts the pen,
Such an intruder on the rights of men,   10
Such a presumptuous Creature, is esteem'd,
The fault, can by no vertue be redeem'd.
They tell us, we mistake our sex and way;
Good breeding, fashion, dancing, dressing, play
Are the accomplishments we shou'd desire;   15
To write, or read, or think, or to enquire
Wou'd cloud our beauty, and exaust our time,
And interrupt the Conquests of our prime;
Whilst the dull mannage, of a servile house
Is held by some, our outmost art, and use.   20
     Sure 'twas not ever thus, nor are we told
Fables, of Women that excell'd of old;
To whom, by the diffusive hand of Heaven
Some shares of witt, and poetry was given.
On that glad day, on which the Ark return'd,   25
The holy pledge, for which the Land had mourn'd,
The joyfull Tribes, attend itt on the way,
The Levites do the sacred Charge convey,
Whilst various Instruments, before itt play;
Here, holy Virgins in the Concert joyn,   30
The louder notes, to soften, and refine,
And with alternate verse, compleat the Hymn Devine.
Loe! the young Poet, after Gods own heart,
By Him inspired, and taught the Muses Art,
Return'd from Conquest, a bright Chorus meets,   35
That sing his slayn ten thousand in the streets.
In such loud numbers they his acts declare,
Proclaim the wonders, of his early war,
That Saul upon the vast applause does frown,
And feels, itts mighty thunder shake the Crown.   40
What, can the threat'n'd Judgment now prolong?
Half of the Kingdom is already gone;

The fairest half, whose influence guides the rest,
Have David's Empire, o're their hearts confess't.
    A Woman here, leads fainting Israel on,   45
She fights, she wins, she tryumphs with a song,
Devout, Majestick, for the subject fitt,
And far above her arms, exalts her witt,
Then, to the peacefull, shady Palm withdraws,
And rules the rescu'd Nation, with her Laws.   50
How are we fal'n, fal'n by mistaken rules?
And Education's, more then Nature's fools,
Debarr'd from all improve-ments of the mind,
And to be dull, expected and dessigned;
And if some one, wou'd Soar above the rest,   55
With warmer fancy, and ambition press't,
So strong, th' opposing faction still appears,
The hopes to thrive, can ne're outweigh the fears,
Be caution'd then my Muse, and still retir'd;
Nor be dispis'd, aiming to be admir'd;   60
Conscious of wants, still with contracted wing,
To some few friends, and to thy sorrows sing;
For groves of Lawrell, thou wert never meant;
Be dark enough thy shades, and be thou there content.

The Apology

'Tis true I write and tell me by what Rule
I am alone forbid to play the fool
To follow through the Groves a wand'ring Muse
And fain'd Idea's for my pleasures chuse
Why shou'd it in my Pen be held a fault   5
Whilst Mira paints her face, to paint a thought
Whilst Lamia to the manly Bumper flys
And borrow'd Spiritts sparkle in her Eyes
Why shou'd itt be in me a thing so vain
To heat with Poetry my colder Brain   10

But I write ill and there-fore shou'd forbear
Does Flavia cease now at her fortieth year
In ev'ry Place to lett that face be seen
Which all the Town rejected at fifteen
Each Woman has her weaknesse; mine indeed   15
Is still to write tho' hoplesse to succeed
Nor to the Men is this so easy found
Ev'n in most Works with which the Witts abound
(So weak are all since our first breach with Heav'n)
Ther's lesse to be Applauded then forgiven.   20

Ardelia to Melancholy

At last, my old inveterate foe,
No opposition shalt thou know.
Since I by struggling, can obtain
Nothing, but encrease of pain,
I will att last, no more do soe,   5
Tho' I confesse, I have apply'd
Sweet mirth, and muscik, and have try'd
A thousand other arts beside,
To drive thee from my darken'd breast,
Thou, who hast banish'd all my rest.   10
But, though sometimes, a short repreive they gave,
Unable they, and far to weak, to save;
All arts to quell, did but augment thy force,
As rivers check'd, break with a wilder course.

Freindship, I to my heart have laid,   15
Freindship, th' applauded sov'rain aid,
And thought that charm so strong wou'd prove,
As to compell thee, to remove;
And to myself, I boasting said,
Now I a conqu'rer sure shall be,   20
The end of all my conflicts, see,
And noble tryumph, wait on me;
My dusky, sullen foe, will sure

N'er this united charge endure.
But leaning on this reed, eve'n whilst I spoke   25
It peirc'd my hand, and into peices broke.
Still, some new object, or new int'rest came
And loos'd the bonds, and quite disolv'd the claim.

These failing, I invok'd a Muse,
And Poetry wou'd often use,   30
To guard me from thy Tyrant pow'r;
And to oppose thee ev'ry hour
New troups of fancy's, did I chuse.
Alas! in vain, for all agree
To yeild me Captive up to thee,   35
And heav'n, alone, can sett me free.
Thou, through my life, wilt with me goe,
And make ye passage, sad, and slow.
All, that cou'd ere thy ill gott rule, invade.
Their uselesse arms, before thy feet have laid;   40
The Fort is thine, now ruin'd, all within,
Whilst by decays without, thy Conquests too, is seen.

On Myselfe

Good Heav'n, I thank thee, since it was design'd
I shou'd be fram'd, but of the weaker kinde,
That yet, my Soul, is rescu'd from the Love
Of all those Trifles, which their Passions move.
Pleasures, and Praise, and Plenty have with me   5
But their just value. If allow'd they be,
Freely, and thankfully as much I tast,
As will not reason, or Religion wast.
If they're deny'd, I on my selfe can live,
And slight those aids, unequal chance does give.   10
When in the Sun, my wings can be display'd,
And in retirement, I can bless the shade.

Clarinda's Indifference at
Parting with Her Beauty

Now, age come on, and all the dismal traine
That fright the vitious, and afflicte the vaine.
Departing beauty, now Clarinda spies
Pale in her cheeks, and dying in her eyes;
That youthfull air, that wanders ore the face,   5
That undescrib'd, that unresisted grace,
Those morning beams, that strongly warm, and shine,
Which men that feel and see, can ne're define,
Now, on the wings of restlesse time, were fled,
And ev'ning shades, began to rise, and spread,   10
When thus resolv'd, and ready soon to part,
Slighting the short repreives of proffer'd art
She spake—
And what, vain beauty, didst thou 'ere atcheive,
When at thy height, that I thy fall shou'd greive,   15
When, did'st thou e're succesfully persue?
When, did'st thou e're th' appointed foe subdue?
'Tis vain of numbers, or of strength to boast,
In an undisciplin'd, unguided Host,
And love, that did thy mighty hopes deride,   20
Wou'd pay no sacrafice, but to thy pride.
When, did'st thou e're a pleasing rule obtain,
A glorious Empire's but a glorious pain,
Thou, art indeed, but vanity's cheife sourse,
But foyle to witt, to want of witt a curse,   25
For often, by thy gaudy sign's descry'd
A fool, which unobserv'd, had been untry'd,
And when thou doest such empty things adorn,
'Tis but to make them more the publick scorn.
I know thee well, but weak thy reign wou'd be   30
Did n'one adore, or prize thee more then me.
I see indeed, thy certain ruine neer,
But can't affoard one parting sigh, or tear,
Nor rail at Time, nor quarrell with my glasse,
But unconcern'd, can lett thy glories passe.   35

The Unequal Fetters

Cou'd we stop the time that's flying
    Or recall itt when 'tis past
Put far off the day of Dying
    Or make Youth for ever last
To love wou'd then be worth our cost.   5

But since we must loose those Graces
    Which at first your hearts have wonne
And you seek for in new Faces
    When our Spring of Life is done
It wou'd but urdge our ruine on   10

Free as Nature's first intention
    Was to make us, I'll be found
Nor by subtle Man's invention
    Yeild to be in Fetters bound
By one that walks a freer round.   15

Mariage does but slightly tye Men
    Whil'st close Pris'ners we remain
They the larger Slaves of Hymen
    Still are begging Love again
At the full length of their chain.   20

To the Nightingale

Exert thy Voice, sweet Harbinger of Spring!
    This Moment is thy Time to sing,
    This Moment I attend to Praise,
And set my Numbers to thy Layes.
    Free as thine shall be my Song;   5
    As thy Musick, short, or long.
Poets, wild as thee, were born,
    Pleasing best when unconfin'd,
    When to Please is least design'd,
Soothing but their Cares to rest;   10

Cares do still their Thoughts molest,
And still th' unhappy Poet's Breast,
Like thine, when best he sings, is plac'd against a Thorn.
She begins, Let all be still!
Muse, thy Promise now fulfill!   15
Sweet, oh! sweet, still sweeter yet
Can thy Words such Accents fit,
Canst thou Syllables refine,
Melt a Sense that shall retain
Still some Spirit of the Brain,   20
Till with Sounds like these it join.
'Twill not be! then change thy Note;
Let division shake thy Throat.
Hark Division now she tries;
Yet as far the Muse outflies.   25
Cease then, prithee, cease thy Tune;
Trifler, wilt thou sing till *June?*
Till thy Bus'ness all lies waste,
And the Time of Building past!
Thus we Poets that have Speech   30
Unlike what thy Forest teach,
If a fluent Vein be shown
That's transcendent to our own,
Criticize, reform, or preach,
Or censure what we cannot reach.   35

A Letter to Dafnis April: 2d 1685

This to the Crown, and blessing of my life,
The much lov'd husband, of a happy wife.
To him, whose constant passion found the art
To win a stubborn, and ungratefull heart;
And to the World, by tend'rest proof discovers   5
They err, who say that husbands can't be lovers.
With such return of passion, as is due,
Daphnis I love, Daphnis my thoughts persue,
Daphnis, my hopes, my joys, are bounded all in you:
Ev'n I, for Daphnis, and my promise sake,   10

What I in women censure, undertake.
But this from love, not vanity, proceeds;
You know who writes; and I who 'tis that reads.
Judge not my passion, by my want of skill,
Many love well, though they express itt ill;   15
And I your censure cou'd with pleasure bear,
Wou'd you but soon return, and speak itt here.

Life's Progress

How gayly is at first begun
      Our *Life's* uncertain Race!
Whilst yet that sprightly Morning Sun,
With which we just set out to run
      Enlightens all the Place.   5

How smiling the World's Prospect lies
      How tempting to go through!
Not *Canaan* to the Prophet's Eyes,
From *Pisgah* with a sweet Surprize,
      Did more inviting shew.   10

How promising's the Book of Fate,
      Till thoroughly understood!
Whilst partial Hopes such Lots create,
As may the youthful Fancy treat
      With all that's Great and Good.   15

How soft the first Ideas prove,
      Which wander through our Minds!
How full the Joys, how free the Love,
Which do's that early Season move;
      As Flow'rs the Western Winds!   20

Our Sighs are then but Vernal Air;
      But *April*-drops our Tears,
Which swiftly passing, all grows Fair,
Whilst Beauty compensates our Care,
      And Youth each Vapour clears.   25

But oh! too soon, alas, we climb;
    Scarce feeling we ascend
The gently rising Hill of *Time*,
From whence with Grief we see that Prime,
    And all its Sweetness end.   30

The Die now cast, our Station known,
    Fond Expectation past;
The Thorns, which former days had sown,
To Crops of late Repentance grown,
    Thro' which we toil at last.   35

Whilst ev'ry Care's a driving Harm,
    That helps to bear us down;
Which faded Smiles no more can charm,
But ev'ry Tear's a Winter-Storm,
    And ev'ry Look's a Frown.   40

Till with succeeding Ills opprest,
    For Joys we hop'd to find;
By Age too, rumpl'd and undrest,
We gladly sinking down to rest,
    Leave following Crouds behind.   45

A Nocturnal Reverie

In such a night, when every louder wind
Is to its distant cavern safe confined;
And only gentle Zephyr fans his wings,
And lonely Philomel, still waking, sings;
Or from some tree, famed for the owl's delight,   5
She, hollowing clear, directs the wanderer right:
In such a night, when passing clouds give place,
Or thinly veil the heavens' mysterious face;
When in some river, overhung with green,
The waving moon and trembling leaves are seen;   10

When freshened grass now bears itself upright,
And makes cool banks to pleasing rest invite,
Whence springs the woodbind, and the bramble-rose,
And where the sleepy cowslip sheltered grows;
Whilst now a paler hue the foxglove takes,   15
Yet checkers still with red the dusky brakes:
When scattered glow-worms, but in twilight fine,
Show trivial beauties watch their hour to shine;
Whilst Salisbury stands the test of every light,
In perfect charms, and perfect virtue bright: 20
When odors, which declined repelling day,
Through temperate air uninterrupted stray;
When darkened groves their softest shadows wear,
And falling waters we distinctly hear;
When through the gloom more venerable shows   25
Some ancient fabric, awful in repose,
While sunburnt hills their swarthy looks conceal,
And swelling haycocks thicken up the vale:
When the loosed horse now, as his pasture leads,
Comes slowly grazing through the adjoining meads,   30
Whose stealing pace, and lengthened shade we fear,
Till torn-up forage in his teeth we hear:
When nibbling sheep at large pursue their food,
And unmolested kine rechew the cud;
When curlews cry beneath the village walls,   35
And to her straggling brood the partridge calls;
Their shortlived jubilee the creatures keep,
Which but endures, whilst tyrant man does sleep;
When a sedate content the spirit feels,
And no fierce light disturbs, whilst it reveals;   40
But silent musings urge the mind to seek
Something, too high for syllables to speak;
Till the free soul to a composedness charmed,
Finding the elements of rage disarmed,
O'er all below a solemn quiet grown,   45
Joys in the inferior world, and thinks it like her own:
In such a night let me abroad remain,
Till morning breaks, and all's confused again;
Our cares, our toils, our clamors are renewed,
Or pleasures, seldom reached, again pursued.   50

LADY RACHEL RUSSELL

(1636–1723)

Remembered chiefly for her letters, Rachel Russell came from an aristocratic family, married among the aristocracy, and seemed destined to live a comfortable and sheltered life. But tragedy followed her from her first marriage through her second. Rachel Russell's father was Thomas Wriothesley, Earl of Southampton, and her mother was Rachel de Ruvigny, a French Huguenot known for her beauty and virtue. Russell first married Francis, Lord Vaughan, eldest son of the Earl of Carbery, when she was seventeen. After twelve years of marriage, she bore a child who died at birth; her husband died two years later, the same year that she also lost her father. During her early widowhood, she lived with her sister Lady Elizabeth Noel, wife of the later first Earl of Gainsborough.

In 1669, when she was thirty-three, Rachel married thirty-year-old William Russell, who subsequently succeeded his elder brother as Earl of Bedford. They were a happy couple, united as well in their political and religious sympathies. Both ardently supported the Whig party at a time when it could be dangerous to do so. The English historian Thomas Macaulay wrote that Lord Russell was "Driven into opposition by dread of popery, by dread of France, and by disgust at the extravagance, dissoluteness, and faithlessness of the court." His strong opposition to the government led to his arrest for high treason in 1683. Lady Russell worked tirelessly to free him, taking notes at his trial, helping to assemble his defense, and trying to convince Charles II, whom her father had faithfully served, to aid her husband. All her efforts failed; in 1683, Lord Russell was beheaded.

Devastated by her loss, Lady Russell devoted herself to restoring his good name, which was cleared in 1689, a year after the Glorious Revolution in which James II resigned the throne to William and Mary. Her letters, discovered after her death by her steward Thomas Sellwood, tell in unaffected prose the poignant story of her struggle to clear her husband, arrange secure marriages for their three children, and attain peace of mind. Half a century after her death, Russell's letters were published as a vindication of her husband's reputation. During her long lifetime, Russell remained a well known and highly esteemed figure. She died at eighty-seven, having outlived all but one of her children, and is buried beside Lord Russell.

EDITION USED: *Letters of Lady Rachel Russell*, 4th ed. (London, 1792).

FROM LETTERS OF LADY RACHEL RUSSELL

Lady Russell to Dr. Fitzwilliam*

YOUR LETTERS are still the welcome messengers of good news to me, good Doctor, and the good will I know you send them with, engages my receiving them the more kindly; and my best thanks due to you for them; but where our chiefest thanks should be paid, I desire that neither myself, nor those concerned near as I was, may forget our duty. With your usual favour, oblige me by presenting my service chearfully to my brother; I hope he still improves in his health. That they may both rejoice many years in the well-being of one another, is the earnest prayer of

Their humble servant and yours,
Tuesday Morning.   R. RUSSELL.

Lady Russell's Letter to the King
(Charles II)*

MAY IT PLEASE YOUR MAJESTY,

I FIND my husband's enemies are not appeased with his blood, but still continue to misrepresent him to your Majesty. 'Tis a great addition to my sorrows, to hear your Majesty is prevailed upon to believe, that the paper he delivered to the Sheriffe at his death, was not his own. I can truly say, and am ready in the solemnest manner to attest that [during his imprisonment] I often heard him discourse the chiefest matters contained in that paper, in the same expressions he therein uses, as some of those few relations that were admitted to him, can likewise aver. And sure 'tis an argument of no great force, that there is a phrase or two in it another uses, when nothing is more common than to take up such words we like, or are accustomed to in our conversation. I beg leave further to avow to your Majesty, that al that is set down in the paper read to your Majesty on

---

*Reverend John Fitzwilliam, chaplain to Lady Russell's father, was her trusted correspondent and confidant until his death in 1699.
*"My Letter to the King a few days after my dear Lord's [husband's] death [execution]"

Sunday night, to be spoken in my prefence, is exactly true; as I doubt not but the rest of the paper is, which was written at my request; and the author of it in al his conversation with my husband, that I was privy to, showed himselfe a loyal subject to your Majesty, a faithful friend to him, and a most tender and conscientious minister to his soule. I do therefore humbly beg your Majesty would be so charitable to beleve, that he who in al his life was observed to act with the greatest clearnesse and sincerity, would not at the point of death doe so disingenious and false a thing as to deliver for his own, what was not properly and expressly so. And if, after the losse in such a manner of the best husband in the world, I were capable of any consolation, your Majesty only could afford it by having better thoughts of him, which when I was so importunat to speak with your Majesty, I thought I had som reason to beleve I should have inclined you to, not from the credit of my word, but upon the evidence of what I had to say. I hope I have writ nothing in this that wil displease your Majesty. If I have, I humbly beg of you to consider it as coming from a woman amazed with grief; and that you wil pardon the daughter of a person who served your Majesty's father in his greatest extremityes, [and your Majesty in your greatest posts] and one that is not conscious of having ever done any thing to offend you [before]. I shall ever pray for your Majesty's long life and happy reign.

    Who am, with al humility,

      May it please your Majesty, &c.

Lady Russell to Dr. Fitzwilliam

I NEED not tell you, good Doctor, how little capable I have been of such an exercise as this*. You will soon find how unfit I am still for it, since my yet disordered thoughts can offer me no other than such words as express the deepest sorrows, and confused, as my yet amazed mind is. But such men as you, and particularly one so much my friend, will, I know, bear with my weakness, and compassionate my distress, as you have already done by your good letter, and excellent prayer. I endeavour to make the best use I can of both; but I am so evil and unworthy a creature, that though I have desires, yet I have no dispositions, or worthiness, towards receiving comfort. You that knew us both, and how we lived, must allow

---

*Lord Russell, her husband, was executed July 21, 1683.

I have just cause to bewail my loss. I know it is common with others to lose a friend; but to have lived with such a one, it may be questioned how few can glory in the like happiness, so consequently lament the like loss. Who can but shrink at such a blow, till by the mighty aids of his holy spirit, we will let the gift of God, which he hath put into our hearts, interpose? That reason which sets a measure to our souls in prosperity, will then suggest many things which we have seen and heard, to moderate us in such sad circumstances as mine. But, alas! my understanding is clouded, my faith weak, sense strong, and the devil busy to fill my thoughts with false notions, difficulties, and doubts, as of a future condition* of prayer: but this I hope to make matter of humiliation, not sin. Lord let me understand the reason of these dark and wounding providences, that I sink not under the discouragements of my own thoughts: I know I have deserved my punishment, and will be silent under it; but yet secretly my heart mourns, too sadly I fear, and cannot be comforted, because I have not the dear companion and sharer of all my joys and sorrows. I want him to talk with, to walk with, to eat and sleep with; all these things are irksome to me now; the day unwelcome, and the night so too; all company and meals I would avoid, if it might be; yet all this is, that I enjoy not the world in my own way, and this sure hinders my comfort; when I see my children before me, I remember the pleasure he took in them; this makes my heart shrink. Can I regret his quitting a lesser good for a bigger? O! if I did stedfastly believe, I could not be dejected; for I will not injure myself to say, I offer my mind any inferior consolation to supply this loss. No; I most willingly forsake this world— this vexatious, troublesome world, in which I have no other business, but to rid my soul from sin; secure by faith and a good conscience my eternal interests; with patience and courage bear my eminent misfortunes, and ever hereafter be above the smiles and frowns of it. And when I have done the remnant of the work appointed me on earth, then joyfully wait for the heavenly perfection in God's good time, when by his infinite mercy I may be accounted worthy to enter into the same place of rest and repose, where he is gone, for whom only I grieve I do* fear. From that contemplation must come my best support. Good Doctor, you will think, as you have reason, that I set no bounds, when I let myself loose to my

---

*Two or three words torn off.
*A word torn off.

complaints; but I will release you, first fervently asking the continuance of your prayers for

> Your infinitely afflicted,
> But very faithful servant,

Woborne Abby,   R. RUSSELL,
30 *September*, 1683.

Lady Russell to Dr. Fitzwilliam

'TIS ABOVE a fortnight, I believe, good Doctor, since I received your comforting letter; and 'tis displeasing to me that I am now but sitting down to tell you so; but it is allotted to persons under my dismal title, and yet more dismal circumstances, to have additional cares, from which I am sure I am not exempt, but am very unfit to discharge well or wisely, especially under the oppressions I feel; however, 'tis my lot, and a part of my duty remaining to my choicest friend, and those pledges he has left me. That remembrance makes me do my best, and so occasions the putting by such employments as suit better my present temper of mind, as this I am now about; since if, in the multitude of those sorrows that possess my soul, I find any refreshments, though, alas! such as are but momentary, 'tis but casting off some of my crouded thoughts to compassionate friends, such as deny not to weep with those that weep; or in reading such discourses and advices as your letter supplies me with, which I hope you believe I have read more than once; and if I have more days to pass upon this earth, I mean to do so often, since I profess, of all those have been offered me, (in which charity has been most abounding to me) none have in all particulars more suited my humour. You deal with me, Sir, just as I would be dealt withall; and 'tis possible I feel the more smart from my raging griefs, because I would not take them off, but upon fit considerations: as 'tis easiest to our natures to have our sore in deep wounds gently handled; yet, as most profitable, I would yield, nay desire, to have mine searched, that, as you religiously design by it, they may not fester. 'Tis possible I grasp at too much of this kind, for a spirit so broke by affliction; for I am so jealous, that time, or necessity, the ordinary abater of all violent passions, (nay even employment, or company of such friends as I have left) should do that, my reason or religion ought to do, as makes me covet the best advices, and use all methods to obtain such a relief, as I can ever hope for, a silent submission to this severe and terrible providence, without any ineffective unwillingness to bear what I must suffer; and such a victory over myself, that, when once allayed, immoderate passions may not be apt to break out again upon fresh occasions and accidents, offering to my memory that dear object of my desires, which must happen every day, I may say every hour, of the longest life I can live; that so, when I must return into the world, so far as to act that part is incumbent upon me in faithfulness to him I owe as much as can be due to man, it may be with great strength of spirits, and grace to live a stricter life of holiness to my God, who will not always let me cry to him in vain. On him I will wait, till he have pity on me, humbly imploring, that by the mighty aids of his most holy spirit, he will touch my heart with greater love to himself. Then I shall be what he would have me. But I am unworthy of such a spiritual blessing, who remain so unthankful a creature for those earthly ones I have enjoyed, because I have them no longer. Yet God, who knows our frames, will not expect that when we are weak, we should be strong. This is much comfort under my deep dejections, which are surely increased by the subtil malice of that great enemy of souls, taking all advantages upon my present weakened and wasted spirits, assaulting with divers temptations, as, when I have in any measure overcome one kind, I find another in the room, as when I am less afflicted, (as I before complained) then I find reflections troubling me, as omissions of some sort or other; that if either greater persuasions had been used, he had gone away; or some errors at the tryal amended, or other applications made, he might have been acquitted, and so yet have been in the land of the living; (tho' I discharge not these things as faults upon myself, yet as aggravations to my sorrows) so that not being certain of our time being appointed, beyond which we cannot pass, my heart shrinks to think his time possibly was shortened by unwise management. I believe I do ill to torment myself with such unwist management. I believe I do ill to torment myself with such unprofitable thoughts[.]

Lady Russell to Dr. Fitzwilliam

BELIEVE ME, good Doctor, I find myself uneasy at reading your short letter of 8th April, (which I have but newly received) before I had answered yours of the 11th March. I have several times taken a pen in my hand to do it, and been prevented by dispatching less pleasing dispatches first, and so my time was spent before I came to that I intended before I laid away the pen.

The future part of my life will not I expect pass, as perhaps I would just choose; sense has been long enough gratified; indeed so long, I know not how to live by faith; yet the pleasant stream that fed it near fourteen years together, being gone, I have no sort of refreshment, but when I can repair to that living fountain, from whence all flows; while I look not at the things which are seen, but at those which are not seen, expecting that day which will settle and compose all my tumultuous thoughts in perpetual peace and quiet; but am undone, irrecoverably so, as to my temporal longings and concerns. Time runs on, and usually wears off some of that sharpness of thought inseparable with my circumstances, but I cannot experience such an effect, every week making me more and more sensible of the miserable change in my condition; but the same merciful hand which has held me up from sinking in the extremest calamities, will (I verily believe) do so still, that I faint not to the end in this sharp conflict, nor add sin to my grievous weight of sorrows, by too high a discontent, which is all I have now to fear. You do, I doubt not, observe I let my pen run too greedily upon this subject: indeed 'tis very hard upon me to restrain it, especially to such as pity my distress, and would assist towards my relief any way in their power. I am glad I have so expressed myself to you, as to fix you in resolving to continue the course you have begun with me, which is to set before me plainly my duty in all kinds: 'twas my design to engage you to it; nor shall you be less successful with me, in your desires, could there happen occasion for it, which is most unlikely, Doctor Fitzwilliam understanding himself and the world so well. On neither of the points, I believe, I shall give you reason to complain, yet please myself in both, so far of one mind we shall be.

I am entertaining some thoughts of going to that now desolate place Straton, for a few days, where I must expect new amazing reflections at first, it being a place where I have lived in sweet and full content; considered the condition of others, and thought none deserved my envy: but I must pass no more such days on earth; however, places are indeed nothing. Where can I dwell that his figure is not present to me! Nor would I have it otherwise; so I resolve that shall be no bar, if it proves requisite for the better acquitting any obligation upon me. That which is the immediate one, is settling, and indeed giving up the trust, my dear Lord had from my best sister. Fain would I see that performed, as I know he would have done it had he lived. If I find I can do as I desire in it, I will (by God's permission) infallibly go; but indeed not to stay more than two or three weeks, my children remaining here, who shall ever have my diligent attendance, therefore shall hasten back to them.

I do not admit one thought of accepting your kind and religious offer, knowing it is not proper. I take, if I do go, my sister Margaret, and believe Lady Shaftsbury will meet me there. This I choose, as thinking some persons being there to whom I would observe some rules, will engage me to restrain myself, or keep in better bounds my wild and sad thoughts. This is all I can do for myself. But blessed by the good prayers of others for me, they will, I hope, help me forward towards the great end of our creation.

> I am, most cordially, good Doctor,
> Your ever mournfull, but
> Ever faithfull friend, to serve you,
>
> R. RUSSELL.

I hear my Lord Gainsborough and my Lady will be shortly at Chilten. She is one I do truly respect: I can never regret being near her, though my design is to converse with none but lawyers and accountants.

Woborne Abby, 20 *April*, 1684.

Lady Russell to Dr. Fitzwilliam

YOU PURSUE, good Doctor, all ways of promoting comfort to my afflicted mind, and will encourage me to think the better of myself, for that better temper of mind you judge you found me in, when you so kindly gave me a week of your time in London. You are highly in the right, that as quick a sense as sharpness on the one hand, and tenderness on the other, can cause, I labour under, and shall, I believe, to the end of my life, so eminently unfortunate in the close of it.

But I strive to reflect how large my portion of good things has been, and though they are passed away no more to return; yet I have a pleasant work to do, dress up my soul for my desired change, and fit it for the converse of angels and the spirits of just men made perfect; amongst whom my hope is my loved Lord is one; and my often repeated prayer to my God is, that if I have a reasonable ground for that hope, it may give a refreshment to my poor soul.

Do not press yourself, Sir, too greatly in seeking my advantage, but when your papers do come, I expect and hope they will prove such. The accidents of every day tell us of what a tottering clay our bodies are made. Youth nor beauty, greatness nor wealth, can prop it up. If it could, the

Lady Offory had not so early left this world; she died (as an express acquainted her father this morning) on Sunday last, of a flux and miscarrying. I heard also this day of a kinsman that is gone; a few years ago I should have had a more concerned sense for Sir Thomas Vernon; his unfitness (as I doubt) I do lament indeed.

Thus I treat you, as I am myself, with objects of mortification; but you want none such in your solitude, and I being unprovided of other, will leave you to your own thoughts, and ever continue,

Sir your obliged servant,

31 *January*, 1684–5.   R. RUSSELL.

Lady Russell to Dr. Fitzwilliam

NEVER SHALL I, good Doctor, I hope, forget your work (as I may term it) of labour and love, so instructive and comfortable do I find it, that at any time, when I have read any of your papers, I feel a heat within me to be repeating my thanks to you anew, which is all I can do towards the discharge of a debt you have engaged me in; and though nobody loves more than I to stand free from engagements I cannot answer, yet I do not wish for it here; I would have it as it is; and although I have the present advantage, you will have the future reward; and if I can truly reap what I know you design me by it, a religious and quiet submission to all providences, I am assured you will esteem to have attained it here in some measure. Never could you more seasonably have fed me with such discourses, and left me with expectations of new repasts, in a more seasonable time, than these my miserable months, and in those this very week in which I have lived over again that fatal day that determined what fell out a week after, and that has given me so long and so bitter a time of sorrow. But God has a compass in his providences, that is out of our reach, and as he is all good and wife, that consideration should in reason slacken the fierce rages of grief. But sure, Doctor, 'tis the nature of sorrow to lay hold on all things which give a new ferment to it, then how could I chuse but feel it in a time of so much confusion as these last weeks have been, closing so tragically as they have done; and sure never any poor creature, for two whole years together, has had more awakers to quicken and revive the anguish of its soul than I have had; yet I hope I do most truly desire that nothing may be so bitter to me, as to think that I have in the least offended thee, O my God! and that nothing may be so marvelous in my eyes as the exceeding love of my Lord Jesus; that heaven being my aim, and the longing expectations of my soul, I may go through honour and dishonour, good report and bad report, prosperity and adversity, with some evenness of mind. The inspiring me with these desires is, I hope, a token of his never-failing love towards me, though an unthankful creature for all the good things I have enjoyed, and do still in the lives of hopefull children by so beloved a husband. God has restored me my little girl; the surgeon says she will do well. I should now hasten to give them the advantage of the country air, but am detained by the warning to see my uncle Ruvigny here, who comes to me; so I know not how to quit my house till I have received him, at least into it; he is upon his journey.

My Lady Gainsborough came to this town last night, and I doubt found neither her own daughter nor Lady Jane in a good condition of health. I had carried a surgeon on the day before to let my niece blood, by Dr. Loure's direction, who could not attend, by reason my Lord Radnor lay in extremity, and he was last night past hopes. My niece's complaint is a neglected cold, and he fears her to be something hectick, but I hope youth will struggle and overcome; they are children whose least concerns touch me to the quick; their mother was a delicious friend; sure nobody has enjoyed more pleasure in the conversations and tender kindnesses of a husband and a sister than myself, yet how apt am I to be fretfull that I must not still do so! but I must follow that which seems to be the will of God, how unacceptable soever it may be to me. I must stop, for if I let my pen run on I know not where it will end.

I am, good Doctor,
    With great faithfullness,
        Your affectionate friend to serve you,
Southampton-house   R. RUSSELL.
17 *July*, 1685.

Lady Russell to Dr. Fitzwilliam

NOW I know where to find you, good Doctor, (which I do by your letter writ at my Cousin Spenser's) you must be sure to hear from her who is still not ashamed to be on the receiving hand with you. God has given you the abilities, and opportunity for it, and not to me; and what am I, that I should say, Why is it not otherwise?—No, I do not, nor do I grudge or envy you the pious and ingenious pleasure you have in it; my part in this world is of another nature, and I thank you, Sir, (but God must give you the recompense) you instruct me admirably how to overcome, that I may once make application of that text, Revel. iii. 12. and raise such hopes as cannot miscarry. The great thing is to acquiesce with all one's heart to the good pleasure of God, who will prove us by the ways and dispensations He sees best, and when He will break us to pieces we must be broken. Who can tell his works from the beginning to the end? But who can praise his mercys more than wretched I, that He has not cut me off in anger, who have taken his chastisements so heavily, not weighing his mercys in the midst of judgments! The stroke was of the fiercest sure; but had I not then a reasonable ground to hope, that what I loved as I did my own soul, was raised from a prison to a throne? Was I not enabled to shut up my own sorrows, that I encreased not his sufferings by seeing mine? How were my sinking spirits supported by the early compassions of excellent and wise christians, without ceasing, admonishing me of my duty; instructing, reproving, comforting me! You know, Doctor, I was not destitute; and I must acknowledge that many others like yourself, with devout zeal, and great charity, contributed to the gathering together my scattered spirits, and then subjecting them by reason to such a submission as I could obtain under so astonishing a calamity: and further, he has spared me hitherto the children of so excellent a friend, giving them hopefull understandings, and yet very tractable and sweet dispositions; spared my life in usefulness I trust to them; and being I am to linger in a world I can no more delight in, has given me a freedom from bodily pain to a degree I almost never knew, not so much as a strong fit of the head-ach have I felt since that miserable time, who used to be tormented with it very frequently. This calls for praises my dead heart is not exercised in, but I hope this is my infirmity; I bewail it. He that took our nature, and felt our infirmities, knows the weakness of my person, and the sharpness of my sorrows.

I should not forget to mention, Sir, I did receive your papers and a letter I never had the opportunity to tell you of, dated 13 August; and another letter after that, where you write of your being in London within a fortnight; so that time slipping, I know not where to find you, nor how I came to let time do so.

I know not if you have heard some unwisht for accidents in my family have hurried me into new disorders. A young lady my Uncle Ruvigny brought with him falling ill of the small pox, I first removed my children to Bedford-house, then followed myself, for the quieting of my good uncle's mind, who would have it so; from thence I brought my little tribe down to Woborne, and when I heard how fatal the end was of the young lady's distemper, I returned myself to Bedford-house to take my last leave (for so I take it to be) of as kind a relation, and as zealous tender a friend as ever any body had. To my uncle and aunt their niece was an inexpressible loss, but to herself death was the contrary. She died (as most do) as she lived, a pattern to all who knew her. As her body grew weak, her faith and hope grew strong, comforting her comforters, and edifying all about her; ever magnifying the goodness of God, that she died in a country, where she could in peace give up her soul to him that made it. What a glorious thing, Doctor, 'tis to live and die as sure as she did! I heard my uncle and aunt say, that in seven years she had been with them, they never could tax her with a failure in her piety or worldly prudence, yet she had been roughly attackt, as the French Gazettes will tell you, if you have leisure to look over them now they are so many; however I keep them together, and so send them to you, who shall ever be gratified in what you ask from me, as a recompense of all your labours; 'tis a poor one indeed, the weak unworthy prayers of

Your very much obliged servant,
Woborne Abby, 11 *Oct.* 1685.   R. RUSSELL.

Lady Russell to Dr. Fitzwilliam

AS YOU profess, good Doctor, to take pleasure in your writings to me, from the testimony of a conscience, to forward my spiritual welfare, so do I to receive them as one to me of your friendship in both worldly and spiritual concernments: doing so, I need not waste my time nor yours to tell you they are very valuable to me. That you are so contented to read mine, I make the just allowance for; not for the worthiness of them, I know it cannot be, but however, it enables me to keep up an advantageous conversation without scruple of being too troublesome. You say some things sometimes by which I should think you season'd, or rather tainted with being so much where compliment or praising is best learned; but I conclude, that often, what one heartily wishes to be in a friend, one is apt to believe is so. The effect is not nought towards me, whom it animates to have a true not false title to the least virtue you are disposed to attribute to me. Yet I am far from such a vigour of mind as surmounts the secret discontent so hard a destiny as mine has fixt in my breast; but there are times the mind can hardly feel displeasure, as while such friendly conversation entertaineth it; then a grateful sense moves one to exprefs the courtesie.

If I could contemplate the conducts of Providence with the uses you do, it would give ease indeed, and no disasterous events should much affect us. The new scenes of each day, make me often conclude myself very void of temper and reason, that I still shed tears of sorrow, and not of joy, that so good a man is landed safe on the happy shore of a blessed eternity; doubtless he is at rest, tho' I find none without him, so true a partner he was in all my joys and griefs; I trust the Almighty will pass by this my infirmity; I speak it in respect to the world, from whose inticing delights I can now be better weaned. I was too rich in possessions whilst I possest him; all relish now is gone, I bless God for it, and pray and ask of all good people, (do it for me from such you know are so) also to pray that I may more and more turn the stream of my affections upwards, and set my heart upon the ever satisfying perfections of God; not starting at his darkest providences, but remembering continually either his glory, justice, or power, is advanced by every one of them, and that mercy is over all his works, as we shall one day with ravishing delight see. In the mean time, I endeavour to suppress all wild imaginations a melancholy fancy is apt to let in; and say with the man in the Gospel, "I believe, help thou my unbelief."

If any thing I say suggest to you matter for a pious reflection, I have not hurt you but ease myself, by letting loose some of my crowded thoughts. I must not finish without telling you, I have not the book you mention of Seraphical Meditations of the Bishop of B. and Wells, and should willingly see one here, since you design the present. I have sent you the last sheet of your papers, as the surest course; you can return it with the book. You would, Sir, have been welcome to Ld. Bedford, who expresses himself hugely obliged to the Bishop of Ely your friend; to whom you justly give the title of good, if the character he has very generally, belongs to him. And who is good is happy; for he is only truly miserable or wretchedly so, that has no joy here, nor hopes for any hereafter. I believe it may be near Christmas before my Lord Bedford removes for the winter, but I have not yet discours'd him about it, nor how long he desires our company; so whether I will come before him, or make one company, I know not; he shall please himself, for I have no will in these matters, nor can like one thing or way better than another, if the use and conveniencies be

alike to the young creatures, whose service is all the business I have in this
world, and for their good I intend all diligence in the power of,
　　　　Sir,
　　Your obliged friend to serve you,
　　　　　　　　　　　　　　　　　　　　　　R. RUSSELL.

Lady Russell to Dr. Fitzwilliam

I PRESUME, Doctor, you are now so settled in your retirement (for such 'tis
in comparison of that you can obtain at London) that you are at leisure to
peruse the inclosed papers; hereafter I will send them once a week, or
oftener if you desire it.

Yesterday the Lord Delamere passed his tryal, and was acquitted. I do
bless God that he has caused some stop to the effusion of blood has been
shed of late in this poor land. But, Doctor, as diseased bodys turn the
best nourishments, and even cordials into the same sour humour that
consumes and eats them up, just so do I. When I should rejoyce with
them that do rejoyce, I seek a corner to weep in. I find I am capable of no
more gladness; but every new circumstance, the very comparing my night
of sorrow after such a day, with theirs of joy, does, from a reflection of
one kind or other, rack my uneasy mind. Though I am far from wishing
the close of theirs like mine, yet I can't refrain giving some time to lament
mine was not like theirs; but I certainly took too much delight in my lot,
and would too willingly have built my tabernacle here; for which I hope
my punishment will end with life.

The accounts from France are more and more astonishing; the perfect-
ing the work is vigorously persued, and by this time compleated 'tis
thought; all without exception, having a day given them; only these I am
going to mention have found so much grace as I'll tell you. The Countess
de Roy is permitted, with two daughters, to go within 14 days to her
husband, who is in Denmark, in that King's service; but five other of her
children are put into monasterys. Mareschal Schomberg and his wife are
commanded to be prisoners in their house, in some remote part of France
appointed them. My uncle and his wife are permitted to come out of
France. This I was told for a truth last night, but I hope it needs a
confirmation.

'Tis enough to sink the strongest heart to read the relations are sent
over. How the children are torn from their mothers, and sent into monas-

terys; their mothers to another. The husband to prison, or the gallies. These are amazing providences, Doctor! God out of infinite mercy stengthen weak believers. I am too melancholy an intelligencer to be very long, so will hasten to conclude, first telling you Lord Talbot is come out of Ireland, and brought husbands for his daughters-in-law; one was married on Tuesday to a Lord Roffe; the other Lord is Dungan; Walgrave that married the King's daughter, is made a Lord. The brief for the poor Protestants was not sealed on Wednesday, as was hoped it would be; the Chancellour bid it be laid by, when it was offered him to seal.

    I am very really, Doctor,
       Your affectionate friend and servant,
15 *Jan.* 1685–6.   R. RUSSELL.

Lady Russell to the Dean of St. Paul's*

YOUR LETTERS will never trouble me, Dr. Dean; on the contrary, they are comfortable refreshments to my, for the most part, overburthened mind, which both by nature and by accident, is made so weak, that I can't bear, with that constancy I should, the losses I have lately felt; I can say, friends and acquaintances thou hast hid out of my sight, but I hope it shall not disturb my peace. These were young, and as they had began their race of life after me, so I desired they might have ended it also. But happy are those whom God retires in his grace — I trust these were so and then no age can be amiss: to the young 'tis not too early, nor to the aged too late. Submission and prayer is all we know that we can do towards our own relief in our distresses, or to disarm God's anger, either in our public or private concerns. The scene will soon alter to that peaceful and eternal home in prospect. But in this time of our pilgrimage, vicissitudes of all sorts are every one's lot. And this leads me to your case, Sir.

    The time seems to be come that you must put anew in practice that submission, you have so powerfully both try'd yourself, and instructed others to; I see no place to escape at; you must take up the cross, and bear it; I faithfully believe it has the figure of a very heavy one to you, though not from the cares of it; since, if the King guesses right, you toil more now; but this work is of your own choosing, and the dignity of the other is what

---

*Dr. John Tillotson (1630–94), later archbishop of Canterbury, years earlier had testified in behalf of Lord Russell at his trial for treason.

you have bent your mind against, and the strong resolve of your life has been to avoid it. Had this even proceeded to a vow, 'tis, I think, like the virgins of old, to be dissolved by the father of your country. Again, tho' contemplation, and a few friends well chosen, would be your grateful choice, yet, if charity, obedience, and necessity, call you into the great world, and where enemies encompass round about, must not you accept it? And each of these, in my mean apprehension, determines you to do it. In short, 'twill be a noble sacrifice you will make, and I am confident you will find as a reward, kind and tender supports, if you do take the burthen upon you; there is, as it were, a commanding Providence in the manner of it. Perhaps I do as sincerely wish your thoughts at ease as any friend you have, but I think you may purchase that too dear; and if you should come to think so too, they would then be as restless as before.

Sir, I believe you would be as much a common good as you can; consider how few of ability and integrity this age produces. Pray do not turn this matter too much in your head; when one has once turn'd it every way, you know that more does but perplex, and one never sees the clearer for it. Be not stiff if it be still urged to you. Conform to the Divine Will, which has set it so strongly into the others mind, and be content to endure; 'tis God calls you to it. I believe 'twas wisely said, that when there is no remedy they will give it over, and make the best of it, and so I hope no ill will terminate on the King; and they will lay up their arrows, when they perceive they are shot in vain at him or you, upon whom no reflection that I can think of can be made that is ingenious; and what is pure malice you are above being affected with.

I wish, for many reasons, my prayers were more worthy, but such as they are, I offer them with a sincere zeal to the throne of grace for you in this strait, that you may be led out of it, as shall best serve the great ends and designs of God's glory.

[*About the middle of October*, 1690.]

Lady Russell to (*supposed*) the Bishop of Salisbury

I HAVE, my Lord, so upright an heart to my friends, that tho' your great weight of business had forced you to a silence of this kind, yet I should have had no doubt, but that one I so distinguished in that little number God has yet left me, does joyn with me to lament my late losses. The one was a just, sincere man, and the only son of a sister and a friend I loved with too much passion; the other my last sister, and I ever lov'd her tenderly.

It pleases me to think that she deserves to be remembered by all those that knew her. But after above 40 years acquaintance with so amiable a creature, one must needs, in reflecting, bring to remembrance so many engaging endearments as are yet at present imbittering and painfull; and indeed we may be sure, that when any thing below God is the object of our love, at one time or another it will be a matter of our sorrow. But a little time will put me again into my settled state of mourning; for a mourner I must be all my days upon earth, and there is no need I should be other[.] My glass runs low: the world does not want me, nor I want that; my business is at home, and within a narrow compass. I must not deny, as there was something so glorious in the object of my biggest sorrow, I believe that in some measure, kept me from being then overwhelmed. So now it affords me, together with the remembrance how many easy years we lived together, thoughts that are joy enough for one, who looks no higher than a quiet submission to her lot, and such pleasures in educating the young folks as surmounts the cares that it will afford. If I shall be spared the tryal, where I have most thought of being prepared to bear the pain, I hope I shall be thankfull, and I think I ask it faithfully, that it may be in mercy not in judgment. Let me rather be tortured here, than they or I be rejected in that other blessed peacefull home to all ages, to which my soul aspires. There is something in the younger going before me, that I have observed all my life to give a sense I can't describe; it is harder to be borne than a bigger loss, where there has been spun out a longer thread of life. Yet I see no cause for it, for every day we see the young fall with the old; but methinks 'tis a violence upon nature.

A troubled mind has a multitude of these thoughts. Yet I hope I master all murmurings; if I have had any I am sorry, and will have no more, assisted by God's grace; and rest satisfied that whatever I think, I shall one day be entirely satisfied what God has done and shall do, will be best, and justify both his justice and mercy. I meant this as a very short epistle; but you have been some years acquainted with my infirmity, and have endured it, tho' you never had waste time, I believe, in your life; and better times do not, I hope, make your patience less. However it will become me to put an end to this, which I will do, signing myself cordially

16 *Oct.* 1690.   Your, &c.

ELIZABETH TOLLET

(1694–1754)

A poet, Elizabeth Tollet was the daughter of George Tollet, a commissioner of the navy during the reigns of William III and Queen Anne. She spent her earliest years at his home in the Tower of London, but later moved to another part of London, then Stratford, and finally West Ham where she spent the end of her life. Her father's friend, the physicist Sir Isaac Newton, urged him to give Elizabeth a good education that emphasized history and mathematics rather than the usual feminine pursuits of music, drawing, and fancy needlework, with a little fashionable French thrown in. Newton was also one of the first to read her work.

Until recently, scholars believed that Tollet had not published her poetry during her lifetime, supposedly according to her expressed wishes. Recently, however, Roger Lonsdale discovered a substantial collection of her work published anonymously in 1724 and entitled *Poems on Several Occasions. With Anne Boleyn to King Henry VIII. An Epistle.* It contained poems about Lady Mary Wortley Montagu, William Congreve, and Anne Finch (reprinted here), as well as some translations of the Psalms and a musical drama *Susanna, or Innocence Preserv'd*. Few copies were printed, and it seems to have received little notice. The same volume with a few omissions and some later verse was published posthumously in 1755 with the same title. A later undated reissue of her *Poems* (c. 1760) contained additional translations of the Psalms. Her work received mixed reviews during her lifetime. The *Monthly Review* found her verse harmonious and solemn, but not of the first rank. John Nichols, publisher of *The Gentleman's Magazine*, commended her depth of thought and reprinted a number of her poems in his eight-volume *Select Collection of Poems* (1780–84), including "On a Death's Head." She lived a solitary life, never marrying and apparently belonging to no literary circle.

EDITION USED: *Poems on Several Occasions,* 2nd ed. (London, n. d.).

In Memory of the Countess of Winchelsea

Sad *Cypress* and the Muses Tree
    Shall shade *Ardelia's* sacred Urn:
These with her Fame and Fate agree,
    And ever live, and ever mourn.

While ev'ry Muse with vocal breath   5
    In moving Strains recites her Praise:
And there assumes the *Cypress* Wreath,
    And on her Tomb resigns the Bays.

What Pow'r shall aid the Virgin Choir
    To make her Worth and Virtue known?   10
Who shall the Sculptor's Art inspire
    To write them on the lasting Stone?

The honour'd Streams of antient Blood,
    And Titles, are by Fortune giv'n:
But to be virtuous, wise, and good,   15
    Derives a Kindred Claim from Heav'n.

Virtue, and Wit in Courts admir'd,
    The shining Pattern shall diffuse:
Nor, tho' to private Life retir'd,
    Are lost, but flourish with her Muse.   20

Of those the *Sister-Nine* shall sing,
    Yet with their Voice their Verse shall pass:
And Time shall sure Destruction bring
    To wounded Stone, or molten Brass.

Tho' Titles grace the stately Tomb,   25
    Vain Monument of mortal Pride!
The Ruins of the mould'ring Dome
    Its undistinguish'd Heap shall hide.

Wit, which outlasts the firmest Stone,
    Shall *Phoenix*-like, its life prolong: 30
No verse can speak her but her own,
    The Spleen must be her fun'ral Song.

On a Death's Head

On this Resemblance, where we find
A Portrait drawn for all Mankind,
Fond lover! gaze a while, to see
What Beauty's Idol charms shall be.
Where are the Balls that once cou'd dart   5
Quick lightning thro' the Wounded Heart?
The Skin, whose Teint cou'd once unite
The glowing Red and polish'd White?
The Lip in brighter Ruby drest?
The Cheek with dimpled Smiles imprest?   10
The rising Front, where Beauty sate
Thron'd in her Residence of State;
Which, half-disclos'd and half-conceal'd,
The hair in flowing Ringlets veil'd;
'Tis vanish'd all! remains alone   15
This eyeless Scalp of Naked Bone:
The vacant Orbits sunk within:
The Jaw that offers at a Grin.
Is this the Object then that claims
The Tribute of our youthful Flames?   20
Must am'rous Hopes and fancy'd Bliss,
Too dear Delusions! end in this?
How high does Melancholy swell!
Which Sighs can more than Language tell:
Till Love can only grieve or fear;   25
Reflect a while, then drop a Tear
For all that's beautiful or dear.

Untitled

Adieu my Friend! and may thy Woes
    Be all in long Oblivion lost:
If Innocence can give Repose;
    Or gentle Verse can please thy Ghost.

No pious Rite, no solemn Knell   5
    Attended thy belov'd Remains:
Nor shall the letter'd Marble tell
    What silent Earth the Charge contains.

Obscure, beneath the nameless Stone,
    With thee shall Truth and Virtue sleep: 10
While, with her Lamp, the Muse alone,
    Shall watch thy sacred Dust and weep.

Blue violets, and Snow-drops pale,
    In pearly Dew for thee shall mourn:
And humble Lillies of the Vale   15
    Shall cover thy neglected Urn.

The Monument

In vain the stately Monument you raise,
Inscrib'd with pompous Epitaphs of Praise:
By waste of Time, or sacrilege o'erthrown,
A nameless Ruin shall remain alone.
Let servile Poets, in a fawning Strain,
Applaud the Mighty, and delude the vain:
Let curious Art inspire the breathing Bust;
And marble Urns enshrine the mould'ring Dust.
Can these, alas! an after Being buy?
Or raise the Man above Mortality?
May I, in Death that useless Pride resign;
The humble Surface of the Earth be mine:
The Hand which made can recollect the Frame,
Without the Guidance of a Stone or Name.

ELIZABETH SINGER ROWE

(1674–1737)

Self-styled Philomela (nightingale), Elizabeth Rowe was a poet and religious writer. She was the eldest of the three children of Walter and Elizabeth Singer. Her father, a nonconformist minister, had been in prison for his religious views when his future wife met him on a charity visit. Elizabeth Rowe's education was primarily religious, but she was also accomplished in music and drawing. In her early twenties, she began writing poems and sent them anonymously to John Dunton's *Athenian Mercury*. Dunton published her volume of *Poems on Several Occasions. Written by Philomela* (1696). It attracted favorable attention and was reissued twice during her lifetime. The poet Matthew Prior found her work so entrancing that he reprinted one of her poems and added verses of his own declaring his desperate love for her. She became acquainted with Dr. Isaac Watts, the nonconformist minister and hymn writer, who addressed a poem to her. In 1710, Elizabeth married Thomas Rowe, a classical scholar and son of a nonconformist minister. Although he was thirteen years younger than she, he died after their fifth year of marriage, a tragedy from which she never recovered and which gave rise to some of her most moving poems.

Alexander Pope and Samuel Johnson both thought highly of her writing. Pope imitated some of her lines and appended her "Elegy on the Death of Mr. Rowe" to the second edition of his "Eloisa to Abelard" (1720). Her most popular compositions were in religious prose cast in the form of letters. These include *Friendship in Death, or Letters from the Dead to the Living* (1728), which was reprinted many times, and *Letters Moral and Entertaining* (1729–32). Samuel Johnson said of this latter work that it successfully employed "the ornaments of romance in the decoration of religion" (Boswell, *Life*, ed. G.B. Hill, 1:312). She also wrote paraphrases of parts of the Bible and prayers. At her request, upon her death Isaac Watts revised and published her prayers as *Devout Exercises of the Heart* (1737). Her works continued to be popular after her death.

EDITION USED: *Miscellaneous Works in Prose and Verse*, 4th ed. (London, 1756).

The Vision

'TWAS in the close recesses of a shade,
A shade for sacred contemplation made;
No beauteous branch, no plant, or fragrant flow'r,
But flourish'd near the fair, delicious bow'r;
With charming state its lofty arches rise   5

Adorn'd with blossoms, as with stars the skies;
All pure and fragrant was the air I drew,
Which winds thro' myrtle groves and orange blew;
Clear waves along with pleasing murmur rush,
And down the artful falls in noble cat'racts gush.   10

    'TWAS here, within this happy place retir'd,
Harmonious pleasures all my soul inspir'd;
I take my lyre, and try each tuneful string,
Now war, now love, and beauty's force would sing:
To heav'nly subjects now, in serious lays,   15
I strive my faint, unskilful voice to raise:
But as I unresolv'd and doubtful lay,
My cares in easy slumbers glide away;
Nor with such grateful sleep, such soothing rest,
And dreams like this I e'er before was bless'd;   20
No wild, uncouth chimera's intervene,
To break the perfect intellectual scene.

    THE place was all with heav'nly light o'er-flown,
And glorious with immortal splendor shone;
When! lo a bright ethereal youth drew near,   25
Ineffable his motions and his air.
A soft, beneficent, expressless grace,
With life's most florid bloom adorn'd his Face;
Wreaths of immortal palm his temples bind,
And long his radiant hair fell down behind,   30
His azure robes hung free, and waving to the wind.
Angelic his address, his tuneful voice
Inspir'd a thousand elevating joys:
When thus the wond'rous youth his silence broke,
And with an accent all celestial spoke.   35

    TO heav'n, nor longer pause, devote thy songs,
To heav'n the muse's sacred art belongs;
Let his unbounded glory be thy theme,
Who fills th' eternal regions with his fame;
And when death's fatal sleep shall close thine eyes,   40

In triumph we'll attend thee to the skies;
We'll crown thee there with everlasting bays,
And teach thee all our celebrated lays.
This spoke, the shining vision upward flies,
And darts as lightning thro' the cleaving skies.   45

Hymn 5

1

IN vain the dusky night retires,
    And sullen shadows fly:
In vain the morn with purple light
    Adorns the eastern sky.

2

In vain the gaudy rising sun   5
    The wide horizon gilds,
Comes glitt'ring o'er the silver streams,
    And chears the dewy fields.

3

In vain, dispensing vernal sweets
    The morning breezes play;   10
In vain the birds with chearful songs
    Salute the new-born day;

4

In vain! unless my Saviour's face
    These gloomy clouds controul,
And dissipate the sullen shades   15
    That press my drooping soul.

5

O! visit then thy servant, Lord,
    With favour from on high;
Arise, my bright, immortal sun!
    And all these shades will die.   20

6

When, when, shall I behold thy face
  All radiant and serene,
Without these envious dusky clouds
  That makes a veil between?

7

When shall that long-expected day   25
  Of sacred vision be,
When my impatient soul shall make
  A near approach to thee?

A Description of Hell
in Imitation of Milton

DEEP, to unfathomable spaces deep,
Descend the dark, detested paths of hell,
The gulphs of execration and despair,
Of pain, and rage, and pure unmingled woe;
The realms of endless death, and seats of night,   5
Uninterrupted night, which sees no dawn,
Prodigious darkness! which receives no light,
But from the sickly blaze of sulph'rous flames,
That cast a pale and dead reflection round,
Disclosing all the desolate abyss,   10
Dreadful beyond what human thought can form,
Bounded with circling seas of liquid fire:
Aloft the blazing billows curl their heads,
And form a roar along the direful strand;
While ruddy cat'racts from on high descend,   15
And urge the fiery ocean's stormy rage.
Impending horrors o'er the region frown,
And weighty ruin threatens from on high;
Inevitable snares, and fatal pits,
And gulphs of deep perdition, wait below;   20
Whence issue long, remedyless complaints,

With endless groans, and everlasting yells.
Legions of ghastly fiends (prodigious sight!)
Fly all confus'd across the sickly air,
And roaring horrid, shake the vast extent.   25
Pale, meagre spectres wander all around,
And pensive shades, and black deformed ghosts:
With impious fury some aloud blaspheme,
And wildly staring upwards, curse the skies:
While some, with gloomy terror in their looks,   30
Trembling all over, downward cast their eyes,
And tell, in hollow groans, their deep despair.

CONVINC'D by fatal proofs, the atheist here
Yields to the sharp tormenting evidence;
And of an infinite eternal Mind,   35
At last the challeng'd demonstration meets.

THE libertine his folly here laments,
His blind extravagance, that made him sell
Unfading bliss, and everlasting crowns,
Immortal transports, and celestial feasts,   40
For the short pleasure of a sordid sin,
For one fleet moment's despicable joy.
Too late, all lost, for ever lost! he sees
Th' envy'd saints triumphing from afar,
And angels basking in the smiles of God.   45
But oh! that all was for a trifle lost,
Gives to his bleeding soul perpetual wounds.

THE wanton beauty, whose bewitching arts
Have drawn ten thousand wretched souls to hell,
Depriv'd of ev'ry blandishment and charm,   50
All black, and horrid, seeks the darkest shades,
To shun the fury of revengeful ghosts,
That with vindictive curses still pursue,
The author of their miserable fate,
Who from the paths of life seduc'd their souls,   55
And led them down to these accurst abodes.

THE fool that sold his heav'n for gilded clay,
The scorn of all the damn'd, ev'n here laments
His sordid heaps; which still to purchase, he
A second time would forfeit all above;   60
Nor covets fields of light, nor starry wreaths,
Nor angels songs, nor pure unmingled bliss,
But for his darling treasures still repines;
Which from afar, to aggravate his doom,
He sees some thoughtless prodigal consume.   65

BEYOND them all, a miserable hell
The execrable persecutor finds;
No spirit howls among the shades below
More damn'd, more fierce, nor more a fiend than he.
Aloud he heav'n and holiness blasphemes,   70
While all his enmity to good appears,
His enmity to good; once falsly call'd
Religious warmth, and charitable zeal.
On high, beyond th' unpassable abyss,
To aggravate his righteous doom, he views   75
The blissful realms, and there the schismatic,
The visionary, the deluded saint,
By him so often hated, wrong'd, and scorn'd,
So often curs'd, and damn'd, and banish'd thence:
He sees him there possess'd of all that heav'n,   80
Those glories, those immortal joys, which he,
The orthodox, unerring catholic,
The mighty fav'rite, and elect of God,
With all his mischievous, converting arts,
His killing charity, and burning zeal,   85
His pompous creeds, and boasted faith, has lost.

Despair

OH! lead me to some solitary gloom,
Where no enliv'ning beams, nor chearful echoes come;
But silent all, and dusky let it be,
Remote, and unfrequented but by me;

Mysterious, close, and sullen as that grief,   5
Which leads me to its covert for relief.
Far from the busy world's detested noise,
Its wretched pleasures, and distracted joys;
Far from the jolly fools, who laugh, and play, ⎫
And dance, and sing, impertinently gay,   ⎬   10
Their short, inestimable hours away;   ⎭
Far from the studious follies of the great,
The tiresome farce of ceremonious state:
There, in a melting, solemn, dying strain,
Let me, all day, upon my lyre complain,   15
And wind up all its soft, harmonious strings,
To noble, serious, melancholy things.
And let no human foot, but mine, e'er trace
The close recesses of the sacred place:
Nor let a bird of chearful note come near,   20
To whisper out his airy raptures here.
Only the pensive songstress of the grove,
Let her, by mine, her mournful notes improve;
While drooping winds among the branches sigh,
And sluggish waters heavily roll by.   25
Here, to my fatal sorrows let me give
The short remaining hours I have to live.
Then, with a sullen, deep-fetch'd groan expire,
And to the grave's dark solitude retire.

On the Anniversary Return of
the Day on Which Mr. Rowe Died

UNHAPPY day! with what a dismal light
Dost thou appear to my afflicted sight?
In vain the chearful spring returns with thee,
There is no future chearful spring for me.

WHILE my *Alexis* withers in the tomb,   5
Untimely cropt, nor sees a second bloom,

The fairest season of the changing year,
A wild and wintry aspect seems to wear;
The flow'rs no more their former beauty boast,
Their painted hue, and fragrant scents are lost;   10
The joyous birds their harmony prolong,
But, oh! I find no music in their song.

    YE mossy caves, ye groves, and silver streams,
(The muses lov'd retreats, and gentle themes)
Ye verdant fields, no more your landscapes please,   15
Nor give my soul one interval of ease;
Tranquility and pleasure fly your shades,
And restless care your solitude invades.
Nor the still ev'ning, nor the rosy dawn,
Nor moon-light glimm'ring o'er the dewy lawn,   20
Nor stars, nor sun, my gloomy fancy chear;
But heav'n and earth a dismal prospect wear:
That hour that snatch'd *Alexis* from my arms,
Rent from the face of nature all its charms.

    UNHAPPY day! be sacred still to grief,   25
A grief too obstinate for all relief;
On thee my face shall never wear a smile,
No joy on thee shall e'er my heart beguile.
Why does thy light again my eyes molest?
Why am I not with thee, dear youth, at rest?   30
When shall I, stretch'd upon my dusty bed,
Forget the toils of life, and mingle with the dead?

Canticle I.vii

O TELL me thou, for whom I prove
The softest languishments of love,
Thou, dearer than all human things,
From whom my purest pleasure springs,
Thou lovely object of my care,   5
Whom more than life I prize by far;

O tell me in what verdant mead,
Or flow'ry vale, thy flocks are fed;
Or by what silver current's side,
Thou gently dost their footsteps guide?   10
Instruct me to what shade they run,
The noon-day's scorching heat to shun.
They follow thee, they hear thy voice,
And at the well known sound rejoice:
O let me too that music hear,   15
Let one kind whisper reach mine ear;
My soul shall that soft call obey,
Nor longer from thee wildly stray.

Canticle II.viii, ix.

IS it a dream? or does my ravish'd ear
The charming voice of my beloved hear?
Is it his face? or are my eager eyes
Deluded by some vision's bright disguise?
'Tis he himself! I know his lovely face,   5
It's heav'nly lustre, and peculiar grace.
I know the sound, 'tis his transporting voice,
My heart assures me by its rising joys.
He comes, and wing'd with all the speed of love,
His flying feet along the mountains move;   10
He comes, and leaves the panting hart behind,
His motion swift and fleeting as the wind.
O welcome, welcome, never more to part!
I'll lodge thee now for ever in my heart;
My doubtful heart, which trembling scarce believes,   15
And scarce the mighty ecstasy receives.

The Submission

HOWEVER hard, my God, thy terms appear,
Howe'er to sense afflicting and severe,

To any articles I can agree,
Rather than bear the thoughts of losing thee:
Exact whate'er thou wilt, we'll never part,   5
Nothing shall force thy image from my heart.
Thou still art good, howe'er thou deal with me.
Spotless thy truth, unstain'd thy purity:
Amidst my suff'rings still I'll own thee just,
And in thy wonted mercy firmly trust.   10
Whate'er becomes of such a wretch as me,
Thy equal ways shall still unblemish'd be;
The sons of men shall still thy grace proclaim,
And place their refuge to thy mighty name;
Thro' all the wide-extended realms above,   15
Bright angels shall proclaim thy wond'rous love:
Ev'n I shall yet adore thy wonted grace,
Tho' darkness now conceals thy lovely face.
But, oh! how long shall I thy absence mourn?
When, when wilt thou, my sun, my life, return?   20
Thou only can'st my drooping soul sustain,
Of nothing but thy distance I complain.

ELIZABETH CARTER

(1717–1806)

Elizabeth Carter was a poet, scholar, translator, essayist, and letter writer. Carter's mother died when she was ten, and her father, an Anglican clergyman, undertook her education in Latin, Greek, and Hebrew, but found her a slow scholar and discouraged continuation of her studies. She persevered, however, staying up late to study and taking snuff to keep awake. She mastered Latin, Greek, and Hebrew, and went on to learn French, Italian, Spanish, German, Portuguese, and Arabic. She also studied history, astronomy, and ancient geography, played the flute, and was a lifelong student of the Bible. The oldest of a large family, she managed her father's household from an early age until his death in 1774. She did not marry, although she had suitors, one of whom she refused because of the "light and licentious turn of mind" revealed in some poems he had published. She was as accomplished in the domestic arts as she was in scholarship. Samuel Johnson meant to give her a high compliment when he said she "could make a pudding as well as translate Epictetus from the Greek" (Boswell, *Life*, ed. G. B. Hill, 1:123n.). Her translation of *All of the Works of Epictetus* (1758) established her reputation as a scholar. It ran to three editions during her life and a fourth just after her death.

Her poems were also popular. She began writing poetry in her teens; her early work was printed by Edward Cave, publisher of the *Gentleman's Magazine* and a friend of her father's. In 1762 she published *Poems on Several Occasions*, from which the following selections are taken. Samuel Johnson thought very highly of her intellectual abilities and included two of her essays in his *Rambler* (Nos. 44 and 100). She was a central member of the *Bas Bleu* (the Bluestockings), a group of eighteenth-century women (as well as a few men) who met socially for intellectual conversation rather than for gossip and cards. Carter corresponded voluminously on literary and moral subjects with the "Queen of the Blues," Elizabeth Montagu. Her letters to her dearest friend Catherine Talbot, whose work she published posthumously, show her relaxed and playful side. Her ready and subtle wit comes out especially in her private letters which she wrote, as she insisted, with no idea that they would be made public. Thus, we glimpse her amused reaction to a friend who, dazzled by her accomplishments, persisted in writing her obsequious letters:

> It is with the utmost diffidence that I venture to do myself the high honour of writing to you, when I consider my own nothingness and utter incapacity of doing any one thing upon earth. Unless I had as many tongues in my head as there are grains of dust between this and Canterbury, it is impossible for me to express the millionth part of the obligations I have to you, therefore I must content myself with assuring you that I am, with the sublimest veneration and most profound humility,

213

Your most devoted, obsequious, respectful, obedient, obliged, and dutiful
humble servant,

                                                                    E. Carter

I shall die with envy if you outdo this.

Carter's mentor in poetry was Elizabeth Rowe, whom she memorialized in "On
the Death of Mrs. Rowe."

EDITION USED: *Poems on Several Occasions* (London, 1762).

On the Death of Mrs. Rowe

Oft' did Intrigue it's guilty Arts unite,
To blacken the Records of female Wit:
The tuneful Song lost ev'ry modest Grace,
And lawless Freedoms triumph'd in their Place:
The Muse, for Vices not her own accus'd,   5
With Blushes view'd her sacred Gifts abus'd;
Those Gifts for nobler Purposes assign'd,
To raise the Thoughts, and moralize the Mind;
The chaste Delights of Virtue to inspire,
And warm the Bosom with seraphic Fire;   10
Sublime the Passions, lend Devotion Wings,
And celebrate the first great CAUSE of Things.
      These glorious Tasks were *Philomela'*s Part,
Who charms the Fancy, and who mends the Heart.
In her was ev'ry bright Distinction join'd,   15
Whate'er adorns, or dignifies the Mind:
Her's ev'ry happy Elegance of Thought,
Refin'd by Virtue, as by Genius wrought.
Each low-born Care her pow'rful Strains controul,
And wake the nobler Motions of the Soul.   20
When to the vocal Wood or winding Stream,
She hymn'd th' Almighty AUTHOR of it's Frame,
Transported Echoes bore the Sounds along,
And all Creation listen'd to the Song:
Full, as when raptur'd Seraphs strike the Lyre;   25

Chaste, as the Vestal's consecrated Fire;
Soft as the balmy Airs, that gently play
In the calm Sun-set of a vernal Day;
Sublime as Virtue; elegant as Wit;
As Fancy various; and as Beauty sweet.   30
Applauding Angels with Attention hung,
To learn the heav'nly Accents from her Tongue:
They, in the midnight Hour, beheld her rise
Beyond the Verge of sublunary Skies;
Where, rap'd in Joys to mortal Sense unknown,   35
She felt a Flame extatic as their own.
    O while distinguish'd in the Realms above,
The blest Abode of Harmony and Love,
Thy happy Spirit joins the heav'nly Throng,
Glows with their Transports, and partakes the Song,   40
Fixt on my Soul shall thy Example grow,
And be my Genius and my Guide below;
To this I'll point my first, my noblest Views,
Thy spotless Verse shall regulate my Muse.
And O forgive, tho' faint the Transcript be,   45
That copies an Original like thee:
My justest Pride, my best Attempt for Fame,
That joins my own to *Philomela's* Name.

To ⸺

While thus my Thoughts their softest Sense express,
And strive to make the tedious Hours seem less,
Say, shall these Lines the Name, I hide impart,
And point their Author to my *Cynthia's* Heart?
Will she, by correspondent Friendship, own   5
A Verse the Muse directs to her alone?
    Dear Object of a Love whose fond Excess
No studied Forms of Language can express,
How vain those Arts which vulgar Cares controul
To banish thy Remembrance from my Soul!   10

Which fixt and constant to it's fav'rite Theme,
In spite of Time and Distance is the same:
Still feels thy Absence equally severe,
Nor tastes without thee a Delight sincere.
    Now cold *Aquarius* rules the frozen Sky,   15
And with pale Horrors strikes the chearless Eye;
Sooth'd by the melancholy Gloom I rove,
With lonely Footsteps thro' the leafless Grove;
While sullen Clouds the Face of Heav'n invest,
And, in rude Murmurs, howls the bleak *North-east*:   20
Ev'n here thy Image rises to my Sight,
And gilds the Shade with momentary Light:
It's magic Pow'r transforms the wintry Scene,
And gay as *Eden* blooms the faded Plain.
    From Solitude to busy Crowds I fly,   25
And there each wild Amusement idly try:
Where laughing Folly sports in various Play,
And leads the Chorus of the Young and Gay.
But here the Fancy only takes a Part,
The giddy Mirth ne'er penetrates my Heart,   30
Which, cold, unmov'd, by all I hear or see,
Steals from the Circle to converse with thee.
    To calm Philosophy I next retire,
And seek the Joys, her sacred Arts inspire,
Renounce the Frolics of unthinking Youth,   35
To court the more engaging Charms of Truth:
With *Plato* soar on Contemplation's Wing,
And trace Perfection to th' eternal Spring:
Observe the vital Emanations flow,
That animate each fair Degree below: 40
Whence Order, Elegance, and Beauty move
Each finer Sense, that tunes the Mind to Love;
Whence all that Harmony and Fire that join,
To form a Temper, and a Soul like thine.
    Thus thro' each diff'rent Track my Thoughts pursue,   45
Thy lov'd Idea ever meets my View,
Of ev'ry Joy, of ev'ry Wish a Part,
And rules each varying Motion of my Heart.
    May Angels guard thee with distinguish'd Care,

And ev'ry Blessing be my *Cynthia*'s Share!   50
Thro' flow'ry Paths securely may she tread,
By Fortune follow'd, and by Virtue led;
While Health and Ease, in ev'ry Look express,
The Glow of Beauty, and the Calm of Peace.
Let one bright Sunshine form Life's vernal Day,   55
And clear and smiling be it's Ev'ning Ray.
Late may she feel the softest Blast of Death,
As Roses droop beneath a Zephyr's Breath.
Thus gently fading, peaceful rest in Earth,
'Till the glad Spring of Nature's second Birth: 60
Then quit the transient Winter of the Tomb
To rise and flourish in immortal Bloom.

On a WATCH [1]

Unlike the Triflers whose contracted View
Ne'er looks beyond a glitt'ring outside Show,
In this Machine with moral Eyes survey
How gliding Life steals silently away,
And, mindful of it's short determin'd Space,   5
Improve the flying Moments, as they pass.
    See rolling Years with quick Dispatch, decide
The transient Date of sublunary Pride:
See Beauty, Genius, Fortune, Fair, Sublime,
Borne headlong down the rapid Stream of Time: 10
O'er their sad Wrecks, along the fatal Shore,
Rapacious Death asserts his tyrant Pow'r;
There all their momentary Glories fade,
In dull Oblivion's everlasting Shade.
    Is all, that Nature or that Art can boast   15
In undistinguish'd, final Ruin lost?
Must All partake the same unalter'd Doom,
The Sport of Time, and Victims of the Tomb?
One only Good secure, unchang'd, defies
The giddy Whirl of sublunary Skies;   20
Which see, uninfluenc'd by their wild Controul,

Offspring of Heav'n, the Undecaying Soul.
    To this unfailing Excellence devote
The Morn of Reason, and the Prime of Thought.
Tho' Youth and Beauty diff'rent Tasks persuade,   25
That Youth must languish, and that Beauty fade:
Destructive Years no Graces leave behind,
But those, which Virtue fixes in the Mind.
How vain the want of real Worth to hide,
Each flatter'd Talent's superficial Pride!   30
It's Touch in vain the mimic Pencil tries,
And Sounds harmonious from the Lyre arise.
As some fair Structure, rais'd by skilful Hand,
But weakly founded on the shaking Sand,
Securely stands, in sculptur'd Foliage gay,   35
While vernal Airs around it's Columns play:
But soon the Rains descend, the Tempests beat,
And each unsolid Ornament defeat:
The faithless Base betrays it's feeble Trust,
And all the beauteous Trifle sinks in Dust: 40
So sinks each Grace of Nature, and of Art,
Unprop'd by strong Integrity of Heart!
    Let idle Flutt'rers, miserably gay,
In Dress and Trifling waste their useless Day;
That Day, for nobler Exercises givn',   45
T' adorn the Soul for Happiness and Heav'n:
Beyond the Triumph of these shadowy Charms,
Which ev'ry beating Pulse of Time alarms,
To fairer Views let thy Ambition tend,
Our Nature's Glory, and our Being's End;   50
And seek from Beauties form'd on Virtue's Rules,
Th' Applause of Angels, not the Gaze of Fools.

To _____

The Midnight Moon serenely smiles,
    O'er Nature's soft Repose;
No low'ring Cloud obscures the Sky,
    Nor ruffling Tempest blows.

Now ev'ry Passion sinks to Rest,   5
    The throbbing Heart lies still:
And varying Schemes of Life no more
    Distract the lab'ring Will.

In Silence hush'd, to Reason's Voice,
    Attends each mental Pow'r: 10
Come dear *Emilia*, and enjoy
    Reflexion's fav'rite Hour.

Come: while the peaceful Scene invites,
    Let's search this ample Round,
Where shall the lovely fleeting Form   15
    Of *Happiness* be found?

Does it amidst the frolic Mirth
    Of gay Assemblies dwell?
Or hide beneath the solemn Gloom,
    That Shades the Hermit's Cell?   20

How oft the laughing Brow of Joy
    A sick'ning Heart conceals!
And thro' the Cloister's deep Recess,
    Invading Sorrow steals.

In vain thro' Beauty, Fortune, Wit,   25
    The Fugitive we trace:
It dwells not in the faithless Smile,
    That brightens *Clodio*'s Face.

Perhaps the Joy to these deny'd,
    The Heart in Friendship finds: 30
Ah! dear Delusion! gay Conceit
    Of visionary Minds!

Howe'er our varying Notions rove,
    Yet all agree in one,
To place it's Being in some State,   35
    At Distance from our own.

O blind to each indulgent Aim,
 Of Pow'r supremely wise,
Who fancy Happiness in ought
 The Hand of Heav'n denies!   40

Vain is alike the Joy we seek,
 And vain what we possess,
Unless harmonious Reason tunes
 The Passions into Peace.

To temper'd Wishes, just Desires   45
 Is Happiness confin'd,
And deaf to Folly's Call, attends
 The Music of the Mind.

On a WATCH [2]

While this gay Toy attracts thy Sight,
 Thy Reason let it warn;
And seize, my Dear, that rapid Time
 That never must return.

If idly lost, no Art or Care   5
 The Blessing can restore:
And Heavn' exacts a strict Account
 For ev'ry mis-spent Hour.

Short is our longest Day of Life,
 And soon its Prospects end: 10
Yet on that Day's uncertain Date
 Eternal Years depend.

Yet equal to our Being's Aim
 The Space to Virtue giv'n:
And ev'ry Minute well improv'd   15
 Secures an Age in Heav'n.

[Untitled]

While Night in solemn Shade invests the Pole,
And calm Reflexion soothes the pensive Soul;
While Reason undisturb'd asserts her Sway,
And Life's deceitful Colours fade away:
To Thee! all-conscious Presence! I devote   5
This peaceful Interval of sober Thought.
Here all my better Faculties confine,
And be this Hour of sacred Silence thine.
    If by the Day's illusive Scenes misled,
My erring Soul from Virtue's Path has stray'd: 10
Snar'd by Example, or by Passion warm'd,
Some false Delight my giddy Sense has charm'd,
My calmer Thoughts the wretched Choice reprove,
And my best Hopes are center'd in thy Love.
Depriv'd of this, can Life one Joy afford!   15
It's utmost Boast a vain unmeaning Word.
    But ah! how oft' my lawless Passions rove,
And break those awful Precepts I approve!
Pursue the fatal Impulse I abhor,
And violate the Virtue I adore!   20
Oft' when thy better Spirit's guardian Care
Warn'd my fond Soul to shun the tempting Snare,
My stubborn Will his gentle Aid represt,
And check'd the rising Goodness in my Breast,
Mad with vain Hopes, or urg'd by false Desires,   25
Still'd his soft Voice, and quench'd his sacred Fires.
    With Grief opprest, and prostrate in the Dust,
Should'st thou condemn, I own the Sentence just.
But oh thy softer Titles let me claim,
And plead my Cause by *Mercy*'s gentle Name.   30
Mercy, that wipes the penitential Tear,
And dissipates the Horrors of Despair:
From rig'rous *Justice* steals the vengeful Hour;
Softens the dreadful Attribute of Power;
Disarms the Wrath of an offended God,   35
And seals my Pardon in a *Saviour*'s Blood.
    All pow'rful Grace, exert thy gentle Sway,

And teach my rebel Passions to obey:
Lest lurking Folly with insidious Art
Regain my volatile inconstant Heart.   40
Shall ev'ry high Resolve Devotion frames,
Be only lifeless Sounds and specious Names?
Oh rather while thy Hopes and Fears controul,
In this still Hour each Motion of my Soul,
Secure it's Safety by a sudden Doom,   45
And be the soft Retreat of Sleep my Tomb.
Calm let me slumber in that dark Repose,
'Till the last Morn it's orient Beam disclose:
Then, when the great Archangel's potent Sound,
Shall echo thro' Creation's ample Round,   50
Wak'd from the Sleep of Death, with Joy survey
The op'ning Splendors of eternal Day.

CATHERINE TALBOT
(1721–1770)

Catherine Talbot was a poet, essayist, and letter writer. Her father, an Anglican bishop, died a few months before her birth. She and her mother lived in the household of Thomas Secker, who became Archbishop of Canterbury. Secker guided Catherine's education which centered on the Bible and languages. In 1741 she met Elizabeth Carter, who became her intimate friend. Moving in the intellectual and high Anglican society of Secker's home, she became acquainted with the well-known Bluestocking, Elizabeth Montagu, as well as with such literary men as Samuel Johnson and Samuel Richardson. Richardson discussed the creation of his novel *Sir Charles Grandison* with Talbot and Elizabeth Carter and adopted some of their suggestions. Talbot's delicate health prevented her from continuous literary work, but she encouraged Elizabeth Carter to translate the works of Epictetus and wrote her own essays, "occasional thoughts," and a few poems when her strength allowed. Despite the urging of friends, who thought highly of her abilities, she did not publish her works during her lifetime, although she contributed an essay to Samuel Johnson's *Rambler* (No. 30). On Secker's death in 1768, she and her mother inherited £13,000, a sizeable fortune which allowed them to set up their own home in London's Lower Grosvenor Square. She died of cancer at forty-nine, and her mother entrusted Elizabeth Carter with her manuscripts.

In 1770 Carter published, at her own expense, Miss Talbot's *Reflections on the Seven Days of the Week*, a work which ran to ten editions in fifteen years. Also published after her death were Talbot's works in two volumes, an undertaking begun by Elizabeth Carter and finished by Carter's nephew Montagu Pennington. These volumes contain her poems, essays, imitations of Ossian, a fairy tale, prose pastorals, and allegories. Talbot's letters to Elizabeth Carter, which show her delightfully informal side, were published separately in four volumes in 1809.

EDITION USED: *The Works of Miss Catharine Talbot*, 8th ed. (London, 1812).

ALLEGORY 1
Life Compared to a Play

IF I was not quite sick of the number of stupid dreams, which have been writ in imitation of those excellent ones published in the Spectators, Tatlers, and some later periodical papers, I should be exceedingly tempted to fall into some allegorical slumbers. After this declaration, I know not why I may not actually do it; since I see people in a hundred

223

other instances, seem to imagine that censuring any thing violently, is amply sufficient to excuse their being guilty of it.

Suppose me then composed in my easy chair, after having long meditated on that old and threadbare comparison of human Life to a Play. To this, my imagination furnishes abundance of scenery; and the train of my thoughts go on just as well, after my eyes are closed, as it did before.

As I have yet but a very inconsiderable part in the performance, I have leisure enough to stand between the scenes, and to amuse myself with various speculations. Fortunately for me, I am placed near a person, who can give me sufficient information of the whole matter; since indeed this venerable person is no other, than the originally intended directress of the theatre, *Wisdom* by name: but being of a temper above entering into all the little disputes of the actors, she has suffered her place to be usurped by a multitude of pretenders, who mix the vilest of farces, and the absurdest of tragedies, with the noblest drama in the world.

These destructive interlopers were busily instructing all the actors, as they appeared upon the stage, and indeed one might easily see the effects of their teaching. Scarce one in fifty repeated a single line with a natural and unaffected air. Every feature was distorted by grimace: many a good sentiment *outrée*, by the emphasis with which it was pronounced.

Would it not put one quite out of patience, said my neighbour, to see that fellow there, so entirely spoil one of the finest passages in the play, by turning it into a mere rant? Is there any bearing that man, who pretending to act the lover, puts on all the airs of a madman? Why Sir, do you think that graceful figure, that sense, and all those advantages you were drest with, in order to do honour to my company, were given you, only that you might walk about the stage, sighing and exclaiming? Pray let me cast an eye upon your part.—Look ye, are here any of those soliloquies that you are every moment putting in?—Why, here is not a single word of misery, death, torment—The lover waking out of his reverie, pointed to a prompter that stood at a little distance, when *Wisdom* perceived it to be busy *Imagination*. She only, with an air of compassion, drew the poor youth to her side of the stage, and begged he would keep out of the hearing of so bad a director.

The next, we happened to attend to, was a young woman, of a most amiable figure, who stood pretty near us, but the good-nature in her countenance was mixed with a kind of haughty disdain, whenever she turned towards *Imagination*, that did not absolutely please me. I remarked upon it to my friend, and we jointly observed her stealing leisure from her part, to look over the whole scheme of the Drama. That actress, says she, has a most charming genius, but she too has a *Travers* in it. Because she has seen some love scenes, in the play, ridiculously acted, and heard them censured by those, whose judgment she respects, and especially because she is very justly displeased with all the bombast stuff, *Imagination* puts into them, she will, against her senses believe, there is scarce a single line about it, in the whole Drama: and there you may see her striking out for spurious, passages that have warmed the noblest hearts with generous sentiments, and gained a just applause from Socrates and Plato themselves: two of the finest actors I ever had. This is, however, an error on the right side. Happy for you, young actress, if you never fall into a worse. She may indeed miss saying an agreeable thing, but she never will say an absurd one.

Look yonder, and you will see more dangerous, and more ridiculous mistakes. That group of young actors, just entering on the stage, who cannot possibly have beheld more than half a scene, pretend already in a decisive way, to give their judgment of the whole. They do not so much as wait for their cue (which years and discretion ought to give them) but thrust forward into the very middle of the action. Some of them, displeased with the decorations of their part of the theatre, are busied in hurrying the tinsel ornaments, from the other corners of it, where they were much more becomingly placed. That man yonder, who ought to be acting the part of a hero, is so taken up with adjusting his dress, and that of his companions, that he never once seems to think of the green-room, where all these robes must soon be laid aside.

Look yonder, look yonder! This is a pitiable sight indeed. Behold that woman exquisitely handsome still, though much past the bloom of youth, and formed to shine in any part, but so unhappily attached to that she has just left, that her head is absolutely turned behind her: so unwilling is she to lose sight of her beloved gaieties.

In another place you may see persons, who, sensible that the splendid dresses of the theatre are only lent them, for a time, disdain, with a sullen ill-judged pride, to put them on at all, and so disgrace the parts that were allotted them for their own advantage.

Alas! what a different prompter has that actor got! He was designed to represent a character of generosity, and, for that purpose, furnished with a large treasure of counters, which it was his business to dispose of in the most graceful manner, to those actors engaged in the same scene with him. Instead of this, that old fellow, *Interest*, who stands at his elbow, has prompted him to put the whole bag into his pocket, as if the counters themselves were of real value: whereas the moment he sets his foot off the stage, or is hurried down, through some of those trap-doors, that are every moment opening round him, these tinsel pieces are no longer current. To conceal, in some measure, the falseness of this behaviour, he is forced to leave out a hundred fine passages, intended to grace his character, and to occasion unnumbered chasms, and inconsistencies, which not only make him hissed, but the very scheme of the Drama murmured at. Yet still he persists: and see! just now, when he ought to be gracefully treading the stage with a superior air; he is stooping down to pick up some more counters that happen to be fallen upon the dirty floor, made dirty on purpose for the disgrace of those who chuse to grovel there.

You can scarce have an idea, added my instructress, how infinitely the harmony of the whole piece is interrupted, by the misuse which these wrong-headed actors make of its mere decorations. The part you have to act, child, is a very small one. But remember, it is infinitely superior to every such attachment. Fix your attention upon its meaning; not its ornaments. Let your manner be just, and unaffected; your air cheerful and disengaged. Never pretend to look beyond the present page: and above all, trust the great Author of the Drama, with his own glorious work: and never think to mend what is above your understanding, by minute criticisms, that are below it.

ALLEGORY 2

The Danger of Indulgence of the Imagination

METHOUGHT as I was sitting at work, a young woman came into the room, clothed in a loose green garment. Her long hair fell in ringlets upon her shoulders: her head was crowned with roses and myrtles. A prodigious sweetness appeared in her countenance, and notwithstanding the irregularity of her features, and a certain wildness in her eyes, she seemed to me the most agreeable person I had ever beheld.

When she was entered, she presented me with a little green branch, upon which was a small sort of nut enclosed in a hard black shell, which she said was both wholesome and delicious, and bid me follow her, and not be afraid, for she was going to make me happy.

I did as she commanded me, and immediately a chariot descended and took us up. It was made of the richest materials, and drawn by four milk-white turtles. Whilst we were hurried with a rapid motion, over vast oceans, boundless plains, and barren desarts, she told me, that her name was *Imagination*; that she was carrying me to Parnassus, where she herself lived.

I had scarce time to thank her before we arrived at the top of a very high mountain, covered with very thick woods. Here we alighted; and my guide taking me by the hand, we passed through several beautiful groves of myrtle, bays, and laurel, separated from one another by little green alleys, enamelled with the finest flowers. Nothing was to be heard but the rustling of leaves, the humming of bees, the warbling of birds, and the purling of streams: and in short, this spot seemed to be a Paradise.

After wandering some time in this delightful place, we came to a long grasswalk; at the further end of which, in a bower of jassamins and woodbines strewed with flowers, sat a woman of a middle age, but of a pleasing countenance. Her hair was finely braided: and she wore a habit of changeable silk.

When we approached her she was wearing nets of the finest silk, which she immediately threw down, and embraced me. I was surprized at so much civility from a stranger; which she perceiving, bid me not wonder at the kindness she showed for me, at first sight, since, besides my being in the company of that lady, (pointing to *Imagination*) which was recommendation enough, my own person would entitle me to the favour of all who saw me: but, added she, you have had a long walk, and want rest; come and sit down in my bower.

Though this offer would, at another time, have been very acceptable to me, yet so great was my desire of seeing the Muses, that I begged to be excused, and to have permission to pursue my journey. Being informed by *Imagination* where we were going, she commended my laudable curiosity, and said, she would accompany us. As we went along, she told me her name was *Good Will*, and that she was a great friend to the Muses, and to the lady who brought me hither, whom she had brought up from a child: and had saved her from being carried away by *Severity* and *Ill-Humour*, her inveterate enemies.

When she had done speaking, we arrived at the happy place I had so much wished to see. It was a little circular opening, at the upper end of which sat, on a throne of the most fragrant flowers, a young man in a flame-coloured garment, of a noble, but haughty countenance. He was crowned with laurel, and held a harp in his hand. Round him sat nine beautiful young women, who all played upon musical instruments. These, *Imagination* told me, were *Apollo* and the *Muses*. But above all the rest, there were three that I most admired, and who seemed fondest of me.

One of these was clothed in a loose and careless manner; she was reposed on a bank of flowers, and sung with a sweeter voice than any of the others. The garment of the second was put on with the greatest care and exactness, and richly embroidered with the gayest colours, but it did not seem to fit her. But it was the third whom I most admired. She was crowned with roses and a variety of other flowers. She played upon all the instruments, and never staid five minutes in a place.

Just as I was going to sit down to a fine repast, which they had prepared for me of the fruits of the mountain, we saw two grave-looking men advancing towards us. Immediately *Imagination* shrieked out and *Good-Will* said she had great reason, for those were *Severity* and *Ill-Humour*, who had like to have run away with her when but a child, as she had told me before. You too, added she, may be in danger, therefore come into the midst of us.

I did so: and by this time the two men were come up. One of them was completely armed, and held a mirror in his hand. The other wore a long robe, and held, in one hand, a mariner's compass, and in the other, a lanthorn. They soon pierced to the center of our little troop: and the first, with much ado, at length forced me from the only two, who still held out against them, and made me hearken to the other, who bid me not be afraid, and told me, though I might be prejudiced against him and his companion, by those I had lately been with, yet they had a greater desire of my happiness, and would do more towards it. But, said he, if you have eat any of that fruit, which you have in your hand, of which the real name is *Obstinacy*, all I can say will be ineffectual.

I assured him, I had not tasted this fatal fruit. He said he was very glad of it, and bid me throw it down and follow him, which I did, till by a shorter way, we came to the brow of the mountain. When we were there, he told me, the only way to deliver myself from the danger I was then in, was to leap down into the plain below. As the mountain seemed very steep, and the plain very barren, I could neither persuade myself to obey, nor had I courage to disobey him.

I thus stood wavering for some time, till the man in armour pushed me down, as Mentor did Telemachus. When I was recovered from the first shock of my fall, how great was my surprize to find this paradise of the world, this delightful mountain, was raised to that prodigious height, by mere empty clouds.

After they had given me some time to wonder, he, who held the lanthorn in his hand, told me that the place before me was the Mount of *Folly*. That *Imagination* was *Romance*, *Good-Will* was *Flattery*, *Apollo* was *Bombast*, That the two false Muses who tried most to keep me from coming with them, were *Self-Conceit* and *Idleness*: that the others were *Inconstancy*, *False-Taste*, *Ignorance*, and *Affectation* her daughter, *Enthusiasm* of Poetry, *Credulity* a great promoter of their despotic dominion, and *Fantasticalness*, who took as many hearts as any of the rest.

I thanked him for this information, and told him, that it would almost equal the joy of my deliverance, to know the names of my deliverers. He told me his own was *Good-Advice*, and his companion's *Good-Sense* his brother, and born at the same time. He added, that if I liked their company, they would, after having shewn me the many thousand wretches, whom my false friends had betrayed, conduct me to the abode of *Application* and *Perseverance*, the parents of all the virtues.

I told him that nothing could afford me a more sensible pleasure. Then, said he, prepare yourself for a scene of horror: and immediately, with the help of his brother, he lifted up the mountain, and discovered to my sight a dark and hollow vale, where under the shade of cypress and yew, lay in the utmost misery, multitudes of unhappy mortals, mostly young women, run away with by *Romance*. When I had left this dreadful spot, and the mountain was closed upon them, just as I was going to be good and happy, some unhappy accident awakened me.

[Untitled]

Awake my Laura, break the silken chain,
Awake my Friend, to hours unsoil'd by pain:
Awake to peaceful joys and thought refin'd,
Youth's cheerful morn, and Virtue's vigorous mind:
Wake to all joys, fair friendship can bestow,   5
All that from health, and prosp'rous fortune flow.
    Still dost thou sleep? awake, imprudent fair,
    Few hours has life, and few of those can spare.

Forsake thy drowsy couch, and sprightly rise
While yet fresh morning streaks the ruddy skies: 10
While yet the birds their early mattins sing,
And all around us blooming as the spring.

Ere sultry Phœbus with his scorching ray
Has drank the dew-drops from their mansion gay,
Scorch'd ev'ry flow'r, embrown'd each drooping green,   15
Pall'd the pure air, and chas'd the pleasing scene.
    Still dost thou sleep? O rise, imprudent fair,
    Few hours has life, nor of those few can spare.*

    But this, perhaps, was but a summer song,
And winter nights are dark, and cold and long: 20
Weak reason that, for sleeping past the morn
Yet urg'd by sloth, and by indulgence born.
Oh rather haste to rise, my slumb'ring friend,
While feeble suns their scanty influence lend;
While cheerful day-light yet adorns the skies,   25
Awake, my Friend! my Laura haste to rise.
For soon the uncertain short-liv'd day shall fail,
And soon shall night extend her sooty veil*:
Blank nature fades, black shades and phantoms drear
Haunt the sick eye, and fill the court of fear.   30
    O therefore sleep no more, imprudent fair,
    Few hours has day, few days the circling year,
    Few years has life, and few of these can spare.

    Think of the task those hours have yet in view,
Reason to arm, and passion to subdue;   35
While life's fair calm, and flatt'ring moments last,
To fence your mind against the stormy blast:
Early to hoard blest Wisdom's peace-fraught store,
Ere yet your bark forsakes the friendly shore,
And the winds whistle, and the billows roar.   40

---

*For is there aught in sleep can charm the wise?
To lie in dull oblivion, losing half
The fleeting moments of too short a life!

THOMAS SUMMER.

*"The night cometh when no man can work"

JOHN 9.4

Imperfect beings! weakly arm'd to bear
Pleasure's soft wiles, or sorrow's open war:
Alternate shocks from diff'rent sides to feel,
Now to subdue the heart, and now to steel:
Yet fram'd with high aspirings, strong desires,   45
How mad th' attempt to quench celestial fires!
Still to perfection tends the restless mind,
And happiness its bright reward assign'd.
And shall dull sloth obscure the Heav'n beam'd ray ⎫
That guides our passage to the realms of day,   ⎬   50
Cheers the faint heart, and points the dubious way! ⎭
Not weakly arm'd, if ever on our guard,
Nor to the worst unequal if prepar'd:
Not unsurmountable the task, if lov'd,
Nor short the time, if ev'ry hour improv'd.   55
O rouse thee then, nor shun the glorious strife,
Extend, improve, enjoy thy hours of life:
Assert thy reason, animate thy heart,
And act thro' life's short scene the useful part:
Then sleep in peace, by gentlest mem'ry crown'd,   60
Till time's vast year hast fill'd its perfect round.

Elegy

O Form'd for boundless bliss! Immortal soul,
    Why dost thou prompt the melancholy sigh
While evening shades disclose the glowing pole,
    And silver moon-beams tremble o'er the sky.

These glowing stars shall fade, this moon shall fall,   5
    This transitory sky shall melt away,
Whilst thou triumphantly surviving all
    Shalt glad expatiate in eternal day.

Sickens the mind with longings vainly great,
    To trace mysterious wisdom's secret ways,   10

While chain'd and bound in this ignoble state,
      Humbly it breaths sincere, imperfect praise!

Or glows the beating heart with sacred fires,
      And longs to mingle in the worlds of love?
Or, foolish trembler, feeds its fond desires   15
      Of earthly good? or dreads life's ill to prove?

Back does it trace the flight of former years,
      The friends lamented, and the pleasures past?
Or wing'd with forecast vain, and impious fears,
      Presumptuous to the cloud hid future haste;   20

Hence, far begone, ye fancy-folded pains,
      Peace, trembling heart, be ev'ry sigh supprest:
Wisdom supreme, eternal goodness reigns,
      Thus far is sure: to Heav'n resign the rest*.

Moral Stanzas

1

Welcome the real state of things
          Ideal world adieu,
Where clouds pil'd up by fancy's hand
          Hang lou'ring o'er each view.

2

Here the gay sunshine of content   5
          Shall gild each humble scene:
And life steal on with gentle pace,
          Beneath a sky serene.

---

*Thus far was right; The rest belongs to Heaven.

                                        POPE
                                        Prol. to the Sat.

3

Hesperian trees amidst my grove
    I ask not to behold,
Since ev'n from Ovid's song I know,
    That dragons guard the gold.

4

Nor would I have the phœnix build
    In my poor elms his nest,
For where shall odorous gums be found
    To treat the beauteous guest?

5

Henceforth no pleasure I desire
    In any wild extreme,
Such as should lull the captiv'd mind
    In a bewitching dream.

6

Friendship I ask, without caprice,
    When faults are over-seen:
Errors on both sides mix'd with truth
    And kind good-will between.

7

Health, that may best its value prove,
    By slight returns of pain:
Amusements to enliven life,
    Crosses to prove it vain.

8

Thus would I pass my hours away,
    Extracting good from all:
Till time shall from my sliding feet
    Push this uncertain ball.

JANE COLLIER

(1709?–1754?)

A satirist, Jane Collier was born in Salisbury to Arthur and Margaret Collier. Her father, the rector of Langford Magna and a philosopher, was forced by his debts to sell his property, leaving Jane and her brother and sister, Arthur and Margaret, to fend for themselves. Little is known about Collier, including the exact dates of her birth and death. She and her sister shared a life marked by struggle and poverty. They became friends of Sarah Fielding, whose brother, the novelist Henry Fielding, befriended the family after their father died. The son Arthur, following in his father's feckless footsteps, saddled Fielding with a £400 debt.

The two Collier sisters and Sarah Fielding also became friends with another famous eighteenth-century novelist, Samuel Richardson. Jane Collier offered Richardson suggestions about his novel *Clarissa*, and he valued her intellect so much that he listed her among the thirty-six examples of superior women that he sent to a friend in 1750. A year after publishing *An Essay on the Art of Ingeniously Tormenting* (1753) excerpted here, Collier and Sarah Fielding wrote *The Cry: A New Dramatic Fable* (1754), a prose work that satirized the public's taste for scandal and sensationalism. Soon after publishing *The Cry*, it appears that Collier died—still in her forties and in poverty.

EDITION USED: *An Essay on the Art of Ingeniously Tormenting* (London, 1753).

FROM AN ESSAY ON THE ART OF TORMENTING

ENGLAND HAS ever been allowed to excel most other nations in her improvements of arts and sciences, although she seldom claims to herself the merit of invention: to her improvements also are many of her neighbours indebted, for the exercise of some of their most useful arts.

'Tis not the benefit that may arise to the few from any invention, but its general utility, which ought to make such invention of universal estimation. Had the art of navigation gone no higher than to direct the course of a small boat by oars, the Low Countries only could have been the better for it. Again, should the inhabitants of Lapland invent the most convenient method for warming their houses by stoves, bringing them, by their improvements, to the utmost perfection; yet could not those who live within the Tropics receive the least benefit from such their improvements; any more than the Laplanders could, from the invention of fans, umbrella's, and cooling grottos.

But as the science recommended in this short essay will be liable to no such exceptions; being, we presume, adapted to the circumstances, genius, and capacity, of every nation under heaven, why should I doubt of that deserved fame, generally given to those

> *Inventas aut qui vitam excoluere per artes,*
> *Quique fui memores alios fecere merendo?*
> [Who graced their age with new invented art;
> Those who to worth their bounty did extend]
>
> VIRG. 1. 6. v. 663.

Unless, indeed, I should be told, that mankind are already too great adepts in this art, to need any farther instructions.

May I hope that my dear countrymen will pardon me for presuming (by the very publication of these rules) that they are not already absolutely perfect in this our art? Or at least, that they may not always have an ingenious Torment ready at hand to inflict?

By the common run of servants, it might have been presumed, that Dean Swift's instructions to them were unnecessary; but I dare believe no one ever read over that ingenious work, without finding there some inventions for idleness, carelessness, and ill-behaviour, which had never happened within his own experience.

Although I do not suppose mankind in general to be thorough proficients in this our art; yet wrong not my judgment so much, gentle reader, as to imagine, that I would write *institutes* of any science, to those who are unqualified for its practice, or do not shew some genius in themselves towards it. Should you observe in one child a delight of drawing, in another a turn towards music, would you not do your utmost to assist their genius, and to further their attempts? 'Tis the great progress that I have observed to be already made in this our pleasant art, and the various attempts that I daily see towards bringing it to perfection, that encouraged me to offer this my poor assistance.

One requisite for approbation I confess, is wanting in this work; for, alas! I fear it will contain nothing new. But what is wanting in novelty, shall be made up in utility; for, although I may not be able to shew one new and untried method of plagueing, teazing, or tormenting; yet will it not be a very great help to any one, to have all the best and most approved methods collected together, in one small pocket volume? Did I promise a new set of rules, then, whatever was not mine, might be claim'd by its proper owner; and, like the jay in the fable, I should justly be stripped of my borrowed plumes: but, as I declare myself only an humble collector, I doubt not, but every one, who has practised, or who in writing has described, an ingenious Torment, will thank me for putting it into this my curious collection.

That a love to this science is implanted in our natures, or early inculcated, is very evident, from the delight many children take in teazing and tormenting little dogs, cats, squirrels, or any other harmless animal, that they get into their power.

This love of Tormenting may be said to have one thing in common with what, some writers affirm, belongs to the true love of virtue; namely, that it is exercised for its own sake, and no other: For, can there be a clearer proof, that, for its own sake alone, this art of Tormenting is practised, than that it never did, nor ever can, answer any other end? I know that the most expert practitioners deny this; and frequently declare, when they whip, cut, and slash, the body, or when they teaze, vex, and torment, the mind, that 'tis done for the good of the person that suffers. Let the vulgar believe this if they will; but I, and my good pupils, understand things better; and, while we can enjoy the high pleasure of Tormenting, it matters not what the objects of our power either feel, think, or believe.

With what contempt may we, adepts in this science, look down on the tyrants of old! On Nero, Caligula, Phalaris, and all such paltry pretenders to our art! Their inventions ending in death, freed the sufferer from any farther Torments; or, if they extended only to broken bones, and bodily wounds, they were such as the skill of the surgeon could rectify, or heal: But where is the hand can cure the wounds of unkindness, which our ingenious artists inflict?

The practice of tormenting the body is not now, indeed, much allowed, except in some particular countries, where slavery and ignorance subsist: but let us not, my dear countrymen, regret the loss of that trifling branch of our power, since we are at full liberty to exercise ourselves in that much higher pleasure, the tormenting the mind. Nay, the very laws themselves, although they restrain us from being too free with our bastinado, pay so much regard to this our strong desire of Tormenting, that, in some instances, they give us the fairest opportunities we could wish, of legally indulging ourselves in this pleasant sport.

To make myself clearly understood, examine the case, as it stands (if I mistake not) between the debtor and creditor.

If a person owes me a thousand pounds (which perhaps, too, may be my all), and has an estate of yearly that value, he may, if he pleases, and has a mind to plague, distress, and vex me, refuse paying me my money. Arrest him, then, cry you. — If he be not in parliament, I do — He gives bail; and, with my own money, works me through all the quirks of the law. — At last (if he be of the true blood of those my best disciples, who would hang themselves to spite their neighbours) he retires into the liberties of the Fleet, or King's-bench; lives at his ease, and laughs at me and my family, who are starving. However, as some inconveniences attend such a proceeding, this method of plaguing a creditor is not very often practised.

But on the other hand, how can I be thankful enough to our good laws, for indulging me in the pleasure of persecuting and tormenting a man who is indebted to me, and who does not want the Will, but the Power, to pay me!

As soon as I perceive this to be the case, I instantly throw him in gaol, and there I keep him to pine away his life in want and misery. — How will my pleasure be increased, if he should be a man in any business or profession! For I then rob him of all probable means of escaping my power. It may be objected, perhaps, that in this last instance I act imprudently; that I defeat my own ends, and am myself the means of my losing my whole money. — How ignorant of the true joys of Tormenting is such an objector! You mistake greatly, my friend, if you think I defeat my own ends; — for my ends are to plague and torment, not only a fellow-creature, but a fellow-christian. — And are there not instances enough of this kind of practice, to make us fairly suppose, that the value of one thousand, or ten thousand pounds, is nothing, compared to the excessive delight of Tormenting?

But let me raise this joyous picture a little higher. — Let me suppose, that this wretched man, now pining in a prison, has a wife and children, whom he fondly loves — Must not my pleasure be doubled and trebled by the consideration, that his children are starving; that his wife is in the same condition, oppressed also with unspeakable anguish for not being able to give her helpless infants any relief? — Suppose, too, that the husband, with the reflexion of all this, and his own incapacity to help them, should be driven to distraction! Would not this exceed the most malicious transports of revenge ever exercised by an antient or modern tyrant?

If there are some odd sort of people, who have no great relish for this kind of happiness, which I have here attempted to describe; yet let them not hastily condemn it, as unnatural: for I appeal to the experience of mankind; and ask—Whether there is any one who has not heard of, at least, one instance of distress, near as high as the scene before described? And that the love of Tormenting must have been the sole motive to a creditor's acting in such a manner, when his debtor could not pay him, is evident, from the impossibility of reasonably assigning any other cause.

One strong objection, I know, will be made against my whole design, by people of weak consciences; which is, that every rule I shall lay down will be exactly opposite to the doctrine of Christianity. Greatly, indeed, in a Christian country, should I fear the force of such an objection, could I perceive, that any one vice was refrained from on that account only. Both Theft and Murder are forbidden by God himself: yet can any one say, that our lives and properties would be in the least secure, were it not for the penal laws of our country? Who is there, that having received a blow on one cheek, will turn the other, while revenge can be had from the law of assault and battery? Are there any who exercise the virtues of patience and forgiveness, if they can have legal means of punishing the aggressor, and revenging themselves tenfold on the person who gives them the most slight offence? Innumerable are the instances that could be given to shew, that the doctrine of the Gospel has very little influence upon the practice of its *followers*; unless it be on a few obscure people, that *nobody knows*. The foregoing formidable objection, therefore, we hope, is pretty well got over, except with the *obscure few* above-mentioned.

But as I would willingly remove every the least shadow of an objection that I am acquainted with, I must take notice of one which was made by a person very zealous indeed for our cause; but who feared, he said, that people would not bear publicly to avow their love of Tormenting, and their disregard of that very religion which they profess. This, at first, almost stagger'd me, and I was going to throw by my work, till I recollected several books (some too written by divines) that had been extremely well received, although they struck at the very foundation of our religion. These precedents are surely sufficient to make me depend upon coming off with impunity, let me publish what I will, except a libel against any great man. For to abuse Chrift himself is not, at present, esteem'd so high an offence, as to abuse one of his followers; or, rather, one of his Abusers; for such may we term all those, who, without observing his laws, call themselves after his name.

It has been already observed, that the torments of the body are not much allowed in civilized nations: but yet, under the notion of punishments for faults, such as whipping and picketing amongst the soldiers; with some sorts of curious marine discipline, as the cat-of-nine-tails, keel-hawling, and the like; a man may pick out some excellent fun; for if he will now-and-then inflict those punishments on the good, which were intended for the chastisement and amendment of the bad, he will not only work the flesh, but vex the spirit, of an ingenuous youth; as nothing can be more grating to a liberal mind, than to be so unworthily treated.

If I should be so happy, my good pupils, by these my hearty endeav-ours, as to instruct you thoroughly in the ingenious art of plaguing and tormenting the mind, you will have also more power over the body than you are at first aware of. You may take the Jew's forfeit of a pound of flesh, without incurring the imputation of barbarity which was cast on him for that diverting joke. He was a mere mongrel at Tormenting, to think of cutting it off with a knife; no—your true delicate way is to waste it off by degrees. —For has not every creditor (by the pleasant assistance of a prison) the legal power of taking ten or twenty pounds of Christian flesh, in forfeit of his bond?

However, without such violent measures, you may have frequent opportunities (by teazing and tormenting) of getting out of your friends a good pretty picking. But be very careful daily to observe, whether your patient continues in good health, and is fat and well-liken: if so, you may be almost certain, that your whole labour is thrown away. As soon, therefore, as you perceive this to be the case, you must (to speak in the phrase of surgeons, when they hack and hue a human body) immediately choose another Subject.

CHAPTER 3

To Parents

IT HAS been said, that the state of children when very young, with regard to their parents, is like the state of a blind man, in the hands of a friend who has the use of his eyes. Children want both protection from harms, and direction in every step they are to take. They are perfectly helpless, and incapable of supporting themselves, even one day, without a parental care over them; and where that care is exerted for their benefit, there they undoubtedly owe the highest duty and regard imaginable.

The most unlimited power was ever given to parents over their children: and in antient Rome, it was said to extend to life and death. This most probably must arise from a knowlege of the great natural affection and tenderness, that is in almost every living creature towards its offspring; and to such parents as possess this true affection, I direct not my precepts; for where real love and affection towards the children (which must exert itself for their good) is in the heart, all my instructions will be thrown away. But as for you, O ye parents, who are willing to learn, and who intend to make a proper use of your power, let me remind you, that even in this age you are invested, both by law and custom, with the strongest outward and visible power I know of in this land. Purchased slaves are not allowed: your servants if you use them ill may leave you, or can, in many cases, have better redress against you from the magistrate, than you can procure against them. Your children have nobody to fly to, nobody even to complain to! and as it is in your power to take care of these, or cruelly to neglect them; their very lives, whilst infants, are still, in a manner, at your disposal. It is at your own option to feed them on bread and water, the hard fare appointed for criminals, or to pamper them (if you can afford it) with all the dainties of the land. The reins of restraint are yours. The rod of correction is given into your hands: who shall set bounds to your strokes?

These my rules — which positively forbid, not only all manual correction, but every the least degree of restraint or contradiction, to the infant's wayward will, if you intend to breed them up properly, so as to be a torment to themselves if they live, and a plague to all your acquaintance.

Severity to children, when carried to excess, may, indeed, render the lives of those children very miserable; and I allow it to be *one* method of Tormenting: but, in my opinion, by no means the best.

Yet, if you intend to follow this method, let me give you one necessary piece of advice: which is, never to strike or whip a child, but when you are angry, and in a violent passion with that child; nor ever let this correction come for lying, obstinacy, or disobedience, in the child, but for having torn or dirted her white frock, if it be a girl; or for having accidentally broke a china cup at play; or any such trifling offence. But there is one strong reason still remains against the least degree of general severity; which is, the regard you ought to have for your own reputation. If your intention be to indulge yourself, without any regard to your child's welfare, why should you take a method by which you may incur the censure of cruelty, when you can more effectually answer your own purpose, and be called kind? Therefore, by all means, humour every child you have to the highest degree, till they attain the age of five or six years; by which time you will be able to judge, whether your indulgence has had a proper effect. If you see them possessed with a due degree of obstinacy, wilfulness, perverseness, and ill-humour; if you find, that the passions of pride, cruelty, malice, and envy, have, like rank weeds, flourished, for want of rooting up, and overwhelmed every spark of goodness in the mind; then may you (as my true disciples) rejoice in having so far done your duty by them, as to have laid the proper foundation for their becoming no small adepts in this our useful science.

If, notwithstanding the uncontroulled liscense you have given to your children, of indulging every rising passion, one of them should chance to be endued with such a mildness of disposition, and so much in-bred good-nature, as to have grown up gentle, against your consent; then, to that child, immediately change your method; grow morose and severe; make favourites of all the rest, and encourage them to teaze and insult it, till you have quite broke its spirit, and got the better of its natural placidness of disposition, so as to turn it into a dejected mope.

But take another view of this extreme indulgence to children; and it is hoped this picture will confirm you in such a practice.

Suppose your stock of children too large; and that, by your care for their support, you should be abridged of some of your own luxuries and pleasures. To make away with the troublesome and expensive brats, I allow, would be the desireable thing: but the question is, how to effect this without subjecting yourself to that punishment which the law has thought proper to affix to such sort of jokes. Whipping and starving, with some caution, might do the business: but, since a late execution for a fact of that kind may have given a precedent for the magistrates to examine into such affairs, you may, by these means, find your way to the gallows, if you are low enough for such a scrutiny into your conduct: and, if you are too high to have your actions punished, you may possibly be a little ill spoken of amongst your acquaintance. I think, therefore, it is best not to venture, either your neck, or your reputation, by such a proceeding; especially as you may effect the thing, full as well, by following the directions I have given, of holding no restraint over them.

Suffer them to climb, without contradiction, to heights from whence they may break their necks: let them eat every thing they like, and at all times; not refusing them the richest meats, and highest sawces, with as great a variety as possible; because even excess in one dish of plain meat cannot, as I have been told by physicians, do much harm. Suffer them to sit up as late as they please at night, and make hearty meat-suppers; and even in the middle of the night, if they call for it, don't refuse the poor things some victuals. By this means, nobody can say you starve your children: and if they should chance to die of a surfeit, or of an ill habit of body, contracted from such diet, so far will you be from censure, that your name will be recorded for a kind and indulgent parent. If any impertinent person should hint to you, that this manner of feeding your children was the high road to their destruction, you may answer, "That the poor people suffer their children to eat and drink what they please, not feeding them upon bread-pudden, milk and water, and such stuff, as the physicians advise; and (you may say) where do you see any thing more healthful, than the children of the poor?" Take my word for it, you may make this appeal without fear of contradiction; for often have I heard it made in company, and never yet did I hear it observed, that the poor, in truth, had not the hurtful things to give their children, which it is in the power of the rich to indulge them in; that the food of these healthy poor children generally is bread-and-cheese, plain bread, and little fat bacon, clear water, or some small-beer, hardly removed one degree from water itself; and not roast-meat, fish hashes, soups, &c. &c. But to return to my farther directions.

On no account miss that useful season of the year the summer; in which you may give your children as much fruit as they can cram down their throats: then be sure not to contradict the poor little things, if they should choose to play about, and overheat themselves, in the middle of the day; and afterwards should choose to cool their limbs, by sprawling about on the wet grass, after the dew is fallen. If they should chance, after all this, to outlive the month of September, without the worms, a fever, the small-pox, or a general corruption of blood, that no medicine can purify, you must wait the event of another summer. From having indulged them in all their humours, you have one chance more of losing them in sickness than those parents have, who controul them; which is, that it is not (you know) in the power of medicine to cure, when it is not in your power to get that medicine down the child's throat. On all considerations, therefore, I believe, we may venture to affirm, that letting children entirely alone to their own wills, without the least degree of restraint or contradiction, is the surest road to lead them to their own destruction.

If parents, in the foregoing process, should be able, with truth, to deny the motive I have assigned, can they, with equal truth, deny the probable consequence, here shewn, of such indulgence?

Supposing your child, or children, to outlive all these your kind indulgences, encourage them in all sorts of cruelty; first to flies and birds, then to dogs, cats, or any other animals, that come in their way. This will habituate them to that true hardness of heart, which is the foundation of our science.

So pleasant is the sport of Tormenting domestic animals under our protection, that a whole chapter of instructions for that purpose should have been inserted, had it not been already very well exemplified in Pompey the Little. And if my readers have the gift of imitation, they may, by many pleasant examples, becomes perfect in this practice.

Although I would have you inculcate the love of cruelty, yet, by no means, call it by its true name; but encourage them in the practice of it under the name of FUN. When they are well versed in this sport of Tormenting amongst animals, they may introduce it, under the aforesaid name, amongst their friends and acquaintance. It will equally answer in all stations; for how many hurt shins, bloody noses, broken heads, if not broken bones, has this sport caused at a country wake? and, in politer life, how many heavy hearts have retired from company, by the means of joke, repartee, and Fun?

And that this kind of FUN is allowed to be extremely diverting, appears, from its being so very common to hear people publicly declare, that they always laugh at mifchief.

If your children happen to have but weak understandings, upbraid them with every excellence you see abroad; and lament your own hard fate in being plagued with idiots. But,

If you see a rising genius in any child (especially if it be a girl), unless you can in some way turn it to your own profit, give that child no assistance nor encouragement; but browbeat all endeavours towards striking out of the common road.

When once your children are grown up to men or womens estate, let the very appearance of indulgence vanish; and, as soon as they are come to a relish of this world's enjoyment, restrain them with a heavy hand. Upbraid them, also, with your former kindness; lament that your past indulgence to them, when children, has made them ungrateful; and declare them to be the grief and torment of your old age.

As you never contradicted or rebuked them, when children, remember that you have in store a large quantity of contradiction and rebukes at their service; of both which be as lavish as possible, particularly of the latter, which will now be of no sort of service; especially if you bestow such rebukes on them before company, and in the roughest terms.

Study the tempers of your sons and daughters, to see what they most delight in; and, as you have an absolute restraining power, exercise it where it will be most strongly felt.

If gaiety and publick diversion are their delight, confine them constantly at home; or let them out with such restrictions as will damp all their joy. But if they have no immoderate love for such amusement, and could be as well contented at home, from the satisfaction they would take in doing their duty, let your chief point be to dress them out, and send them abroad, for your own honour and credit; and receive them with ill-humour when they come home. If their chief joy be in endeavouring, by their chearful conversation, to please and amuse you, put on such a rigid austerity, as shall make them afraid to open their lips before you; and with-hold from them the least appearance of pleasure or good-humour in yourself, for their readiness in all things to comply with your will.

Spare no expence in dress or equipage for them, provided their dispositions are such, that it will give them no pleasure: for how must an old Harlowe enjoy himself in loading a Clarissa with money, clothes, jewels, &c. whilst he knows, that all she wants from him, is kind looks, and kind words!

When your daughter comes to be old enough to marry, if she should happen to have fixed her affections on a real deserving young man, and you should be bent upon her giving her hand to one whose only merit is his riches, the behaviour of old Western to his daughter Sophia, in Tom Jones, will shew you how a fond father should treat a deserving child.

There is more difficulty in giving positive rules for the Tormenting children, than any other connexion whatever; as my pupils must have two points to carry: one is, the child's own discomfort; and the other is, the Use they are of in Tormenting all your friends and acquaintance. Should you follow the road of those parents, who hold a proper restraint, and keep a watchful eye, over their children, in order to prevent their hurting themselves; should you make that parent your example, who, by carefully watching every rising passion, accustoms the child (if not to subdue) at least to keep it within proper bounds; should you act in the manner of those parents, who, by cultivating and encouraging every good disposition in their children, breed them up with modesty and gentleness of mind; and who, by well-placed kindness and REAL indulgence, have inspired them with a grateful and affectionate regard towards themselves; children thus educated would, I confess, when grown up, in all probability, be more fitted to receive your Torments, than those bred up by my rules. But many contingencies might then arise to prevent the exercise of your power: as your own death, your son's going out in the world, or your daughter's marriage. I give it once more, therefore, as my advice, that you should leave such kind of education for those who have no relish for our sport; and that you pursue the method called INDULGENCE, which I have already marked out. This will infallibly make them miserable while infants; as common experience must shew you, that no children are so fretful, peevish, and uneasy, as those who are so indulged. And although you may, by this means, breed up a parcel of head-strong, hard-hearted cubs, who, when old enough, will defy your power; yet you may, in the mean time, amuse yourself with your servants, your acquaintance, and your friends, who may chance to be more fitted by nature, or education, for your purpose. You may go out of the world, also, with the pleasing reflexion, that you have left behind you a set of wolves, cats, and foxes, of your own educating; who will help to plague and torment all the rest of mankind.

The reason there is no chapter of instructions to children, how to plague their parents, we presume, is pretty obvious. First, because, when they are very young, they cannot read. It lies, therefore, upon you, O ye parents! to make them, in their infancy, both a plague to themselves, and all around them. In the next place, when they are grown old enough to profit by my instructions, they may find, in some of the succeeding chapters, most of the rules that could possibly be given them: which, it is hoped, they will be so kind as to practise on all those parents, who, by departing from my institutes, have given their children an affection-power over them: for such power will the children gain, if you turn your parental authority into an affectionate friendship towards them.

Could I be so happy as to prevail with you to follow my directions, no other instructions would hereafter be necessary. For ye must be sensible, O ye parents! how much it is in your power to form the minds of your children so as to inrol them under my list, or to guard their tender minds against my precepts, if Solomon was in the right when he said, *Train up your child*, &c.

LADY MARY WORTLEY MONTAGU

(1689–1762)

Essayist, poet, letter writer and journalist, Lady Mary Wortley Montagu was the eldest child of Evelyn Pierrepont (later Earl of Kingston, Marquess of Dorchester, and Duke of Kingston) and Lady Mary Fielding. Her mother died when she was very young, and Lady Mary and the three other Pierrepont children were raised by their energetic and forceful paternal grandmother. Mary supplemented her governess's conventional lessons by teaching herself Latin and reading extensively in her father's library, in which she was encouraged by her uncle, William Fielding, and Bishop Burnet. She later wrote of female education: "We are educated in the grossest ignorance, and no art omitted to stifle our natural reason."

Although Pierrepont was an absentee father, he was proud of Lady Mary's wit and beauty. His position enabled her to meet prominent writers such as Congreve, Steele, Addison, and Garth. Among her own close friends was Anne Montagu, whose brother, Edward Wortley Montagu, she married in 1712, overriding her father's vigorous objections to her suitor's rather ungenerous marriage settlement. The story of their on-again, off-again courtship and later marital discord is an object lesson in the problems besetting an eighteenth-century woman in courtship and marriage. A well-born and wealthy young woman all too often became simply a commodity in the marriage market.

Her husband's position with the government took Lady Mary and their infant son to London, where Lady Mary met and became close friends with the poets Alexander Pope and John Gay. In 1715, Lady Mary was stricken with smallpox, which ruined her beauty but which strengthened those inner resources of mind and wit for which she is known today. Montagu is credited with introducing into England the Turkish practice of smallpox inoculation. Her husband became ambassador to Turkey in 1716, and Lady Mary's residence there produced the lively and unconventional *Embassy Letters* (published posthumously, 1763) excerpted here. The Montagus returned to London in 1718 where she resumed her life in Court circles. She became renowned for her wit, met the celebrated French author Voltaire, gave literary advice to the poet Edward Young, acted as patron for her second cousin Henry Fielding, and became acquainted with Mary Astell, who urged her to publish her letters from Turkey. Her friendship with Pope, however, had deteriorated, perhaps because she had humorously rebuffed his affections, and she soon became the target of his scathing satire in the *Dunciad* (1729). She retaliated in her *Verses Addressed to the Imitator of . . . Horace* (1733), possibly a joint collaboration with Lord Hervey, but whose style, according to Robert Halsband (*Lord Hervey* [New York and Oxford, 1974]), "has a crude vitality and masculine robustness more characteristic of Lady Mary" (143).

In 1736, at forty-seven, her attentions turned to Francesco Algarotti, a twenty-four-year-old, bisexual Italian writer. As her children were grown and her hus-

band indifferent, she made plans to join Algarotti in Italy, leaving in 1739.
While the romance with Algarotti never materialized, Lady Mary remained
abroad for twenty years, primarily in Italy. She never saw her husband again,
returning to England only after his death in 1761. A year after her return, she
died of breast cancer. A scorn for publicity and a fear of compromising her social
position had prevented Lady Mary from issuing her works during her lifetime.
However, she was determined that her works eventually become public and
arranged for posthumous publication of the *Embassy Letters*. The first collection
of her verse was published in 1768.

EDITION USED: *The Works of Mary Wortley Montagu*, 5 vols. (London, 1803).

To the Imitator of the First Satire
of the Second Book of Horace

In two large Columns, on thy motly Page,
Where *Roman* Wit is stripe'd with *English* Rage;
Where Ribaldry to Satire makes pretence,
And modern Scandal rolls with ancient Sense:
Whilst on one side we see how *Horace* thought;   5
And on the other, how he never wrote:
Who can believe, who view the bad and good,
That the dull Copist better understood
That *Spirit*, he pretends to imitate,
Than heretofore that *Greek* he did translate?   10
    Thine is just such an Image of *his* Pen,
As thou thy self art of the Sons of Men:
Where our own Species in Burlesque we trace, ⎫
A Sign-Post Likeness of the noble Race;   ⎬
That is at once Resemblance and Disgrace.   ⎭   15
    Horace can laugh, is delicate, is clear;
You, only coarsely rail, or darkly sneer:
His Style is elegant, his Diction pure,   ⎫
Whilst none thy crabbed Numbers can endure; ⎬
Hard as thy Heart, and as thy Birth obscure.   ⎭   20
    If *He* has Thorns, they all on Roses grow;
Thine like rude Thistles, and mean Brambles show;
With this Exception, that tho' rank the Soil,
Weeds, as they are, they seem produc'd by Toil.
    Satire shou'd, like a polish'd Razor keen,   25

Wound with a Touch, that's scarcely felt or seen.
Thine is an Oyster-Knife, that hacks and hews; ⎫
The Rage, but not the Talent of Abuse; ⎬
And is in *Hate*, what Love is in the Stews. ⎭
'Tis the gross *Lust* of Hate, that still annoys,   30
Without distinction, as gross Love enjoys.
Neither to Folly, nor to Vice confin'd;
The Object of thy Spleen is Human Kind:
It preys on all, who yield, or who resist;
To Thee 'tis Provocation to exist.   35
     But if thou see'st a great and gen'rous Heart,
Thy Bow is doubly bent to force a Dart.
Nor only Justice vainly we demand,
But even Benefits can't rein thy Hand:
To this or that alike in vain we trust,   40
Nor find Thee less Ungrateful than Unjust.
     Not even Youth and Beauty can controul
The universal Rancour of thy Soul;
Charms that might soften Superstition's Rage,
Might humble Pride, or thaw the Ice of Age.   45
But how should'st thou by Beauty's Force be mov'd,
No more for loving made, than to be lov'd?
It was the Equity of righteous Heav'n,
That such a Soul to such a Form was giv'n;
And shews the Uniformity of Fate,   50
That one so odious, shou'd be born to hate.
     When God created Thee, one would believe,
He said the same as to *the Snake of Eve*;
To human Race Antipathy declare,
'Twixt them and Thee be everlasting War.   55
But oh! the Sequel of the Sentence dread,
And whilst you *bruise their Heel*, beware your Head.
     Nor think thy Weakness shall be thy Defence;
The Female Scold's Protection in Offence.
Sure 'tis as fair to beat who cannot fight,   60
As 'tis to libel those who cannot write.
And if thou drawst thy Pen to aid the Law,
Others a Cudgel, or a Rod, may draw.
     If none with Vengeance yet thy Crimes pursue,

Or give thy manifold Affronts their due;   65
If Limbs unbroken, Skin without a Stain,   ⎫
Unwhipt, unblanketed, unkick'd, unslain;   ⎬
That wretched little Carcass you retain: ⎭
The Reason is, not that the World wants Eyes;
But thou'rt so mean, they see, and they despise.   70
When fretful *Porcupines*, with rancorous Will,
From mounted Backs shoot forth a harmless Quill,
Cool the Spectators stand; and all the while,
Upon the angry little Monster smile.
Thus 'tis with thee: — whilst impotently safe,   75
You strike unwounding, we unhurt can laugh.
Who but must laugh, this Bully when he sees,
A little Insect shiv'ring at a Breeze?
One over-match'd by ev'ry Blast of Wind,
Insulting and provoking all Mankind.   80
        Is this the *Thing* to keep Mankind in awe,
To make those tremble who escape the Law?
Is this *the Ridicule* to live so long,
The deathless Satire, and *immortal Song?*
No: like thy self-blown Praise, thy Scandal flies;   85
And, as we're told of Wasps, it stings and dies.
        If none do yet return th' intended Blow;
You all your Safety, to your Dullness owe:
But whilst that Armour thy poor Corps defends,
'Twill make thy Readers few, as are thy Friends;   90
Those, who thy Nature loath'd, yet lov'd thy Art,
Who lik'd thy Head, and yet abhor'd thy Heart;
Chose thee, to read, but never to converse,
And scorn'd in Prose, him whom they priz'd in Verse.
Even they shall now their partial Error see,   95
Shall shun thy Writings like thy Company;
And to thy Books shall ope their Eyes no more,
Than to thy Person they wou'd do their Door.
        Nor thou the Justice of the World disown,
That leaves Thee thus an Out-cast, and alone;   100
For tho' in Law, to murder be to kill,
In Equity the Murder's in the Will:
Then whilst with Coward Hand you stab a Name,

And try at least t'assassinate our Fame;
Like the first bold Assassin's be thy Lot,   105
Ne'er be thy Guilt forgiven, or forgot;
But as thou hate'st, be hated by Mankind
And with the Emblem of thy crooked Mind,
Mark'd on thy Back, like *Cain*, by God's own Hand;
Wander like him, accursed through the Land.   110

An Epistle from Pope to Lord Bolingbroke

CONFESS, dear Lælius!* pious, just, and wise,
Some self-content does in that bosom rise,
When you reflect, as sure you sometimes must,
What talents Heaven does to thy virtue trust,
While with contempt you view poor human-kind,   5
Weak, wilful, sensual, passionate, and blind.
Amid these errors thou art faultless found,
(The moon takes lustre from the darkness round)
Permit me too, a small attendant star,
To twinkle, tho' in a more distant sphere;   10
Small things with great, we Poets oft compare.
With admiration all your steps I view,
And almost envy what I can't pursue.
The world must grant, and ('tis no common fame)
My courage and my probity the same;   15
But you, great Lord, to nobler scenes were born;
Your early youth did Anna's court adorn.
Let Oxford own, let Catalonia tell,
What various victims to your wisdom fell;
Let vows or benefits the vulgar bind,   20
Such ties can never chain th' intrepid mind.
Recorded be that memorable hour,
When, to elude exasperated pow'r,

---

*Pope first addressed his Essay on Man to Lord Bolingbroke as Lælius.

With blushless front, you durst your friend betray,
Advise the whole confederacy to stay,   25
While with sly courage you run brisk away.
By a deserted court with joy receiv'd
Your projects all admir'd, your oaths believ'd;
Some trust obtain'd, of which good use you made,
To gain a pardon where you first betray'd.   30
But what is pardon to th' aspiring breast?
You shou'd have been First Minister at least:
Failing of that, forsaking and depress'd,
Sure any soul but your's had sought for rest;
And mourn'd in shades, far from the public eye,   35
Successless fraud, and useless infamy.
And here, my Lord! let all mankind admire
The bold efforts of unexhausted fire;
You stand the champion of the people's cause,
And bid the mob reform defective laws.   40
Oh! was your pow'r, like your intention, good!
Your native land wou'd stream with civic blood.
I own these glorious schemes I view with pain;
My little mischiefs to myself seem mean.   45
Such ills are humble tho' my heart is great,
All I can do is flatter, lie, and cheat;
Yet I may say 'tis plain that you preside
O'er all my morals, and 'tis much my pride
To tread with steps unequal where you guide.
My first subscribers, I have first defam'd,   50
And when detected, never was asham'd;
Rais'd all the storms I could in private life,
Whisper'd the husband to reform the wife;
Outwitted Lintot in his very trade,
And charity with obloquy repaid.   55
Yet while you preach'd in prose, I scold in rhymes
Against the injustice of flagitious times.
You, learned Doctor of the public stage,
Give gilded poison to corrupt the age;
Your poor toad-eater I, around me scatter   60
My scurril jests, and gaping crowds bespatter.
This may seem envy to the formal fools,

Who talk of virtue's bounds and honour's rules;
We, who with piercing eyes look nature through,
We know that all is right, in all we do.   65

    Reason's erroneous—honest instinct right—
Monkeys were made to grin and fleas to bite.
Using the spite by the Creator given,
We only tread the path that's mark'd by Heaven.
And sure with justice 'tis that we exclaim,   70
Such wrongs must e'en your modesty inflame;
While blockheads, court-rewards and honours share, ⎫
You, poet, patriot, and philosopher,   ⎬
No bills in pocket, nor no garter wear.   ⎭

    When I see smoking on a booby's board,   75
Fat Ortolans and pye of Perigord,
Myself am mov'd to high poetic rage,
(The Homer and the Horace of the age)
Puppies who have the insolence to dine
With smiling beauties, and with sparkling wine.   80
While I retire, plagu'd with an empty purse,
Eat broccoli, and kiss my ancient nurse.
But had we flourish'd when stern Harry reign'd,
Our good designs had been but ill explain'd;
The axe had cut your solid reas'nings short,   85
I, in the porter's lodge, been scourg'd at court,
To better times kind Heav'n reserv'd our birth,
Happy for you such coxcombs are on earth!
Mean spirits seek their villainy to hide;   ⎫
We show our venom'd souls with nobler pride,   ⎬   90
And in bold strokes have all mankind defy'd.   ⎭
Past o'er the bounds that keep mankind in awe,
And laugh'd at justice, liberty, and law.
While our admirers stare with dumb surprize,
Treason and scandal we monopolize.   95
Yet this remains our more peculiar boast,
You 'scape the block, and I the whipping-post.

The Lover: A Ballad

At length, by so much importunity pressed,
Take, (Molly), at once, the inside of my breast;
This stupid indifference so often you blame
Is not owing to nature, to fear, or to shame;
I am not as cold as a Virgin in lead,   5
Nor is Sunday's sermon so strong in my head;
I know but too well how time flies along,
That we live but few years and yet fewer are young.

But I hate to be cheated, and never will buy
Long years of repentance for moments of joy.   10
Oh was there a man (but where shall I find
Good sense and good nature so equally joined?)
Would value his pleasure, contribute to mine,
Not meanly would boast, nor lewdly design,
Not over severe, yet not stupidly vain,   15
For I would have the power though not give the pain;

No pedant yet learnèd, not rakehelly gay
Or laughing because he has nothing to say,
To all my whole sex obliging and free,
Yet never be fond of any but me;   20
In public preserve the decorums are just,
And show in his eyes he is true to his trust,
Then rarely approach, and respectfully bow,
Yet not fulsomely pert, nor yet foppishly low.

But when the long hours of public are past   25
And we meet with champagne and a chicken at last,
May every fond pleasure that hour endear,
Be banished afar both discretion and fear,
Forgetting or scorning the airs of the crowd
He may cease to be formal, and I to be proud,   30
Till lost in the joy we confess that we live,
And he may be rude, and yet I may forgive.

And that my delight may be solidly fixed,
Let the friend and the lover be handsomely mixed,
In whose tender bosom my soul might confide,   35
Whose kindness can sooth me, whose counsel could guide.
From such a dear lover as here I describe
No danger should fright me, no millions should bribe;
But till this astonishing creature I know,
As I long have lived chaste, I will keep myself so.   40

I never will share with the wanton coquette,
Or be caught by a vain affectation of wit.
The toasters and songsters may try all their art
But never shall enter the pass of my heart.
I loathe the lewd rake, the dressed fopling despise;   45
Before such pursuers the nice virgin flies;
And as Ovid has sweetly in parables told
We harden like trees, and like rivers are cold.

TO THE COUNTESS OF _____

I AM now preparing to leave Constantinople, and perhaps you will
accuse me of hypocrisy, when I tell you, 'tis with regret; but as I am used
to the air, and have learnt the language, I am easy here; and as much as
I love travelling, I tremble at the inconveniences attending so great a
journey, with a numerous family, and a little infant hanging at the
breast. However, I endeavour, upon this occasion, to do as I have hitherto done in all the odd turns of my life; turn them, if I can to my
diversion. In order to this, I ramble every day, wrapped up in my Ferige
and Asmack, about Constantinople, and amuse myself with seeing all
that is curious in it. I know you will expect that this declaration should
be followed with some account of what I have seen. But I am in no
humour to copy what has been writ so often over. To what purpose
should I tell you, that Constantinople is the antient Bizantium? that 'tis
at present the conquest of a race of people, supposed Scythians; that
there are five or six thousand mosques in it? that Sancta Sophia was
founded by Justinian, &c. I'll assure 'tis not for want of learning, that I
forbear writing all these bright things. I could also, with very little
trouble, turn over Knolles and Sir Paul Rycaut, to give you a list of

Turkish Emperors; but I will not tell you what you may find in every author that has writ of this country. I am more inclined, out of a true female spirit of contradiction, to tell you the falsehood of a great part of what you find in authors; as for instance, in the admirable Mr. Hill, who so gravely asserts, that he saw in Sancta Sophia, a sweating pillar, very balsamic for disordered heads. There is not the least tradition of any such matter; and I suppose it was revealed to him in vision, during his wonderful stay in the Egyptian Catacombs; for I am sure he never heard of any such miracle here. 'Tis also very pleasant to observe how tenderly he and all his brethren voyage-writers, lament the miserable confinement of the Turkish ladies, who are perhaps more free than any ladies in the universe, and are the only women in the world, that lead a life of uninterrupted pleasure, exempt from cares, their whole time being spent in visiting, bathing, or the agreeable amusement of spending money and inventing new fashions. A husband would be thought mad that exacted any degree of æconomy from his wife, whose expences are no way limited but by her own fancy. 'Tis his business to get money, and her's to spend it; and this noble prerogative extends itself to the very meanest of the sex. Here is a fellow that carries embroidered handkerchiefs upon his back to sell. And as miserable a figure as you may suppose such a mean dealer; yet I'll assure you his wife scorns to wear any thing less than cloth of gold; has her ermine furs and a very handsome set of jewels for her head. 'Tis true, they have no places but the bagnios, and these can only be seen by their own sex; however, that is a diversion they take great pleasure in.

I was, three days ago, at one of the finest in the town, and had the opportunity of seeing a Turkish bride received there, and all the ceremony used on that occasion, which made me recollect the Epithalamium of Helen, by Theocritus; and it seems to me, that the same customs have continued ever since. All the she friends, relations and acquaintance of the two families, newly allied, meet at the bagnio; several others go, out of curiosity, and I believe there were that day two hundred women. Those that were, or had been married, placed themselves round the rooms on the marble sofas; but the virgins very hastily threw off their cloaths, and appeared without other ornament or covering, than their own long hair braided with pearl or ribbon. Two of them met the bride at the door, conducted by her mother and another grave relation. She was a beautiful maid of about seventeen, very richly dressed, and shining with jewels, but was presently reduced to the state of nature. Two others filled silver gilt pots with perfume, and began the procession, the rest following in pairs, to the number of thirty. The leaders sung an Epithalamium, answered by the others in chorus, and the two last led the fair bride, her eyes fixed on the ground, with a charming affectation of modesty. In this order they marched round the three large rooms of the Bagnio. 'Tis not easy to represent to you the beauty of this sight, most of them being well proportioned and white skinn'd; all of them perfectly smooth, and polished by the frequent use of bathing. After having made their tour, the bride was again led to every matron round the rooms, who saluted her with a compliment and a present, some of jewels, others of pieces of stuff, handkerchiefs, or little gallantries of that nature, which she thanked them for, by kissing their hands. I was very well pleased with having seen this ceremony; and you may believe me, that the Turkish ladies have, at least, as much wit and civility, nay, liberty, as among us. 'Tis true, the same customs that give them so many opportunities of gratifying their evil inclinations (if they have any) also put it very fully in the power of their husbands to revenge themselves, if they are discovered; and I do not doubt but they suffer some times for their indiscretions in a very severe manner. About two months ago, there was found at day-break, not very far from my house, the bleeding body of a young woman, naked, only wrapped in a coarse sheet, with two wounds of a knife, one in her side, and another in her breast. She was not quite cold, and was so surprizingly beautiful, that there were very few men in Pera that did not go to look upon her; but it was not possible for any body to know her, no woman's face being known. She was supposed to have been brought, in the dead of night, from the Constantinople side, and laid there. Very little enquiry was made about the murderer, and the corpse was privately buried without noise. Murder is never pursued by the King's officers, as with us. 'Tis the business of the next relations to revenge the dead person; and if they like better to compound the matter for money (as they generally do) there is no more said of it. One would imagine this defect in their government, should make such tragedies very frequent, yet they are extremely rare; which is enough to prove the people not naturally cruel. Neither do I think in many other particulars, they deserve the barbarous character we give them. I am well acquainted with a Christian woman of quality, who made it her choice to live with a Turkish husband, and is a very agreeable sensible lady. Her story is so extraordinary, I cannot forbear relating it; but I promise you it shall be in as few words as I can possibly express it.

She is a Spaniard, and was at Naples with her family, when that kingdom was part of the Spanish dominion. Coming from thence in a Felucca, accompanied by her brother, they were attacked by the Turkish Admiral, boarded and taken. — And now how shall I modestly tell you the rest of her adventure? The same accident happened to her, that happened to the fair Lucretia so many years before her. But she was too good a Christian to kill herself, as that heathenish Roman did. The Admiral was so much charmed with the beauty, and long-suffering of the fair captive, that, as his first compliment, he gave immediately liberty to her brother and attendants, who made haste to Spain, and in a few months sent the sum of four thousand pounds sterling, as a ransom for his sister. The Turk took the money, which he presented to her, and told her she was at liberty. But the lady very discreetly weighed the different treatment she was likely to find in her native country. Her relations (as the kindest thing they could do for her in her present circumstances) would certainly confine her to a nunnery for the rest of her days. — Her infidel lover was very handsome, very tender, very fond of her, and lavished at her feet all the Turkish magnificence. She answered him very resolutely, that her liberty was not so precious to her as her honour, that he could no way restore that but by marrying her, and she therefore desired him to accept the ransom as her portion, and give her the satisfaction of knowing that no man could boast of her favours without being her husband. The admiral was transported at this kind offer, and sent back the money to her relations, saying he was too happy in her possession. He married her, and never took any other wife, and (as she says herself) she never had reason to repent the choice she made. He left her some years after, one of the richest widows in Constantinople. But there is no remaining honourably a single woman, and that consideration has obliged her to marry the present Capitan Bassa, (i.e. Admiral) his successor. — I am afraid that you will think my friend fell in love with her ravisher; but I am willing to take her word for it, that she acted wholly on principles on honour, tho' I think she might be reasonably touched at his generosity, which is often found amongst the Turks of rank.

'Tis a degree of generosity to tell the truth, and 'tis very rare that any Turk will assert a solemn falsehood. I don't speak of the lowest sort; for as there is a great deal of ignorance, there is very little virtue amongst them; and false witnesses are much cheaper than in Christendom, those wretched not being punished (even when they are publicly detected) with the rigour they ought to be.

Now I am speaking of their law, I don't know, whether I have ever mentioned to you one custom peculiar to their country, I mean adoption, very common amongst the Turks, and yet more amongst the Greeks and Armenians. Not having it in their power to give their estates to a friend or distant relation, to avoid its falling into the Grand Signior's treasury, when they are not likely to have any children of their own, they chuse some pretty child of either sex, amongst the meanest people, and carry the child and its parents before the Cadi, and there declare they receive it for their heir. The parents, at the same time, renounce all future claim to it; a writing is drawn and witnessed, and a child thus adopted cannot be disinherited. Yet I have seen some common beggars, that have refused to part with their children in this manner, to some of the richest among the Greeks; (so powerful is the instinctive affection that is natural to parents!) though the adopting fathers are generally very tender to these children of their souls, as they call them. I own this custom pleases me much better than our absurd one of following our name. Methinks, 'tis much more reasonable to make happy and rich, an infant whom I educate after my own manners brought up (in the Turkish phrase) upon my knees, and who has learnt to look upon me with a filial respect, than to give an estate to a creature without other merit or relation to me than that of a few letters. Yet this is an absurdity we see frequently practised. — Now I have mentioned the Armenians, perhaps it will be agreeable to tell you something of that nation, with which I am sure you are utterly unacquainted. I will not trouble you with the geographical account of the situation of their country, which you may see in the maps; or a relation of their ancient greatness, which you may read in the Roman History. They are now subject to the Turks; and, being very industrious in trade, and encreasing and multiplying, are dispersed in great numbers through all the Turkish dominions. They were, as they say, converted to the Christian religion by St. Gregory, and are perhaps the devoutest Christians in the whole world. The chief precepts of their priests enjoin the strict keeping of their Lents, which are, at least, seven months in every year, and are not to be dispensed with on the most emergent necessity; no occasion whatever can excuse them if they touch any thing more than mere herbs or roots (without oil) and plain dry bread. That is their constant diet. — Mr. W——y has one of his interpreters of this nation, and the poor fellow was brought so low by the severity of his fasts, that his life was despaired of. Yet neither his master's commands, nor the doctors entreaties (who declared nothing else could save his life) were powerful enough to prevail with him to take two or three spoonfuls of broth. Excepting this, which may rather be called a custom, than an article of faith, I see very little in their religion different from ours. 'Tis true, they seem to incline very much to Mr. Whiston's doctrine; neither do I think the Greek church very distant from it, since 'tis certain, the Holy Spirit's proceeding only from the Father, is making a plain subordination in the Son. — But the Armenians have no notion of Transubstantiation, whatever account Sir Paul Rycaut gives of them (which account I am apt to believe was designed to compliment our court in 1679) and they have a great horror for those amongst them that change to the Roman religion. What is most extraordinary in their customs, is their matrimony; a ceremony, I believe, unparallel'd all over the world. They are always promised very young; but the espoused never see one another, till three days after their marriage. The bride is carried to church with a cap on her head, in the fashion of a large trencher, and over it a red silken veil, which covers her all over to her feet. The priest asks the bridegroom whether he is contented to marry that woman, be she deaf, be she blind? These are the litteral words; to which having answered yes; she is led home to his house, accompanied with all the friends and relations on both sides, singing and dancing, and is placed on a cushion in the corner of the sofa; but her veil is not lifted up, not even by her husband. There is something so odd and monstrous in these ways, that I could not believe them till I had enquired of several Armenians myself, who all assured me of the truth of them, particularly one young fellow who wept when he spoke of it, being promised by his mother to a girl that he must marry in this manner, tho' he protested to me, he had rather die than submit to this slavery, having already figured his bride to himself, with all the deformities in nature. — I fancy I see you bless yourself at this terrible relation. I cannot conclude my letter with a more surprizing story, yet 'tis as seriously true, as that I am,

Dear sister,
Yours, &c. &c,

CONCERNING MONSIEUR DE LA ROCHEFOUCAULT'S MAXIM—"THAT MARRIAGE IS SOMETIMES CONVENIENT, BUT NEVER DELIGHTFUL"

IT MAY be thought a presumptuous attempt in me to controvert a maxim advanced by such a celebrated genius as Monsieur Rochefoucault, and received with such implicit faith by a nation which boasts of superior politeness to the rest of the world, and which for a long time past has prescribed the rules of gallantry to all Europe.

Nevertheless, prompted by that ardour which truth inspires, I dare to maintain the contrary, and resolutely insist, that there are some marriages formed by love, which may be delightful, where the affections are sympathetic. Nature has presented us with pleasures suitable to our species, and we need only to follow her impulse, refined by taste and exalted by a lively and agreeable imagination, in order to attain the most perfect felicity of which human nature is susceptible: ambition, avarice, vanity, when enjoyed in the most exquisite perfection, can yield but trifling and tasteless pleasures, which will be too inconfiderable to affect a mind of delicate sensibility.

We may consider the gifts of fortune as so many steps necessary to arrive at felicity, which we can never attain, being obliged to set bounds to our desires, and being only gratified with some of her frivolous favours, which are nothing more than the torments of life, when they are considered as the necessary means to acquire or preserve a more exquisite felicity.

This felicity consists alone in friendship founded on mutual esteem, fixed by gratitude, supported by inclination, and animated by the tender solicitudes of Love, whom the ancients have admirably described under the appearance of a beautiful infant; it is pleased with infantine amusements, it is delicate and affectionate, incapable of mischief, delighted with trifles; its pleasures are gentle and innocent.

They have given a very different representation of another passion too gross to be mentioned, but of which alone men in general are susceptible. This they have described under the figure of a satyr, who has more of the brute than of the man in his composition. By this fabulous animal they have expressed a passion, which is the real foundation of all the fine exploits of modish gallantry, and which only endeavours to glut its appetite with the possession of the object which is most lovely in its estimation: a passion founded in injustice, supported by deceit, and attended by crimes, remorse, jealousy and contempt. Can such an affection be delightful to a virtuous mind? Nevertheless such is the delightful attendant on all illicit engagements; gallants are obliged to abandon all those sentiments of honour which are inseparable from a liberal education, and are doomed to live wretchedly in the constant pursuit of what reason condemns, to have all their pleasures embittered by remorse, and to be reduced to the deplorable condition of having renounced virtue, without being able to make vice agreeable.

It is impossible to taste the delights of love in perfection, but in a well assorted marriage; nothing betrays such a narrowness of mind as to be governed by words. What though custom, for which good reasons may be assigned, has made the words husband and wife somewhat ridiculous: A husband, in common acceptation, signifies a jealous brute, a surly tyrant: or at best a weak fool, who may be made to believe any thing. A wife is a domestic termagant, who is destined to deceive or torment the poor devil of a husband. The conduct of married people in general sufficiently justifies these two characters.

But, as I said before, Why should words impose upon us? A well regulated marriage is not like these connections of interest or ambition. A fond couple attached to each other by mutual affection, are two lovers who live happily together. Though the priest pronounces certain words, though the lawyer draws up certain instruments; yet I look on these preparatives in the same light as a lover considers a rope-ladder which he fastens to his mistress's window: If they can but live together, what does it signify by what price or by what means their union is accomplished? Where love is real and well founded, it is impossible to be happy but in the quiet enjoyment of the beloved object, and the price at which it is obtained does not lessen the vivacity and delights of a passion such as my imagination conceives. If I was inclined to romance, I would not picture images of true happiness in Arcadia. I am not prudish enough to confine the delicacy of affection to wishes only. I would open my romance with the marriage of a couple united by sentiment, taste and inclination. Can we conceive a higher felicity than the blending of their interests and lives in such an union? The lover has the pleasure of giving his mistress the last testimony of esteem and confidence, and she in return commits her peace and liberty to his protection. Can they exchange more dear and affectionate pledges? Is it not natural, to give the most incontestable proofs of that tenderness with which our minds are impressed? I am sensible that some are so nice as to maintain that the pleasures of love are derived from the dangers and difficulties with which it is attended; they very pertly observe that a rose would not be a rose without thorns. There are a thousand insipid remarks of this sort, which make so little impression on me, that I am persuaded, was I a lover, the dread of injuring my mistress would make me unhappy, if the enjoyment of her was attended with danger to herself.

Two married lovers lead very different lives: they have the pleasure to pass their time in a successive intercourse of mutual obligations, and marks of benevolence, and they have the delight to find that each forms the entire happiness of the beloved object. Herein consists perfect felicity. The most trivial concerns of oeconomy become noble and elegant when they are exalted by sentiments of affection; to furnish an apartment, is not barely to furnish an apartment; it is a place where I expect my lover; to prepare a supper is not merely giving orders to my cook; it is an amusement to regale the object I doat on. In this light a woman considers these necessary occupations as more lively and affecting pleasures, than those gaudy fights which amuse the greater part of the sex, who are incapable of true enjoyment.

A fixed and affectionate attachment softens every emotion of the soul, and renders every object agreeable which presents itself to the happy lover (I mean one who is married to his mistress.) If he exercises any employment, the fatigues of the camp, the troubles of the court, all become agreeable when he reflects that he endures these inconveniencies to serve the object of his affections. If fortune is favourable to him, for success does not depend on merit, all the advantages it procures, are so many tributes which he thinks due to the charms of the lovely fair; and in gratifying this ambition, he feels a more lively pleasure, and more worthy of an honest man, than that of raising his fortune and gaining public applause. He enjoys glory, titles, and riches no farther than as they regard her he loves; and when he attracts the approbation of a senate, the applause of an army, or the commendation of his prince, it is her praises which ultimately flatter him.

In a reverse of fortune, he has the consolation of retiring to one who is affected by his disgrace; and, locked in her embraces, he has the satisfaction of giving utterance to the following tender reflections. "My happiness does not depend on the caprice of fortune; I have a constant asylum against inquietude. Your esteem renders me insensible of the injustice of a court, or the ingratitude of a master, and my losses afford me a kind of pleasure, since they furnish me with fresh proofs of your virtue and affection. Of what use is grandeur to those who are already happy? We have no need of flatterers, we want no equipages, I reign in your affections, and I enjoy every delight in the possession of your person."

In short there is no situation in which melancholy may not be assuaged by the company of the beloved object. Sickness itself is not without its alleviation, when we have the pleasure of being attended by her we love. I should never conclude, if I attempted to give a detail of all the delights of an attachment, wherein we meet with every thing which can flatter the senses with the most lively and diffusive raptures. But I must not omit taking notice of the pleasure of beholding the lovely pledges of a tender friendship, daily growing up, and of amusing ourselves, according to our different sexes, in training them to perfection. We give way to this agreeable instinct of nature, refined by love. In a daughter we praise the beauty of her mother; in a son, we commend the understanding, and the appearance of innate probity which we esteem in his father. It is a pleasure which, according to Moses, the Almighty himself enjoyed, when he beheld the work of his hands, and saw that all was good.

Speaking of Moses, I cannot forbear observing that the primitive plan of felicity infinitely surpasses all others, and I cannot form an idea of Paradise, more like a Paradise, than the state in which our first parents were placed: that proved of short duration, because they were unacquainted with the world, and it is for the same reason that so few love-matches prove happy. Eve was like a silly child, and Adam was not much enlightened. When such people come together, their being amorous is to no purpose, for their affections must necessarily be short-lived. In the transports of their love, they form supernatural ideas of each other. The man thinks his mistress an angel because she is handsome, and she is enraptured with the merit of her lover, because he adores her. The first decay of her complexion deprives her of his adoration, and the husband being no longer an adorer, becomes hateful to her, who had no other foundation for her love. By degrees they grow disgustful to each other, and after the example of our first parents they do not fail to reproach each other with the crime of their mutual imbecility. After indifference, contempt comes apace, and they are convinced that they must hate each other, because they are married. Their smallest defects swell in each other's view, and they grow blind to those charms which, in any other object, would affect them. A commerce founded merely on sensation can be attended with no other consequences.

A man, when he marries the object of his affections, should forget that she appears to him adorable, and should consider her merely as a mortal, subject to disorders, caprice and ill-temper; he should arm himself with fortitude to bear the loss of her beauty, and should provide himself with a fund of complaisance which is requisite to support a constant intercourse with a person even of the highest understanding and the greatest equanimity. The wife, on the other hand, should not expect a continued course of adulation and obedience; she should dispose herself to obey in her turn with a good grace; a science very difficult to attain, and consequently the more estimable in the opinion of a man who is sensible of the merit. She should endeavour to revive the charms of the mistress, by the solidity and good sense of the friend.

When a pair, who entertain such rational sentiments, are united by indissoluble bonds, all nature smiles upon them, and the most common appear delightful. In my opinion, such a life is infinitely more happy and more voluptuous, than the most ravishing and best regulated gallantry.

A woman, who is capable of reflection, can consider a gallant in no other light than that of a seducer, who would take advantage of her weakness, to procure a momentary pleasure at the expence of her glory, her peace, her honour, and perhaps her life. A highwayman who claps a pistol to your breast, to rob you of your purse, is less dishonest and less guilty; and I have so good an opinion of myself as to believe that if I was a man, I should be as capable of assuming the character of an assassin, as that of defiling an honest woman, esteemed in the world and happy in her husband, by inspiring her with a passion to which she must sacrifice her honour, her tranquility and her virtue.

Should I make her despicable, who appears amiable in my eyes? Should I reward her tenderness, by making her abhorred by her family, by rendering her children indifferent to her, and her husband detestable? I believe that these reflections would have appeared to me in as strong a light, if my sex had not rendered them excusable in such cases; and I hope that I fhould have had more sense than to imagine vice the less vicious because it is the fashion.

N. B. I am much pleased with the Turkish manners: a people, though ignorant, yet in my judgment extremely polite. A gallant convicted of having debauched a married woman is regarded as a pernicious being, and held in the same abhorrence as a prostitute with us. He is certain of never making his fortune, and they would deem it scandalous to confer any considerable employment on a man suspected of having committed such enormous injustice.

What would these moral people think of our anti-knights errant, who are ever in pursuit of adventures to reduce innocent virgins to distress, and to rob virtuous women of their honour; who regard beauty, youth, rank, nay virtue itself, as so many incentives, which inflame their desires, and render their efforts more eager; and who, priding themselves in the glory of appearing expert seducers, forget that with all their endeavours, they can only acquire the second rank in that noble order, the Devil having long since been in possession of the first.

Our barbarous manners are so well calculated for the establishment of vice and wretchedness, which are ever inseparable, that it requires a degree of understanding and sensibility infinitely above the common, to relish the felicity of a marriage such as I have described. Nature is so weak, and so prone to change, that it is difficult to maintain the best grounded constancy, in the midst of those dissipations, which our ridiculous customs have rendered unavoidable.

It must pain an amorous husband to see his wife take all the fashionable liberties; it seems harsh not to allow them, and to be conformable he is reduced to the necessity of letting every one take them that will, to hear her impart the charms of her understanding to all the world, to see her display her bosom at noon-day, to behold her bedeck herself for the ball, and for the play, and attract a thousand and a thousand adorers, and listen to the insipid flattery of a thousand and a thousand coxcombs. Is it possible to preserve an esteem for such a creature, or at least must not her value be greatly diminished by such a commerce?

I must still resort to the maxims of the East, where the most beautiful women are content to confine the power of their charms to him who has a right to enjoy them; and they are too sincere not to confess, that they think themselves capable of exciting desires.

I recollect a conversation that I had with a lady of great quality at Constantinople, (the most amiable woman I ever knew in my life, and with whom I afterwards contracted the closest friendship.) She frankly acknowledged that she was satisfied with her husband. What libertines, said she, you Christian ladies are! You are permitted to receive visits from as many men as you think proper, and your laws allow you the unlimitted use of love and wine. I assured her that she was wrong informed, and that it was criminal to listen to, or to love, any other than our husbands. "Your husbands are great fools, she replied smiling, to be content with so precarious a fidelity. Your necks, your eyes, your hands, your conversation are all for the publick, and what do you pretend to reserve for them?

Pardon me, my pretty Sultana, she added, embracing me, I have a strong inclination to believe all that you tell me, but you would impose impossibilities upon me. I know the filthiness of the infidels; I perceive that you are ashamed, and I will say no more."

I found so much good sense and propriety in what she said, that I knew not how to contradict her, and at length I acknowledged that she had reason to prefer the Mahometan manners to our ridiculous customs, which form a confused medley of the rigid maxims of Christianity, with all the libertinism of the Spartans: And notwithstanding our absurd manners, I am persuaded that a woman who is determined to place her happiness in her husband's affections, should abandon the extravagant desire of engaging public adoration; and that a husband who tenderly loves his wife, should, in his turn, give up the reputation of being a gallant. You find that I am supposing a very extraordinary pair; it is not very surprising therefore, that such an union should be uncommon in those countries, where it is requisite to conform to established customs in order to be happy.

LADY SARAH PENNINGTON

(1725?–1783)

Author of conduct books, letters, and epistolary fiction, Lady Sarah Pennington began her writing career as a notorious woman and lived to be renowned for her piety, charity, benevolence, and resignation under great affliction. Little is known about the details of her life, including the date of her birth, although it must have been about 1725. She lost her mother before she was nineteen and had only a distant relationship with her otherwordly father. She felt the lack of practical social guidance in her life, which probably contributed to the failure of her marriage. Her husband was Sir Joseph Pennington, whom she married in about 1746. After several children and twelve years of marriage, they separated apparently because she conducted herself with unbecoming freedom in public. Sir Joseph's response to her behavior is not clear. Lady Pennington indicates that he encouraged it, but also that he used it as a reason to treat her in a way that endangered her safety. Whether or not he actually beat her, he subjected her to mental and emotional abuse which he continued after their separation by attempting to deprive her of a small inheritance and keeping her apart from her children.

Pennington's writing stemmed from remorse for past errors, from which she wished to save her children and others like herself, as well as from the need to justify her past conduct and, at times, to put food on the table. She wrote four works, of which the first, *An Unfortunate Mother's Advice to Her Absent Daughters* (1761) is the most famous. Reprinted often, *An Unfortunate Mother's Advice* in later editions had appended to it her *Letter to Miss Louisa on the Management and Education of Children*. Other works that Pennington wrote are *Letters on Different Subjects, in Four Volumes; Amongst which are interspers'd the Adventures of Alphonso, After the Destruction of Lisbon* (1766), and *The Child's Conductor* (1777).

EDITION USED: *An Unfortunate Mother's Advice to Her Absent Daughters* (London, 1761).

FROM AN UNFORTUNATE MOTHER'S ADVICE TO HER ABSENT DAUGHTERS

MY DEAR JENNY,

Was there any Probability that a Letter from me would be permitted to reach your Hand alone, I should not have chosen this least eligible Method of writing to you. The Public is no way concerned in Family Affairs, nor ought to be made a Party in them; but my Circumstances are

269

such, as lay me under a Necessity of either communicating my Sentiments to the World, or concealing them from you; the latter would, I think, be the Breach of an indispensible Duty, which obliges me to wave the Impropriety of the former.

A long Train of Events, of a most extraordinary Nature, conspired to remove you, very early, from the tender Care of an affectionate Mother; you were then too young to be able to form any right Judgment of her Conduct, and since that Time it is very probable that it has been represented to you in the most unfavourable Light. The general Prejudice against me I never gave myself the useless Trouble of any Endeavour to remove. — I do not mean to infer from hence that the Opinion of others is of no material Confequence; on the contrary, I would advise you always to remember, that, next to the Consciousness of acting Right, the Public Voice should be regarded, and to endeavour, by a prudent Behaviour, (even in the most trifling Instances) to secure it in your Favour. 'Twas my Misfortune to be educated in a different Opinion: I was early and wisely taught, that Virtue was the one Thing necessary, and without it no Happiness could be expected either in this, or in any future State of Existence; but with this good Principle, a mistaken one was at the same Time inculcated; namely, that the Self-approbation arising from conscious Virtue was alone sufficient, and the Censures of an ill-natured World, ever ready to calumniate, when not founded on Truth, were beneath the Concern of a Person whose Actions were guided by the superior Motive of Obedience to the Will of Heaven: This Notion, strongly imbibed before Reason had gained sufficient Strength to discover its Fallacy, was the Cause of an inconsiderate Conduct in my subsequent Life, which stampt my Character with a disadvantageous Impression. To you I speak with the utmost Sincerity, nor will conceal a Fault that you may profit by the Knowledge of, and therefore freely own, that in my younger Years, satisfied with keeping strictly within the Bounds of Virtue, I took a foolish Pleasure in exceeding those of Prudence, and was ridiculously vain of indulging a Latitude of Behaviour that others of my Age were afraid of launching into; but then, in Justice to myself, I must at the same Time declare, that this Freedom was only taken in public Company, and so extremely cautious was I of giving, what to me appeared any just Ground for Censure, that I call Heaven to witness, your Pappa was the first Man I ever made any private Assignation with, or met in a Room alone, nor with him, 'till after the most solemn mutual Engagement, that of the matrimonial Ceremony, had bound us to each other. My Behaviour then, was such, as, he has frequently since acknowledged, fully convinced him that I was not only innocent of any criminal Act, but of every vicious Thought, and that the outward Freedom of my Deportment proceeded merely from great Gaiety of Temper, and a very high flow of Spirits; never broke (if the Expression may be allowed) into the formal Rules of Decorum. To sum up the whole in a few Words, my private Conduct, was what the severest Prude could not condemn; my public, such as the most finished Coquet alone would have ventured upon; the latter only could be known to the World, and, consequently, from thence must their Opinion be taken, which, you will easily see, could not be favourable to me, but, on the contrary, gave a general Prejudice, that has since been made an Argument to gain Credit for the malicious Falshoods laid to my Charge: For this Reason (convinced by long Experience that the greater Part of Mankind are so apt to receive, and so willing to retain a Bad Impression of others, that when such Prepossessions are once established, there is hardly a Possibility through Life of removing them) I have, for some Years past, silently acquiesced in the Dispensations of Providence, without attempting any Justification of myself, and being conscious that the infamous Aspersions cast on my Character were not founded on Truth, have set down content with the Certainty of an open and perfect Acquittal of all Vicious Dispositions, or Criminal Conduct, at that great Day when all Things shall appear as they really are, and both our Actions and the most secret Motives of them, be made manifest to Men and Angels. Had your Pappa been amongst the Number of those who were deceived by Appearances, I should have thought it my Duty to leave no Method unessayed to clear myself in his Opinion; — but that was not the Case: He knows that many of those Appearances, urged against me, were given, not only under his Direction, but by his absolute Command, (which, contrary to Reason and my own Interest I was, for more than twelve Years, weak enough implicitly to obey) and that others, even since our Separation, were occasioned by some particular Instances of His Behaviour, which rendered it impossible for me to act with Safety in any other Manner; to him I appeal for the Truth of this Assertion, who is conscious of the Meaning, that may hereafter be explained to you. Perfectly acquainted with my Principles and natural Disposition, his Heart, I am convinced, never here condemned me. Being greatly incensed that my Father's Will gave to me an independent Fortune, which Will he imagined I was accessary to, or at least, could have prevented; he was thereby laid open to the Arts of designing Men (who having their own Interest solely in View) worked him up into a Desire of Revenge, and from thence (upon probable Circumstances) into a public Accusation; though that was supported only by the single Testimony of a Person whose known Falshood had made him a thousand Times declare, that he would not credit her Oath in the most trifling Incident; yet when he was disappointed of the additional Evidence he might have been flattered with the Hope of obtaining, — 'twas too late to recede. — This I sincerely believe to be the Truth of the Case, tho' too well know his *tenacious* Temper to expect a present Justification; but whenever he arrives on the Verge of Eternity, if Reason holds her Place to that awful Moment, and Religion has any Power on his Heart, I make no doubt, he will then acquit me to his Children, and with Truth confess that no Part of my Behaviour to him ever deserved the Treatment I have met with. — Sorry am I to be under the Necessity of pointing out Faults in the Conduct of another, which are perhaps long since repented of, and ought then to be as much forgot as they are most truly forgiven: Heaven knows, that so far from retaining any Degree of Resentment in my Heart, the Person breathes not whom I wish to hurt, or to whom I would not this Moment render every Service in my Power. The Injuries by me sustained, had I no Children, should contentedly be buried in Silence 'till the great Day of Retribution; but the false Impressions which, by such Silence, might be fixed on your Mind and those of your Brothers and Sisters, whom I include with you, 'tis incumbent on me in Justice to you, to them, and to myself, as far as possible, to efface. To this End it will be necessary to enter into a circumstantial History of near Fifteen Years, full of Incidents of a Nature so uncommon as to be scarcely credible, which I am convinced will effectually clear me, in your Opinions, of the Imputations I now lie under, and prove, almost to a Demonstration, the true Cause of those Proceedings against me that were couched under pretended Motives, as injurious to my Reputation as they were false in themselves. But this must be deferred some Time longer; you are all yet too young to enter into Things of this Kind, or to judge properly of them. When a few Years shall, by ripening your Understandings, remove this Objection, you shall be informed of the whole Truth without Disguise or Partiality, — 'till then suspend your Belief of all that may have reached your Ears with regard to me, and wait the Knowledge of those Facts my future Letter will reveal for your Information.

Thus much I thought it necessary to premise concerning myself, tho' foreign to the Design of this Epistle, which is only to remind you that you have still an affectionate Mother, anxious for your Welfare, to give you some Advice with regard to your Conduct in Life, — and to lay down a few Precepts that, if attended to, will in the best Manner in my Power supply the Deprivation of a constant tender maternal Care: The Address is to you in particular, your Sisters being yet too young to receive it, but my Intention for the equal Service of you all.

You are just entering, my dear Girl, into a World full of Deceit and Falshood, where few Persons or Things appear as they really are: Vice hides her Deformity with the borrowed Garb of Virtue; and though discernable, by the unbecoming Aukwardness of her Deportment under it, passes on Thousands undetected: Every present Pleasure usurps the Name of Happiness, and as such deceives the unwary Pursuer; thus one general Mask disguises the Whole, and it requires a long Experience, and a penetrating Judgment to discover the Truth. — Thrice happy those whose docile Tempers improve the Instructions of maturer Age, and thereby attain some Degree of this necessary Knowledge while it may be chiefly useful in directing their Conduct!

The Turn your Mind now takes, fixes the Happiness or Misery of your whole future Life, and I am too nearly concerned for your Welfare not to be most solicitously anxious that you may early be led into so just a way of Thinking as will be productive of a prudent, rational Behaviour, and secure to yourself a lasting Felicity. You was old enough, before our Separation, to convince me that Heaven had not denied you a good natural Understanding, which, properly cultivated, will set you above that trifling Disposition too common among the Female World, that makes Youth ridiculous, Maturity insignificant, and old Age contemptible; 'tis therefore needless to enlarge on that Head, since good Sense is there the best Adviser, and without it all Admonitions or Directions on the Subject would be as fruitless as to lay down Rules for an Idiot not to act foolishly.

There is no room to doubt but that sufficient Care will be taken to give you a polite Education; but a religious one is of still greater Consequence; necessary as the former is toward your making a proper Figure in the World, and being well accepted in it, the latter is yet more so, as that only can secure to you the Approbation of the greatest and best of Beings, on whose Favour depends your everlasting Happiness: Let, therefore, your Duty to God be ever the first and principal Object of your Care; as your Creator and Governor, he claims Adoration and Obedience; as your Father and Friend, submissive Duty and Affection: Remember that from this common Parent of the Universe you received your Life, that to His general Providence you owe the Continuance of it, and to his Bounty, all the Health, Ease, Advantages, or Enjoyments which help to make that Life agreeable. A sense of Benefits received naturally inspires a grateful Disposition, with a Desire of making some suitable Returns; all that can here be made, for innumerable Favours every Moment bestowed, is a thankful Acknowledgment, and a willing Obedience; in These be never wanting: Make it an invariable Rule to begin and End the Day with a solemn Address to the Deity; I mean not by this, what is commonly with too much Propriety called saying of Prayers, viz. a customary Repetition of a few good Words without either Devotion or Attention, than which, nothing is more inexcusable and affrontive; 'tis the Homage of the Heart that can alone be accepted.

*   *   *

The sincere Practice of these religious Duties naturally leads to the proper Discharge of the social ones, which may be all comprehended in that one great general Rule of doing unto others as you would they should do unto you; — but of these more particularly hereafter. I shall first give you my Advice concerning Employment, it being of great Moment to set out in Life in such a Method as may be useful to yourself and Beneficial to others. Time is invaluable, its Loss irretrievable! the Remembrance of having made an ill Use of it must be one of the sharpest Tortures to those who are on the Brink of Eternity! and what can yield a more unpleasing Retrospect, than whole Years idled away in an irrational insignificant Manner! Examples of which are continually before our Eyes. Look on every Day as a Blank Sheet of Paper put into your Hands to be filled up; remember the Characters will remain to endless Ages, and can never be expunged; be careful therefore not to write any thing but what you may read with Pleasure a thousand Years hence: I would not be understood in a Sense so strict as might debar you from any Innocent Amusement suitable to your Age, and agreeable to your Inclination; Diversions, properly regulated, are not only allowable, they are absolutly necessary to Youth, and are never criminal but when taken to Excess; that is, when they engross the whole Thought, are made the chief Business of Life, give a distaste to every valuable Employment; and by a Sort of Infatuation leave the Mind in a State of restless Impatience from the Conclusion of one 'till the Commencement of another: This is the unfortunate Disposition of many; guard most carefully against it; for nothing can be attended with more pernicious Consequences: A little Observation will convince you, that there is not, amongst the Human Species, a Set of more miserable Beings than those who cannot live out of a constant Succession of Diversions: These People have no Comprehension of the more satisfactory Pleasures to be found in Retirement; Thought is insupportable to them, and consequently Solitude must be intolerable; they are a Burthen to Themselves, and a Pest to their Acquaintance, by vainly seeking for Happiness in Company where they are seldom acceptable (I say vainly, for true Happiness exists only in the Mind, nothing foreign can give it: The utmost to be attained by what is called a gay Life, is a short Forgetfulness of Misery to be felt with accumulated Anguish in every Interval of Reflection) this restless Temper is frequently the Product of a too eager Pursuit of Pleasure in the early Part of Life, to the Neglect of those valuable Improvements which would lay the Foundation of a more Solid and Permanent Felicity. Youth is the Season for Diversions, but 'tis also the Season for acquiring Knowledge, for fixing Useful Habits, and laying in a Stock of such well-chosen Materials, as may grow into a serene Happiness that will encrease with every added Year of Life, and bloom in the fullest Perfection at the Decline of it. The great Art of Education consists in assigning to each its proper Place, in such a Manner that the one shall never become irksome by intrenching on the other: Our Separation having taken from me the pleasing Task of endeavouring, to the best of my Ability, to suit them occasionally, as might be most conducive both to your Profit and Pleasure, it only remains to give you general Rules, which Accidents may make it necessary sometimes to vary; — that must be left to your own Discretion, and I am convinced you have a sufficient Share of Understanding to be very capable of making such casual Regulations advantageously to yourself, if the Inclination is not wanting.

* * *

Happy is her Lot, who in an Husband finds this invaluable Friend! yet so great is the Hazard, so disproportioned the Chances, that I could almost wish the dangerous Die was never to be thrown for any of you! but as most probably it may, let me conjure ye all, my dear Girls, if ever any of you take this most important Step in Life, to proceed with the utmost Care, and deliberate Circumspection. Fortune and Family it is the sole Province of your Pappa to direct in, who certainly has always an undoubted Right to a Negative Voice, though not to a Compulsive One; as a Child is very justifiable in the Refusal of her Hand, even to the absolute Command of a Father, where her Heart cannot go with it; so is she extremely culpable, by giving it contrary to his Approbation. Here I must take Shame to myself! and for this unpardonable Fault, do justly acknowledge the subsequent ill Consequences of a most unhappy Marriage were the proper Punishment: this and every other Error in my own Conduct, I do, and shall, with the utmost Candour, lay open to you, sincerely praying, that you may reap the Benefit of my Experience, and avoid those Rocks I have, either by Carelessness, or sometimes, alas! by too much Caution split against.

But to return. — The chief Point to be regarded in the Choice of a Companion for Life, is a real virtuous Principle, an unaffected Goodness of Heart; without this you will be continually shocked by Indecency, and pained by Impiety. So numerous have been the unhappy Victims to the ridiculous Opinion, that a reformed Libertine makes the best Husband; that, did not Experience daily evince the contrary, one would believe it impossible for a Girl, who has a tolerable Degree of common Understanding, to be made the Dupe of so erroneous a Position, that has not the least Shadow of Reason for its Foundation, and which a small Share of Observation will prove to be false in Fact. A Man who has been long conversant with the worst Sort of Women, is very apt to contract a bad Opinion of, and a Contempt for the Sex in general; incapable of esteeming any, he is suspicious of all; jealous without Cause, angry without Provocation, and his own disturbed Imagination is a continual Source of ill Humour; to this is frequently joined a bad Habit of Body, the natural Consequence of an irregular Life, which gives an additional Sourness to the Temper. What rational Prospect of Happiness can there be with such a Companion? And that this is the general Character of those who are called reformed Rakes, Observation will certify: but admit there may be some Exceptions, it is a Hazard that no considerate Woman would venture the Peace of her whole future Life upon. The Vanity of those Girls who believe themselves capable of working Miracles of this Kind, and give up their Persons to a Man of libertine Principles, upon the wild Expectation of reclaiming him, justly deserve the Disappointment they will generally meet with; for, believe me, a Wife is, of all others, the least likely to succeed in such an Attempt. — Be it your Care to find that Virtue in a Lover, which you must never hope to form in an Husband. Good Sense and good Nature are almost equally requisite; if the former is wanting, it will be next to impossible for you to esteem the Person of whose Behaviour you may have Cause to be ashamed; (and mutual

Esteem is as necessary to Happiness in the married State, as mutual Affection) without the latter, every Day will bring with it some fresh Cause of Vexation; 'till repeated Quarrels produce a Coldness, that will settle into an irreconcilable Aversion, and you not only become each others Torment, but the Object of Contempt to your Family and Acquaintance.

This Quality of good Nature, is, of all others, the most difficult to be ascertained; which proceeds from the general Mistake of blending it with good Humour, as in themselves the same, though, in fact, no two Principles of Action are more essentially different; this may require some Explanation. — By good Nature, then, I mean, that true Benevolence which partakes the Felicity of all Mankind, that promotes the Satisfaction of every Individual within the Reach of its Ability, that relieves the Distressed, comforts the Afflicted, diffuses Blessings, and communicates Happiness, far as its Sphere of Action can extend, and in the private Scenes of Life, will shine conspicuous in the dutiful Son, the affectionate Husband, the indulgent Father, the faithful Friend, and the compassionate Master, both to Man and Beast; whilst good Humour is nothing more than a chearful, pleasing Deportment, arising either from a natural Gaiety of Mind, or an Affectation of Popularity, joined to an Affability of Behaviour, the Result of good Breeding, and a ready Compliance with the Taste of every Company. This Kind of mere good Humour, is, by far, the most striking Quality, 'tis frequently mistaken for, and complimented with the superior Name of real good Nature; a Man by this specious Appearance has often acquired that Appellation, who in all the Actions of his private Life, has been a Morose, Cruel, Revengeful, Sullen, Haughty Tyrant. — Let them put on the Cap whose Temples fit the galling Wreath! — On the contrary, a Man of a true benevolent Disposition, and formed to promote the Happiness of all around him, may sometimes, perhaps, from an ill Habit of Body, an accidental Vexation, or a commendable Openness of Heart, above the Meanness of Disguise, be guilty of little Sallies of Peevishness, or ill Humour, that may carry the Appearance of, and be unjustly thought to proceed from ill Nature, by Persons who are unacquainted with his true Character, and take them for synonimous Terms; though in Reality they bear not the least Analogy to each other. In order to the forming a right Judgment, it is absolutely necessary to observe this Distinction, which will effectually secure you from the dangerous Error of taking the Shadow for the Substance; an irretrievable Mistake! Pregnant with innumerable consequent Evils.

From what has been said, it plainly appears, that the Criterion of this amiable Virtue, is not to be taken from the general Opinion; mere good Humour being, to all Intents and Purposes, sufficient, in this Particular, to establish the public Voice in favour of a Man utterly devoid of every humane and benevolent Affection of Heart. It is only from the less conspicuous Scenes of Life, the more retired Sphere of Action, the artless Tenor of domestic Conduct, that the real Character can, with any Certainty, be drawn; these undisguised proclaim the Man; but as they shun the Glare of Light, nor court the Noise of popular Applause; obscure, they pass unnoted, and are seldom known 'till after an intimate Acquaintance; the best Method, therefore, to avoid Deception in this Case, is to lay no Stress on outward Appearances, too often fallacious, but to take the Rule of judging from the simple, unpolished Sentiments of those whose dependent Connections give them an undeniable Certainty; who not only see, but hourly feel, the good or bad Effects of that Disposition they are subjected to: by this I mean, that if a Man is equally respected, esteemed and beloved by his Tenants, his Dependents and Domestics, from the substantial Farmer to the laborious Peasant, from the proud Steward to the submissive Wretch, who, thankful for Employment, humbly obeys the menial Tribe; you may justly conclude, he has that true good Nature, that real Benevolence, which delights in communicating Felicity, and enjoys the Satisfaction it diffuses; but if by these he is despised and hated, served merely from a Principle of Fear, devoid of Affection, which is very easily discoverable, whatever may be his public Character, however favourable the general Opinion, be assured, his Disposition is such, as can never be productive of domestic Happiness. I have been the more particular on this Head, as it is one of the most essential Qualifications to be regarded, and of all others the most liable to be mistaken.

Never be prevailed with, my Dear, to give your Hand to a Person defective in these material Points; secure of Virtue, good Nature, and Understanding, in an Husband, you may be secure of Happiness; without the two former it is unattainable, without the latter, in a tolerable Degree, it must be very imperfect.

* * *

I have been thus particular on the Choice of an Husband, and the material Parts of Conduct in a married Life, as thereon depends not only the temporal, but often the eternal Felicity of those who enter into that

State; a constant Scene of Disagreement, ill Nature and Quarrels necessarily unfitting the Mind for every religious and social Duty, by keeping it
in a Disposition diametrically opposite to that Christian Piety, that practical Benevolence and rational Composure which alone can prepare it for
everlasting Happiness.

Instructions on this Head, considering your tender Age, may seem
premature, and should have been deferred, 'till Occasion called for them,
had our Situation allowed me frequent Opportunities of communicating
my Sentiments to you; but that not being the Case, I have chose in this
Epistle, at once, to offer you my best Advice in every Circumstance of
great Moment to your well Being both here and hereafter, lest, at a more
proper Season, it might not happen to be in my Power. This Part you may
defer the Consideration of, 'till the Design of entring into a new Scene of
Life may make it useful to you; which I hope will not be yet some Years;
an unhappy Marriage being generally the Consequence of a too early
Engagement, before Reason has gained sufficient Strength to form a
solid Judgment, on which only a proper Choice can be determined. Great
is the Hazard of a Mistake, and irretrievable the Effects of it! Many are
the Degrees between Happiness and Misery: absolute Misery, I will venture to affirm, is to be avoided by a proper Behaviour, even under all the
complicated Ills of human Life; but to arrive at that proper Behaviour,
requires the highest Degree of Christian Philosophy; and who would
voluntarily put themselves upon a State of Trial, so severe, that not one in
a Thousand have been found able to come off victorious? Betwixt this
and positive Happiness, there are innumerable Steps of comparative Evil;
each has its separate Conflict, variously difficult, differently painful,
under all which a patient Submission, and a conscious Propriety of Behaviour, is the only attainable Good: far short of possible temporal Felicity,
is the Ease arising from hence! rest not content with the Prospect of such
Ease, but fix on a more eligible Point of View, by aiming at true Happiness; and, take my Word, that can never be found in a married State,
without the three essential Qualifications already mentioned, Virtue,
good Nature, and good Sense, in an Husband: remember, therefore, my
dear Girl, this repeated Caution, if you ever resolve on Marriage, never to
give your Hand to a Man who wants either of them; whatever other
Advantages he may be possessed of, so shall you not only escape all those
Vexations, which Thousands of unthinking Mortals hourly repent the
having brought upon themselves, but most assuredly, if it is not your own
Fault, enjoy that uninterrupted domestic Harmony, in the affectionate

Society of a virtuous Companion, that constitutes the highest Satisfaction of human Life. Such an Union, founded on Reason and Religion, cemented by mutual Esteem and Tenderness, is a Kind of faint Emblem (if the Comparison may be allowed) of the promised Reward of Virtue in a future State; and, most certainly, an excellent Preparative for it, by keeping the Mind in a constant Equanimity, a regular Composure, that naturally leads to the proper discharge of all the Religious and Social Duties of Life; the unerring Road to everlasting Peace.

* * *

Examine every Part of your Conduct towards others by the unerring Rule, of supposing a Change of Places; this will certainly lead to an impartial Judgment; do then what appears to you right, or in other Words, what you would they should do unto you; which comprehends every Duty relative to Society.

Aim at Perfection, or you will never reach to an attainable Height of Virtue. Be Religious without Hypocrisy, Pious without Enthusiasm. Endeavour to merit the Favour of God, by a sincere and uniform Obedience to whatever you know, or believe, to be his Will: and should afflictive Evils be permitted to cloud the sun-shine of your brightest Days, receive them with Submission; satisfied that a Being, equally wise, omniscient, and beneficent, at once sees, and intends the Good of his whole Creation; and that every General or Particular Dispensation of his Providence towards the rational Part of it, is so calculated as to be productive of ultimate Happiness, which nothing but the Misbehaviour of Individuals can prevent to themselves. This Truth is surely an unanswerable Argument for absolute Resignation to the Will of God; and such a Resignation, founded upon Reason and Choice, not enforced by Necessity, is unalterable Peace of Mind, fixed on too firm a Basis to be shaken by Adversity: Pain, Poverty, Ingratitude, Calumny, and even the Loss of those we hold most dear, may each transiently affect, but united cannot mortally wound it. Upon this Principle you will find it possible not only to be content, but chearful under all the disagreeable Circumstances this State of Probation is liable to; and by making a proper Use of them, effectually remove the Garb of Terror from the last of all temporal Evils, and learn with grateful Pleasure, to meet approaching Death as the kind Remover of every painful Sensation, the friendly Guide to perfect and everlasting Happiness.

Believe me this is not mere Theory; my own Experience every Moment proves the Fact undeniably true; my Conduct (in all those Relations which still with me subsist, nearly as human Imperfection will allow) is governed by the Rules here laid down for you; which produces the constant rational Composure, that constitutes the most perfect Felicity of human Life; and with Truth I can aver, that I daily feel incomparably more real Satisfaction, more true Contentment in my present Retirement, than the gayest Scenes of Festive Mirth ever afforded me; am pleased with this Life, without an anxious Thought for the Continuance of it, and happy in the Hope, of hereafter exchanging it for an infinitely better. My Soul, unstained by the Crimes unjustly imputed to me, most sincerely forgives the malicious Authors of those Imputations, anticipates the future Pleasure of an open Acquittal, and in that Expectation looses the Pain of present undeserved Censure: by this is meant the Instance that was made the supposed Foundation for the last of innumerable Injuries received through him from whom I am conscious of having deserved the kindest Treatment: other Faults, no Doubt, I might have many, to him had very few; nay, for several Years cannot, upon Reflection, accuse myself of any Thing, but too absolute, too unreserved an Obedience to every Injunction, even where they were plainly contrary to the Dictates of my own Reason. — How wrong such a Compliance, was clearly evinced by many Instances of it, having been since most ungenerously, and most ungratefully urged as circumstantial Arguments against myself.

It must indeed be owned, that for the two or three last Years, tired with a long Series of repeated Insults of a Nature almost beyond the Power of Imagination to conceive, my Temper became soured; a constant fruitless Endeavour to oblige, was changed into an absolute Indifference about it; and ill Humour, occasioned by frequent Disappointments (a Consequence I have experimentally warned you against) was, perhaps, sometimes too much indulged; how far the unequalled Provocations may be allowed as an Excuse for this, Heaven only must determine, whose Goodness has thought fit to release me from the painful Situation, though by a Method, at present, not the most eligible, as it is the Cause of a Separation from my Children also, and thereby has put it out of my Power to attend, in the Manner I could have wished, to their Education; a Duty that Inclination would have led me with equal Care and Pleasure, more amply to fulfil, had they continued under my Jurisdiction. — But as Providence has thought fit otherways to determine, contented I submit to every Dispensation, convinced that all things are ordered for the best, and will, in the End, work together for Good to them that fear God, and sincerely endeavour to keep his Commandments. If in these I err, am certain it is owing to a Mistake in the Judgment, not a Defect of the Will.

Thus have I endeavoured, my dear Girl, in some Measure, to compensate both to you and your Sisters, the Deprivation of a constant maternal Care, by advising you, according to my best Ability, in the most material Parts of your Conduct through Life, as particularly as the Compass of a Letter would allow. May these few Instructions be as serviceable to you, as my Wishes would make them! and may that Almighty Being, to whom my daily Prayers ascend for your Preservation, grant you his heavenly Benediction, keep you from all moral Evil, lead you into the Paths of Righteousness, and Peace; and give us all an happy Meeting in those Regions of unalterable Felicity, *prepared for those, who by patient Continuance in well-doing, seek after Glory and Immortality.*

HANNAH COWLEY

(1743–1809)

Playwright and poet, Hannah Cowley was the daughter of Philip Parkhouse, a bookseller who had been educated as a clergyman. Her mother is believed to have been a relative of the poet John Gay. Her father encouraged her writing. Almost nothing is known about her early life. At about twenty-five, she married Thomas Cowley, a clerk in the Stamp Office, and settled with him in London. She probably wrote her first play to earn money, of which the Cowleys were apparently often in need. A well-known anecdote attributes her first play to her having heard about a play her husband had seen and declaring that she could write a play at least as good as that. She was right. Garrick produced *The Runaway*, probably after having revised it somewhat, in 1776. She claimed to have written it in two weeks and is said to have received 800 guineas which, as she said, "opened a new prospect of advantage to my Family." She pursued this advantage eagerly, producing thirteen plays, all but two of which were comedies, and becoming the most important English woman dramatist since Aphra Behn. Her poetry is less well known. She wrote several long romances as well as a number of poems in the florid Della Cruscan style under the name "Anna Matilda." Cowley's career as a playwright did not always run smoothly. Apparently she was easily riled and quarreled publicly with both Hannah More and David Garrick.

In 1783, Cowley's husband joined the East India Company as a soldier and left for India, apparently not because of any problems with the marriage. He died there in 1797 while traveling to Calcutta to visit their daughter. Hannah Cowley remained in London, although she may have visited her husband once in India. A few years after her husband's death, Cowley retired to her birthplace, Tiverton, where she lived another twenty-four years, dying at sixty-five. Her social habits there, as in London, were by contemporary standards unusual. She avoided fashionable evening entertainments and card parties, but opened her house one morning a week for "ladies only" who attended in crowds.

Today her best known play is *The Belle's Stratagem*, first produced in 1780 and continuing in the British repertoire well into the nineteenth century. It shows her talent for creating easy, natural dialogue, as well as plots that avoid the period's all too prevalent sentimental excesses. The witty and self-reliant heroine fulfills Cowley's ideal of "A creature for whom nature has done much, and education more; she has taste, elegance, spirit, understanding. In her manner she is free, in her morals nice." Moreover, she "is the life of conversation, the spirit of society, the joy of the public!"

EDITION USED: *The Belle's Stratagem*, ed. W. Oxberry (*New English Drama* [London, 1819]).

THE BELLE'S STRATAGEM

Dramatis Personae

DORICOURT
HARDY
SIR GEORGE TOUCHWOOD
FLUTTER
SAVILLE
VILLERS
COURTALL
SILVERTONGUE
CROWQUILL
FIRST GENTLEMAN
SECOND GENTLEMAN
MOUNTEBANK
FRENCH SERVANT

LETITIA HARDY
MRS. RACKETT
LADY FRANCES
MISS OGLE
KITTY WILLIS
LADY

Prologue

[*Speaker from without*]
    Make way—make way good folks! I must appear—
Nay, let me pass—You won't—why then [*Enters*] I'm here.
Pray welcome me; I've had a *squeedging* bout;
You'd bless your eyes, could they but see our rout;
We've all the company behind the scenes,   5
Up from their train-bearers to tragic queens;
There's Harlequin, and Punch, and Banquo's ghost,
And all the soldiers—Richmond's conquering host;
And Richard's troops—nay, honest Bayes's too,
Must all this night perform a grand review.   10

Then all are angry — low'ring discontent
Sits on each brow — when thus they gave it vent:
There, there's a part! just two lines and a letter!
And mine cry'd one, is rather worse than better;
I'm three times doubled — twice I'm deaf and dumb;   15
Nod, smile, bow round, look grave, and bite my thumb;
The third — a miracle! like Bacon's head,
Utter three words, and these three words are lead.
  You grumble! said a third; then I should rave;
A part like mine no author ever gave: 20
A lord I'm titled, and, to speak out plain,
Few on these boards could half so well sustain
The grace and proper action of a peer,
The ease, the loll, the shrug, the careless sneer,
But though our author thinks in wise debate,   25
In senate seated, on affairs of state
I might hold forth — yet in her cursed play,
The deuce a word am I allow'd to say;
Or rather coop'd, like other folks we know,
Between two barren adverbs — *Ay* and *no*.   30
Tis thus we're serv'd, when saucy women write —
Grant me, ye gods, no more to see the night,
When lady writers crowd our Covent stage! —
Yet *other* gods assist my mighty rage!
  Another cries, Why friend, some folks are out;   35
About a comedy make all this rout;
A pantomime indeed, 'twere sense and reason;
They bring the chink, boys — they'll run through a season.
A comedy may yawn its nine nights through,
And then to mortal troubles bid adieu;   40
Secure upon its shelf supinely lie,
Remov'd from ev'ry thought and ev'ry eye.
  No, no, a fifth man cry'd, the press succeeds,
Tis then we know its merits and its deeds:
Actors are thank'd for having done so well,   45
And told how *monstrously* they all excel;
The town is thank'd for having shown its taste,
In clapping, bravoing —

[PROMPTER, *Without.*] Pray, sir, make haste!

A long-spun prologue isn't worth a pin.

    D'ye think so, Mr. Wild? then I'll go in: 50
Yet here permit me, each succeeding day,
To *damn* this author—but, oh! *save* her play.

Act I.

SCENE I.—*Lincoln's Inn*

[*Enter* SAVILLE, *followed by a Servant, at the top of the stage, looking round, as if at a loss.*]

SAV. Lincoln's Inn!—Well, but where to find him, now I am in Lincoln's-Inn?—Where did he say his master was?

SERV. He only said in Lincoln's-Inn, sir.

SAV. That's pretty! And your wisdom never inquired at whose chambers?

SERV. Sir, you spoke to the servant yourself.

SAV. If I was too impatient to ask questions, you ought to have taken directions, blockhead!

    [*Enter* COURTALL, *singing*]

Ha, Courtall!—Bid him keep the horses in motion, and then inquire at all the chambers round. [*Exit* SERVANT]

What the devil brings you to this part of the town? Have any of the Long Robes handsome wives, sisters, or chambermaids?

COURT. Perhaps they have;—but I came on a different errand; and had thy good fortune brought thee here half an hour sooner, I'd have given thee such a treat, ha! ha! ha!

SAV. I'm sorry I miss'd it: what was it?

COURT. I was informed a few days since, that my cousins Fallow were come to town, and desired earnestly to see me at their lodgings in Warwick-Court, Holborn. Away drove I, painting them all the way as so many Hebes. They came from the furthest part of Northumberland, had never been in town, and in course were made up of rusticity, innocence, and beauty.

SAV. Well!

COURT. After waiting thirty minutes, during which there was a violent bustle, in bounced five sallow damsels, four of them Maypoles;—the fifth, Nature, by way of variety, had bent the Æsop style.—But they all opened at once, like hounds on a fresh scent:—"Oh, cousin Courtall!—How do you do, cousin Courtall! Lord, Cousin, I am glad you are come! We want you to go with us to the Park, and the plays, and the opera, and Almack's, and all the fine places!"—The devil, thought I, my dears, may attend you, for I am sure I wont. — However, I heroically stayed an hour with them, and discovered the virgins were all come to town with the hopes of leaving it — Wives: — their heads full of knight-baronights, fops, and adventures.

SAV. Well, how did you get off?

COURT. Oh, pleaded a million engagements. — However, conscience twitched me; so I breakfasted with them this morning, and afterwards 'squired them to the gardens here, as the most private place in town; and then took a sorrowful leave, complaining of my hard, hard fortune, that obliged me to set off immediately for Dorsetshire, ha! ha! ha!

SAV. I congratulate your escape! — Courtall at Almack's, with five aukward country cousins! ha! ha! ha! — Why, your existence, as a man of gallantry, could never have survived it.

COURT. Death, and fire! had they come to town, like the rustics of the last age, to see St. Paul's, the lions, and the wax-work — at their service; but the cousins of our days come up ladies — and, with the knowledge they glean from magazines and pocket-books, fine ladies; laugh at the bashfulness of their grandmothers, and boldly demand their entrees in the first circles.

SAV. Come, give me some news. — I have been at war with woodcocks and partridges these two months and am a stranger to all that has passed out of their region.

COURT. Oh! enough for three gazettes. The ladies are going to petition for a bill, that, during the war every man may be allowed two wives.

SAV. 'Tis impossible they should succeed, for the majority of both houses know what it is to have one?

COURT. But pr'ythee, Saville, how came you to town.

SAV. I came to meet my friend Doricourt, who, you know, is lately arrived from Rome.

COURT. Arrived! Yes, faith, and has cut us all out! — His carriage, his liveries, his dress, himself, are the rage of the day! His first appearance set the whole ton in a ferment, and his valet is besieged by levees of taylors, habit-makers, and other ministers of fashion, to gratify the impatience of their customers for becoming a la mode de Doricourt. Nay, the beautiful lady Frolic t'other night, with two sister countesses, insisted upon his waistcoat for muffs; and their snowy arms now bear it in triumph about town, to the heart-rending affliction of all our Beaux Garcons.

SAV. Indeed! Well, those little gallantries will soon be over; he's on the point of marriage.

COURT. Marriage! Doricourt on the point of marriage! 'Tis the happiest tidings you could have given, next to his being hanged. Who is the bride elect?

SAV. I never saw her; but 'tis miss Hardy, the rich heiress—the match was made by the parents, and the courtship begin on their nurses knees; Master used to crow at miss, and miss used to chuckle at master.

COURT. Oh! then by this time they care no more for each other, than I do for my country cousins.

SAV. I don't know that; they have never met since thus high, and so, probably, have some regard for each other.

COURT. Never met! Odd!

SAV. A whim of Mr. Hardy's; he thought his daughter's charms would make a more forcible impression, if her lover remained in ignorance of them till his return from the continent.

[*Enter* SAVILLE'S SERVANT]

SERV. Mr. Doricourt, sir, has been at counsellor Pleadwell's, and gone about five minutes. [*Exit* SERVANT]

SAV. Five minutes! Zounds! I have been five minutes too late all my life-time!—Good morrow, Courtall; I must pursue him. [*Going*]

COURT. Promise to dine with me to-day; I have some honest fellows.

[*Going off on the opposite side.*]

SAV. Can't promise; perhaps I may.—See there, there's a bevy of female Patagonians, coming down upon us.

COURT. By the lord, then, it must be my strapping cousins.—I dare not look behind me—Run, man, run. [*Exit on the same side*]

SCENE II.—*An Apartment at Doricourt's.*

[*Enter* DORICOURT]

DORIC. [*Speaking to a servant behind.*] I shall be too late for St. James's; bid him come immediately.

[*Enter* SAVILLE]

DORIC. Most fortunate! My dear Saville, let the warmth of this embrace speak the pleasure of my heart.

SAV. Well, this is some comfort, after the scurvy reception I met with in your hall.—I prepared my mind, as I came up stairs, for a bon jour, a grimace, and an adieu.

DORIC. Why so?

SAV. Judging of the master from the rest of the family. What the devil is the meaning of that flock of foreigners below, with their parchment faces and snuffy whiskers? What! can't an Englishman stand behind your carriage, buckle your shoe, or brush your coat?

DORIC. Stale, my dear Saville, stale! Englishmen make the best soldiers, citizens, artizans, and philosophers in the world; but the very worst footmen. I keep French fellows and Germans, as the Romans kept slaves; because their own countrymen had minds too enlarged and haughty to descend with a grace to the duties of such a station.

SAV. A good excuse for a bad practice.

DORIC. On my honour, experience will convince you of its truth. A Frenchman neither hears, sees, nor breathes, but as his master directs; and his whole system of conduct is compriz'd in one short word, obedience! An Englishman reasons, forms opinions, cogitates, and disputes; he is the mere creature of your will: the other, a being conscious of equal importance in the universal scale with yourself, and is therefore your judge, whilst he wears your livery, and decides on your actions with the freedom of a censor.

SAV. And this in defence of a custom I have heard you execrate, together with all the adventitious manners imported by our travell'd gentry. Now to start a subject which must please you. When do you expect miss Hardy.

DORIC. Oh, the hour of expectation is past. She is arrived, and I this morning had the honour of an interview at Pleadwell's. The writings were ready; and, in obedience to the will of Mr. Hardy, we met to sign and seal.

SAV. Has the event answer'd? Did your heart leap, or sink, when you beheld your mistress?

DORIC. Faith, neither one nor t'other: she's a fine girl, as far as mere flesh and blood goes. — But —

SAV. But what?

DORIC. Why, she's only a fine girl; complexion, shape, and features; nothing more.

SAV. Is not that enough?

DORIC. No! she should have spirit! fire! l'air enjoue! that something, that nothing, which every body feels, and which nobody can describe, in the resistless charmers of Italy and France.

SAV. Thanks to the parsimony of my father, that kept me from travel! I would not have lost my relish for true unaffected English beauty, to have been quarrell'd for by all the Belle's of Versailles and Florence.

DORIC. Pho! thou hast no taste. English beauty! 'Tis insipidity; it wants the zest, it wants poignancy, Frank! Why, I have known a French-woman indebted to nature for no one thing but a pair of decent eyes, reckon in her suite as many counts, marquisses, and petits maitres, as would satisfy three dozen of our first-rate toast. I have known an Italian marquizina make ten conquests in stepping from her carriage, and carry her slaves from one city to another, whose real, intrinsic beauty would have yielded to half the little Grisettes that pace your Mall on a Sunday.

SAV. And has miss Hardy nothing of this?

DORIC. If she has, she was pleased to keep it to herself. I was in the room half an hour before I could catch the colour of her eyes; and every attempt to draw her into conversation occasioned so cruel an embar-rassment, that I was reduced to the necessity of news, French fleets, and Spanish captures, with her father.

SAV. So miss Hardy, with only beauty, modesty, and merit, is doom'd to the arms of a husband who will despise her.

DORIC. You are unjust. Though she has not inspir'd me with violent passion, my honour secures her felicity.

SAV. Come, come, Doricourt, you know very well that when the honour of a husband is locum-tenens for his heart, his wife must be as indiffer-ent as himself, if she is not unhappy.

DORIC. Pho! never moralize without spectacles. But as we are upon the tender subject, how did you bear Touchwood's carrying lady Frances?

SAV. You know I never looked up to her with hope; and sir George is every way worthy of her.

DORIC. A la mode Angloise, a philosopher, even in love.

SAV. Come, I detain you—you seem dressed at all points, and of course have an engagement.

DORIC. To St. James's. I dine at Hardy's, and accompany them to the masquerade in the evening—but breakfast with me to-morrow, and we'll talk of our old companions—for I swear to you, Saville, the air of the continent has not effaced one youthful prejudice or attachment.

SAV. With an exception to the case of ladies and servants.

DORIC. True; there I plead guilty:—but I have never yet found any man, whom I could cordially take to my heart and call friend, who was not born beneath a British sky, and whose heart and manners were not truly English. [*Exeunt* DOR. *and* SAV.]

SCENE III. – *An Apartment in* MR. HARDY's *House.*
VILLERS *seated on a Sofa, reading.*

[*Enter* FLUTTER]

FLUT. Ha, Villers, have you seen Mrs. Rackett? – miss Hardy, I find, is out.

VIL. I have not seen her yet. I have made a voyage to Lapland since I came in. [*Flinging away the Book.*] A lady at her toilette is as difficult to be moved as a quaker. [*Yawning.*] What events have happened in the world since yesterday? have you heard?

FLUT. Oh, yes; I stopped at Tattersall's, as I came by, and there I found lord James Jessamy, sir William Wilding, and Mr. – . But, now I think on't, you shan't know a syllable of the matter; for I have been informed you never believe above one-half of what I say.

VIL. My dear fellow, somebody has imposed upon you most egregiously! Half! Why, I never believe one-tenth part of what you say: that is according to the plain and literal expression; but, as I understand you, your intelligence is amusing.

FLUT. That's very hard now, very hard. I never related a falsity in my life, unless I stumbled on it by mistake; and if it were otherwise, your dull matter-of-fact people are infinitely obliged to those warm imaginations which soar into fiction to amuse you; for, positively, the common events of this little dirty world are not worth talking about, unless you embellish them! – Ha! here comes Mrs. Rackett: Adieu to weeds, I see! All life!

[*Enter* MRS. RACKETT]

Enter, madam, in all your charms! Villers has been abusing your toilette, for keeping you so long; but I think we are much obliged to it, and so are you.

MRS. R. How so, pray? Good morning t'ye both. Here, here's a hand a piece for you. [*They kiss her hands.*]

FLUT. How so: Because it has given you so many beauties.

MRS. R. Delightful compliment! what do you think of that, Villers?

VIL. That he and his compliments are alike – showy, but won't bear examining. – So you brought miss Hardy to town last night?

MRS. R. Yes, I should have brought her before, but I had a fall from my horse, that confined me a week – I suppose in her heart she wished me hanged a dozen times an hour.

FLUT. Why?

MRS. R. Had she not an expecting lover in town all the time? she meets him this morning at the lawyer's. — I hope she'll charm him; she's the sweetest girl in the world.

VIL. Vanity, like murder, will out. — You have convinced me you think yourself more charming.

MRS. R. How can that be?

VIL. No woman ever praises another, unless she thinks herself superior in the very perfections she allows.

FLUT. Nor no man ever rails at the sex, unless he is conscious he deserves their hatred.

MRS. R. Thank ye, Flutter — I'll owe ye a bouquet for that. I am going to visit the new married lady Frances Touchwood — Who knows her husband?

FLUT. Every body.

MRS. R. Is there not something odd in the character?

VIL. Nothing, but that he is passionately fond of his wife; — and so petulent in his love, that he opened the cage of a favourite bullfinch, and set it to catch butterflies, because she rewarded its song with her kisses.

MRS. R. Intolerable monster! Such a brute deserves —

VIL. Nay, nay, nay, nay, this is your sex now. Give a woman but one stroke of character, off she goes, like a ball from a racket; sees the whole man, marks him down for an angel or a devil, and so exhibits him to her acquaintance. — This monster! this brute! is one of the worthiest fellows upon earth: sound sense, and a liberal mind; but dotes on his wife to such excess, that he quarrels with every thing she admires, and is jealous of her tippet and nosegay.

MRS. R. Oh, less love for me, kind Cupid! I can see no difference between the torment of such an affection, and hatred.

FLUT. Oh, pardon me, inconceivable difference, inconceivable; I see it as clearly as your bracelet. In the one case the husband would say, as Mr. Snapper said t'other day; zounds! madam, do you suppose that my table, and my house, and my pictures! — Apropos, des Bottes; — There was the divinest plague of Athens sold yesterday at Langford's! the dead figures so natural; you would have sworn they had been alive. Lord Primrose bid five hundred — Six, said lady Carmine — A thousand, said Ingot the nabob. — Down went the hammer. — A rouleau for your bargain, said sir Jeremy Jingle. And what answer do you think Ingot made him?

MRS. R. Why, took the offer.

FLUT. Sir, I would oblige you, but I buy this picture to place in the nursery; the children have already got Whittington and his cat! 'tis just this size, and they'll make good companions.

MRS. R. Ha, ha, ha! Well, I protest that's just the way now—the nabobs and their wives outbid one at every sale, and the creatures have no more taste—

VIL. There again! You forget this story is told by Flutter, who always remembers every thing but the circumstances and the person he talks about;—'twas Ingot who offered a rouleau for the bargain, and sir Jeremy Jingle who made the reply.

FLUT. 'Egad, I believe you are right—Well, the story is as good one way as 'tother, you know. Good morning. I am going to Mrs. Crotchet's.

VIL. I'll venture every figure in your tailor's bill you make some blunder there.

FLUT. [*Turning back.*] Done! my tailor's bill has not been paid these two years; and I'll open my mouth with as much care as Mrs. Bridget Button, who wears cork plumpers in each cheek, and never hazards more than six words, for fear of showing them. [*Exit*]

MRS. R. 'Tis a good-natured insignificant creature! let in every where, and cared for no where.—There's miss Hardy returned from Lincon's-inn: she seems rather chagrined.

VIL. Then I leave you to your communications.

[*Enter* LETITIA, *followed by her* MAID]

Adieu! I am rejoiced to see you so well, madam? but I must tear myself away.

LET. Don't vanish in a moment.

VIL. Oh, inhuman! you are two of the most dangerous women in town— Staying here to be cannonaded by four such eyes, is equal to a rencontre with Paul Jones or a midnight march to a Omoa!—They'll swallow the nonsense for the sake of the compliment. [*Aside.*] [*Exit.*]

LET. [*Gives her Cloak to the* MAID.] Order Du Quesne never more to come again; he shall positively dress my hair no more. [*Exit* MAID] And this odious silk, how unbecoming it is!—I was bewitched to choose it. [*Throwing herself on a Chair, and looking in a pocket Glass;* MRS. RACKETT *staring at her*] Did you ever see such a fright as I am to day?

MRS. R. Yes, I have seen you look much worse.

LET. How can you be so provoking? If I do not look this morning worse than ever I looked in my life, I am naturally a fright. You shall have it which way you will.

MRS. R. Just as you please; but pray what is the meaning of all this?

LET. [*Rising.*] Men are all dissemblers, flatterers, deceivers! Have I not heard a thousand times of my air, my eyes, my shape—all made for victory! and to-day, when I bent my whole heart on one poor conquest, I have proved that all those imputed charms amount to nothing; for Doricourt saw them unmoved. — A husband of fifteen months could not have examined me with more cutting indifference.

MRS. R. Then you return it like a wife of fifteen months, and be as indifferent as he.

LET. Ay, there's the sting! the blooming boy that left his image in my young heart, is at four and twenty improved in every grace that fixed him there. It is the same face that my memory and my dreams constantly painted to me; but its graces are finished, and every beauty heightened. How mortifying, to feel myself at the same moment his slave, and an object of perfect indifference to him!

MRS. R. How are you certain that was the case? Did you expect him to kneel down before the lawyer, his clerks, and your father, to make oath of your beauty?

LET. No; but he should have looked as if a sudden ray had pierced him; he should have been breathless! speechless! for, oh! Caroline, all this was I!

MRS. R. I am sorry you was such a fool. Can you expect a man, who has courted and been courted by half the fine women in Europe, to feel like a girl from a boarding school? He is the prettiest fellow you have seen, and in course bewilders your imagination; but he has seen a million of pretty women, child, before he saw you; and his first feelings have been over long ago.

LET. Your raillery distresses me; but I will touch his heart, or never be his wife.

MRS. R. Absurd and romantic! If you have no reason to believe his heart pre-engaged, be satisfied; if he is a man of honour, you'll have nothing to complain of.

LET. Nothing to complain of? Heavens! shall I marry the man I adore with such an expectation as that?

MRS. R. And when you have fretted yourself pale, my dear, you'll have mended your expectation greatly.

LET. [*Pausing.*] Yet I have one hope. If there is any power whose peculiar care is faithful love, that power I invoke to aid me.

    [*Enter* MR. HARDY]

HAR. Well, now, was'nt I right? Ay, Letty! Ay, cousin Rackett! was'nt I right? I knew 'twould be so. He was all agog to see her before he went abroad; and if he had, he'd have thought no more of her face, may be, than his own.

MRS. R. May be not half so much.

HAR. Ay, may be so—but I see into things; exactly as I foresaw, to day he fell desperately in love with the wench, he, he, he!

LET. Indeed, sir! how did you perceive it?

HAR. That's a pretty question! How do I perceive every thing? How did I foresee the fall of corn, and the rise of taxes? How did I know that if we quarrelled with America, Norway deals would be dearer? How did I foretel that a war would sink the funds? How did I forewarn parson Homily, that if he did'nt some way or other contrive to get more votes than Rubric, he'd lose the lectureship? How did I—But what the devil makes you so dull, Letitia? I thought to have found you popping about, as brisk as the jacks of your harpsichord.

LET. Surely, sir, 'tis a very serious occasion.

HAR. Pho, pho! girls should never be grave before marriage. How did you feel, cousin, beforehand, ay?

MRS. R. Feel! why exceedingly full of cares.

HAR. Did you?

MRS. R. I could not sleep for thinking of my coach, my liveries, and my chairmen; the taste of cloaths I should be presented in, distracted me for a week; and whether I should be married in white or lilac, gave me the most cruel anxiety.

LET. And is it possible that you felt no other care?

HAR. And pray, of what sort may your cares be, Mrs. Letitia? I begin to foresee now that you have taken a dislike to Doricourt.

LET. Indeed, sir, I have not.

HAR. Then what's all this melancholy about? An't you a going to be married? and what's more, to a sensible man, and what's more to a young girl, to a handsome man? And what's all this melancholy for, I say?

MRS. R. Why because he is handsome and sensible, and because she's over head and ears in love with him; all which, it seems, your foreknow-ledge had not told you a word of.

LET. Fie, Caroline!

HAR. Well, come, do you tell me what's the matter then? If you don't like him, hang the signing and sealing, he shan't have you,—and yet I can't say that neither; for you know that estate, that cost his father and me upwards of fourscore thousand pounds, must go all to him if you won't have him: if he won't have you indeed, 'twill be all yours. All that's clear, engrossed upon parchment, and the poor dear man set his hand to it whilst he was a-dying. — Ah! said I, I foresee you'll never live to see them come together; but their first son shall be christened Jeremiah, after you, that I promise you. — But come, I say, what is the matter? Dont you like him?

LET. I fear, sir — if I must speak — I fear I was less agreeable in Mr. Doricourt's eyes, than he appeared in mine.

HAR. There you are mistaken; for I asked him, and he told me he liked you vastly. Don't you think he must have taken a fancy to her? [*To* MRS. R.]

MRS. R. Why really I think so, as I was not by.

LET. My dear sir, I am convinced he has not; but if there is spirit or invention in woman, he shall.

HAR. Right, girl; go to your toilette —

LET. It is not my toilette that can serve me: but a plan has struck me, if you will not oppose it, which flatters me with brilliant success.

HAR. Oppose it! Not I indeed! What is it?

LET. Why, sir — it may seem a little paradoxical; but as he does not like me enough, I want him to like me still less, and will at our next interview endeavour to heighten his indifference into dislike.

HAR. Who the devil could have foreseen that?

MRS. R. Heaven and earth! Letitia, are you serious?

LET. As serious as the most important business of my life demands.

MRS. R. Why endeavour to make him dislike you?

LET. Because 'tis much easier to convert a sentiment into its opposite, than to transform indifference into tender passion.

MRS. R. That may be good philosophy, but I'm afraid you'll find it a bad maxim.

LET. I have the strongest confidence in it. I am inspired with unusual spirits, and on this hazard willingly stake my chance for happiness. I am impatient to begin my measures. [*Exit*]

HAR. Can you foresee the end of this, cousin?

MRS. R. No, sir; nothing less than your penetration can do that, I am sure; and I can't stay now to consider it. I am going to call on the Ogles, and then to lady Frances Touchwood's, and then to an action, and then — I don't know where — but I shall be at home time enough to witness this extraordinary interview. Good bye. [*Exit*]

HAR. Well 'tis an odd thing—I can't understand it,—but I foresee Letty will have her way, and so I shan't give myself the trouble to dispute it.

Act II.

SCENE I. [*Sir George Touchwood's House.*]

[*Enter* DORICOURT, *and* SIR GEORGE TOUCHWOOD]

DORIC. Married, ha, ha, ha! you whom I heard in Paris say such things of the sex, are in London a married man.

SIR G. The sex is still what it has ever been since la petite morale banished substantial virtues; and rather than have given my name to one of your high-bred, fashionable dames, I'd have crossed the line in a fireship, and married a Japanese.

DORIC. Yet you have married an English beauty; yea, and a beauty born in high life.

SIR G. True; but she has a simplicity of heart and manners, that would have become the fair Hebrew damsels toasted by the patriarchs.

DORIC. Ha, ha! Why, thou art a downright, matrimonial Quixote. My life on't she becomes as mere a town lady in six months, as though she had been bred to the trade.

SIR G. Common—common—[*Contemptuously*]—No, sir, lady Frances despises high life so much from the ideas I have given her, that she'll live in it like a salamander in fire.

DORIC. I'll send thee off to St. Evreux this night, drawn at full length, and coloured after nature.

SIR G. Tell him then, to add to the ridicule, that Touchwood glories in the name of husband; that he has found in one Englishwoman more beauty than Frenchmen ever saw, and more goodness than Frenchwomen can conceive.

DORIC. Well—enough of description. Introduce me to this phœnix; I came on purpose.

SIR G. Introduce!—oh, ay, to be sure!—I believe lady Frances is engaged just now—but another time.—How handsome the dog looks to-day! [*Aside.*]

DORIC. Another time!—but I have no other time. 'Sdeath! this is the only hour I can command this fortnight.

SIR G. I am glad to hear it, with all my soul! [*Aside.*] So then you can't dine with us to-day? That's very unlucky.

DORIC. Oh, yes—as to dinner—yes, I can, I believe, contrive to dine with you to-day.

SIR G. Pshaw! I didn't think on what I was saying; I meant supper. — You can't sup with us?

DORIC. Why supper will be rather more convenient than dinner. — But you are fortunate — if you had asked me any other night, I could not have come.

SIR G. To-night! — 'Gad, now I recollect, we are particularly engaged to-night. — But to-morrow night —

DORIC. Why, lookye, sir George, 'tis very plain you have no inclination to let me see your wife at all; so here I sit. [*Throws himself on the sofa.*] There's my hat, and here are my legs — Now I shan't stir till I have seen her; and I have no engagements; I'll breakfast, dine, and sup with you, every day this week.

SIR G. Was there ever such a provoking wretch! [*Aside.*] But to be plain with you, Doricourt, I and my house are at your service: but you are a damned agreeable fellow; and the women, I observe, always simper when you appear. For these reasons, I had rather, when lady Frances and I are together, that you should forget that we are acquainted, further than a nod, a smile, or a how d'ye?

DORIC. Very well.

SIR G. It is not merely yourself, in propria persona, that I object to; but, if, you are intimate here, you'll make my house still more the fashion than it is; and it is already so much so, that my doors are of no use to me. I married lady Frances to engross her to myself; yet, such is the blessed freedom of modern manners, that in spite of me, her eyes, thoughts, and conversation, are continually divided amongst all the flirts and coxcombs of fashion.

DORIC. To be sure, I confess that kind of freedom is carried rather too far. 'Tis hard one can't have a Jewel in one's cabinet, but the whole town must be gratified with its lustre. — He shan't preach me out, of seeing his wife though. [*Aside.*]

SIR G. Well, now, that's reasonable. When you take time to reflect, Doricourt, I always observe you decide right; and therefore I hope —

[*Enter* GIBSON]

GIB. Sir, my lady desires —

SIR G. I am particularly engaged.

DORIC. Oh, Lord, that shall be no excuse in the world. [*Leaping from the sofa.*] Lead the way, John. — I'll attend your lady. [*Exit, following* GIBSON]

SIR G. What devil possessed me to talk about her! — Here, Doricourt! [*Running after him*] Doricourt!

[*Enter* MRS. RACKETT *and* MISS OGLE, *followed by a Servant*]

MRS. R. Acquaint your lady that Mrs. Rackett and Miss Ogle are here. [*Exit Servant*]

MISS O. I shall hardly know lady Frances, 'tis so long since I was in Shropshire.

MRS. R. And I'll be sworn you never saw her out of Shropshire. — Her father kept her locked up with his caterpillars and shells; and loved her beyond any thing but a blue butterfly and a petrified frog!

MISS O. Ha, ha, ha! — Well, 'twas a cheap way of breeding her: — you know he was very poor, though a lord; and very high spirited, though a virtuoso. — In town, her pantheons, operas, and robes de cour, would have swallowed his sea-weeds, moths, and monsters, in six weeks! — Sir George, I find, thinks his wife a most extraordinary creature: he has taught her to despise every thing like fashionable life, and boasts that example will have no effect on her.

MRS. R. There's a great degree of impertinence in all that. — I'll try to make her a fine lady to humble him.

MISS O. That's just the thing I wish.

[*Enter* LADY FRANCES TOUCHWOOD]

LADY F. I beg ten thousand pardons, my dear Mrs. Rackett — Miss Ogle, I rejoice to see you: I should have come to you sooner, but I was detained in conversation by Mr. Doricourt.

MRS. R. Pray make no apology; I am quite happy that we have your lady ship in town at last. — What stay do you make?

LADY F. A short one! Sir George talks with regret of the scenes we have left; and as the ceremony of presentation is over, will, I believe, soon return.

MISS O. Sure he can't be so cruel. Does your ladyship wish to return so soon?

LADY F. I have not the habit of consulting my own wishes; but I think, if they decide, we shall not return immediately. I have yet hardly formed an idea of London.

MRS. R. I shall quarrel with your lord and master, if he dares to think of depriving us of you so soon. How do you dispose of yourself to-day?

LADY F. Sir George is going with me this morning to the mercers, to choose a silk; and then —

MRS. R. Choose a silk for you! Ha, ha, ha! sir George chooses your laces too, I hope; your gloves, and your pincushions!

LADY F. Madam!

MRS. R. I am glad to see you blush, my dear lady Frances. These are strange homespun ways! If you do these things, pray keep them secret. Lord bless us! If the town should know your husband chooses your gowns!

MISS O. You are very young, my lady, and have been brought up in solitude. The maxims you learnt among wood nymphs, in Shropshire, won't pass current here, I assure you.

MRS. R. Why, my dear creature, you look quite frightened. — Come, you shall go with us to an exhibition and an auction. Afterwards, we'll take a turn in the Park, and then drive to Kensington; so we shall be at home by four to dress; and in the evening I'll attend you to lady Brilliant's masquerade.

LADY F. I shall be very happy to be of your party, if sir George has no engagements.

MRS. R. What! do you stand so low in your own opinion, that you dare not trust yourself without sir George? If you choose to play Darby and Joan, my dear, you should have staid in the country; — 'tis an exhibition not calculated for London, I assure you.

MISS O. What, I suppose, my lady, you and sir George will be seen pacing it comfortably round the canal, arm in arm, and then go lovingly into the same carriage; dine tête-a-tête, spend the evening at piquet, and so go soberly to bed at eleven! — Such a snug plan may do for an attorney and his wife; but, for lady Frances Touchwood, 'tis as unsuitable as linsey-woolsey, or a black bonnet at the opera!

LADY F. These are rather new doctrines to me! — But, my dear Mrs. Rackett, you and miss Ogle must judge of these things better than I can. As you observe, I am but young, and may have caught absurd opinions. — Here is sir George!

[*Re-enter* SIR GEORGE TOUCHWOOD]

SIR G. 'Sdeath, another room full! [*Aside.*]

LADY F. My love! Mrs. Rackett and miss Ogle.

MRS. R. 'Give you joy, sir George. — We came to rob you of lady Frances for a few hours.

SIR. G. A few hours.

LADY F. Oh, yes! I am going to an exhibition, and an auction, and the Park, and Kensington, and a thousand places! — It is quite ridiculous, I find, for married people to be always together. — We shall be laughed at!

SIR G. I am astonished! — Mrs. Rackett, what does the dear creature mean?

MRS. R. Mean, sir George! — What she says, I imagine.

MISS O. Why, you know, sir, as lady Frances had the misfortune to be bred entirely in the country, she cannot be supposed to be versed in fashionable life.

SIR G. No; heaven forbid she should! — If she had madam, she would never have been my wife!

MRS. R. Are you serious?

SIR G. Perfectly so. — I should never had the courage to have married a well-bred fine lady.

MISS O. Pray, sir, what do you take a fine lady to be, that you express such fear of her? [*Sneeringly.*]

SIR G. A being easily described, madam, as she is seen every where but in her own house. She sleeps at home, but she lives all over the town. In her mind every sentiment gives place to the lust of conquest, and the vanity of being particular. The feelings of wife and mother are lost in the whirl of dissipation. If she continues virtuous, 'tis by chance — and, if she preserves her husband from ruin, 'tis by her dexterity at the card table! — Such a woman I take to be a perfect fine lady.

MRS. R. And you I take to be a slanderous cynic of two-and-thirty. — Twenty years hence, one might have forgiven such a libel! — Now, sir, hear my definition of a fine lady: — She is a creature for whom nature has done much, and education more; she has taste, elegance, spirit, understanding. In her manner she is free, in her morals nice. Her behaviour is undistinguishingly polite to her husband and all mankind — her sentiments are for their hours of retirement. In a word, a fine lady is the life of conversation, the spirit of society, the joy of the public! — Pleasure follows wherever she appears, and the kindest wishes attend her slumbers. — Make haste, then my dear lady Frances, commence fine lady, and force your husband to acknowledge the justness of my picture.

LADY F. I am sure 'tis a delightful one. How can you [*Looks at him.*] dislike it, sir George? You painted fashionable life in colours so disgusting, that I thought I hated it; but, on a nearer view it seems charming. I have hitherto lived in obscurity; 'tis time that I should be a woman of the world. I long to begin; — my heart pants with expectation and delight!

MRS. R. Come, then, let us begin directly. I am impatient to introduce you to that society which you were born to ornament and charm.

LADY F. Adieu, my love!—We shall meet again at dinner. [*Going.*]

SIR G. Sure, I am in a dream—Fanny!

LADY F. [*Returning.*] Sir George!

SIR G. Will you go without me?

MRS. R. Will you go without me!—Ha, ha, ha! what a pathetic address! Why, sure you would not always be seen side by side, like two beans upon a stalk. Are you afraid to trust lady Frances with me, sir?

SIR G. Heaven and earth! with whom can a man trust his wife, in the present state of society? Formerly there were distinctions of character amongst ye; every class of females had its particular description! grandmothers were pious, aunts discreet, old maids censorious! but now, aunts, grandmothers, girls, and maiden gentlewomen are all the same creature;—a wrinkle more or less is the sole difference between ye.

MRS. R. That maiden gentlewomen have lost their censoriousness is surely not in your catalogue of grievances.

SIR G. Indeed it is—and ranked amongst the most serious grievances.— Things went well, madam, when the tongues of three or four old virgins kept all the wives and daughters of a parish in awe. They were the dragons that guarded the Hesperian fruit; and I wonder they have not been obliged by act of parliament to resume their function.

MRS. R. Ha, ha, ha! and pensioned, I suppose, for making strict inquiries into the lives and conversations of their neighbours.

SIR G. With all my heart, and empowered to oblige every women to conform her conduct to her real situation. You, for instance, are a widow; your air should be sedate, your dress grave, your deportment matronly, and in all things an example to the young women growing up about you!—Instead of which, you are drest for conquest, think of nothing but ensnaring hearts; are a coquette, a wit, and a fine lady.

MRS. R. Bear witness to what he says! A coquette, a wit, and fine lady! Who would have expected an eulogy from such an ill-natur'd mortal?—Valour to a soldier, wisdom to a judge, or glory to a prince, is not more than such a character to a woman.

MISS O. Sir George, I see, languishes for the charming society of a century and a half ago; when a grave squire, and a still graver dame, surrounded by a sober family, formed a stiff group, in a mouldly old house, in the corner of a park.

MRS. R. Delightful serenity! Undisturbed by any noise but the cawing of rooks, and the quarterly rumbling of an old family coach on a state visit; with the happy intervention of a friendly call from the parish apothecary, or the curate's wife.

SIR G. And what is the society of which you boast?—a mere chaos, in which all distinction of rank is lost in a ridiculous affectation of ease. In the same select party, you will often find the wife of a bishop and a sharper, of an earl and a fiddler. In short, 'tis one universal masquerade, all disguised in the same habits and manners.

[*Enter* GIBSON]

GIB. Mr. Flutter. [*Exit*]

SIR G. Here comes an illustration. Now I defy you to tell, from his appearance, whether Flutter is a privy counsellor or a mercer, a lawyer or a grocer's 'prentice.

[*Enter* FLUTTER]

FLUT. Oh, just which you please, sir George; so you don't make me a lord mayor. Ah, Mrs. Rackett—Lady Frances, your most obedient; you look—now hang me, if that's not provoking?—had your gown been of another colour, I should have said the prettiest thing you ever heard in your life.

MISS O. Pray give it us.

FLUT. I was yesterday at Mrs. Bloomer's. She was dressed all in green; no other colour to be seen but dressed all in green; no other colour to be seen but that of her face and bosom. "So," says I, "My dear Mrs. Bloomer; you look like a carnation just bursting from its pod." Wasn't that pretty?

SIR G. And what said her husband?

FLUT. Her husband! why, her husband laughed, and said, a cucumber would have been a better simile.

SIR G. But there are husbands, sir, who would rather have corrected than amended your comparison; I, for instance, should consider a man's complimenting my wife as an impertinence.

FLUT. Why, what harm can there be in compliments? Sure they are not infectious; and if they were, you, sir George, of all people breathing, have reason to be satisfied about your lady's attachment; every body talks of it: that little bird there, that she killed out of jealousy, the most extraordinary instance of affection that ever was given.

LADY F. I kill a bird through jealousy! heavens! Mr. Flutter, how can you impute such a cruelty to me?

SIR G. I could have forgiven you, if you had.

FLUT. Oh, what a blundering fool! — No, no — now I remember — 'twas your bird, lady Frances — that's it, your bullfinch, which sir George, in one of the refinements of his passion, sent into the wide world to seek its fortune — He took it for a knight in disguise.

LADY F. Is it possible? Oh, sir George, could I have imagin'd it was you who deprived me of a creature I was so fond of?

SIR G. Mr. Flutter, you are one of those busy, idle, meddling people, who, from mere vacuity of mind, are the most dangerous inmates in a family. You have neither feelings nor opinions of your own; but like a glass in a tavern, bear about those of every blockhead who gives you his; and, because you mean no harm, think yourselves excused, though broken friendships, discords, and murders, are the consequences of your indiscretions.

FLUT. [*Taking out his Tablets.*]Vacuity of mind! What was next? I'll write down this sermon; 'tis the first I have heard since my grandmother's funeral.

MISS O. Come, lady Frances, you see what a cruel creature your loving husband can be: so let us leave him.

SIR G. Madam, lady Frances shall not go.

LADY F. Shall not, sir George? — This is the first time such an expression — [*Weeping.*]

SIR G. My love! my life!

LADY F. Don't imagine I'll be treated like a child! denied what I wish, and then pacified with sweet words.

MISS O. [*Apart.*] The bullfinch! that's an excellent subject; never let it down.

LADY F. I see plainly you would deprive me of every pleasure, as well as of my sweet bird — out of pure love! — Barbarous man!

SIR G. 'Tis well, madam; — your resentment of that circumstance proves to me, what I did not before suspect, that you are deficient both in tenderness and understanding — Tremble to think the hour approaches, in which you would give worlds for such a proof of my love. Go, madam, give yourself to the public; abandon your heart to dissipation, and see if in the scenes of gaiety and folly that await you, you can find a recompense for the lost affection of a doating husband. [*Exit.*]

FLUT. Lord, what a fine thing it is to have the gift of speech! I suppose sir George practices at Coachmakers'-hall, or the Black-horse in Bond-street.

LADY F. He is really angry; I cannot go.

MRS. R. Not go! foolish creature! you are arrived at the moment which, sometime or other, was sure to happen, and every thing depends on the use you make of it.

MISS O. Come, lady Frances, don't hesitate; the minutes are precious.

LADY F. I could find in my heart! — and yet I won't give up neither. — If I should in this instance, he'll expect it for ever. [*Exit with* MRS. RACKETT]

MISS O. Now you act like a woman of spirit. [*Exit.*]

FLUT. A fair tug, by Jupiter — between duty and pleasure! — Pleasure beats, and off we go. Io triumphe! [*Exit.*]

SCENE II. — *An Auction Room: Busts, Pictures, &c.* SILVERTONGUE *discovered, with* COMPANY, PUFFERS, *&c.*

[*Enter* LADY FRANCES TOUCHWOOD, MRS. RACKETT, *and* MISS OGLE]

SIL. Yes, sir, this is to be the first lot: — the model of a city, in wax.

2 GENT. The model of a city! What city!

SIL. That I have not been able to discover; but call it Rome, Pekin, or London, 'tis still a city; you'll find in it the same virtues, and the same vices, whatever the name.

LADY F. I wish sir George was here. — This man follows me about, and stares at me in such a way, that I am quite uneasy.

[LADY FRANCES *and* MISS OGLE *come forward, followed by* COURTALL.]

MISS O. He has travelled, and is heir to an immense state; so he is impertinent by patent.

COURT. You are very cruel, ladies. Miss Ogle — will not let me speak to you. As to this little scornful beauty, she has frowned me dead fifty times.

LADY F. Sir — I am a married woman. [*Confused.*]

COURT. A married woman! a good hint. [*Aside.*] It would be a shame if such a charming woman was not married. But I see you are a Daphne just come from your sheep and your meadows, your crook and your waterfalls. Pray now who is the happy Damon, to whom you have vowed eternal truth and constancy?

MISS O. 'Tis lady Frances Touchwood, Mr. Courtall, to whom you are speaking.

COURT. Lady Frances! By heaven, that's Saville's old flame. [*Aside.*]I beg your ladyship's pardon. I ought to have believed, that such beauty could belong only to your name — a name I have long been enamour'd

of because I knew it to be that of the finest woman in the world. [MRS.
RACKETT *comes forward*]

LADY F. [*Apart.*] My dear Mrs. Rackett, I am so frightened! Here's a man
making love to me, though he knows I am married.

MRS. R. Oh, the sooner for that, my dear; don't mind him. — Was you at
the Cassino last night, Mr. Courtall?

COURT. I looked in. — 'Twas impossible to stay. Nobody there but
antiques. You'll be at lady Brilliant's to-night, doubtless?

MRS. R. Yes, I go with lady Frances.

LADY F. Bless me! I did not know this gentleman was acquainted with Mrs.
Rackett. — I behaved so rude to him. [*To* MISS OGLE.]

MRS. R. Come, ma'am; [*Looking at her Watch.*] 'tis past one. I protest if we
don't fly to Kensington, we shan't find a soul there.

LADY F. Won't this gentleman go with us?

COURT. [*Looking surprized*] To be sure, you make me happy, madam,
beyond description.

MRS. R. Oh never mind him — he'll follow. [*Exeunt* LADY FRANCES, MRS.
RACKETT, and MISS OGLE]

COURT. Lady Touchwood, with a vengeance! But 'tis always so; your
reserved ladies are like ice, 'egad! — no sooner begin to soften than
they melt! [*Following*]

Act III.

SCENE I. — *Mr. Hardys'.*

[*Enter* MRS. RACKETT *and* LETITIA]

MRS. R. Come, prepare, prepare, your lover is coming.

LET. My lover! confess now that my absence at dinner was a severe mortification to him.

MRS. R. I can't absolutely swear it spoiled his appetite; he ate as if he was
hungry, and drank his wine as though he liked it.

LET. What was the apology?

MRS. R. That you were ill; — but I gave him a hint that your extreme
bashfulness could not support his eye.

LET. If I comprehend him, awkwardness and bashfulness are the last faults
he can pardon in a woman; so expect to see me transformed into the
veriest maukin.

MRS. R. You persevere then?

LET. Certainly. I know the design is a rash one, and the event
important; — it either makes Doricourt mine by all the tenderest ties of

passion, or deprives me of him for ever; and never to be his wife will afflict me less than to be his wife, and not be beloved.

MRS. R. So you won't trust to the good old maxim, — Marry first, and love will follow?

LET. As readily as I would venture my last guinea, that good fortune might follow. The woman that has not touched the heart of a man, before he leads her to the altar, has scarcely a chance to charm it, when possession and security turn their powerful arms against her — But here he comes — I'll disappear for a moment. Don't spare me. [*Exit*]

[*Enter* DORICOURT *not seeing* MRS. RACKETT.]

DORIC. So! [*Looking at a Picture.*] This is my mistress, I presume. Ma foi! the painter has hit her off. The downcast eye — the blushing cheek — timid — apprehensive — bashful — A tear and a prayer-book, would have made her La Bella Magdalena —

Give me a woman, in whose touching mein

A mind, a soul, a polished art is seen;

Whose motion speaks, whose poignant air can move;

Such are the darts, to wound with endless love.

MRS. R. Is that an impromptu?

[*Touching him on the Shoulder with her Fan*]

DORIC. [*Starting.*] Madam! Finely caught! [*Aside.*] — Not absolutely — it struck me during the desert, as a motto for your picture.

MRS. R. Gallantly turned! — I perceive, however, miss Hardy's charms have made no violent impression on you. — And who can wonder? — the poor girl's defects are so obvious.

DORIC. Defects!

MRS. R. Merely those of education — Her father's indulgence ruined her. — Mauvaise honte — conceit and ignorance all unite in the lady you are to marry.

DORIC. Marry! I marry such a woman! — Your picture, I hope, is overcharged. — I marry mauvaise honte, pertness, and ignorance!

MRS. R. Thank your stars, that ugliness and ill temper are not added to the list. — You must think her handsome.

DORIC. Half her personal beauty would content me; — but could the Medicean Venus be animated for me, and endowed with a vulgar soul, I should become the statue, and my heart transformed to marble.

MRS. R. Bless us! — We are in a hopeful way, then!

DORIC. There must be some envy in this. I see she is a coquette — [*Aside.*] — Ha, ha, ha! and you imagine I am persuaded of the truth of your character! ha, ha, ha! Miss Hardy, I have been assured, madam, is elegant and accomplished — but one must allow for a lady's painting.

MRS. R. I'll be even with him for that. [*Aside.*] Ha, ha, ha! and so you have found me out? — Well, I protest, I meant no harm; 'twas only to increase the eclat of her appearance, that I threw a veil over her charms. — Here comes the lady: her elegance and accomplishments will announce themselves.

[*Enter* LETITIA, *running.*]

LET. La, cousin, do you know that our John — Oh dear heart! — I didn't see you, sir. [*Hanging down her head, and dropping behind* MRS. R.]

MRS. R. Fie, Letitia — Mr. Doricourt thinks you a woman of elegant manners. Stand forward and confirm his opinion.

LET. No, no; keep before me. — He's my sweetheart, and 'tis impudent to look one's sweetheart in the face, you know.

MRS. R. You'll allow in future for a lady's painting, sir — Ha, ha, ha!

DORIC. I am astonished!

LET. Well, hang it, I'll take heart. — Why, he is but a man, you know, cousin — and I'll let him see, I wasn't born in a wood to be scared by an owl. [*Half apart; advances, and looks at him through her Fingers*] He, he, he! [*Goes up to him, and makes a very stiff, formal courtesy; he bows.*] You have been a great traveller, sir, I hear. I wish you'd tell us about the fine sights you saw when you went over sea — I have read in a book, that there are some other countries, where the men and women are all horses. — Did you see any of them?

MRS. R. Mr. Doricourt is not prepared my dear, for these inquiries — he is reflecting on the importance of the question, and will answer you — when he can.

LET. When he can! Why, he's as slow in speech as aunt Margery when she's reading Thomas Aquinas — and stands gaping like mumchance.

MRS. R. Have a little discretion.

LET. Hold your tongue! — Sure I may say what I please before I am married, if I can't afterwards — D'ye think a body does not know how to talk to a sweetheart? — He is not the first I have had.

DORIC. Indeed!

LET. Oh, lud, he speaks! — Why if you must know — there was the curate at home — When papa was a hunting, he used to come a suitoring, and make speeches to me out of books — Nobody knows what a mort of fine things he used to say to me — and call me Venis, and Jubah, and Dinah.

DORIC. And pray, fair lady, how did you answer him?

LET. Why, I used to say, "Look you, Mr. Curate, don't think to come over me with your flim-flams, for a better man than ever trod in your shoes is coming over-sea to marry me." — but, 'ifags, I begin to think I was out. — Parson Dobbins was the sprightfuller man of the two.

DORIC. Surely this cannot be miss Hardy?

LET. Laws, why don't you know me? — You saw me to-day — but I was daunted before my father, and the lawyer, and all them; and did not care to speak out — so, may be, you thought I couldn't — but I can talk as fast as any body, when I know folks a little — And now I have shown my parts, I hope you'll like me better.

[*Enter* HARDY]

HAR. I foresee this won't do — Mr. Doricourt, may be, you take my daughter for a fool, but you are mistaken — she's as sensible a girl as any in England.

DORIC. I am convinced she has a very uncommon understanding, sir. — I did not think he had been such an ass! [*Aside.*]

LET. My father will undo the whole [*Aside.*] Laws, papa, how can you think he can take me for a fool when every body knows, I beat the 'pothecary at conundrums, last Christmas-time? — And didn't I make a string of names, all in riddles, for the Lady's Diary? — There was a little river and a great house — that was Newcastle. — There was what a lamb says, and three letters, that was ba, and k-e-r, ker-baker. There was —

HAR. Don't stand ba-a-ing there — you'll make me mad in a moment — I tell you, sir, that for all that, she's dev'lish sensible.

DORIC. Sir, I give all possible credit to your assertions.

LET. Laws, papa, do come along. If you stand watching, how can my sweetheart break his mind, and tell me how he admires me?

DORIC. That would be difficult, indeed, madam.

HAR. I tell you, Letty, I'll have no more of this. — I see well enough —

LET. Laws, don't snub me before my husband — that is to be. — You'll teach him to snub me too — and, I believe, by his looks, he'd like to begin now. So let us go — cousin, you may tell the gentleman what a genus I have — how I can cut watch papers, and work catgut — make quadrille baskets with pins, and take profiles in shade — ay, as well as the lady at No. 62, South Moulton-street, Grosvenor-square.

[*Exeunt* HAR. *and* LET.]

MRS. R. What think you of my painting now?

DORIC. Oh, mere water colours, madam — The lady has caricatured your picture.

MRS. R. And how does she strike you on the whole?

DORIC. Like a good design, spoiled by the incapacity of the artist. Her faults are evidently the result of her father's weak indulgence. I observed an expression in her eye, that seemed to satirize the folly of her lips.

MRS. R. But at her age, when education is fixed, and manner becomes nature, hopes of improvement —

DORIC. Would be absurd — Besides, I can't turn schoolmaster — Doricourt's wife must be incapable of improvement — but it must be, because she's got beyond it.

MRS. R. I am pleased your misfortune sits no heavier.

DORIC. Your pardon, madam — so mercurial was the hour in which I was born, that misfortunes always go plump to the bottom of my heart, like a pebble in water, and leave the surface unruffled —! shall certainly set off for Bath, or the other world to-night — but whether I shall use a chaise with four swift coursers, or go off in a tangent — from the aperture of a pistol, deserves consideration — so I make my adieus. [Going]

MRS. R. Oh, but I entreat you, postpone your journey till to-morrow — determine on which you will — you must be this night at the masquerade.

DORIC. Masquerade!

MRS. R. Why not? — If you resolve to visit the other world, you may as well take one night's pleasure first in this, you know.

DORIC. Faith, that's very true; — ladies are the best philosophers after all — Expect me at the masquerade. [Exit]

MRS. R. He's a charming fellow — I think Letitia shan't have him. [Going.]
        [Enter HARDY]

HAR. What's he gone?

MRS. R. Yes; and I am glad he is — You would have ruined us! — Now I beg, Mr. Hardy, you won't interfere in this business; it is a little out of your way. [Exit]

HAR. Hang me, if I don't, though — I foresee very clearly what will be the end of it, if I leave you to yourselves; so I'll e'en follow him to the masquerade, and tell him all about it. — Let me see — what shall my dress be — A great mogul? No — A grenadier? No — no — that, I foresee, would make a laugh — Hang me, if I don't send to my favourite little Quick, and borrow his Jew Isaac's dress — I know the dog likes a glass of good wine; so I'll give him a bottle of my forty-eight, and he shall teach me—Ay, that's it—I'll be cunning little Isaac—If they complain of my want of wit, I'll tell them, the cursed Duenna wears the breeches, and has spoiled my parts. [*Exit*]

SCENE II.—*Courtalls'*.

[*Enter* COURTALL, SAVILLE, *and three Gentlemen, from an Apartment in the back Scene. The last three Tipsy.*]

COURT. You shan't go yet—Another catch and another bottle.

1 GENT. May I be a bottle, and an empty bottle, if you catch me at that!—Why, I am going to the masquerade; Jack —, you know who I mean, is to meet me, and we are to have a leap at the new lustres.

2 GENT. And I am going to—a pilgrim—[*Hickups.*]—Am not I in a pretty pickle for a pilgrim?—And Tony, here—he is going in the disguise—in the disguise—of a gentleman!

1 GENT. We are all very disguised—so bid them draw up—Dy'e hear?
[*Exeunt the Three Gentlemen*]

SAV. Thy skull, Courtall, is a lady's thimble.—no, an egg shell.

COURT. Nay, then you are gone too: you never aspire to similes, but in your cups.

SAV. No, no; I am steady enough—but the fumes of the wine pass directly through thy egg-shell, and leave thy brain as cool as—Hey! I am quite sober; my similes fail me.

COURT. Then we'll sit down here, and have one sober bottle.
[*Enter* DICK]
Bring a bottle and glasses. [*Exit* DICK]

SAV. I'll not swallow another drop; no, though the juice should be the true Falernian.

COURT. By the bright eyes of her you love, you shall drink her health.
[*Re-enter* DICK, *with Bottle and Glasses.*]

SAV. Ah! [*Sitting down.*] Her I loved is gone—[*Sighing.*]—She's married!
[*Exit* DICK]

COURT. Then bless your stars you are not her husband! I would be husband to no woman in Europe, who was not dev'lish rich, and dev'lish ugly.

SAV. Wherefore ugly?

COURT. Because she could not have the conscience to exact those attentions that a pretty wife expects; or if she should, her resentments would be perfectly easy to me, nobody would undertake to revenge her cause.

SAV. Thou art a most licentious fellow.

COURT. I should hate my own wife, that's certain; but I have a warm heart for those of other people; and so here's to the prettiest wife in England—lady Frances Touchwood.

SAV. Lady Frances Touchwood! I rise to drink her, [*Drinks.*] How the devil came lady Frances in your head? I never knew you give a woman of chastity before.

COURT. That's odd, for you have heard me give half the women of fashion in England. —But, pray now what do you take a woman of chastity to be? [*Sneeringly.*]

SAV. Such a woman as lady Frances Touchwood, sir.

COURT. Oh, you are grave, sir; I remember you was an adorer of hers— Why didn't you marry her?

SAV. I had not the arrogance to look so high. —Had my fortune been worthy of her, she should not have been ignorant of my admiration.

COURT. Precious fellow! What, I suppose you would not dare tell her now that you admire her?

SAV. No, nor you.

COURT. By the lord, I have told her so.

SAV. Have? Impossible!

COURT. Ha, ha, ha! —Is it so?

SAV. How did she receive the declaration?

COURT. Why in the old way; blushed and frowned, and said she was married.

SAV. What amazing things thou art capable of! I could more easily have taken the Pope by the beard, than profaned her ears with such a declaration.

COURT. I shall meet her at lady Brilliant's to-night, where I shall repeat it; and I'd lay my life, under a mask, she'll hear it all without a blush or frown.

SAV. [*Rising.*] 'Tis false, sir! —She won't.

COURT. She will! [*Rising.*] Nay, I'll venture to lay a round sum that I prevail on her to go out with me—only to taste the fresh air I mean.

SAV. Preposterous vanity! from this moment I suspect that half the victories you have boasted are as false and slanderous as your pretended influence with lady Frances.

COURT. Pretended! —How should such a fellow as you now, who never soared beyond a cherry-checked daughter of a ploughman, in Norfolk, judge of the influence of a man of my figure and habits? I could show

thee a list, in which there are names to shake thy faith in thy whole
sex; — and, to that list I have no doubt of adding the name of lady —

SAV. Hold, sir! My ears cannot bear the profination; — you cannot — dare
not approach her! — For your soul you dare not mention love to her!
Her look would freeze the word, whilst it hovered on thy licentious
lips.

COURT. Whu! whu! Well, we shall see — this evening, by Jupiter, the trial
shall be made. — If I fail — I fail.

SAV. I think thou dar'st not! But my life, my honour, on her purity. [*Exit*]

COURT. Hot-headed fool! But since he has brought it to this point, by gad
I'll try what can be done with her ladyship — [*Musing — Rings.*] She's
frost-work, and the prejudices of education yet strong: ergo, passionate professions will only inflame her pride, and put her on her
guard. — For other arts then!

[*Enter* DICK]

Dick, do you know any of the servants at sir George Touchwood's?

DICK. Yes, sir, I knows the groom, and one of the housemaids; for the
matter o'that, she's my own cousin; and it was my mother that helped
her to the place.

COURT. Do you know lady Frances's maid?

DICK. I can't say as how I know she.

COURT. Do you know sir George's valet?

DICK. No, sir; but Sally is very thick with Mr. Gibson, sir George's
gentleman.

COURT. Then go there directly, and employ Sally to discover whether her
master goes to lady Brilliant's this evening; and if he does, the name of
the shop that sold his habit.

DICK. Yes, sir.

COURT. Be exact in your intelligence, and come to me at Boodle's. [*Exit.*
DICK] — If I cannot otherwise succeed, I'll beguile her as Jove did
Alcmena, in the shape of her husband. The possession of so fine a
woman — the triumph over Saville, are each a sufficient motive; and
united, they shall be resistless. [*Exit*]

SCENE III. — *The Street.*

[*Enter* SAVILLE]

SAV. The air has recovered me! What have I been doing? Perhaps my
petulance may be the cause of her ruin, whose honour I asserted: his
vanity is piqued; — and where women are concerned, Courtall can be a
villain.

[*Enter* DICK. *Bows and passes hastily.*]

Ha! That's his servant! — Dick!

DICK. [*Returning.*] Sir!

SAV. Where are you going, Dick?

DICK. Going! I am going, sir, where my master sent me.

SAV. Well answered — but I have a particular reason for my inquiry, and you must tell me.

DICK. Why then, sir, I am going to call upon a cousin of mine, that lives at sir George Touchwood's.

SAV. Very well. — There, [*Gives him Money*] you must make your cousin drink my health. — What are you going about?

DICK. Why, sir, I believe 'tis no harm, or elseways I am sure I would not blab — I am only going to ax if sir George goes to the masquerade to-night, and what dress he wears!

SAV. Enough! Now, Dick, if you will call at my lodgings in your way back, and acquaint me with your cousin's intelligence, I'll double the trifle I have given you.

DICK. Bless your honour, I'll call — never fear. [*Exit*]

SAV. Surely the occasion may justify the means; — 'tis doubly my duty to be lady Frances's protector. Courtall, I see, is planning an artful scheme: but Saville shall out plot-him. [*Exit*]

SCENE IV. — *Sir George Touchwood's.*

[*Enter* SIR GEORGE *and* VILLIERS]

VIL. For shame, sir George; you have left lady Frances in tears. — How can you afflict her?

SIR G. 'Tis I that am afflicted; — my dream of happiness is over — Lady Frances and I are disunited.

VIL. The devil! Why, you have been in town but ten days: she can have made no acquaintance for a commons affair yet.

SIR G. Pho! 'tis our minds that are disunited: she no longer places her whole delight in me; she has yielded herself up to the world!

VIL. Yielded herself up to the world! Why did you not bring her to town in a cage? Then she might have taken a peep at the world! — But, after all, what has the world done? A twelvemonth since you was the gayest fellow in it: — If any body ask'd who dresses best? — Sir George Touchwood. — Who is the most wedded to amusement and dissipation? Sir George Touchwood — And now Sir George is metamorphosed into a sour censor: and talks of fashionable life with as much bitterness as the old crabbed fellow in Rome.

ISIR G. The moment I became possessed of such a jewel as lady Frances, every thing wore a different complexion; that society in which I liv'd, with so much eclat; became the object of my terror; and I think of the manners of polite life as I do of the atmosphere of a Pest-house. — My wife is already infected; she was set upon this morning by maids, widows, and batchelors, who carried her off in triumph in spite of my displeasure.

VIL. Aye, to be sure; there would have been no triumph in the case, if you had not oppos'd it: — but I have heard the whole story from Mrs. Rackett; and I assure you, lady Frances didn't enjoy the morning at all; — she wish'd for you fifty times.

SIR G. Indeed! Are you sure of that?

VIL. Perfectly sure.

SIR G. I wish I had known it: — my uneasiness at dinner was occasioned by very different ideas.

VIL. Here then she comes to receive your apology; but if she is true woman, her displeasure will rise in proportion to your contrition; — and till you grow careless about her pardon, she won't grant it: — however, I'll leave you. — Matrimonial duties are seldom set in the style I like. [*Exit* VILLERS]

[*Enter* LADY FRANCES]

SIR G. The sweet sorrow that glitters in these eyes, I cannot bear [*Embracing her.*] Look cheerfully, you rogue.

LADY F. I cannot look otherwise if you are pleas'd with me.

SIR G. Well, Fanny, to-day you made your entree in the fashionable world; tell me honestly the impressions you receiv'd.

LADY F. Indeed, sir George, I was so hurried from place to place, that I had not time to find out what my impressions were.

SIR G. That's the very spirit of the life you have chosen.

LADY F. Every body about me seem'd happy — but every body seem'd in a hurry to be happy somewhere else.

SIR G. And you like this?

LADY F. One must like what the rest of the world likes.

SIR G. Pernicious maxim!

LADY F. But, my dear sir George, you have not promised to go with me to the masquerade.

SIR G. 'Twould be a shocking indecorum to be seen together, you know.

LADY F. Oh, no; I ask'd Mrs. Rackett, and she told me we might be seen together at the masquerade — without being laughed at.

SIR G. Really?

LADY F. Indeed, to tell you the truth, I could wish it was the fashion for married people to be inseparable: for I have more heart felt satisfaction in fifteen minutes with you at my side, than fifteen days of amusement could give me without you.

SIR G. My sweet creature! How that confession charms me! — Let us begin the fashion.

LADY F. O, impossible! we should not gain a single proselyte; and you can't conceive what spiteful things, would be said of us. — At Kensington to day a lady met us, whom we saw at court, when we were presented; she lifted up her hands in amazement! — Bless me! said she to her companion, here's lady Frances without sir Hurlo Thrumbo! — My dear Mrs. Rackett consider what an important charge you have! for heaven's sake take her home again, or some enchanter on a flying dragon will descend and carry her off — Oh, said another, I dare say lady Frances has a clue at her heel, like the peerless Rosamond: — her tender swain would never have trusted her so far without such a precaution.

SIR G. Heaven and earth! — How shall innocence preserve its lustre amidst manners so corrupt! — My dear Fanny, I feel a sentiment for thee at this moment, tenderer than love — more animated than passion. — I could weep over that purity, expos'd to the ? breath of fashion, and the ton, in whose latitudinary vortex chastity herself can scarcely move unspotted.

   [*Enter* GIBSON]

GIB. Your honour talk'd, I thought, something about going to the masquerade?

SIR G. Well.

GIB. Isn't it? — hasn't your honour? — I thought your honour had forgot to order a dress.

LADY F. Well consider'd, Gibson. — Come, will you be Jew, Turk, or Heretic; Chinese Emperor, or a ballad-singer: a rake, or a watchman?

SIR G. Oh, neither, my love; I can't take the trouble to support a character.

LADY F. You'll wear a domino then: — I saw a pink domino trimmed with blue at the shop where I bought my habit. — Would you like it?

SIR G. Any thing, any thing.

LADY F. Then go about it directly, Gibson. — A pink domino trimm'd with blue, and a hat of the same — Come, you have not seen my dress yet —

it is most beautiful; I long to have it on.

[*Exeunt* SIR GEORGE *and* LADY FRANCES]

Act IV.

SCENE I. — *A Masquerade.*

[*A party dancing Cotillions in front — a variety of Characters pass and repass.*]

MOUNT. Who'll buy my nostrums? Who'll buy my nostrums?

MASK. What are they? [*They all come round him*]

MOUNT. Different sorts, and for different customs. Here's a liquor for ladies — it expells the rage of gaming and gallantry. Here's a pill for members of parliament — good to settle consciences. Here's an eye-water for jealous husbands — it thickens the visual membrane, through which they see too clearly. Here's a decoction for the clergy — it never sits easy, if the patient has more than one living. Here's a draught for lawyers — a great promoter of modesty. Here's a powder for projectors — 'twill rectify the fumes of an empty stomach, and dissipate their airy castles.

MASK. Have you a nostrum that can give patience to young heirs, whose uncles and fathers are stout and healthy?

MOUNT. Yes; and I have an infusion for creditors — it gives resignation and humility, when fine gentlemen break their promises, or plead their privilege.

MASK. Come along: — I'll find you customers for your whole cargo. [*They retire*]

[*Enter* HARDY, *in the dress of Isaac Mendoza.*]

HAR. Why isn't it a shame to see so many stout, well-built young fellows, masquerading, and cutting Couranta's here at home — instead of making the French cut capers to the tune of your cannon — or sweating the Spaniards with an English Fandango? — I foresee the end of all this.

MASK. Why, thou little testy Israelite! back to Duke's Place; and preach your tribe into a subscription for the good of the land on whose milk and honey ye fatten. — Where are your Joshuas and your Gideons, aye! What! all dwindled into stockbrokers, Pedlars, and Rag-men?

HAR. No, not all. Some of us turn Christians, and by degrees grow into all the privileges of Englishmen! In the second generation we are patriots, rebels, courtiers, and husbands. [*Puts his fingers to his forehead.*]

[*Mask advances.*]

2d MASK. What, my little Isaac! — How the devil came you here? Where's your old Margaret?

HAR. Oh, I have got rid of her.

2d MASK. How?

HAR. Why, I persuaded a young Irishman that she was a blooming plump beauty of eighteen; so they made an elopement, ha! ha! ha! and she is now the toast of Tipperary. Ha! there's cousin Rackett and her party; they sha'nt know me. [*Aside. —Puts on his Mask*]

[*Enter* FOLLY *on a Hobby-horse, with Cap and Bells.*]

MASK. Hey! Tom fool! what business have you here?

FOLLY. What sir! affront a Prince in his own dominion! [*Struts off*]

[*Enter* MRS. RACKETT, LADY FRANCES, SIR GEORGE *and* FLUTTER]

MRS. R. Look at this dumpling Jew; he must be a Levite by his figure. You have surely practised the flesh-hook a long time, friend, to have raised that goodly presence.

HAR. About as long, my brisk widow, as you have been angling for a second husband; but my hook has been better baited than yours. — You have only caught gudgeons, I see. [*Pointing to Flutter.*]

FLUT. Oh! this is one of the geniuses they hire to entertain the company with their accidental sallies —Let me look at your common-place book, friend. —I want a few good things.

HAR. I'd oblige you, with all my heart but you'll spoil them in repeating — or, if you should not, they'll gain you no reputation —for nobody will believe they are your own.

SIR G. He knows ye, Flutter! —the little gentleman fancies himself a wit, I see.

HAR. There's no depending on what you see —eyes of the jealous are not to be trusted —Look to your lady.

FLUT. He knows ye, sir George.

HAR. I can neither see Doricourt nor Letty. [*Aside.*] I must find them out. [*Aside.*] —[*Exit* HARDY]

MRS. R. Well, lady Frances, is not all this charming? Could you have conceived such a brilliant assemblage of objects?

LADY F. Delightful. The days of enchantment are restor'd; the columns glow with saphires and rubies, emperors and fairies, beauties and dwarfs, meet me at every step.

SIR G. How lively are first impressions on sensible minds! In four hours, vapidity and languor will take place of that exquisite sense of joy which flutters your little heart.

MRS. R. What an inhuman creature! Fate has not allowed us these sensations above ten times in our lives and would you have us shorten them by anticipation? [SIR G. *and* MRS. R. *talk apart.*]

FLUT. O lord! your wise men are the greatest fools upon earth; they reason about their enjoyments, and analyse their pleasures, whilst the essence escapes. Look, lady Frances: D'ye see that figure strutting in the dress of an emperor? His father retails oranges in Botolph-Lane. That gipsey is a maid of honour, and that rag-man a physician.

LADY F. Why, you know every body!

FLUT. Oh, every creature. — A mask is nothing at all to me. — I can give you the history of half the people here. In the next apartment there is a whole family, and, to my knowledge, have lived on water-cresses this month, to make a figure here to-night; — but, to make up for that, they'll cram their pockets with cold ducks and chickens, for a carnival to-morrow.

LADY F. Oh, I should like to see this provident family.

FLUT. Honour me with your arm. [*Exeunt* FLUT. *and* LADY F—MRS. R. *advances*]

MRS. R. Come, sir George, you shall be my beau. — We'll make the tour of the rooms, and meet them. Oh! your pardon, you must follow lady Frances; or the wit and fine parts of Mr. Flutter may drive you out of her head. Ha! ha! ha! [*Exit* MRS. RACKETT]

SIR G. I was going to follow her, and now I dare not. How can I be such a fool as to be governed by the fear of that ridicule which I despise? [*Exit* SIR G.]

[*Enter* DORICOURT *meeting at Mask.*]

DORIC. Ha! my lord; — I thought you had been engaged at Westminster on this important night.

MASK. So I am — I slipt out as soon as lord Trope got upon his legs; I can badiner here an hour or two, and be back again before he is down. — There's a fine figure! I'll address her.

[*Enter* LETITIA]

Charity, fair lady! Charity for a poor pilgrim.

LET. Charity! If you mean my prayers, heaven grant thee wit, pilgrim.

MASK. That blessing would do from a devotee: from you I ask other charities; — such charities as beauty should bestow — soft looks — sweet words — and kind wishes.

LET. Alas! I am bankrupt of these, and forced to turn beggar myself. — There he is! — how shall I catch his attention? [*Aside.*]

MASK. Will you grant me no favour?

LET. Yes, one—I'll make you my partner—not for life, but through the soft mazes of a minuet.—Dare you dance?

DORIC. Some spirit in that.

MASK. I dare do any thing you command. That lady is against my vow—but here comes a man of the world.

DORIC. Do you know her, my lord?

MASK. No. Such a woman as that would formerly have been known in any disguise; but beauty is not common—Venus seems to have given her cestus to the whole sex.

[A Minuet.]

DORIC. [During the Minuet.] She dances divinely. [When ended.] Somebody must know her! Let us inquire who she is. [Retires]

[Enter SAVILLE and KITTY WILLIS, habited like Lady Frances]

SAV. I have seen Courtall in sir George's habit, though he endeavoured to keep himself concel'd. Go, and seat yourself in the tea-room, and on no account discover your face;—remember too, Kitty, that the woman you are to personate is a woman of virtue.

KITTY. I am afraid I shall find that a difficult character; indeed I believe it is seldom kept up through a whole masquerade.

SAV. Of that you can be no judge.—Follow my directions, and you shall be rewarded.

[Exit KITTY]

[Enter DORICOURT]

DORIC. Ha! Saville! Did you see a lady dance just now?

SAV. No.

DORIC. Very odd. Nobody knows her.

SAV. Where is miss Hardy?

DORIC. Cutting watch-papers, and making conundrums, I suppose.

SAV. What do you mean?

DORIC. Faith, I hardly know. She's not here, however, Mrs. Rackett tells me.—I ask'd no further.

SAV. Your indifference seems increas'd.

DORIC. Quite the reverse; 'tis advanced thirty-two degrees towards hatred.

SAV. You are jesting?

DORIC. Then it must be with a very ill grace, my dear Saville; for I never felt so seriously: Do you know the creature's almost an idiot?

SAV. What!

DORIC. An idiot. What the devil shall I do with her? Egad! I think I'll feign myself mad—and then Hardy will propose to cancel the engagements.

SAV. An excellent expedient. I must leave you; you are mysterious, and I can't stay to unravel ye.—I came here to watch over innocence and beauty.

DORIC. The guardian of innocence and beauty at three-and-twenty! Is there not a cloven foot under that black gown, Saville?

SAV. No, faith, Courtall is here on a most detestable design.—I found means to get a knowledge of the lady's dress, and have brought a girl to personate her, whose reputation cannot be hurt. You shall know the result to-morrow. Adieu. [*Exit* SAVILLE]

DORIC. [*Musing.*] Yes, I think that will do.—I'll feign myself mad, fee the doctor to pronounce me incurable, and when the parchments are destroyed— [*Stands in a musing Posture.*]

[*Enter* LETITIA]

LET. You have chosen an odd situation for study. Fashion and taste preside in this spot:—They throw their spells around you:—ten thousand delights spring up at their command;—and you, a stoic—a being without senses, are wrapt in reflection.

DORIC. And you, the most charming being in the world, awaken me to admiration. Did you come from the stars?

LET. Yes, and I shall re-ascend in a moment.

DORIC. Pray show me your face before you go.

LET. Beware of imprudent curiosity; it lost Paradise.

DORIC. Eve's curiosity was raised by the devil—'tis an angel tempts mine.—So your allusion is not in point.

LET. But why would you see my face?

DORIC. To fall in love with it.

LET. And what then?

DORIC. Why then—Ay, curse it! there's the rub! [*Aside.*]

LET. Your mistress will be angry;—but perhaps you have no mistress?

DORIC. Yes, yes, and a sweet one it is!

LET. What! is she old?

DORIC. No.

LET. Ugly?

DORIC. No.

LET. What then?

DORIC. Pho! don't talk about her; but show me your face.

LET. My vanity forbids it—'twould frighten you.

DORIC. Impossible! Your shape is graceful, your air bewitching, your bosom transparent, and your chin would tempt me to kiss it, if I did not see a pouting, red lip above it, that demands—[*Going to kiss.*]

LET. You grow too free.

DORIC. Show me your face then—only half a glance.

LET. Not for worlds!

DORIC. What! you will have a little gentle force? [*Attempts to seize her Mask.*]

LET. I am gone for ever? [*Exit*]

DORIC. 'Tis false—I'll follow to the end— [*Exit*]
          [*Music. Re-enter* FLUTTER, LADY FRANCES TOUCHWOOD, *and* SAVILLE]

LADY F. How can you be thus interested for a stranger?

SAV. Goodness will have interest; its home is heaven: so earth 'tis but a wanderer. Where is your husband?

FLUT. Why, what's that to him?

LADY F. Surely it can't be merely his habit;—there's something in him that awes me.

FLUT. Pho! 'tis only his grey beard. I know him; he keeps a lottery-office on Cornhill.

SAV. My province as an enchanter lays open every secret to me, lady! there are dangers abroad—Beware! [*Exit*]

LADY F. 'Tis very odd; his manner has made me tremble. Let us seek sir George.

FLUT. He is coming towards us.
          [*Enter* COURTALL, *habited like sir George Touchwood*]

COURT. There she is! If I can but disengage her from that fool, Flutter— crown me, ye schemers, with immortal wreaths!

LADY F. Oh, my dear sir George! I rejoice to meet you—an old conjurer has been frightening me with his prophecies.—Where's Mrs. Rackett?

COURT. In the dancing-room.—I promised to send you to her, Mr. Flutter.

FLUT. Ah! she wants me to dance. With all my heart. [*Exit*]

LADY F. Why do you keep on your mask?—'tis too warm.

COURT. 'Tis very warm—I want air—let us go.

LADY F. You seem agitated.—Shan't we bid our company adieu?

COURT. No, no—there's not time for forms. I'll just give directions to the carriage, and be with you in a moment. [*Going, steps back.*] Put on your mask! I have a particular reason for it. [*Exit*]

[*Re-enter* SAVILLE, *with* KITTY]

SAV. Now, Kitty, you know your lesson. Lady Frances, [*Takes off his Mask.*] let me lead you to your husband.

LADY F. Heavens! Is Mr. Saville the conjurer? sir George is just stepp'd to the door, to give directions—We are going home immediately.

SAV. No, madam, you are deceived: sir George is this way.

LADY F. This is astonishing!

SAV. Be not alarmed: you have escaped a snare, and shall be in safety in a moment. [*Exeunt* SAVILLE *and* LADY FRANCES]

[*Re-enter* COURTALL, *and seizes* KITTY'S *hand*]

COURT. Now!

KITTY. 'Tis pity to go so soon.

COURT. Perhaps I may bring you back, my angel—but go now you must.

[*Exeunt* COURTALL *and* KITTY]

[*Music. Re-enter* DORICOURT *and* LETITIA]

DORIC. By heavens! I never was charmed till now.—English beauty—French vivacity—wit—elegance.—Your name, my angel! tell me your name, though you persist in concealing your face.

LET. My name has a spell in it.

DORIC. I thought so; it must be charming.

LET. But if revealed, the charm is broke.

DORIC. I'll answer for its force.

LET. Suppose it Harriet, or Charlotte, or Maria, or—

DORIC. Hang Harriet, and Charlotte, and Maria—the name your father gave ye!

LET. That can't be worth knowing; 'tis so transient a thing.

DORIC. How, transient?

LET. Heaven forbid my name should be lasting till I am married.

DORIC. Married! the chains of matrimony are too heavy and vulgar for such a spirit as yours. The flowery wreaths of Cupid are the only bands you should wear.

LET. They are the lightest, I believe; but 'tis possible to wear those of marriage gracefully.—Throw them loosely round, and twist them in a true-lover's knot for the bosom.

DORIC. An angel! But what will you be when a wife?

LET. A woman.—If my husband should prove a churl, a fool, or a tyrant, I'd break his heart, ruin his fortune, elope with the first pretty fellow that asked me—and return the contempt of the world with scorn, whilst my feelings preyed upon my life.

DORIC. Amazing! [*Aside.*] What if you loved him, and he were worthy of your love?

LET. Why, then I'd be anything—and all!—grave, gay, capricious—the soul of whim, the spirit of variety—live with him in the eye of fashion, or in the shade of retirement—change my country, my sex—feast with him in an Equimaux hut, or a Persian pavilion—join him in the victorious war-dance on the borders of Lake Ontario, or sleep to the soft breathings of the flute in the cinnamon groves of Ceylon—dig with him in the mines of Golconda, or enter the dangerous precincts of the mogul's seraglio—cheat him of his wishes, and overturn his empire, to restore the husband of my heart to the blessings of liberty and love.

DORIC. Delightful wildness! oh, to catch thee, and hold thee for ever in this little cage! [*Attempting to clasp her.*]

LET. Hold, sir. Though Cupid must give the bait that tempts me to the snare, 'tis Hymen must spread the net to catch me.

DORIC. 'Tis in vain to assume airs of coldness—Fate has ordained you mine.

LET. How do you know?

DORIC. I feel it here. I never met with a woman so perfectly to my taste; and I won't believe it formed you so, on purpose to tantalize me.

LET. This moment is worth a whole existence! [*Aside.*]

DORIC. Come, show me your face, and rivet my chains.

LET. To-morrow you shall be satisfied.

DORIC. To-morrow, and not to-night?

LET. No.

DORIC. Where then shall I wait on you to-morrow?—Where see you?

LET. You shall see me at an hour when you least expect me.

DORIC. Why all this mystery?

LET. I like to be mysterious. At present be content to know that I am a woman of family and fortune.

DORIC. Let me see you to your carriage.

LET. As you value knowing me, stir not a step. If I am followed, you never see me more. Adieu. [*Exit*]

    [*Enter* HARDY]

HAR. Adieu! then I'm come in at the fag end! [*Aside.*]

DORIC. Barbarous creature! she's gone! what, and is this really serious?— Am I in love?—Pho! it can't be.

    [*Enter* FLUTTER]

O Flutter, do you know that charming creature?

FLUT. What charming creature? I passed a thousand,

DORIC. She went out at that door, as you entered.

FLUT. Oh, yes; — I know her very well.

DORIC. Do you, my dear fellow, who?

FLUT. She's kept by lord George Jennett.

HAR. Impudent scoundrel! — I foresee I shall cut his throat! [*Aside.*]

DORIC. Kept!

FLUT. Yes; colonel Gorget had her first; — then Mr. Loveill; — then — I forget exactly how many; and at last she's lord George's. [*Talks to other Masks.*]

DORIC. I'll murder Gorget, poison lord George, and shoot myself.

HAR. Now's the time, I see, to clear up the whole. Mr. Doricourt! — I say — Flutter was mistaken; I know who you are in love with.

DORIC. A strange rencontre! Who?

HAR. My Letty.

DORIC. Oh! I understand your rebuke; — 'tis too soon, sir, to assume the father-in-law.

HAR. Zounds! what do you mean by that? I tell you that the lady you admire is Letitia Hardy.

DORIC. I am glad you are so well satisfied with the state of my heart. — I wish I was! [*Exit*]

HAR. Stop a moment. — Stop, I say! what, you won't? very well — if I don't play you a trick for this, may I never be a grandfather! I'll plot with Letty now, and not against her; ay, hang me if I don't! There's something in my head, that shall tingle in his heart. He shall have a lecture upon impatience, that I foresee he'll be the better for as long as he lives.

[*Re enter* SAVILLE, *with Gentlemen.*]

SAV. Flutter, come with us; we're going to raise a laugh at Courtall's.

FLUT. With all my heart. "Live to live," was my father's motto: "Live to laugh," is mine. [*Music. — Exeunt*]

SCENE II. — *Courtall's.*

[*Enter* KITTY *and* COURTALL]

KITTY. Where have you brought me, sir George? This is not our home!

COURT. 'Tis my home, beautiful lady Frances! [*kneels and takes off his Mask.*] Oh, forgive the ardency of my passion, which has compelled me to deceive you!

KITTY. Mr. Courtall! what will become of me?

COURT. Oh, say but that you pardon the wretch who adores you. Did you but know the agonizing tortures of my heart, since I had the felicity of conversing with you this morning—or the despair that now— [*Knock.* COURTALL *rises*]

KITTY. Oh, I'm undone!

COURT. Zounds! my dear lady Frances! I am not at home! [*Calls to a servant without*] Rascal! do you hear?—Let nobody in; I am not at home!

SERV. [*Without.*] Sir, I told the gentlemen so.

COURT. Eternal curses! they are coming up. Step into this room, adorable creature! one moment; I'll throw them out of the window, if they stay three.

> [*Exit* KITTY, *through the back Scene.*]
> [*Enter* SAVILLE, FLUTTER, *and Gentlemen.*]

FLUT. O Gemini! beg the petticoat's pardon.—Just saw a corner of it.

1 GENT. No wonder admittance was so difficult. I thought you took us for bailiffs.

COURT. Upon my soul, I am devilish glad to see you—but you perceive how I am circumstanced. Excuse me at this moment.

2 GENT. Tell us who 'tis then.

COURT. Oh, fie!

FLUT. We won't blab.

COURT. I can't, upon honour. Thus far—She's a woman of the first character and rank. Saville [*Taking him aside*] have I influence, or have I not?

SAV. Why, sure, you do not insinuate—

COURT. No, not insinuate, but swear, that she's now in my bed-chamber; by gad, I don't deceive you.—There's generalship, you rogue! such an humble, distant, sighing fellow as thou art, at the end of a six months siege, would have boasted of a kiss from her glove. I only give the signal, and—pop! she's in my arms!

SAV. What, lady Fran—

COURT. Hush! You shall see her name to-morrow morning in red letters at the end of my list. Gentlemen, you must excuse me now. Come and drink chocolate at twelve, but—

SAV. Ay, let us go, out of respect to the lady!—'tis a person of rank.

FLUT. Is it?—Then I'll have a peep at her. [*Runs to the door in the back Scene.*]

COURT. This is too much. [*Trying to prevent him.*]

1 GENT. By Jupiter we'll have a peep.

COURT. Gentlemen, consider — for heaven's sake — a lady of quality. What will be the consequences?

FLUT. The consequences! — Why, you'll have your throat cut, that's all — but I'll write your elegy. So now for the door! [*Part open the door, whilst the rest hold* COURTALL] I beg your ladyship's pardon, whoever you are. [*Leads her out*] Emerge from darkness, like the glorious sun, and bless the wond'ring circle with your charms. [*Takes off her Mask.*]

SAV. Kitty Willis! ha, ha, ha!

OMNES. Kitty Willis! ha, ha, ha! Kitty Willis!

1 GENT. Why, what a fellow you are, Courtall, to attempt imposing on your friends in this manner! A lady of quality! — an earl's daughter! — Your ladyship's most obedient — Ha, ha, ha!

SAV. Courtall, have you influence, or have you not?

FLUT. The man's moon-struck.

COURT. Hell and ten thousand furies seize you all together.

KITTY. What, me too, Mr. Courtall? me, whom you have knelt to, prayed to, and adored?

FLUT. That's right, Kitty; give him a little more.

COURT. Disappointed and laughed at!

SAV. Laughed at, and despised. I have fulfilled my design, which was to expose your villainy, and laugh at your presumption. Adieu, sir; remember how you again boast of your influence with women of rank; and when you next want amusement, dare not to look up to the virtuous and to the noble for a companion. [*Exit*]

FLUT. And, Courtall, before you carry a lady into your bed-chamber again, look under her mask; d'ye hear? [*Exit, leading* KITTY]

COURT. There's no bearing this! I'll set off for Paris directly. [*Exit*]

Act V.

SCENE I. — *Hardy's House.*

[*Enter* HARDY *and* VILLERS]

VIL. Whimsical enough! Dying for her, and hates her! Believes her a fool, and a woman of brilliant understanding!

HAR. As true as you are alive — but when I went up to him, last night, at the Pantheon, out of downright good nature, to explain things — my gentleman whips round upon his heel, and snapp'd one as short as if I had been a beggar woman with six children, and he overseer of the parish.

VII. Here comes the wonder-worker.

[*Enter* LETITIA]

Here comes the enchantress, who can go to masquerades, and sing, and dance, and talk a man out of his wits! But, pray, have we morning masquerades?

LET. Oh, no—but I am so enamoured of this all-conquering habit, that I could not resist putting it on the moment I had breakfasted. I shall wear it on the day I am married, and then lay it by in spices—like the miraculous robes of St. Bridget.

VIL. That's as most brides do. The charms that helped to catch the husband are generally laid by, one after another, till the lady grows a downright wife, and then runs crying to her mother, because she has transformed her lover into a downright husband.

HAR. Listen to me.—I han't slept to-night, for thinking of plots to plague Doricourt—and they drove one another out of my head so quick, that I was as giddy as a goose, and could make nothing of them—I wish to goodness you could contrive something.

VIL. Contrive to plague him! Nothing so easy. Don't undeceive him, madam, till he is your husband. Marry him whilst he possesses the sentiments you laboured to give him of miss Hardy—and when you are his wife—

LET. Oh, heavens! I see the whole—that's the very thing. My dear Mr. Villers, you are the divinest man!

VIL. Don't make love to me, hussy.

[*Enter* MRS. RACKETT]

MRS. R. No, pray don't—for I design to have Villers myself in about six years.—There's an oddity in him that pleases me.—He holds women in contempt; and I should like to have an opportunity of breaking his heart for that.

VIL. And when I am heartily tired of life, I know no woman whom I would with more pleasure make my executioner.

HAR. It cannot be—I foresee it will be impossible to bring it about. You know the wedding wasn't to take place this week, or more—and Letty will never be able to play the fool so long.

VIL. The knot shall be tied to-night.—I have it all here; [*Pointing to his Forehead.*] the licence is ready.—Feign yourself ill; send for Doricourt, and tell him you can't go out of the world in peace, except you see the ceremony performed.

HAR. I feign myself ill! I could as soon feign myself a Roman

ambassador. — I was never ill in my life, but with the tooth-ache —
when Letty's mother was a breeding I had all the qualms.

VIL. Oh, I have no fears for you. But what says miss Hardy? Are you
willing to make the irrevocable vow before night?

LET. Oh, heavens! — I — 'Tis so exceeding sudden, that really —

MRS. R. That really she is frightened out of her wits — lest it should be
impossible to bring matters about. But I have taken the scheme into
my protection, and you shall be Mrs. Doricourt before night. Come
[*To* HARDY.] to bed directly: your room shall be crammed with vials,
and all the apparatus of death then, heigh, presto! for Doricourt.

VIL. You go and put off your conquering dress, [*To* LETITIA.] and get all
your awkward airs ready — And you practise a few groans, [*To* HARDY.]
and you, if possible, an air of gravity. [*To* MRS. RACKETT.] I'll answer for
the plot.

LET. Married in jest! 'Tis an odd idea! Well, I'll venture it. [*Exeunt* LETITIA
and MRS. RACKETT]

VIL. Ay, I'll be sworn! [*Looks at his Watch.*] 'Tis past three. The budget's
to be opened this morning. I'll just step down to the house. — Will you
go?

HAR. What! with a mortal sickness?

VIL. What a blockhead! if I believe half of us were to stay away with mortal
sicknesses, it would be for the health of the nation. Good morning. —
I'll call and feel your pulse as I come back. [*Exit*]

HAR. You won't find them over brisk, I fancy. I foresee some ill happening
from this making believe to die before one's time. But hang it —
ahem! — I am a stout man yet; only fifty-six — What's that? In the last
yearly bills there were three lived to above an hundred: Fifty-six!
Fiddle-de-dee! I am not afraid, not I. [*Exit*]

SCENE II. — *Doricourt's Lodgings.*

[DORICOURT *discovered in his Robe de Chambre. Enter* SAVILLE.]

SAV. Undressed so late?

DORIC. I did'nt go to bed till late — 'twas late before I slept — late when I
rose. Do you know lord George Jennett?

SAV. Yes.

DORIC. Has he a mistress?

SAV. Yes.

DORIC. What sort of a creature is she?

SAV. Why, she spends him three thousand a year with the ease of a
duchess, and entertains his friends with the grace of a Ninon. Ergo,

she is handsome, spirited, and clever. [DORICOURT *walks about disordered.*] In the name of caprice, what ails you?

DORIC. You have hit it—Elle est mon caprice.—The mistress of lord George Jennett is my caprice—Oh, insufferable!

SAV. What, you saw her at the masquerade?

DORIC. Saw her, loved her, died for her—without knowing her—and now, the curse is, I can't hate her.

SAV. Ridiculous enough! All this distress about a kept woman, whom any man may have, I dare swear, in a fortnight—They've been jarring some time.

DORIC. Have her! The sentiment I have conceived for the witch is so unaccountable, that, in that line, I cannot bear her idea. Was she a woman of honour, for a wife, I could adore her—but I really believe, if she should send me an assignation, I should hate her.

SAV. Hey-day! This sounds like love. What becomes of poor miss Hardy?

DORIC. Her name has given me an ague! Dear Saville, how shall I contrive to make old Hardy cancel the engagements! The moiety of the estate, which he will forfeit, shall be his the next moment by deed of gift.

SAV. Let me see—Can't you get it insinuated that you are a devilish wild fellow; that you are an infidel, and attached to wenching, gaming, and so forth?

DORIC. Ay, such a character might have done some good two centuries back. But who the devil can it frighten now? I believe it must be the mad scheme at last.—There, will that do for a grin? [*affects madness.*]

SAV. Ridiculous!—But how are you certain that the woman who has so bewildered you belongs to lord George?

DORIC. Flutter told me so.

SAV. Then fifty to one against the intelligence.

DORIC. It must be so. There was a mystery in her manner, for which nothing else can account. [*A violent rap*] Who can this be?

SAV. [*Looks out.*] The proverb is your answer—'to Flutter himself. Tip him a scene of the madman, and see how it takes.

DORIC. I will—a good way to send it about town. Shall it be of the melancholy kind, or the raving?

SAV. Rant!—rant!—Here he comes.

DORIC. Talk not to me, who can pull comets by the beard, and overset an island?

[*Enter* FLUTTER]

There! This is he! — this is he who hath sent my poor soul, without coat
or breeches, to be tossed about in ether like a duck-feather! Villain,
give me my soul again! [*Seizes him.*]

FLUT. Upon my soul, I havn't got it. [*Exceedingly frightened.*]

SAV. Oh, Mr. Flutter, what a melancholy sight! — I little thought to have
seen my poor friend reduced to this.

FLUT. Mercy defend me! What, is he mad?

SAV. You see how it is. A cursed Italian lady — Jealousy — gave him a drug;
and every full of the moon —

DORIC. Moon! Who dares talk of the moon? The patroness of genius — the
rectifier of wits — the — Oh! here she is! — I feel her — she tugs at my
brain — she has it — she has it — Oh! [*Exit*]

FLUT. Well, this is dreadful! exceeding dreadful, I protest. Have you had
Monro?

SAV. Not yet — The worthy miss Hardy — what a misfortune!

FLUT. Ay, very true. — Do they know it?

SAV. Oh, no; the paroxysm seized him but this morning.

FLUT. Adieu; I can't stay. [*Going in great haste*]

SAV. But you must stay, [*Holding him.*] and assist me — perhaps he'll
return again in a moment; and when he is in this way, his strength is
prodigious.

FLUT. Can't, indeed — can't upon my soul. [*Going*]

SAV. Flutter — don't make a mistake now — remember 'tis Doricourt that's
mad.

FLUT. Yes — you mad.

SAV. No, no; Doricourt.

FLUT. Egad, I'll say you are both mad, and then I can't mistake. [*Exeunt,*
FLUT. SAV.]

SCENE III. — *Sir George Touchwood's House.*

[*Enter* SIR GEORGE *and* LADY FRANCES TOUCHWOOD]

SIR G. The bird is escaped — Courtall is gone to France.

LADY F. Heaven and earth! Have you been to seek him?

SIR G. Seek him! Ay.

LADY F. How did you get his name? I should never have told it you.

SIR G. I learn'd it in the first coffee-house I entered. — Every body is full of
the story.

LADY F. Thank heaven he's gone! — But I have a story for you — The Hardy
family are forming a plot upon your friend Doricourt, and we are
expected in the evening to assist.

SIR G. With all my heart, my angel; but I can't stay to hear it unfolded. They told me Mr. Saville would be at home in half an hour, and I am inpatient to see him. The adventure of last night—

LADY F. Think of it only with gratitude. The danger I was in has overset a new system of conduct, that perhaps I was too much inclined to adopt. But henceforward, my dear sir George, you shall be my constant companion and protector. And when they ridicule the unfashionable monsters, the felicity of our hearts will make their satire pointless.

SIR G. Charming angel! You almost reconcile me to Courtall. Hark! Here's company. [*Stepping to the Door*] 'Tis your lively widow—I'll step down the back stairs to escape her. [*Exit*]

    [*Enter* MRS. RACKETT]

MRS. R. Oh, lady Frances! I am shocked to death. — Have you received a card from us?

LADY F. Yes; within these twenty minutes.

MRS. R. Ay, 'tis of no consequence. — 'Tis all over—Doricourt's mad.

LADY F. Mad!

MRS. R. My poor Letitia!—Just as we were enjoying ourselves with the prospect of a scheme that was planned for their mutual happiness, in came Flutter, breathless, with the intelligence; — I flew here to know if you had heard it.

LADY F. No, indeed—and I hope it is one of Mrs. Flutter's dreams.

    [*Enter* SAVILLE]

Apropos; now we shall be informed. Mr. Saville, I rejoice to see you, though sir George will be disappointed; he's gone to your lodgings.

SAV. I should have been happy to have prevented sir George. I hope your ladyship's adventure last night did not disturb your dreams?

LADY F. Not at all; for I never slept a moment. My escape, and the importance of my obligations to you, employed my thoughts. But we have just had shocking intelligence — Is it true that Doricourt is mad?

SAV. So the business is done. [*Aside.*] Madam, I am sorry to say that I have just been a melancholy witness of his ravings; he was in the height of a paroxysm.

MRS. R. Oh, there can be no doubt of it! Flutter told us the whole history. Some Italian princess gave him a drug, in a box of sweetmeats, sent to him by her own page; and it renders him lunatic every month. Poor Miss Hardy! I never felt so much on any occasion in my life.

SAV. To soften your concern, I will inform you, madam, that miss Hardy is less to be pitied than you imagine.

MRS. R. Why so, sir?

SAV. 'Tis rather a delicate subject, but he did not love miss Hardy.

MRS. R. He did love miss Hardy, sir, and would have been the happiest of men.

SAV. Pardon me, madam; his heart was not only free from that lady's chains, but absolutely captivated by another.

MRS. R. No, sir—no. It was miss Hardy who captivated him. She met him last night at the masquerade, and charmed him in disguise. He professed the most violent passion for her; and a plan was laid this evening to cheat him into happiness.

SAV. Ha, ha, ha!—Upon my soul, I must beg your pardon! I have not eaten of the Italian princess's box of sweetmeats, sent by her own page; and yet I am as mad as Doricourt. Ha, ha, ha!

MRS. R. So it appears. What can all this mean?

SAV. Why, madam, he is at present in his perfect senses; but he'll lose them in ten minutes through joy. The madness was only a feint, to avoid marrying miss Hardy, ha, ha, ha! I'll carry him the intelligence directly. [*Going.*]

MRS. R. Not for worlds. I owe him revenge now for what he has made us suffer. You must promise not to divulge a syllable I have told you; and when Doricourt is summoned to Mr. Hardy's, prevail on him to come—madness and all.

LADY F. Pray do. I should like to see him showing off, now I am in the secret.

SAV. You must be obeyed, though 'tis inhuman to conceal his happiness.

MRS. R. I am going home; so I'll set you down in his lodgings, and acquaint you, by the way, with our whole scheme. Allons!

SAV. I attend you. [*Leading her out.*]

MRS. R. You won't fail us?

[*Exeunt* MR. SAVILLE *and* MRS. RACKETT]

LADY F. No; depend on us. [*Exit*]

SCENE IV.—*Doricourt's Lodgings.*

[DORICOURT *seated, reading.*]

DORIC. [*Flings away the Book*] What effect can the morals of fourscore have on a mind torn with passion? [*Musing.*] Is it possible such a soul as hers can support itself in so humiliating a situation? A kept woman! [*Rising.*] Well, well—I am glad it is so—I am glad it is so!

[*Enter* SAVILLE]

SAV. What a happy dog you are, Doricourt! I might have been mad, or beggared, or pistol'd, myself, without its being mentioned — But you, forsooth! the whole female world is concerned for. I reported the state of your brain to five different women. The lip of the first trembled; the white bosom of the second heaved a sigh; the third ejaculated, and turned her eye to — the glass; the fourth blessed herself; and the fifth said, whilst she pinned a curl, well, now perhaps he'll be an amusing companion: his native dulness was intolerable.

DORIC. Envy! sheer envy, by the smiles of Hebe! — There are not less than forty pair of the brightest eyes in town will drop crystals, when they hear of my misfortune.

SAV. Well, but I have news for you: — Poor Hardy is confined to his bed; they say he is going out of the world by the first post, and he wants to give you his blessing.

DORIC. Ill! so ill! I am sorry from my soul. He's a worthy little fellow — if he had not the gift of foreseeing so strongly.

SAV. Well, you must go and take leave.

DORIC. What! to act the lunatic in the dying man's chamber?

SAV. Exactly the thing; and will bring your business to a short issue; for his last commands must be that you are not to marry his daughter.

DORIC. That's true, by Jupiter! — and yet, hang it, impose upon a fellow at so serious a moment! — I can't do it.

SAV. You must, faith. I am answerable for your appearance, though it should be in a straight waist coat. He knows your situation, and seems the more desirous of an interview.

DORIC. I don't like encountering Rackett. — She's an arch little devil, and will discover the cheat.

SAV. There's a fellow! — Cheated ninety-nine women, and now afraid of the hundredth.

DORIC. And with reason — for that hundredth is a widow. [*Exeunt*]

SCENE V. — *Hardy's.*

[*Enter* MRS. RACKETT *and* MISS OGLE]

MISS O. And so miss Hardy is actually to be married to-night?

MRS. R. If her fate does not deceive her. You are apprised of the scheme, and we hope it will succeed.

MISS O. Deuce take her! she's six years younger than I am. [*Aside.*] Is Mr. Doricourt handsome?

MRS. R. Handsome, generous, young, and rich. — There's a husband for ye! Isn't he worth pulling caps for?

MISS O. I'my conscience, the widow speaks as though she'd give cap, ears,

and all for him. [*Aside.*] I wonder you didn't try to catch this wonderful man, Mrs. Rackett?

MRS. R. Really, miss Ogle, I had not time. Besides, when I marry, so many
stout young fellows will hang themselves, that, out of regard to society, in these sad times, I shall postpone it for a few years. — This will
cost her a new lace — I heard it crack, [*Aside.*]

[*Enter* SIR GEORGE *and* LADY FRANCES]

SIR G. Well, here we are. But where's the knight of the woful
countenance?

MRS. R. Here soon, I hope — for a woful night it will be without him.

SIR G. Oh, fie! do you condescend to pun?

MRS. R. Why not? It requires genius to make a good pun — some men of
bright parts can't reach it. I know a lawyer, who writes them on the
back of his briefs; and says they are of great use — in a dry cause.

[*Enter* FLUTTER]

FLUT. Here they come! Here they come! — Their coach stopped as mine
drove off.

SAV. [*Without.*] Come, let me guide you! — This way, my poor friend!
Why are you so furious?

DORIC. [*Without.*] The house of death — to the house of death!

[*Enter* DORICOURT *and* SAVILLE]

Ah! this is the spot!

LADY F. How wild and fiery he looks!

MISS O. Now, I think he looks terrified!

MRS. R. I never saw a madman before — Let me examine him — Will he
bite?

SAV. Pray keep out of his reach, ladies — You don't know your danger. He's
like a wild cat, if a sudden thought seizes him.

MRS. R. You talk like a keeper of wild cats — How much do you demand for
showing the monster?

DORIC. I don't like this — I must rouse their sensibility. [*Aside.*] There!
there she darts through the air in liquid flames. Down again. — Now I
have her — Oh, she burns! she scorches! — Oh! she eats into my very
heart!

OMNES. Ha, ha, ha!

DORIC. I am laughed at!

MRS. R. Laughed at — ay, to be sure; why, I could play the madman better
than you. There! there she is! Now I have her! Ha, ha, ha!

DORIC. I'll leave the house: — I'm covered with confusion. [*Going.*]

SIR G. Stay, sir—You must not go. 'Twas poorly done, Mr. Doricourt, to affect madness rather than fulfil your engagements.

DORIC. Affect madness? Saville, what can I do?

SAV. Since you are discovered, confess the whole.

DORIC. Yes; since my designs have been so unaccountably discovered, I will avow the whole. I cannot love miss Hardy—and I will never—

SAV. Hold, my dear Doricourt? What will the world say to such—

DORIC. Damn the world! What will the world give me for the loss of happiness? Must I sacrifice my peace, to please the world?

SIR G. Yes, every thing, rather than be branded with dishonour.

LADY F. Though our arguments should fail, there is a pleader, whom you surely cannot withstand—the dying Mr. Hardy supplicates you not to forsake his child.

SIR G. The dying Mr. Hardy!

FLUT. The dying Mr. Hardy!

    [*Enter* VILLERS]

VIL. The dying Mr. Hardy requests you to grant him a moment's conversation, Mr. Doricourt, though you should persist to send him miserable to the grave. Let me conduct you to his chamber.

DORIC. Oh, ay, any where; to the antipodes—to the moon—Carry me—Do with me what you will.

MRS. R. I'll follow, and let you know what passes.

    [*Exeunt* VIL. DORIC. MRS. R. *and* MISS O.]

FLUT. Ladies, ladies, have the charity to take me with you, that I may make no blunder in repeating the story. [*Exit*]

LADY F. Sir George, you don't know Mr. Saville. [*Exit*]

SIR G. Ten thousand pardons; I have been with the utmost impatience at your door twice to-day.

SAV. I am concerned you had so much trouble, sir George.

SIR G. Trouble! what a word!—I hardly know how to address you; your having preserved lady Frances in so imminent a danger—Start not, Saville; to protect lady Frances was my right. You have wrested from me my dearest privilege.

SAV. I hardly know how to answer such a reproach.

SIR G. I do not mean to reproach you. I hardly know what I mean. There is one method by which you may restore peace to me. I have a sister, Saville, who is amiable; and you are worthy of her. You must go with us into Hampshire: and, if you see each other with the eyes I do, our felicity will be complete.

SAV. I will attend you to Hampshire with pleasure; but not on the plan of retirement. Society has claims on lady Frances that forbid it.

SIR G. Claims, Saville?

SAV. Yes, claims; lady Frances was born to be the ornament of courts. She is sufficiently alarmed, not to wander beyond the reach of her protector; and, from the British court, the most tenderly anxious husband could not wish to banish his wife. Bid her keep in her eye the bright example who presides there; the splendour of whose rank yields to the superior lustre of her virtue.

[*Re-enter* MRS. RACKETT, LADY FRANCES, MISS OGLE, *and* FLUTTER, R.H.D.]

MRS. R. Oh, heavens! do you know—

FLUT. Let me tell the story. As soon as Doricourt—

MRS. R. I protest you shan't, said Mr. Hardy—

FLUT. No, 'twas Doricourt spoke first—says he—No, 'twas the parson—says he—

MRS. R. Stop his mouth, sir George—he'll spoil the tale.

SIR G. Never heed circumstances—the result—the result.

MRS. R. No, no; you shall have it in form. Mr. Hardy performed the sick man like an angel. He sat up in bed, and talked so pathetically, that the tears stood in Doricourt's eyes.

FLUT. Ay, stood—they did not drop, but stood. I shall in future be very exact: the parson seized the moment; you know they never miss an opportunity.

MRS. R. "Make haste," said Doricourt; "if I have time to reflect, poor Hardy will die unhappy."

FLUT. They were got as far as the day of judgement, when we slipped out of the room.

SIR G. Then, by this time, they must have reached amazement, which every body knows is the end of matrimony.

MRS. R. Ay, the reverend fathers ended the service with that word, prophetically—to teach the bride what a capricious monster a husband is.

SIR G. I rather think it was sarcastically—to prepare the bridegroom for the unreasonable humours and vagaries of his helpmate.

LADY F. Here comes the bridegroom of to-night.

[*Re-enter* DORICOURT *and* VILLERS—VILLERS *whispers* SAVILLE, *who goes out*]

OMNES. Joy! joy! joy!

MISS O. If he's a sample of bridegrooms, keep me single! A younger brother, from the funeral of his father, could not carry a more fretful countenance.

FLUT. Oh! now he's melancholy mad, I suppose.

LADY F. You do not consider the importance of the occasion.

VIL. No; nor how shocking a thing it is for a man to be forced to marry one woman whilst his heart is devoted to another.

MRS. R. Well, now 'tis over, I confess to you, Mr. Doricourt, I thing 'twas a most ridiculous piece of Quixotism, to give up the happiness of a whole life to a man who perhaps has but few moments to be sensible of the sacrifice.

FLUT. So it appeared to me. But, thought I, Mr. Doricourt has travelled — he knows best.

DORIC. Zounds! confusion! did ye not all set upon me? Didn't ye talk to me of honour — compassion — justice?

SIR G. Very true — You have acted according to their dictates, and I hope the utmost felicity of the married state will reward you.

DORIC. Never, sir George! To felicity I bid adieu — but I will endeavour to be content. Where is my — I must speak it — where is my wife?

[*Enter* LETITIA *masked, led by* SAVILLE]

SAV. Mr. Doricourt, this lady was pressing to be introduced to you.

DORIC. Oh! [*Starting.*]

LET. I told you last night you should see me at a time when you least expected me, and I have kept my promise.

VIL. Whoever you are, madam, you could not have arrived at a happier moment. Mr. Doricourt is just married.

LET. Married! impossible! 'tis but a few hours since he swore to me eternal love: I believed him, gave him up my virgin heart — and now! — Ungrateful sex!

DORIC. Your virgin heart! No, lady — my fate, thank heaven! yet wants that torture. Nothing but the conviction that you was another's could have made me think one moment of marriage, to have saved the lives of half mankind. But this visit, madam, is as barbarous as unexpected. It is now my duty to forget you, which, spite of your situation, I found difficult enough.

LET. My situation! what situation?

DORIC. I must apologise for explaining it in this company — but, madam, I am not ignorant that you are the companion of lord George Jennett — and this is the only circumstance that can give me peace.

LET. I—a companion! ridiculous pretence! no, sir, know, to your confusion, that my heart, my honour, my name is unspotted as hers you
have married; my birth equal to your own, my fortune large. That,
and my person, might have been yours. But, sir, farewel! [*Going.*]

DORIC. Oh, stay a moment—Rascal! is she not—

FLUT. Who, she? O lord!—no—'Twas quite a different person that I
meant. I never saw that lady before.

DORIC. Then, never shalt thou see her more. [*Shakes* FLUTTER.]

MRS. R. Have mercy upon the poor man! heavens! He'll murder him.

DORIC. Murder him! Yes, you, myself, and all mankind. Sir George—
Saville—Villers—'twas you who pushed me on this precipice; 'tis you
who have snatched from me joy, felicity, and life.

MRS. R. There! now, how well he acts the madman! This is something like!
I knew he would do it well enough, when the time came.

DORIC. Hard-hearted woman! enjoy my ruin—riot in my wretchedness.

[*Enter* HARDY, *hastily, in his Nightcap and Gown*]

HAR. This is too much. You are now the husband of my daughter; and
how dare you show all this passion about another woman?

DORIC. Alive again!

HAR. Alive! ay, and merry. Here wipe off the flour from my face. I was
never in better health and spirits in all my life. I foresaw 'twould do.
Why, my illness was only a fetch, man! to make you marry Letty.

DORIC. It was! base and ungenerous! Well, sir, you shall be gratified. The
possession of my heart was no object either with you or your daughter.
My fortune and name was all you desired, and these—I leave ye. My
native England I shall quit, nor never behold you more. But, lady,
that, in my exile, I may have one consolation, grant me the favour you
denied last night;—let me behold all that mask conceals, that your
whole image may be impressed on my heart, and cheer my distant
solitary hours.

LET. This is the most awful moment of my life. Oh, Doricourt, the slight
action of taking off my mask stamps me the most blest, or miserable of
women!

DORIC. What can this mean? Reveal your face, I conjure you.

LET. Behold it. [*Unmasks.*]

DORIC. Rapture! transport! heaven!

FLUT. Now for a touch of the happy madman.

LET. This little stratagem arose from my disappointment in not having
made the impression on you I wished. The timidity of the English

character threw a veil over me you could not penetrate. You have forced me to emerge in some measure from my natural reserve, and to throw off the veil that hid me.

DORIC. I am yet in a state of intoxication—I cannot answer you.—Speak on, sweet angel!

LET. You see I can be any thing: choose then my character—you shall fix it. Shall I be an English wife?—or, breaking from the bonds of nature and education, step forth to the world in all the captivating glare of foreign manners?

DORIC. You shall be nothing but yourself—nothing can be captivating that you are not. I will not wrong your penetration, by pretending that you won my heart at the first interview; but you have now my whole soul—your person, your face, your mind, I would not exchange for those of any other woman breathing.

HAR. A dog! how well he makes up for past slights! cousin Rackett, I wish you a good husband, with all my heart. Mr. Flutter, I'll believe every word you say this fortnight. Mr. Villers, you and I have managed this to a T. I never was so merry in my life—'Gad, I believe I can dance. [*Footing.*]

DORIC. Charming, charming creature!

LET. Congratulate me, my dear friends! Can you conceive my happiness?

HAR. No, congratulate me, for mine is the greatest.

FLUT. No, congratulate me, that I have escaped with life, and give me some sticking plaster—this wild cat has torn the skin from my throat.

HAR. Come into the next room; I have ordered out every drop of my forty-eight, and I'll invite the whole parish of St. George's, but we'll drink it out—except one dozen, which I shall keep under three double locks, for a certain christening, that I foresee will happen within this twelvemonth.

DORIC. My charming bride! It was a strange perversion of taste, that led me to consider the delicate timidity of your deportment as the mark of an uninformed mind, or inelegant manners. I feel now it is to that innate modesty, English husbands owe a felicity the married men of other nations are strangers to; it is a sacred veil to your own charms; it is the surest bulwark to your husbands' honour; and curse on the hour—should it ever arrive—in which British ladies shall sacrifice to foreign graces the grace of modesty.

Epilogue.

[*Spoken by* LAETITIA]

Nay, cease, and hear me! — I am come to ask
Why pleas'd at conquest gain'd behind a mask!
Is't strange? Why, pray what lady Bab, or Grace,
E'er won a lover — in her natural face?
Mistake me not! French red and blanching creams 5
I stoop not to — for these are hackneyed themes;
The arts I mean are harder to detect,
Easier put on, displayed to more effect.

Do pride or envy by their horrid lines,
Destroy th' effect of nature's sweet designs? 10
The mask of softness is at once applied,
And gentlest manners decorate the bride!

Does heart in love inspire the vestal's eye,
Or point the glance, or prompt the struggling sigh?
Not Dian's brows more rigid frowns disclose, 15
And timid hues appear, where passion glows.

And you, my gentle sirs, wear vizors too,
But I'll unmask you, and expose to view
Your hidden features. — First, I point at you!
That well-stuff'd waistcoat, and that ruddy cheek, 20
That ample forehead, and that skin so sleek,
Point out good nature and a generous heart —
Tyrant! stand forth, and, conscious, own thy part;
Thy wife, thy children, tremble in thy eye,
And peace is banish'd — when the father's nigh! 25

Sure 'tis enchantment! See, on every side
Your masks fall off! — In charity I hide
The monstrous features rushing to my view —
Fear not there, grand-papa — nor you — nor you,
For, should I show your features to each other, 30
Not one be known would by his friend or brother.

'Tis plain, in real life, from youth to age,
All wear their masks. Here only on the stage,
You see us as we are; here trust your eyes,
Our wish to please cannot be mere disguise! 35

JOANNA BAILLIE

(1762–1851)

Poet, playwright, and dramatic critic, Joanna Baillie was descended from a long-established Scottish family. Her father, James, a Presbyterian clergyman, was descended from the Scotch Patriot William Wallace. Her mother was Dorothy Hunter, whose brothers William and John were famous surgeons. At ten years old Joanna was sent to a boarding school in Glasgow. Her father died in 1778, and her uncle William Hunter took responsibility for the Baillie family, moving them to London the following year. When her uncle married, she moved with her sister and mother to Hampstead and, at her mother's death, she continued to live with her sister. Both women lived long lives, Joanna to eighty-eight (although she had been delicate as a child) and her sister to one hundred.

She apparently began writing songs and ballads at an early age and at twenty-eight she published anonymously *Poems; Wherein it is Attempted to Describe Certain Views of Nature and of Rustic Manners* (1790). William Enfield, in the *Monthly Review*, commented favorably on their "true unsophisticated representations of nature." Fifty years later, Baillie reprinted many of them in *Fugitive Verses* (1840) because, as she noted, the original book was "not noticed by the public, or circulated in any considerable degree." Some of the poems show her interest in contrasting psychological states, an interest she carried over into her plays and dramatic criticism.

Between 1798 and 1812, she published blank verse dramas anonymously as *Series of Plays in which it is attempted to Delineate the Stronger Passions of the Mind* (3 vols.). Her long preface to the *Plays* is reprinted in part here. The first volume of the *Plays* attracted a good deal of attention and gave rise to the belief that the dramas were written by a man. The plays themselves are too stylized for easy performance and were criticized for their implausibility. Few were performed, and those were often failures on stage. Her greatest success was the drama *De Montfort* in which Sarah Siddons played the heroine. Today we find the plays unperformable and generally unreadable, but the theory of passions elaborated in her preface remains of interest. In her day, however, Baillie's reputation as a woman dramatist was unrivalled. She knew many of the literary figures of her time, including Anna Barbauld, Maria Edgeworth, William Wordsworth, and Walter Scott. Her writing career continued for fifty years. The year before her death, she revised the poems she had written some sixty years earlier.

EDITION USED: *A Series of Plays*, 2nd ed. (London, 1799).

INTRODUCTORY DISCOURSE

(Plays on the Passions)

IT IS natural for a writer, who is about to submit his works to the Public, to feel a strong inclination, by some Preliminary Address, to conciliate the favor of his reader, and dispose him, if possible, to peruse them with a favorable eye. I am well aware, however, that his endeavors are generally fruitless: in his situation our hearts revolt from all appearance of confidence, and we consider his diffidence as hypocrisy. Our own word is frequently taken for what we say of ourselves, but very rarely for what we say of our works. Were the three plays which this small volume contains, detached pieces only, and unconnected with others that do not yet appear, I should have suppressed this inclination altogether; and have allowed my reader to begin what is before him and to form what opinion of it his taste or his humor might direct, without any previous trespass upon his time or his patience. But they are part of an extensive design: of one which, as far as my information goes, has nothing exactly similar to it in any language: of one which a whole life's time will be limited enough to accomplish; and which has, therefore, a considerable chance of being cut short by that hand which nothing can resist.

Before I explain the plan of this work, I must make a demand upon the patience of my reader, whilst I endeavour to communicate to him those ideas regarding human nature, as they in some degree affect almost every species of moral writings, but particularly the Dramatic, that induced me to attempt it; and, as far as my judgment enabled me to apply them, has directed me in the execution of it.

From that strong sympathy which most creatures, but the human above all, feel for others of their kind, nothing has become so much an object of man's curiosity as man himself. We are all conscious of this within ourselves, and so constantly do we meet with it in others, that, like every circumstance of continually repeated occurrence, it thereby escapes observation. Every person who is not deficient in intellect, is more or less occupied in tracing amongst the individuals he converses with, the varieties of understanding and temper which constitute the characters of men; and receives great pleasure from every stroke of nature that points out to him those varieties. This is, much more than we are aware of, the occupation of children, and of grown people also, whose penetration is but lightly esteemed; and that conversation which degenerates with them into trivial and mischievous tattling, takes its rise not unfrequently from the same source that supplies the rich vein of the satirist and the wit. That eagerness so universally shown for the conversation of the latter, plainly enough indicates how many people have been occupied in the same way with themselves. Let any one, in a large company, do or say what is strongly expressive of his peculiar character, or of some passion or humor of the moment, and it will be detected by almost every person present. How often may we see a very stupid countenance animated with a smile, when the learned and the wise have betrayed some native feature of their own minds! and how often will this be the case when they have supposed it to be concealed under a very sufficient disguise. From this constant employment of their minds, most people, I believe, without being conscious of it, have stored up in idea the greater part of those strong marked varieties of human character, which may be said to divide it into classes; and in one of those classes they involuntarily place every new person they become acquainted with.

I will readily allow that the dress and the manners of men, rather than their characters and dispositions, are the subjects of our common conversation, and seem chiefly to occupy the multitude. But let it be remembered that it is much easier to express our observations upon these. It is easier to communicate to another how a man wears his wig and cane, what kind of house he inhabits, and what kind of table he keeps, than from what slight traits in his words and actions we have been led to conceive certain impressions of his character: traits that will often escape the memory, when the opinions that were founded upon them remain. Besides, in communicating our ideas of the characters of others, we are often called upon to support them with more expence of reasoning than we can well afford; but our observations on the dress and appearance of men seldom involve us in such difficulties. For these, and other reasons too tedious to mention, the generality of people appear to us more trifling than they are: and I may venture to say, that, but for this sympathetic curiosity towards others of our kind which is so strongly implanted within us, the attention we pay to the dress and manners of men would dwindle into an employment as insipid, as examining the varieties of plants and minerals, is to one who understands not natural history.

In our ordinary intercourse with society, this sympathetic propensity of our minds is exercised upon men under the common occurrences of life, in which we have often observed them. Here, vanity and weakness put themselves forward to view, more conspicuously than the virtues; here, men encounter those smaller trials, from which they are not apt to come off victorious; and here, consequently, that which is marked with the whimsical and ludicrous will strike us most forcibly, and make the strongest impression on our memory. To this sympathetic propensity of our minds, so exercised, the genuine and pure comic of every composition, whether drama, fable, story, or satire, is addressed.

If man is an object of so much attention to man, engaged in the ordinary occurrences of life, how much more does he excite his curiosity and interest when placed in extraordinary situations of difficulty and distress? It cannot be any pleasure we receive from the sufferings of a fellow-creature which attracts such multitudes of people to a public execution, though it is the horror we conceive for such a spectacle that keeps so many more away. To see a human being bearing himself up under such circumstances, or struggling with the terrible apprehensions which such a situation impresses, must be the powerful incentive, that makes us press forward to behold what we shrink from, and wait with trembling expectation for what we dread.* For though few at such a spectacle can get near enough to distinguish the expression of face, or the minuter parts of a criminal's behaviour, yet from a considerable distance will they eagerly mark whether he steps firmly; whether the motions of his body denote agitation or calmness; and if the wind does but ruffle his garment, they will, even from that change upon the outline of his distant figure, read some expression connected with his dreadful situation. Though there is a greater proportion of people in whom this strong curiosity will be overcome by other dispositions and motives; though there are many more who will stay away from such a sight than will go to it; yet there are very few who will not be eager to converse with a person who has beheld it; and to learn, very minutely, every circumstance connected with it, except the very act itself of inflicting death. To lift up the roof of his dungeon, like the *Diable Boiteux* [lame devil], and look upon a criminal the night before he suffers, in his still hours of privacy, when all that disguise is

---

*In confirmation of this opinion I may venture to say, that of the great numbers who go to see a public execution, there are but very few who would not run away from, and avoid it, if they happened to meet with it unexpectedly. We find people stopping to look at a procession, or any other uncommon sight, they may have fallen in with accidentally, but almost never an execution. No one goes there who has not made up his mind for the occasion; which would not be the case, if any natural love of cruelty were the cause of such assemblies.

removed which is imposed by respect for the opinion of others, the strong motive by which even the lowest and wickedest of men still continue to be actuated, would present an object to the mind of every person, not withheld from it by great timidity of character, more powerfully attractive than almost any other.

* * * *

But it is not in situations of difficulty and distress alone, that man becomes the object of this sympathetic curiosity: he is no less so when the evil he contends with arises in his own breast, and no outward circumstance connected with him either awakens our attention or our pity. What human creature is there, who can behold a being like himself under the violent agitation of those passions which all have, in some degree, experienced, without feeling himself most powerfully excited by the sight? I say, all have experienced: for the bravest man on earth knows what fear is as well as the coward; and will not refuse to be interested for one under the dominion of this passion, provided there be nothing in the circumstances attending it to create contempt. Anger is a passion that attracts less sympathy than any other, yet the unpleasing and distorted features of an angry man will be more eagerly gazed upon, by those who are no wise concerned with his fury or the objects of it, than the most amiable placid countenance in the world. Every eye is directed to him; every voice hushed to silence in his presence: even children will leave off their gambols as he passes, and gaze after him more eagerly than the gaudiest equipage. The wild tossings of despair: the gnashing of hatred and revenge; the yearnings of affection, and the softened mien of love; all the language of the agitated soul, which every age and nation understand, is never addressed to the dull or inattentive.

It is not merely under the violent agitations of passion, that man so rouses and interests us; even the smallest indications of an unquiet mind, the restless eye, the muttering lip, the half-checked exclamation, and the hasty start, will set our attention as anxiously upon the watch, as the first distant flashes of a gathering storm. When some great explosion of passion bursts forth, and some consequent catastrophe happens, if we are at all acquainted with the unhappy perpetrator, how minutely shall we endeavour to remember every circumstance of his past behaviour! and with what avidity shall we seize upon every recollected word or gesture, that is in the smallest degree indicative of the supposed state of his mind, at the time when they took place. If we are not acquainted with him, how eagerly shall we listen to similar recollections from another! Let us understand, from observation or report that any person harbours in his breast, concealed from the world's eye, some powerful rankling passion of what kind soever it may be, we shall observe every word, every motion, every look, even the distant gait of such a man, with a constancy and attention bestowed upon no other. Nay, should we meet him unexpectedly on our way, a feeling will pass across our minds as though we found ourselves in the neighborhood of some secret and fearful thing. If invisible, would we not follow him into his lonely haunts, into his closet, into the midnight silence of his chamber? There is, perhaps, no employment which the human mind will with so much avidity pursue, as the discovery of concealed passion, as the tracing the varieties and progress of a perturbed soul.

It is to this sympathetic curiosity of our nature, exercised upon mankind in great and trying occasions, and under the influence of the stronger passions, when the grand, the generous, and the terrible attract our attention far more than the base and depraved, that the high and powerfully tragic, of every composition, is addressed.

*   *   *   *

In proportion as moral writers of every class have exercised within themselves this sympathetic propensity of our nature, and have attended to it in others, their works have been interesting and instructive. They have struck the imagination more forcibly, convinced the understanding more clearly, and more lastingly impressed the memory. If unseasoned with any reference to this, the fairy bowers of the poet, with all his gay images of delight, will be admired and forgotten; the important relations of the historian, and even the reasonings of the philosopher, will make a less permanent impression.

*   *   *   *

If the study of human nature then, is so useful to the poet, the novelist, the historian, and the philosopher, of how much greater importance must it be to the dramatic writer? To them it is a powerful auxiliary, to him it is the centre and strength of the battle. If characteristic views of human nature enliven not their pages, there are many excellencies with which they can, in some degree, make up for the deficiency: it is what we receive from them with pleasure rather than demand. But in his works, no richness of invention, harmony of language, nor grandeur of sentiment will supply the place of faithfully delineated nature. The poet and the novelist may represent to you their great characters from the cradle to the tomb. They may represent them in any mood or temper, and under the influence of any passion which they see proper, without being obliged to put words into their mouths, those great betrayers of the feigned and adopted. They may relate every circumstance, however trifling and minute, that serves to develope their tempers and dispositions. They tell us what kind of people they intend their men and women to be, and as such we receive them. If they are to move us with any scene of distress, every circumstance regarding the parties concerned in it, how they looked, how they moved, how they sighed, how the tears gushed from their eyes, how the very light and shadow fell upon them, is carefully described; and the few things that are given them to say along with all this assistance, must be very unnatural indeed if we refuse to sympathize with them. But the characters of the drama must speak directly for themselves. Under the influence of every passion, humor, and impression; in the artificial veilings of hypocrisy and ceremony, in the openness of freedom and confidence, and in the lonely hour of meditation they speak. He who made us hath placed within our breasts a judge that judges instantaneously of every thing they say. We expect to find them creatures like ourselves; and if they are untrue to nature, we feel that we are imposed upon.

As in other works deficiency in characteristic truth may be compensated by excellencies of a different kind, in the drama, characteristic truth will compensate every other defect. Nay, it will do what appears a contradiction; one strong genuine stroke of nature will cover a multitude of sins, even against nature herself. When we meet in some scene of a good play a very fine stroke of this kind, we are apt to become so intoxicated with it, and so perfectly convinced of the author's great knowledge of the human heart, that we are unwilling to suppose the whole of it has not been suggested by the same penetrating spirit. Many well-meaning enthusiastic critics have given themselves a great deal of trouble in this way; and have shut their eyes most ingeniously against the fair light of nature for the very love of it. They have converted, in their great zeal, sentiments palpably false, both in regard to the character and situation of the persons who utter them, sentiments which a child or a clown would detect, into the most skilful depictments of the heart. I can think of no stronger instance to show how powerfully this love of nature dwells within us.*

Formed as we are with these sympathetic propensities in regard to our own species, it is not at all wonderful that theatrical exhibition has become the grand and favourite amusement of every nation into which it has been introduced. Savages will, in the wild contortions of a dance, shape out some rude story expressive of character or passion, and such a dance will give more delight to their companions than the most artful exertions of agility. Children in their gambols will make out a mimic representation of the manners, characters, and passions of grown men and women; and such a pastime will animate and delight them much more than a treat of the daintiest sweetmeats, or the handling of the gaudiest toys. Eagerly as it is enjoyed by the rude and the young, to the polished and the ripe in years it is still the most interesting amusement. Our taste for it is durable as it is universal. Independently of those circumstances which first introduced it, the world would not have long been without it. The progress of society would soon have brought it forth; and men, in the whimsical decorations of fancy, would have displayed the characters and actions of their heroes, the folly and absurdity of their fellow-citizens, had no Priests or Bacchus ever existed.

In whatever age or country the Drama might have taken its rise, Tragedy would have been the first-born of its children. For every nation has its great men, and its great events upon record, and to represent their own forefathers struggling with those difficulties, and braving those dangers, of which they have heard with admiration, and the effects of which they still, perhaps, experience, would certainly have been the most animating subject for the poet, and the most interesting for his audience, even independently of the natural inclination we all so universally show for scenes of horror and distress, of passion and heroic exertion. Tragedy would have been the first child of the Drama, for the same reasons that

---

*It appears to me a very strong testimony of the excellence of our great national Dramatist, that so many people have been employed in finding out obscure and refined beauties, in what appear to ordinary observation his very defects. Men, it may be said, do so merely to show their own superior penetration and ingenuity. But granting this; what could make other men listen to them, and listen so greedily too, if it were not that they have received from the works of Shakspeare, pleasure far beyond what the most perfect poetical compositions of a different character can afford?

have made heroic ballad, with all its battles, murders, and disasters, the earliest poetical compositions of every country.

We behold heroes and great men at a distance, unmasked by those small but distinguishing features of the mind, which give a certain individuality to such an infinite variety of similar beings, in the near and familiar intercourse of life. They appear to us from this view like distant mountains, whose dark outlines we trace in the clear horizon, but the varieties of whose roughened sides, shaded with heath and brushwood, and seamed with many a cleft, we perceive not. When accidental anecdote reveals to us any weakness or peculiarity belonging to them, we start upon it like a discovery. They are made known to us in history only, by the great events they are connected with, and the part they have taken in extraordinary or important transactions. Even in poetry and romance, with the exception of some love story interwoven with the main events of their lives, they are seldom more intimately made known to us. To Tragedy it belongs to lead them forward to our nearer regard, in all the distinguishing varieties which nearer inspection discovers; with the passions, the humors, the weaknesses, the prejudices of men. It is for her to present to us the great and magnanimous hero, who appears to our distant view as a superior being, as a god, softened down with those smaller frailties and imperfections which enable us to glory in, and claim kindred to his virtues. It is for her to exhibit to us the daring and ambitious man planning his dark designs, and executing his bloody purposes, marked with those appropriate characteristics, which distinguish him as an individual of that class; and agitated with those varied passions, which disturb the mind of man when he is engaged in the commission of such deeds. It is for her to point out to us the brave and impetuous warrior struck with those visitations of nature, which, in certain situations, will unnerve the strongest arm, and make the boldest heart tremble. It is for her to show the tender, gentle, and unassuming mind animated with that fire which, by the provocation of circumstances, will give to the kindest heart the ferocity and keenness of a tiger. It is for her to present to us the great and striking characters that are to be found amongst men, in a way which the poet, the novelist, and the historian can but imperfectly attempt. But above all, to her, and to her only it belongs to unveil to us the human mind under the dominion of those strong and fixed passions, which, seemingly unprovoked by outward circumstances, will from small beginnings brood within the breast, till all the better dispositions, all the fair gifts of nature are borne down before them; those passions which conceal themselves from the observation of men; which cannot unbosom themselves even to the dearest friend; and can, oftentimes, only give their fulness vent in the lonely desert, or in the darkness of midnight. For who hath followed the great man into his secret closet, or stood by the side of his nightly couch, and heard those exclamations of the soul which heaven alone may hear, that the historian should be able to inform us? and what form of story, what mode of rehearsed speech will communicate to us those feelings, whose irregular bursts, abrupt transitions, sudden pauses, and half-uttered suggestions, scorn all harmony of measured verse, all method and order of relation?

*   *   *   *

The Drama improves us by the knowledge we acquire of our own minds, from the natural desire we have to look into the thoughts, and observe the behaviour of others. Tragedy brings to our view, men placed in those elevated situations, exposed to those great trials, and engaged in those extraordinary transactions, in which few of us are called upon to act. As examples applicable to ourselves, therefore, they can but feebly affect us; it is only from the enlargement of our ideas in regard to human nature, from that admiration of virtue and abhorrence of vice which they excite, that we can expect to be improved by them. But if they are not represented to us as real and natural characters, the lessons we are taught from their conduct and their sentiments will be no more to us, than those which we receive from the pages of the poet or the moralist.*

*   *   *   *

---

*I have said nothing here in regard to female character, though in many tragedies it is brought forward as the principal one of the piece, because what I have said of the above characters is likewise applicable to it. I believe there is no man that ever lived, who has behaved in a certain manner on a certain occasion, who has not had amongst women some corresponding spirit, who, on the like occasion, and every way similarly circumstanced, would have behaved in the like manner. With some degree of softening and refinement, each class of the tragic heroes I have mentioned has its corresponding one amongst the heroines. The tender and pathetic no doubt has the most numerous, but the great and magnanimous is not without it, and the passionate and impetuous boasts of one by no means inconsiderable in numbers, and drawn sometimes to the full as passionate and impetuous as itself.

Comedy presents to us men, as we find them in the ordinary inter-course of the world, with all the weaknesses, follies, caprice, prejudices, and absurdities which a near and familiar view of them discovers. It is her task to exhibit them engaged in the busy turmoil of ordinary life, harass-ing and perplexing themselves with the endless pursuits of avarice, van-ity, and pleasure; and engaged with those smaller trials of the mind, by which men are most apt to be overcome, and from which he, who could have supported with honor the attack of great occasions, will oftentimes come off most shamefully foiled. It belongs to her to show the varied fashions and manner of the world, as, from the spirit of vanity, caprice, and imitation they go on in swift and endless succession; and those disagreeable or absurd peculiarities attached to particular classes and conditions in society. It is for her also to represent men under the influ-ence of the stronger passions; and to trace the rise and progress of them in the heart, in such situations, and attended with such circumstances, as take off their sublimity, and the interest we naturally take in a perturbed mind. It is hers to exhibit those terrible tyrants of the soul, whose ungov-ernable rage has struck us so often with dismay, like wild beasts tied to a post, who growl and paw before us, for our derision and sport. In pourtraying the characters of men she has this advantage over tragedy, that the smallest traits of nature, with the smallest circumstances which serve to bring them forth, may by her be displayed, however ludicrous and trivial in themselves, without any ceremony. And in developing the passions she enjoys a similar advantage; for they often more strongly betray themselves when touched by those small and familiar occurrences which cannot, consistently with the effect it is intended to produce, be admitted into tragedy.

As tragedy has been very much cramped in her endeavors to exalt and improve the mind, by that spirit of imitation and confinement in her successive writers, which the beauty of her earliest poets first gave rise to, so comedy has been led aside from her best purposes by a different temptation. Those endless changes in fashions and in manners, which offer such obvious and ever-new subjects of ridicule; that infinite variety of tricks and manœuvres by which the ludicrous may be produced, and curiosity and laughter excited; the admiration we so generally bestow upon satirical remark, pointed repartee, and whimsical combinations of ideas, have too often led her to forget the warmer interest we feel, and the more profitable lessons we receive, from genuine representations of nature. The most interesting and instructive class of comedy, therefore, the real characteristic, has been very much neglected, whilst satirical, witty, sentimental, and, above all, busy or circumstantial comedy, have usurped the exertions of the far greater proportion of Dramatic Writers.

In Satirical Comedy, sarcastic and severe reflections on the actions and manners of men, introduced with neatness, force, and poignancy of expression, into a lively and well-supported dialogue, of whose gay surface they are the embossed ornaments, make the most important and studied part of the work: character is a thing talked of rather than shown. The persons of the drama are indebted for the discovery of their peculiarities to what is said of them, rather than to any thing they are made to say or do for themselves. Much incident being unfavourable for studied and elegant dialogue, the plot is commonly simple, and the few events that compose it neither interesting nor striking. It only affords us that kind of moral instruction which an essay or a poem could as well have conveyed, and, though amusing in the closet, is but feebly attractive in the Theatre.

In what I have termed Witty Comedy, every thing is light, playful, and easy. Strong, decided condemnation of vice is too weighty and material to dance upon the surface of that stream, whose shallow currents sparkle in perpetual sunbeams, and cast up their bubbles to the light. Two or three persons of quick thought, and whimsical fancy, who perceive instantaneously the various connections of every passing idea, and the significations, natural or artificial, which single expressions, or particular forms of speech can possibly convey, take the lead through the whole, and seem to communicate their own peculiar talent to every creature in the play. The plot is most commonly feeble rather than simple, the incidents being numerous enough, but seldom striking or varied. To amuse, and only to amuse, is its aim; it pretends not to interest nor instruct. It pleases when we read, more than when we see it represented; and pleases still more when we take it up by accident, and read but a scene at a time.

Sentimental Comedy treats of those embarrassments, difficulties, and scruples, which, though sufficiently distressing to the delicate minds who entertain them, are not powerful enough to gratify the sympathetic desire we all feel to look into the heart of man in difficult and trying situations, which is the sound basis of tragedy, and are destitute of that seasoning of the lively and ludicrous, which prevents the ordinary transactions of comedy from becoming insipid. In real life, those who, from the peculiar frame of their minds, feel most of this refined distress, are not generally communicative upon the subject; and those who do feel and talk about it at the same time, if any such there be, seldom find their friends much inclined to listen to them. It is not to be supposed, then, long conversations upon the stage about small sentimental niceties, can be generally interesting. I am afraid plays of this kind, as well as works of a similar nature, in other departments of literature, have only tended to increase amongst us a set of sentimental hypocrites; who are the same persons of this age that would have been the religious ones of another; and are daily doing morality the same kind of injury, by substituting the particular excellence which they pretend to possess, for plain simple uprightness and rectitude.

In Busy or Circumstantial Comedy, all those ingenious contrivances of lovers, guardians, governantes, and chambermaids; that ambushed bushfighting amongst closets, screens, chests, easy-chairs, and toilet-tables, form a gay, varied game of dexterity and invention: which, to those who have played at hide and seek, who have crouched down, with beating heart, in a dark corner, whilst the enemy groped near the spot; who have joined their busy school-mates in many a deep-laid plan to deceive, perplex, and torment the unhappy mortals deputed to have the charge of them, cannot be seen with indifference. Like an old hunter, who pricks up his ears at the sound of the chase, and starts away from the path of his journey, so, leaving all wisdom and criticism behind us, we follow the varied changes of the plot, and stop not for reflection. The studious man who wants a cessation from thought, the indolent man who dislikes it, and all those who, from habit or circumstances, live in a state of divorce from their own minds, are pleased with an amusement, in which they have nothing to do but to open their eyes and behold. The moral tendency of it, however, is very faulty. That mockery of age and domestic authority, so constantly held forth, has a very bad effect upon the younger part of an audience; and that continual lying and deceit in the first characters of the piece, which is necessary for conducting the plot, has a most pernicious one.

But Characteristic Comedy, which represents to us this motley world of men and women in which we live, under those circumstances of ordinary and familiar life most favourable to the discovery of the human heart, offers to us a wide field of instruction adapted to general application. We find in its varied scenes an exercise of the mind analogous to that which we all, less or more, find out for ourselves, amidst the mixed groups of people whom we meet with in society; and which I have already mentioned as an exercise universally pleasing to man. As the distinctions which it is its highest aim to discriminate, are those of nature and not situation, they are judged of by all ranks of men; for a peasant will very clearly perceive in the character of a peer those native peculiarities which belong to him as a man, though he is entirely at a loss in all that regards his manners and address as a nobleman. It illustrates to us the general remarks we have made upon men; and in it we behold, spread before us, plans of those original ground-works, upon which the general ideas we have been taught to conceive of mankind, are founded. It stands but little in need of busy plot, extraordinary incidents, witty repartee, or studied sentiments. It naturally produces for itself all that it requires. Characters, who are to speak for themselves, who are to be known by their own words and actions, not by the accounts that are given of them by others, cannot well be developed without considerable variety of judicious incident: a smile that is raised by some trait of undisguised nature, and a laugh that is provoked by some ludicrous effect of passion, or clashing of opposite characters, will be more pleasing to the generality of men, than either the one or the other when occasioned by a play upon words, or a whimsical combination of ideas; and to behold the operation and effects of the different propensities and weaknesses of men, will naturally call up in the mind of the spectator moral reflections more applicable, and more impressive than all the high-sounding sentiments with which the graver scenes of Satirical and Sentimental Comedy are so frequently interlarded. It is much to be regretted, however, that the eternal introduction of love as the grand business of the Drama, and the consequent necessity for making the chief persons in it, such, in regard to age, appearance, manners, dispositions, and endowments, as are proper for interesting lovers, has occasioned so much insipid similarity in the higher characters. It is chiefly, therefore, on the second and inferior characters, that the efforts, even of our best poets, have been exhausted: and thus we are called upon to be interested in the fortune of one man, whilst our chief attention is directed to the character of another, which produces a disunion of ideas in the mind, injurious to the general effect of the whole. From this cause, also, those characteristic varieties have been very much neglected, which men present to us in the middle stages of life; when they are too old for lovers or the confidents of lovers, and too young to be the fathers, uncles, and guardians, who are contrasted with them; but when they are still in full vigour of mind, eagerly engaged with the world, joining the activity of youth to the providence of age, and offer to our attention objects sufficiently interesting and instructive. It is to be regretted that strong contrasts of character are too often attempted, instead of those harmonious shades of it, which nature so beautifully varies, and which we so greatly delight in, whenever we clearly distinguish them. It is to be regretted that in place of those characters, which present themselves to the imagination of a writer from his general observations upon mankind, inferior poets have so often pourtrayed with senseless minuteness the characters of particular individuals. We are pleased with the eccentricities of individuals in real life, and also in history or biography, but in fictitious writings we regard them with suspicion; and no representation of nature, that corresponds not with some of our general ideas in regard to it, will either instruct or inform us. When the original of such characters are known and remembered, the plays in which they are introduced are oftentimes popular; and their temporary success has induced a still inferior class of poets to believe, that, by making men strange, and unlike the rest of the world, they have made great discoveries, and mightily enlarged the boundaries of dramatic character. They will, therefore, distinguish one man from another by some strange whim or imagination, which is ever uppermost in his thoughts, and influences every action of his life; by some singular opinion, perhaps, about politics, fashions, or the position of the stars; by some strong unaccountable love for one thing, or aversion from another; entirely forgetting that, such singularities, if they are to be found in nature, can no where be sought for, with such probability of success, as in Bedlam. Above all it is to be regretted that those adventitious distinctions amongst men, of age, fortune, rank, profession, and country, are so often brought forward in preference to the great original distinctions of nature, and our scenes so often filled with courtiers, lawyers, citizens, Frenchmen, &c. &c. with all the characteristics of their respective conditions, such as they have been represented from time immemorial. This has introduced a great sameness into many of our plays, which all the changes of new fashions burlesqued, and new customs turned into ridicule, cannot conceal.

In comedy, the stronger passions, love excepted, are seldom introduced but in a passing way. We have short bursts of anger, fits of jealousy and impatience; violent passion of any continuance we seldom find. When this is attempted, however, forgetting that mode of exposing the weakness of the human mind, which peculiarly belongs to her, it is too frequently done in the serious spirit of tragedy; and this has produced so many of those serious comic plays, which so much divide and distract our attention. Yet we all know from our own experience in real life, that, in certain situations, and under certain circumstances, the stronger passions are fitted to produce scenes more exquisitely comic than any other: and one well-wrought scene of this kind will have a more powerful effect in repressing similar intemperance in the mind of a spectator, than many moral cautions, or even, perhaps, than the terrific examples of tragedy. There are to be found, no doubt, in the works of our best dramatic writers, comic scenes descriptive of the stronger passions, but it is generally the inferior characters of the piece who are made the subjects of them, very rarely those in whom we are much interested; and consequently the useful effect of such scenes upon the mind is very much weakened. This general appropriation of them has tempted our less skilful Dramatists to exaggerate, and step, in further quest of the ludicrous, so much beyond the bounds of nature, that the very effect they are so anxious to produce is thereby destroyed, and all useful application of it entirely cut off; for we never apply to ourselves a false representation of nature.

*   *   *   *

It was the saying of a sagacious Scotchman, "Let who will make the laws of a nation, if I have the writing of its ballads." Something similar to this may be said in regard to the Drama. Its lessons reach not, indeed, to the lowest classes of the labouring people, who are the broad foundation of society, which can never be generally moved without endangering every thing that is constructed upon it, and who are our potent and formidable ballad-readers; but they reach to the classes next in order to them, and who will always have over them no inconsiderable influence. The impressions made by it are communicated, at the same instant of time, to a greater number of individuals than those made by any other species of writing; and they are strengthened in every spectator, by observing their effects upon those who surround him. From this observation, the mind of my reader will suggest of itself what it would be unnecessary, and, perhaps, improper in me here to enlarge upon. The theatre is a school in which much good or evil may be learned. At the beginning of its career, the Drama was employed to mislead and excite; and, were I not unwilling to refer to transactions of the present times, I might abundantly confirm what I have said by recent examples. The author, therefore, who aims in any degree to improve the mode of its instruction, and point to more useful lessons than it is generally employed to dispense, is certainly praiseworthy, though want of abilities may unhappily prevent him from being successful in his efforts.

MARY WOLLSTONECRAFT

(1759–1797)

Often called the founder of feminism, Mary Wollstonecraft wrote works concerned with improving the education and lot of women. To this end, she wrote book-length essays, moral tales for children, and two novels. She also wrote a long refutation of Edmund Burke's *Reflections on the Revolution in France* and numerous letters. Her mother was Irish, as was her paternal grandfather, who made a fortune as a weaver. Unfortunately, her father wasted his inheritance and became an abusive drunkard. In keeping with the times, he centered what little support he gave to his family on his two sons, leaving Mary and her three sisters to shift for themselves. Although Mary's formal education was scant, her intellectual talents were great and her energy even greater.

At twenty-one, she began earning a living as a gentlewoman's companion. In 1783 she set up a school with her younger sister Eliza, whose disastrous marriage provided the material for the unfinished novel *Maria; or, The Wrongs of Woman*, published posthumously in 1798. The school closed after two years, and Mary became a governess in Lord Kingsborough's household. Her experiences there provided some of the material for her most famous work, *A Vindication of the Rights of Woman* (1792). She settled in London in 1787, and there she met the publisher Joseph Johnson, who employed her as a reader and translator. Johnson published her *Thoughts on the Education of Daughters* (1787) and continued as her publisher and loyal friend until her untimely death ten years later. He also introduced her to important social thinkers such as Thomas Paine and William Godwin (who later became her husband), as well as to the artists Henry Fuseli and William Blake. She became intimate with Fuseli and his wife, but the friendship ended when she proposed a *ménage à trois*.

In 1792, after the publication of *Vindication*, which caused a public outcry, she set off for France, then in the throes of revolution. There she met the adventurer Gilbert Imlay, who became her lover and the father of her first child, Fanny. Her letters to Imlay during the flowering and death of their love affair testify to the intensity of her emotions. After traveling for a few months in Sweden, Denmark and Norway, she returned to London, where in despair over Imlay's indifference she tried to drown herself in the Thames. During all this time of emotional agony, she continued writing and publishing. She also renewed her acquaintance with Godwin, and their friendship soon became love. Neither approved of conventional marriage, and not until the approaching birth of their child did they bow to convention and marry. Mary Wollstonecraft Godwin died as the result of giving birth to Mary Godwin, who later married the poet Shelley and wrote *Frankenstein*. After her death, William Godwin published her *Posthumous Works* (1798), including her passionate letters to Imlay. Their sexual frankness raised a scandal that caused her to be stigmatized as a wanton, "a hyena in petticoats," and eclipsed her real merits for at least a century.

EDITIONS USED: *Vindication of The Rights of Woman* (London, 1792); *Letters Written During A Short Residence in Sweden, Norway, and Denmark* (London, 1796); *Posthumous Works*, 4 vols. (London, 1798).

VINDICATION OF THE RIGHTS OF WOMAN

Of the Pernicious Effects Which Arise from the Unnatural Distinctions Established in Society

FROM THE respect paid to property flow, as from a poisoned fountain, most of the evils and vices which render this world such a dreary scene to the contemplative mind. For it is in the most polished society that noisome reptiles and venomous serpents lurk under the rank herbage; and there is voluptuousness pampered by the still sultry air, which relaxes every good disposition before it ripens into virtue.

One class presses on another; for all are aiming to procure respect on account of their property: and property, once gained, will procure the respect due only to talents and virtue. Men neglect the duties incumbent on man, yet are treated like demi-gods; religion is also separated from morality by a ceremonial veil, yet men wonder that the world is almost, literally speaking, a den of sharpers or oppressors.

There is a homely proverb, which speaks a shrewd truth, that whoever the devil finds idle he will employ. And what but habitual idleness can hereditary wealth and titles produce? For man is so constituted that he can only attain a proper use of his faculties by exercising them, and will not exercise them unless necessity, of some kind, first set the wheels in motion. Virtue likewise can only be acquired by the discharge of relative duties; but the importance of these sacred duties will scarcely be felt by the being who is cajoled out of his humanity by the flattery of sycophants. There must be more equality established in society, or morality will never gain ground, and this virtuous equality will not rest firmly even when founded on a rock, if one half of mankind are chained to its bottom by fate, for they will be continually undermining it through ignorance or pride.

It is vain to expect virtue from women till they are, in some degree, independent of men; nay, it is vain to expect that strength of natural affection, which would make them good wives and mothers. Whilst they are absolutely dependent on their husbands they will be cunning, mean, and selfish, and the men who can be gratified by the fawning fondness of spaniel-like affection, have not much delicacy, for love is not to be bought, in any sense of the words, its silken wings are instantly shrivelled up when any thing beside a return in kind is sought. Yet whilst wealth enervates men; and women live, as it were, by their personal charms, how can we expect them to discharge those ennobling duties which equally requires exertion and self-denial. Hereditary property sophisticates the mind, and the unfortunate victims to it, if I may so express myself, swathed from their birth, seldom exert the locomotive faculty of body or mind; and, thus viewing every thing through one medium, and that a false one, they are unable to discern in what true merit and happiness consist. False, indeed, must be the light when the drapery of situation hides the man, and makes him stalk in masquerade, dragging from one scene of dissipation to another the nerveless limbs that hang with stupid listlessness, and rolling round the vacant eye which plainly tells us that there is no mind at home.

I mean, therefore, to infer that the society is not properly organized which does not compel men and women to discharge their respective duties, by making it the only way to acquire that countenance from their fellow-creatures, which every human being wishes some way to attain. The respect, consequently, which is paid to wealth and mere personal charms, is a true north-east blast, that blights the tender blossoms of affection and virtue. Nature has wisely attached affections to duties, to sweeten toil, and to give that vigour to the exertions of reason which only the heart can give. But, the affection which is put on merely because it is the appropriated insignia of a certain character, when its duties are not fulfilled, is one of the empty compliments which vice and folly are obliged to pay to virtue and the real nature of things.

To illustrate my opinion, I need only observe, that when a woman is admired for her beauty, and suffers herself to be so far intoxicated by the admiration she receives, as to neglect to discharge the indispensable duty of a mother, she sins against herself by neglecting to cultivate an affection that would equally tend to make her useful and happy. True happiness, I mean all the contentment, and virtuous satisfaction, that can be snatched in this imperfect state, must arise from well regulated affections; and an affection includes a duty. Men are not aware of the misery they cause, and the vicious weakness they cherish, by only inciting women to render themselves pleasing; they do not consider that they thus make natural and artificial duties clash, by sacrificing the comfort and respectability of a woman's life to voluptuous notions of beauty, when in nature they all harmonize.

Cold would be the heart of a husband, were he not rendered unnatural by early debauchery, who did not feel more delight at seeing his child suckled by its mother, than the most artful wanton tricks could ever raise; yet this natural way of cementing the matrimonial tie, and twisting esteem with fonder recollections, wealth leads women to spurn. To preserve their beauty, and wear the flowery crown of the day, that gives them a kind of right to reign for a short time over the sex, they neglect to stamp impressions on their husbands' hearts, that would be remembered with more tenderness when the snow on the head began to chill the bosom, than even their virgin charms. The maternal solicitude of a reasonable affectionate woman is very interesting, and the chastened dignity with which a mother returns the caresses that she and her child receive from a father who has been fulfilling the serious duties of his station, is not only a respectable, but a beautiful sight. So singular, indeed, are my feelings, and I have endeavoured not to catch factitious ones, that after having been fatigued with the sight of insipid grandeur and the slavish ceremonies that with cumberous pomp supplied the place of domestic affections, I have turned to some other scene to relive my eye by resting it on the refreshing green every where scattered by nature. I have then viewed with pleasure a woman nursing her children, and discharging the duties of her station with, perhaps, merely a servant maid to take off her hands the servile part of the household business. I have seen her prepare herself and children, with only the luxury of cleanliness, to receive her husband, who returning weary home in the evening found smiling babes and a clean hearth. My heart has loitered in the midst of the group, and has even throbbed with sympathetic emotion, when the scraping of the well known foot has raised a pleasing tumult.

Whilst my benevolence has been gratified by contemplating this artless picture, I have thought that a couple of this description, equally necessary and independent of each other, because each fulfilled the respective duties of their station, possessed all that life could give.—Raised sufficiently above abject poverty not to be obliged to weigh the consequence of every farthing they spend, and having sufficient to prevent their attending to a frigid system of economy, which narrows both heart and mind. I declare, so vulgar are my conceptions, that I know not what is wanted to render this the happiest as well as the most respectable situation in the world, but a taste for literature, to throw a little variety and interest into social converse, and some superfluous money to give to the needy and to buy books. For it is not pleasant when the heart is opened by compassion and the head active in arranging plans of usefulness, to have a prim urchin continually twitching back the elbow to prevent the hand from drawing out an almost empty purse, whispering at the same time some prudential maxim about the priority of justice.

Destructive, however, as riches and inherited honours are to the human character, women are more debased and cramped, if possible, by them, than men, because men may still, in some degree, unfold their faculties by becoming soldiers and statesmen.

As soldiers, I grant, they can now only gather, for the most part, vain glorious laurels, whilst they adjust to a hair the European balance, taking especial care that no bleak northern nook or sound incline the beam. But the days of true heroism are over, when a citizen fought for his country like a Fabricius or a Washington, and then returned to his farm to let his virtuous fervour run in a more placid, but not a less salutary, stream. No, our British heroes are oftener sent from the gaming table than from the plow; and their passions have been rather inflamed by hanging with dumb suspense on the turn of a die, than sublimated by panting after the adventurous march of virtue in the historic page.

The statesman, it is true, might with more propriety quit the Faro Bank, or card-table, to guide the helm, for he has still but to shuffle and trick. The whole system of British politics, if system it may courteously be called, consisting in multiplying dependents and contriving taxes which grind the poor to pamper the rich; thus a war, or any wild goose chace is, as the vulgar use the phrase, a lucky turn-up of patronage for the minister, whose chief merit is the art of keeping himself in place.

It is not necessary then that he should have bowels for the poor, so he can secure for his family the odd trick. Or should some shew of respect, for what is termed with ignorant ostentation an Englishman's birth-right, be expedient to bubble the gruff mastiff that he has to lead by the nose, he can make an empty shew, very safely, by giving his single voice, and suffering his light squadron to file off to the other side. And when a question of humanity is agitated he may dip a sop in the milk of human kindness, to silence Cerberus, and talk of the interest which his heart takes in an attempt to make the earth no longer cry for vengeance as it sucks in its children's blood, though his cold hand may at the very moment rivet their chains, by sanctioning the abominable traffick. A minister is no longer a minister than while he can carry a point, which he is determined to carry. — Yet it is not necessary that a minister should feel like a man, when a bold push might shake his seat.

But, to have done with these episodical observations, let me return to the more specious slavery which chains the very soul of woman, keeping her for ever under the bondage of ignorance.

The preposterous distinctions of rank, which render civilization a curse, by dividing the world between voluptuous tyrants, and cunning envious dependents, corrupt, almost equally, every class of people, because respectability is not attached to the discharge of the relative duties of life, but to the station, and when the duties are not fulfilled the affections cannot gain sufficient strength to fortify the virtue of which they are the natural reward. Still there are some loop-holes out of which a man may creep, and dare to think and act for himself; but for a woman it is an herculean task, because she has difficulties peculiar to her sex to overcome, which require almost superhuman powers.

A truly benevolent legislator always endeavours to make it the interest of each individual to be virtuous; and thus private virtue becoming the cement of public happiness, an orderly whole is consolidated by the tendency of all the parts towards a common centre. But, the private or public virtue of woman is very problematical; for Rousseau, and a numerous list of male writers, insist that she should all her life be subjected to a severe restraint, that of propriety. Why subject her to propriety — blind propriety, if she be capable of acting from a nobler spring, if she be an heir of immortality? Is sugar always to be produced by vital blood? Is one half of the human species, like the poor African slaves, to be subject to prejudices that brutalize them, when principles would be a surer guard, only to sweeten the cup of man? Is not this indirectly to deny woman reason? for a gift is a mockery, if it be unfit for use.

Women are, in common with men, rendered weak and luxurious by the relaxing pleasures which wealth procures; but added to this they are made slaves to their persons, and must render them alluring that man may lend them his reason to guide their tottering steps aright. Or should they be ambitious, they must govern their tyrants by sinister tricks, for without rights there cannot be any incumbent duties. The laws respecting woman, which I mean to discuss in a future part, make an absurd unit of a man and his wife; and then, by the easy transition of only considering him as responsible, she is reduced to a mere cypher.

The being who discharges the duties of its station is independent; and, speaking of women at large, their first duty is to themselves as rational creatures, and the next, in point of importance, as citizens, is that, which includes so many, of a mother. The rank in life which dispenses with their fulfilling this duty, necessarily degrades them by making them mere dolls. Or, should they turn to something more important than merely fitting drapery upon a smooth block, their minds are only occupied by some soft platonic attachment; or, the actual management of an intrigue may keep their thoughts in motion; for when they neglect domestic duties, they have it not in their power to take the field and march and counter-march like soldiers, or wrangle in the senate to keep their faculties from rusting.

I know that as a proof of the inferiority of the sex, Rousseau has exultingly exclaimed, How can they leave the nursery for the camp! — And the camp has by some moralists been termed the school of the most heroic virtues; though, I think, it would puzzle a keen casuist to prove the reasonableness of the greater number of wars that have dubbed heroes. I do not mean to consider this question critically; because, having frequently viewed these freaks of ambition as the first natural mode of civilization, when the ground must be torn up, and the woods cleared by fire and sword, I do not choose to call them pests; but surely the present system of war has little connection with virtue of any denomination, being rather the school of *finesse* and effeminacy, than of fortitude.

Yet, if defensive war, the only justifiable war, in the present advanced state of society, where virtue can shew its face and ripen amidst the rigours which purify the air on the mountain's top, were alone to be adopted as just and glorious, the true heroism of antiquity might again animate female bosoms. — But fair and softly, gentle reader, male or female, do not alarm thyself, for though I have contrasted the character of a modern soldier with that of a civilized woman, I am not going to advise them to turn their distaff into a musket, though I sincerely wish to see the bayonet converted into a pruning-hook. I only recreated an imagination, fatigued by contemplating the vices and follies which all proceed from a feculent stream of wealth that has muddied the pure rills of natural affection, by supposing that society will some time or other be so constituted, that man must necessarily fulfil the duties of a citizen, or be despised, and that while he was employed in any of the departments of civil life, his wife, also an active citizen, should be equally intent to manage her family, educate her children, and assist her neighbours.

But, to render her really virtuous and useful, she must not, if she discharge her civil duties, want, individually, the protection of civil laws; she must not be dependent on her husband's bounty for her subsistence during his life, or support after his death—for how can a being be generous who has nothing of its own? or, virtuous, who is not free? The wife, in the present state of things, who is faithful to her husband, and neither suckles nor educates her children, scarcely deserves the name of a wife, and has no right to that of a citizen. But take away natural rights, and there is of course an end of duties.

Women thus infallibly become only the wanton solace of men, when they are so weak in mind and body, that they cannot exert themselves, unless to pursue some frothy pleasure, or to invent some frivolous fashion. What can be a more melancholy sight to a thinking mind, than to look into the numerous carriages that drive helter-skelter about this metropolis in a morning full of pale-faced creatures who are flying from themselves. I have often wished, with Dr. Johnson, to place some of them in a little shop with half a dozen children looking up to their languid countenances for support. I am much mistaken, if some latent vigour would not soon give health and spirit to their eyes, and some lines drawn by the exercise of reason on the blank cheeks, which before were only undulated by dimples, might restore lost dignity to the character, or rather enable it to attain the true dignity of its nature. Virtue is not to be acquired even by speculation, much less by the negative supineness that wealth naturally generates.

Besides, when poverty is more disgraceful than even vice, is not morality cut to the quick? Still to avoid misconstruction, though I consider that women in the common walks of life are called to fulfil the duties of wives and mothers, by religion and reason, I cannot help lamenting that women of a superiour cast have not a road open by which they can pursue more extensive plans of usefulness and independence. I may excite laughter, by dropping an hint, which I mean to pursue, some future time, for I really think that women ought to have representatives, instead of being arbitrarily governed without having any direct share allowed them in the deliberations of government.

But, as the whole system of representation is now, in this country, only a convenient handle for despotism, they need not complain, for they are as well represented as a numerous class of hard working mechanics, who pay for the support of royalty when they can scarcely stop their children's mouths with bread. How are they represented whose very sweat supports the splendid stud of an heir apparent, or varnishes the chariot of some female favourite who looks down on shame? Taxes on the very necessaries of life, enable an endless tribe of idle princes and princesses to pass with stupid pomp before a gaping crowd, who almost worship the very parade which costs them so dear. This is mere gothic grandeur, something like the barbarous useless parade of having sentinels on horseback at White-hall, which I could never view without a mixture of contempt and indignation.

How strangely must the mind be sophisticated when this sort of state impresses it! But, till these monuments of folly are levelled by virtue, similar follies will leaven the whole mass. For the same character, in some degree, will prevail in the aggregate of society: and the refinements of luxury, or the vicious repinings of envious poverty, will equally banish virtue from society, considered as the characteristic of that society, or only allow it to appear as one of the stripes of the harlequin coat, worn by the civilized man.

In the superior ranks of life, every duty is done by deputies, as if duties could ever be waved, and the vain pleasures which consequent idleness forces the rich to pursue, appear so enticing to the next rank, that the numerous scramblers for wealth sacrifice every thing to tread on their heels. The most sacred trusts are then considered as sinecures, because they were procured by interest, and only sought to enable a man to keep *good company*. Women, in particular, all want to be ladies. Which is simply to have nothing to do, but listlessly to go they scarcely care where, for they cannot tell what.

But what have women to do in society? I may be asked, but to loiter with easy grace; surely you would not condemn them all to suckle fools and chronicle small beer! No. Women might certainly study the art of healing, and be physicians as well as nurses. And midwifery, decency seems to allot to them, though I am afraid the word midwife, in our dictionaries, will soon give place to *accoucheur* [male midwife], and one proof of the former delicacy of the sex be effaced from the language.

They might, also, study politics, and settle their benevolence on the broadest basis; for the reading of history will scarcely be more useful than the perusal of romances, if read as mere biography; if the character of the times, the political improvements, arts, &c. be not observed. In short, if it be not considered as the history of man; and not of particular men, who filled a niche in the temple of fame, and dropped into the black rolling stream of time, that silently sweeps all before it, into the shapeless void called — eternity. — For shape, can it be called, 'that shape hath none?'

Business of various kinds, they might likewise pursue, if they were educated in a more orderly manner, which might save many from common and legal prostitution. Women would not then marry for a support, as men accept of places under government, and neglect the implied duties; nor would an attempt to earn their own subsistence, a most laudable one! sink them almost to the level of those poor abandoned creatures who live by prostitution. For are not milliners and mantua-makers reckoned the next class? The few employments open to women, so far from being liberal, are menial; and when a superiour education enables them to take charge of the education of children as governesses, they are not treated like the tutors of sons, though even clerical tutors are not always treated in a manner calculated to render them respectable in the eyes of their pupils, to say nothing of the private comfort of the individual. But as women educated like gentlewomen, are never designed for the humiliating situation which necessity sometimes forces them to fill; these situations are considered in the light of a degradation; and they know little of the human heart, who need to be told, that nothing so painfully sharpens the sensibility as such a fall in life.

Some of these women might be restrained from marrying by a proper spirit or delicacy, and others may not have had it in their power to escape in this pitiful way from servitude; is not that government then very defective, and very unmindful of the happiness of one half of its members, that does not provide for honest, independent women, by encouraging them to fill respectable stations? But in order to render their private virtue a public benefit, they must have a civil existence in the state, married or single; else we shall continually see some worthy woman, whose sensibility has been rendered painfully acute by unde-served contempt, droop like 'the lily broken down by a plow-share.'

It is a melancholy truth; yet such is the blessed effect of civilization! the most respectable women are the most oppressed; and, unless they have understandings far superiour to the common run of understandings, taking in both sexes, they must, from being treated like contemptible beings, become contemptible. How many women thus waste life away the prey of discontent, who might have practised as physicians, regulated a farm, managed a shop, and stood erect, supported by their own industry, instead of hanging their heads surcharged with the dew of sensibility, that consumes the beauty to which it at first gave lustre; nay, I doubt whether pity and love are so near akin as poets feign, for I have seldom seen much compassion excited by the helplessness of females, unless they were fair; then, perhaps, pity was the soft handmaid of love, or the harbinger of lust.

How much more respectable is the woman who earns her own bread by fulfilling any duty, than the most accomplished beauty! — beauty did I say? — so sensible am I of the beauty of moral loveliness, or the harmonious propriety that attunes the passions of a well-regulated mind, that I blush at making the comparison; yet I sigh to think how few women aim at attaining this respectability by withdrawing from the giddy whirl of pleasure, or the indolent calm that stupifies the good sort of women it sucks in.

Proud of their weakness, however, they must always be protected, guarded from care, and all the rough toils that dignify the mind. — If this be the fiat of fate, if they will make themselves insignificant and contemptible, sweetly to waste 'life away,' let them not expect to be valued when their beauty fades, for it is the fate of the fairest flowers to be admired and pulled to pieces by the careless hand that plucked them. In how many ways do I wish, from the purest benevolence, to impress this truth on my sex; yet I fear that they will not listen to a truth that dear bought experience has brought home to many an agitated bosom, nor willingly resign the privileges of rank and sex for the privileges of humanity, to which those have no claim who do not discharge its duties.

Those writers are particularly useful, in my opinion, who make man feel for man, independent of the station he fills, or the drapery of factitious sentiments. I then would fain convince reasonable men of the importance of some of my remarks, and prevail on them to weigh dispassionately the whole tenor of my observations. — I appeal to their understandings; and, as a fellow-creature claim, in the name of my sex, some interest in their hearts. I entreat them to assist to emancipate their companion, to make her a help meet for them!

Would men but generously snap our chains, and be content with rational fellowship instead of slavish obedience, they would find us more observant daughters, more affectionate sisters, more faithful wives, more reasonable mothers — in a word, better citizens. We should then love them with true affection, because we should learn to respect ourselves; and the peace of mind of a worthy man would not be interrupted by the idle vanity of his wife, nor his babes sent to nestle in a strange bosom, having never found a home in their mother's.

LETTERS WRITTEN DURING A SHORT RESIDENCE IN SWEDEN, NORWAY, AND DENMARK

Letter 1

ELEVEN DAYS of weariness on board a vessel not intended for the accommodation of passengers have so exhausted my spirits, to say nothing of the
other causes, with which you are already sufficiently acquainted, that it is
with some difficulty I adhere to my determination of giving you my
observations, as I travel through new scenes, whilst warmed with the
impression they have made on me.

The captain, as I mentioned to you, promised to put me on shore at
Arendall, or Gothenburg, in his way to Elsineur; but contrary winds
obliged us to pass both places during the night. In the morning, however, after we had lost sight of the entrance of the latter bay, the vessel
was becalmed; and the captain, to oblige me, hanging out a signal for a
pilot, bore down towards the shore.

My attention was particularly directed to the light-house; and you can
scarcely imagine with what anxiety I watched two long hours for a boat to
emancipate me—still no one appeared. Every cloud that flitted on the
horizon was hailed as a liberator, till approaching nearer, like most of the
prospects sketched by hope, it dissolved under the eye into disappointment.

Weary of expectation, I then began to converse with the captain on the
subject; and, from the tenour of the information my questions drew
forth, I soon concluded, that, if I waited for a boat, I had little chance of
getting on shore at this place. Despotism, as is usually the case, I found
had here cramped the industry of man. The pilots being paid by the
king, and scantily, they will not run into any danger, or even quit their
hovels, if they can possibly avoid it, only to fulfil what is termed their
duty. How different is it on the english coast, where, in the most stormy
weather, boats immediately hail you, brought out by the expectation of
extraordinary profit.

Disliking to sail for Elsineur, and still more to lie at anchor, or cruise
about the coast for several days, I exerted all my rhetoric to prevail on the
captain to let me have the ship's boat; and though I added the most
forcible of arguments, I for a long time addressed him in vain.

It is a kind of rule at sea, not to send out a boat. The captain was a
good-natured man; but men with common minds seldom break through
general rules. Prudence is ever the resort of weakness; and they rarely go

as far as they may in any undertaking, who are determined not to go beyond it on any account. If, however, I had some trouble with the captain, I did not lose much time with the sailors; for they, all alacrity, hoisted out the boat, the moment I obtained permission, and promised to row me to the light-house.

I did not once allow myself to doubt of obtaining a conveyance from thence round the rocks—and then away for Gothenburg—confinement is so unpleasant.

The day was fine; and I enjoyed the water till, approaching the little island, poor Marguerite, whose timidity always acts as a feeler before her adventuring spirit, began to wonder at our not seeing any inhabitants. I did not listen to her. But when, on landing, the same silence prevailed, I caught the alarm, which was not lessened by the sight of two old men, whom we forced out of their wretched hut. Scarcely human in their appearance, we with difficulty obtained an intelligible reply to our queries—the result of which was, that they had no boat, and were not allowed to quit their post, on any pretence. But, they informed us, that there was at the other side, eight or ten miles over, a pilot's dwelling; two guineas tempted the sailors to risk the captain's displeasure, and once more embark to row me over.

The weather was pleasant, and the appearance of the shore so grand, that I should have enjoyed the two hours it took to reach it, but for the fatigue which was too visible in the countenances of the sailors who, instead of uttering a complaint, were, with the thoughtless hilarity peculiar to them, joking about the possibility of the captain's taking advantage of a slight westerly breeze, which was springing up, to sail without them. Yet, in spite of their good humour, I could not help growing uneasy when the shore, receding, as it were, as we advanced, seemed to promise no end to their toil. This anxiety increased when, turning into the most picturesque bay I ever saw, my eyes sought in vain for the vestige of a human habitation. Before I could determine what step to take in such a dilemma, for I could not bear to think of returning to the ship, the sight of a barge relieved me, and we hastened towards it for information. We were immediately directed to pass some jutting rocks when we should see a pilot's hut.

There was a solemn silence in this scene, which made itself be felt. The sun-beams that played on the ocean, scarcely ruffled by the lightest breeze, contrasted with the huge, dark rocks, that looked like the rude materials of creation forming the barrier of unwrought space, forcibly struck me; but I should not have been sorry if the cottage had not appeared equally tranquil. Approaching a retreat where strangers, especially women, so seldom appeared, I wondered that curiosity did not bring the beings who inhabited it to the windows or door. I did not immediately recollect that men who remain so near the brute creation, as only to exert themselves to find the food necessary to sustain life, have little or no imagination to call forth the curiosity necessary to fructify the faint glimmerings of mind which entitles them to rank as lords of the creation. — Had they either, they could not contentedly remain rooted in the clods they so indolently cultivate.

Whilst the sailors went to seek for the sluggish inhabitants, these conclusions occurred to me; and, recollecting the extreme fondness which the parisians ever testify for novelty, their very curiosity appeared to me a proof of the progress they had made in refinement. Yes; in the art of living — in the art of escaping from the cares which embarrass the first steps towards the attainment of the pleasures of social life.

The pilots informed the sailors that they were under the direction of a lieutenant retired from the service, who spoke english; adding, that they could do nothing without his orders; and even the offer of money could hardly conquer their laziness, and prevail on them to accompany us to his dwelling. They would not go with me alone, which I wanted them to have done, because I wished to dismiss the sailors as soon as possible. Once more we rowed off, they following tardily, till, turning round another bold protuberance of the rocks, we saw a boat making towards us, and soon learnt that it was the lieutenant himself, coming with some earnestness to see who we were.

To save the sailors any further toil, I had my baggage instantly removed into his boat; for, as he could speak english, a previous parley was not necessary; though Marguerite's respect for me could hardly keep her from expressing the fear, strongly marked on her countenance, which my putting ourselves into the power of a strange man excited. He pointed out his cottage; and, drawing near to it, I was not sorry to see a female figure, though I had not, like Marguerite, been thinking of robberies, murders, or the other evil which instantly, as the sailors would have said, runs foul of a woman's imagination.

On entering, I was still better pleased to find a clean house, with some degree of rural elegance. The beds were of muslin, coarse it is true, but dazzlingly white; and the floor was strewed over with little sprigs of juniper (the custom, as I afterwards found, of the country), which formed a contrast with the curtains and produced an agreeable sensation of freshness, to soften the ardour of noon. Still nothing was so pleasing as the alacrity of hospitality—all that the house afforded was quickly spread on the whitest linen. —Remember I had just left the vessel, where, without being fastidious, I had continually been disgusted. Fish, milk, butter, and cheese, and I am sorry to add, brandy, the bane of this country, were spread on the board. After we had dined, hospitality made them, with some degree of mystery, bring us some excellent coffee. I did not then know that it was prohibited.

The good man of the house apologized for coming in continually, but declared that he was so glad to speak english, he could not stay out. He need not have apologized; I was equally glad of his company. With the wife I could only exchange smiles; and she was employed observing the make of our clothes. My hands, I found, had first led her to discover that I was the lady. I had, of course, my quantum of reverences; for the politeness of the north seems to partake of the coldness of the climate, and the rigidity of its iron sinewed rocks. Amongst the peasantry, there is, however, so much of the simplicity of the golden age in this land of flint—so much overflowing of heart, and fellow-feeling, that only benevolence, and the honest sympathy of nature, diffused smiles over my countenance when they kept me standing, regardless of my fatigue, whilst they dropt courtesy after courtesy.

The situation of this house was beautiful, though chosen for convenience. The master being the officer who commanded all the pilots on the coast, and the person appointed to guard wrecks, it was necessary for him to fix on a spot that would overlook the whole bay. As he had seen some service, he wore, not without a pride I thought becoming, a badge to prove that he had merited well of his country. It was happy, I thought, that he had been paid in honour; for the stipend he received was little more than twelve pounds a year. —I do not trouble myself or you with the calculation of swedish ducats. Thus, my friend, you perceive the necessity of *perquisites*. This same narrow policy runs through every thing. I shall have occasion further to animadvert on it.

Though my host amused me with an account of himself, which gave me an idea of the manners of the people I was about to visit, I was eager to climb the rocks to view the country, and see whether the honest tars had regained their ship. With the help of the lieutenant's telescope I saw the vessel underway with a fair though gentle gale. The sea was calm, playful even as the most shallow stream, and on the vast bason I did not see a dark speck to indicate the boat. My conductors were consequently arrived.

Straying further, my eye was attracted by the sight of some heart's-ease that peeped through the rocks. I caught at it as a good omen, and going to preserve it in a letter that had not conveyed balm to my heart, a cruel remembrance suffused my eyes; but it passed away like an April shower. If you are deep read in Shakspeare, you will recollect that this was the little western flower tinged by love's dart, which "maidens call love in idleness." The gaiety of my babe was unmixed; regardless of omens or sentiments, she found a few wild strawberries more grateful than flowers or fancies.

The lieutenant informed me that this was a commodious bay. Of that I could not judge, though I felt its picturesque beauty. Rocks were piled on rocks, forming a suitable bulwark to the ocean. Come no further, they emphatically said, turning their dark sides to the waves to augment the idle roar. The view was sterile: still little patches of earth, of the most exquisite verdure, enamelled with the sweetest wild flowers, seemed to promise the goats and a few straggling cows luxurious herbage. How silent and peaceful was the scene. I gazed around with rapture, and felt more of that spontaneous pleasure which gives credibility to our expectation of happiness, than I had for a long, long time before. I forgot the horrors I had witnessed in France, which had cast a gloom over all nature, and suffering the enthusiasm of my character, too often, gracious God! damped by the tears of disappointed affection, to be lighted up afresh, care took wing while simple fellow feeling expanded my heart.

To prolong this enjoyment, I readily assented to the proposal of our host to pay a visit to a family, the master of which spoke english, who was the drollest dog in the country, he added, repeating some of his stories, with a hearty laugh.

I walked on, still delighted with the rude beauties of the scene; for the sublime often gave place imperceptibly to the beautiful, dilating the emotions which were painfully concentrated.

When we entered this abode, the largest I had yet seen, I was introduced to a numerous family; but the father, from whom I was led to expect so much entertainment, was absent. The lieutenant consequently was obliged to be the interpreter of our reciprocal compliments. The phrases were awkwardly transmitted, it is true; but looks and gestures were sufficient to make them intelligible and interesting. The girls were all vivacity, and respect for me could scarcely keep them from romping with my host, who, asking for a pinch of snuff, was presented with a box, out of which an artificial mouse, fastened to the bottom, sprung. Though this trick had doubtless been played time out of mind, yet the laughter it excited was not less genuine.

They were overflowing with civility; but to prevent their almost killing my babe with kindness, I was obliged to shorten my visit; and two or three of the girls accompanied us, bringing with them a part of whatever the house afforded to contribute towards rendering my supper more plentiful; and plentiful in fact it was, though I with difficulty did honour to some of the dishes, not relishing the quantity of sugar and spices put into every thing. At supper my host told me bluntly that I was a woman of observation, for I asked him *men's questions.*

The arrangements for my journey were quickly made; I could only have a car with post-horses, as I did not chuse to wait till a carriage could be sent for to Gothenburg. The expense of my journey, about one or two and twenty english miles, I found would not amount to more than eleven or twelve shillings, paying, he assured me, generously. I gave him a guinea and a half. But it was with the greatest difficulty that I could make him take so much, indeed any thing for my lodging and fare. He declared that it was next to robbing me, explaining how much I ought to pay on the road. However, as I was positive, he took the guinea for himself; but, as a condition, insisted on accompanying me, to prevent my meeting with any trouble or imposition on the way.

I then retired to my apartment with regret. The night was so fine, that I would gladly have rambled about much longer; yet recollecting that I must rise very early, I reluctantly went to bed: but my senses had been so awake, and my imagination still continued so busy, that I sought for rest in vain. Rising before six, I scented the sweet morning air; I had long before heard the birds twittering to hail the dawning day, though it could scarcely have been allowed to have departed.

Nothing, in fact, can equal the beauty of the northern summer's evening and night; if night it may be called that only wants the glare of day, the full light, which frequently seems so impertinent; for I could write at midnight very well without a candle. I contemplated all nature at rest; the rocks, even grown darker in their appearance, looked as if they partook of the general repose, and reclined more heavily on their foundation.—What, I exclaimed, is this active principle which keeps me still awake?—Why fly my thoughts abroad when every thing around me appears at home? My child was fleeping with equal calmness—innocent and sweet as the closing flowers.—Some recollections, attached to the idea of home, mingled with reflections respecting the state of society I had been contemplating that evening, made a tear drop on the rosy cheek I had just kissed; and emotions that trembled on the brink of extacy and agony gave a poignancy to my sensations, which made me feel more alive than usual.

What are these imperious sympathies? How frequently has melancholy and even mysanthropy taken possession of me, when the world has disgusted me, and friends have proved unkind. I have then considered myself as a particle broken off from the grand mass of mankind; — I was alone, till some involuntary sympathetic emotion, like the attraction of adhesion, made me feel that I was still a part of a mighty whole, from which I could not sever myself — not, perhaps, for the reflection has been carried very far, by snapping the thread of an existence which loses its charms in proportion as the cruel experience of life stops or poisons the current of the heart. Futurity, what hast thou not to give to those who know that there is such a thing as happiness! I speak not of philosophical contentment, though pain has afforded them the strongest conviction of it.

Letter 2

GOTHENBURG IS a clean airy town, and having been built by the dutch, has canals running through each street, and in some of them there are rows of trees that would render it very pleasant were it not for the pavement, which is intolerably bad.

There are several rich commercial houses, scotch, french, and swedish; but the scotch, I believe, have been the most successful. The commerce and commission business with France since the war, has been very lucrative, and enriched the merchants, I am afraid, at the expence of the other inhabitants, by raising the price of the necessaries of life.

As all the men of consequence, I mean men of the largest fortune, are merchants, their principal enjoyment is a relaxation from business at the table, which is spread at, I think, too early an hour (between one and two) for men who have letters to write and accounts to settle after paying due respect to the bottle. However, when numerous circles are to be brought together, and when neither literature nor public amusements furnish topics for conversation, a good dinner appears to be the only centre to rally round, especially as scandal, the zest of more select parties, can only be whispered. As for politics, I have seldom found it a subject of continual discussion in a country town in any part of the world. The politics of the place being on a smaller scale, suits better with the size of their faculties; for, generally speaking, the sphere of observation deter-mines the extent of the mind.

The more I see of the world, the more I am convinced that civilization is a blessing not sufficiently estimated by those who have not traced its progress; for it not only refines our enjoyments, but produces a variety which enables us to retain the primitive delicacy of our sensations. With-out the aid of the imagination all the pleasures of the senses must sink into grossness, unless continual novelty serve as a substitute for the imagi-nation, which being impossible, it was to this weariness, I suppose, that Solomon alluded when he declared that there was nothing new under the fun! — nothing for the common sensations excited by the senses. Yet who will deny that the imagination and understanding have made many, very many discoveries since those days, which only seem harbingers of others still more noble and beneficial. I never met with much imagination amongst people who had not acquired a habit of reflection; and in that state of society in which the judgment and taste are not called forth, and formed by the cultivation of the arts and sciences, little of that delicacy of feeling and thinking is to be found characterized by the word sentiment. The want of scientific pursuits perhaps accounts for the hospitality, as well as for the cordial reception which strangers receive from the inhabi-tants of small towns.

Hospitality has, I think, been too much praised by travellers as a proof of goodness of heart, when in my opinion indiscriminate hospitality is rather a criterion by which you may form a tolerable estimate of the indolence or vacancy of a head; or, in other words, a fondness for social pleasures in which the mind not having its proportion of exercise, the bottle must be pushed about.

These remarks are equally applicable to Dublin, the most hospitable city I ever passed through. But I will try to confine my observations more particularly to Sweden.

It is true I have only had a glance over a small part of it; yet of its present state of manners and acquirements I think I have formed a distinct idea, without having visited the capital, where, in fact, less of a national character is to be found than in the remote parts of the country.

The swedes pique themselves on their politeness; but far from being the polish of a cultivated mind, it consists merely of tiresome forms and ceremonies. So far indeed from entering immediately into your character, and making you feel instantly at your ease, like the well-bred french, their over-acted civility is a continual restraint on all your actions. The sort of superiority which a fortune gives when there is no superiority of education, excepting what consists in the observance of senseless forms, has a contrary effect than what is intended; so that I could not help reckoning the peasantry the politest people of Sweden, who only aiming at pleasing you, never think of being admired for their behaviour.

*   *   *

A day of this kind you would imagine sufficient—but a to-morrow and a to-morrow—A never ending, still beginning feast may be bearable, perhaps, when stern winter frowns, shaking with chilling aspect his hoary locks; but during a summer, sweet as fleeting, let me, my kind strangers, escape sometimes into your fir groves, wander on the margin of your beautiful lakes, or climb your rocks to view still others in endless perspective; which, piled by more than giant's hand, scale the heavens to intercept its rays, or to receive the parting tinge of lingering day—day that, scarcely softened into twilight, allows the freshening breeze to wake, and the moon to burst forth in all her glory to glide with solemn elegance through the azure expanse.

The cow's bell has ceased to tinkle the herd to rest; they have all paced across the heath. Is not this the witching time of night? The waters murmur, and fall with more than mortal music, and spirits of peace walk abroad to calm the agitated breast. Eternity is in these moments: worldly cares melt into the airy stuff that dreams are made of; and reveries, mild and enchanting as the first hopes of love, or the recollection of lost enjoyment, carry the hapless wight into futurity, who, in bustling life, has vainly strove to throw off the grief which lies heavy at the heart. Good night! A crescent hangs out in the vault before, which woos me to stray abroad:—it is not a silvery reflection of the sun, but glows with all its golden splendour. Who fears the falling dew? It only makes the mown grass smell more fragrant.

Adieu!

Letter 6

THE SEA was boisterous; but, as I had an experienced pilot, I did not apprehend any danger. Sometimes I was told, boats are driven far out and lost. However, I seldom calculate chances so nicely — sufficient for the day is the obvious evil!

We had to steer amongst islands and huge rocks, rarely losing sight of the shore, though it now and then appeared only a mist that bordered the water's edge. The pilot assured me that the numerous harbours on the Norway coast were very safe, and the pilot-boats were always on the watch. The Swedish side is very dangerous, I am also informed; and the help of experience is not often at hand, to enable strange vessels to steer clear of the rocks, which lurk below the water, close to the shore.

There are no tides here, nor in the cattegate; and, what appeared to me a consequence, no sandy beach. Perhaps this observation has been made before; but it did not occur to me till I saw the waves continually beating against the bare rocks, without ever receding to leave a sediment to harden.

The wind was fair, till we had to tack about in order to enter Laurvig, where we arrived towards three o'clock in the afternoon. It is a clean, pleasant town, with a considerable iron-work, which gives life to it.

As the norwegians do not frequently see travellers, they are very curious to know their business, and who they are — so curious that I was half tempted to adopt Dr. Franklin's plan, when travelling in America, where they are equally prying, which was to write on a paper, for public inspection, my name, from whence I came, where I was going, and what was my business. But if I were importuned by their curiosity, their friendly gestures gratified me. A woman, coming alone, interested them. And I know not whether my weariness gave me a look of peculiar delicacy; but they approached to assist me, and enquire after my wants, as if they were afraid to hurt, and wished to protect me. The sympathy I inspired, thus dropping down from the clouds in a strange land, affected me more than it would have done, had not my spirits been harassed by various causes — by much thinking — musing almost to madness — and even by a sort of weak melancholy that hung about my heart at parting with my daughter for the first time.

You know that as a female I am particularly attached to her — I feel more than a mother's fondness and anxiety, when I reflect on the dependent and oppressed state of her sex. I dread lest she should be forced to sacrifice her heart to her principles, or principles to her heart. With trembling hand I shall cultivate sensibility, and cherish delicacy of sentiment, lest, whilst I lend fresh blushes to the rose, I sharpen the thorns that will wound the breast I would fain guard — I dread to unfold her mind, lest it should render her unfit for the world she is to inhabit — Hapless woman! what a fate is thine!

But whither am I wandering? I only meant to tell you that the impression the kindness of the simple people made visible on my countenance increased my sensibility to a painful degree. I wished to have had a room to myself; for their attention, and rather distressing observation, embarrassed me extremely. Yet, as they would bring me eggs, and make my coffee, I found I could not leave them without hurting their feelings of hospitality.

It is customary here for the host and hostess to welcome their guests as master and mistress of the house.

My clothes, in their turn, attracted the attention of the females; and I could not help thinking of the foolish vanity which makes many women so proud of the observation of strangers as to take wonder very gratuitously for admiration. This error they are very apt to fall into; when arrived in a foreign country, the populace stare at them as they pass: yet the make of a cap, or the singularity of a gown, is often the cause of the flattering attention, which afterwards supports a fantastic superstructure of self-conceit.

Not having brought a carriage over with me, expecting to have met a person where I landed, who was immediately to have procured me one, I was detained whilst the good people of the inn sent round to all their acquaintance to search for a vehicle. A rude sort of *cabriole* was at last found, and a driver half drunk, who was not less eager to make a good bargain on that account. I had a danish captain of a ship and his mate with me: the former was to ride on horseback, at which he was not very expert, and the latter to partake of my seat. The driver mounted behind to guide the horses, and flourish the whip over our shoulders; he would not suffer the reins out of his own hands. There was something so grotesque in our appearance, that I could not avoid shrinking into myself when I saw a gentleman-like man in the group which crowded round the door to observe us. I could have broken the driver's whip for cracking to call the women and children together; but seeing a significant smile on the face, I had before remarked, I burst into a laugh, to allow him to do so too, — and away we flew. This is not a flourish of the pen; for we actually went on full gallop a long time, the horses being very good; indeed I have never met with better, if so good, post-horses, as in Norway; they are of a stouter make than the english horses, appear to be well fed, and are not easily tired.

I had to pass over, I was informed, the most fertile and best cultivated tract of country in Norway. The distance was three norwegian miles, which are longer than the swedish. The roads were very good; the farmers are obliged to repair them; and we scampered through a great extent of country in a more improved state than any I had viewed since I left England. Still there was sufficient of hills, dales, and rocks, to prevent the idea of a plain from entering the head, or even of such scenery as England and France afford. The prospects were also embellished by water, rivers, and lakes, before the sea proudly claimed my regard; and the road running frequently through lofty groves, rendered the landscapes beautiful, though they were not so romantic as those I had lately seen with such delight.

It was late when I reached Tonsberg; and I was glad to go to bed at a decent inn. The next morning, the 17th of July, conversing with the gentleman with whom I had business to transact, I found that I should be detained at Tonsberg three weeks; and I lamented that I had not brought my child with me.

The inn was quiet, and my room so pleasant, commanding a view of the sea, confined by an amphitheatre of hanging woods, that I wished to remain there, though no one in the house could speak english or french. The mayor, my friend, however, sent a young woman to me who spoke a little english, and she agreed to call on me twice a day, to receive my orders, and translate them to my hostess.

My not understanding the language was an excellent pretext for dining alone, which I prevailed on them to let me do at a late hour; for the early dinners in Sweden had entirely deranged my day. I could not alter it there, without disturbing the economy of a family where I was as a visitor; necessity having forced me to accept of an invitation from a private family, the lodgings were so incommodious.

Amongst the norwegians I had the arrangement of my own time; and I determined to regulate it in such a manner, that I might enjoy as much of their sweet summer as I possibly could; — short, it is true; but "passing sweet."

I never endured a winter in this rude clime; consequently it was not the contrast, but the real beauty of the season which made the present summer appear to me the finest I had ever seen. Sheltered from the north and eastern winds, nothing can exceed the salubrity, the soft freshness of the western gales. In the evening they also die away; the aspen leaves tremble into stillness, and reposing nature seems to be warmed by the moon, which here assumes a genial aspect; and if a light shower has chanced to fall with the sun, the juniper the underwood of the forest, exhales a wild perfume, mixed with a thousand nameless sweets, that, soothing the heart, leave images in the memory which the imagination will ever hold dear.

Nature is the nurse of sentiment, — the true source of taste; — yet what misery, as well as rapture, is produced by a quick perception of the beautiful and sublime, when it is exercised in observing animated nature, when every beauteous feeling and emotion excites responsive sympathy, and the harmonized soul sinks into melancholy, or rises to extasy, just as the chords are touched, like the æolian harp agitated by the changing wind. But how dangerous is it to foster these sentiments in such an imperfect state of existence; and how difficult to eradicate them when an affection for mankind, a passion for an individual, is but the unfolding of that love which embraces all that is great and beautiful.

When a warm heart has received strong impressions, they are not to be effaced. Emotions become sentiments; and the imagination renders even transient sensations permanent, by fondly retracing them. I cannot, without a thrill of delight, recollect views I have seen, which are not to be forgotten, — nor looks I have felt in every nerve which I shall never more meet. The grave has closed over a dear friend, the friend of my youth; still she is present with me, and I hear her soft voice warbling as I stray over the heath. Fate has separated me from another, the fire of whose eyes, tempered by infantine tenderness, still warms my breast; even when gazing on these tremendous cliffs, sublime emotions absorb my soul. And, smile not, if I add, that the rosy tint of morning reminds me of a suffusion, which will never more charm my senses, unless it reappears on the cheeks of my child. Her sweet blushes I may yet hide in my bosom, and she is still too young to ask why starts the tear, so near akin to pleasure and pain?

I cannot write any more at present. Tomorrow we will talk of Tonsberg.

HINTS

3

It is generally supposed, that the imagination of women is particularly active, and leads them astray. Why then do we seek by education only to exercise their imagination and feeling, till the understanding, grown rigid by disuse, is unable to exercise itself — and the superfluous nourishment the imagination and feeling have received, renders the former romantic, and the latter weak?

4

Few men have risen to any great eminence in learning, who have not received something like a regular education. Why are women expected to surmount difficulties that men are not equal to?

6

It has frequently been observed, that, when women have an object in view, they pursue it with more steadiness than men, particularly love. This is not a compliment. Passion pursues with more heat than reason, and with most ardour during the absence of reason.

9

I know of no other way of preserving the chastity of mankind, than that of rendering women rather objects of love than desire. The difference is great. Yet, while women are encouraged to ornament their persons at the expence of their minds, while indolence renders them helpless and lascivious (for what other name can be given to the common intercourse between the sexes?) they will be, generally speaking, only objects of desire; and, to such women, men cannot be constant. Men, accustomed only to have their senses moved, merely seek for a selfish gratification in the society of women, and their sexual instinct, being neither supported by the understanding nor the heart, must be excited by variety.

12

Children should be taught to feel deference, not to practice submission.

13

It is always a proof of false refinement, when a fastidious taste overpowers sympathy.

14

Lust appears to be the most natural companion of wild ambition; and love of human praise, of that dominion erected by cunning.

15

"Genius decays as judgment increases." Of course, those who have the least genius, have the earliest appearance of wisdom.

16

A knowledge of the fine arts, is seldom subservient to the promotion of either religion or virtue. Elegance is often indecency; witness our prints.

28

Mr. Kant has observed, that the understanding is sublime, the imagination beautiful—yet it is evident, that poets, and men who undoubtedly possess the liveliest imagination, are most touched by the sublime, while men who have cold, enquiring minds, have not this exquisite feeling in any great degree, and indeed seem to lose it as they cultivate their reason.

29

The Grecian buildings are graceful—they fill the mind with all those pleasing emotions, which elegance and beauty never fail to excite in a cultivated mind—utility and grace strike us in unison—the mind is satisfied—things appear just what they ought to be: a calm satisfaction is felt, but the imagination has nothing to do—no obscurity darkens the gloom—like reasonable content, we can say why we are pleased—and this kind of pleasure may be lasting, but it is never great.

31

It is the individual manner of seeing and feeling, pourtrayed by a strong imagination in bold images that have struck the senses, which creates all the charms of poetry. A great reader is always quoting the description of another's emotions; a strong imagination delights to paint its own. A writer of genius makes us feel; an inferior author reason.

HANNAH MORE

(1745–1833)

Hannah More wrote moral and religious works, poetry, and drama. Her father, a high-church Anglican and Tory, kept a free school at Stapleton near Bristol; her mother was the daughter of a farmer. The fourth of five girls, Hannah More and her sisters were educated by their father to earn their living as teachers. A precocious but delicate child, Hannah could read before she was four and later on applied herself so vigorously to her lessons that her father, fearing for her health, tried to discontinue his instruction. Supported by her mother, Hannah persuaded him at least to continue the Latin lessons. Later she learned French from her older sister Mary, who set up a school in Bristol where Hannah continued lessons in Latin and also learned Italian and Spanish. The Bristol school prospered and Hannah, then in her teens, stayed there with her sisters and engaged in the city's lively intellectual and social life. When she was about twenty-two, she was courted and then jilted by a Mr. Turner, who was twenty years older than she. Soured by this experience, she vowed never to marry.

When she was about twenty-nine, she visited London, saw David Garrick play the lead in *King Lear*, and expressed her admiration for him in a letter that came to Garrick's attention and led to her becoming close friends with Garrick and his wife. Garrick nicknamed her "Madam Nine," referring to her resemblance to all of the nine muses. About this time (1774), she also met the statesman and philosopher Edmund Burke, the painter Joshua Reynolds, and Samuel Johnson, who was at the height of his fame as an author, editor, and critic. Johnson praised her poetry in high-flown terms, especially her long poem *The Bas Bleu*, which described the Bluestockings, a group of intellectual women that included Elizabeth Montagu and Elizabeth Carter, and now Hannah More herself. She wrote a more ambitious poem, *Sir Eldred of the Bower* (1776) that, according to Elizabeth Montagu, combined Roman magnanimity with Gothic spirit and earned her 40 guineas.

After Garrick's death in 1779, Hannah More's thoughts turned to the serious matters of life. She gave up playgoing and devoted herself to the charitable and educational work for which she is best known today. Her piety deepened through an association with men high in the Anglican church, and her social conscience was stimulated by her friendship with William Wilberforce, who was beginning his campaign against slavery. Hannah More's writing became centered on religion, morality, and education. Together with her sisters, she wrote and published the *Cheap Repository Tracts* (1795–98) which included moral tales, uplifting ballads, and special readings of sermons, prayers and Bible stories. Millions of copies circulated throughout England and America. Her most successful work was the long didactic tale *Coelebs in Search of a Wife* (1809), which ran to eleven editions in its first nine months. She wrote tracts and poems opposing slavery, treatises on religion, a number of hymns, and many works on education including

385

Strictures on the Modern System of Female Education (1799), which went through thirteen editions during her lifetime. She died at eighty-eight and left a large estate of £30,000 to a number of charities.

EDITION USED: *Strictures on the Modern System of Female Education* (Hartford, 1801).

ON THE DANGER OF
AN ILL-DIRECTED SENSIBILITY

IN CONSIDERING the human character with a view to its improvement, it is prudent to endeavour to discover the natural bent of the mind, and having found it, to direct your force against that side on which the warp lies, that you may lessen by counteraction the defect which you might be promoting, by applying your aid in a contrary direction. But the misfortune is, people who mean better than they judge, are apt to take up a set of general rules good perhaps in themselves, and originally gleaned from experience and observation on the nature of human things but not applicable in all cases. These rules they keep by them as nostrums of universal efficacy, which they therefore often bring out for use in cases to which they do not apply. For to make any remedy effectual, it is not enough to know the medicine, you must study the constitution also; if there be not congruity between the two, you may be injuring one patient by the means which are requisite to raise and restore another, whose temperament is of a contrary description.

It is of importance in forming the female character, that those on whom this task devolves should possess so much penetration as accurately to discern the degree of sensibility, and so much judgment as to accommodate the treatment to the individual character. By constantly stimulating and extolling feelings naturally quick, those feelings will be rendered too acute and irritable. On the other hand, a calm and equable temper will become obtuse by the total want of excitement; the former treatment converts the feelings into a source of error, agitation and calamity: the latter starves their native energy, deadens the affections, and produces a cold, dull, selfish spirit; for the human mind is an instrument which will lose its sweetness if strained too high, and will be deprived of its tone and strength if not sufficiently raised.

It is cruel to chill the precious sensibility of an ingenuous soul, by treating with supercilious coldness and unfeeling ridicule every indication of a warm, tender, disinterested and enthusiastic spirit, as if it exhibited symptoms of a deficiency in understanding or prudence. How many are apt to imitate, with a smile of mingled pity and contempt, that when such a one knows the world, that is, in other words, when she shall be grown cunning, selfish, and suspicious, she will be ashamed of her present glow of honest warmth, and of her lovely susceptibility of heart. May she never know the world, if the knowledge of it must be acquired at such an expense! But to sensible hearts, every indication of genuine feeling will be dear, for they will know that it is this temper which, by the guidance of the Divine Spirit, may make her one day become more enamoured of the beauty of holiness; which, with the co-operation of principle, and under its direction, will render her the lively agent of Providence in diminishing the misery that is in the world: into which misery this temper will give her a quicker intuition than colder characters possess. It is this temper which, when it is touched and purified by a "live coal from the alter,"* will give her a keener taste for the spirit of religion, and a quicker zeal in discharging its duties. But let it be remembered likewise, that as there is no quality in the female character which will be so likely to endanger the peace, and to expose the virtue of the possessor; so there is none which requires to have its luxuriances more carefully watched, and its wild shoots more closely lopped.

For young women of affections naturally warm, but not carefully disciplined, are in danger of incurring an unnatural irritability; and while their happiness falls a victim to the excess of uncontrolled feelings, they are liable at the same time to indulge a vanity of all others the most preposterous, that of being vain of their very defect. They have heard sensibility highly commended, without having heard anything of those bounds and senses which were intended to confine it, and without having been imbued with that principle which would have given it a beneficial direction; conscious that they would possess the quality itself in the extreme, and not aware that they want all that makes that quality safe and delightful, they plunge headlong into those sins and miseries from which they conceitedly imagine, that not principle but coldness has preserved the more sober-minded and well instructed of their sex.

But as it would be foreign to the present design to expatiate on those criminal excesses which are some of the sad effects of ungoverned passion,

---

*Isaiah, 6.6

it is only intended here to hazard a few remarks on those lighter consequences of it which consists in the loss of comfort without ruin of character, and the privation of much of the happiness of life without involving
any very censurable degree of guilt or discredit. Let it, however, be
incidentally remarked and let it be carefully remembered, that if no
women have risen so high in the scale of moral excellence as those whose
natural warmth has been conscientiously governed by its true guide, and
directed to its true end; so none have furnished such deplorable instances
of extreme depravity as those who, through the ignorance of the derelic-
tion of principle, have been abandoned by the excess of this very temper
to the violence of ungoverned passions and uncontrolled inclinations.
Perhaps, if we were to inquire into the remote cause of some of the
blackest crimes which stain the annals of mankind, profligacy, murder,
and especially suicide, we might trace them back to this original principle, an ungoverned Sensibility.

Notwithstanding all the fine theories in prose and verse to which this
topic has given birth, it will be found that very exquisite sensibility
contributes so little to *happiness* and may yet be made to contribute so
much to *usefulness* that it may perhaps, be considered as bestowed for an
excercise to the possessor's own virtue, and as a keen instrument with
which they may better work for the good of others.

Women of this cast of mind are less careful to avoid the charge of
unbounded extremes, than to escape at all events the imputation of
insensibility. They are little alarmed at the danger of *exceeding*, though
terrified at the suspicion of *coming short*, of what they take to be the
extreme point of feeling. They will even resolve to prove the warmth of
their sensibility, though at the expense of their judgment, and sometimes
also of their justice. Even when they earnestly desire to *be* and to *do* right,
they are apt to employ the wrong instrument to accomplish the right end.
They employ the passions to do the work of the judgment; forgetting, or
not knowing, that the passions were not given us to be used in the search
and discovery of truth, which is the office of a cooler and more discriminating faculty; but that they were given to animate us to warmer zeal in
the pursuit and practice of truth, when the judgment shall have pointed
out what *is* truth.

Through this natural warmth, which they have been justly told is so
pleasing, but which, perhaps, they have not been told will be continually
exposing them to peril and to suffering, their joys and sorrows are excessive. Of this extreme irritability, as was before remarked, the ill-educated

learn to boast as if it were a decided indication of superiority of soul, instead of labouring to restrain it as the excess of a temper which ceases to be amiable, when it is no longer under the control of the governing faculty. It is misfortune enough to be born more liable to suffer and to sin, from this conformation of mind; it is too much to nourish the evil by unrestrained indulgence: it is still worse to be proud of so misleading a quality.

Flippancy, impetuosity, resentment, and violence of spirit, grow out of this disposition, which will be rather promoted than corrected, by the system of education on which we have been animadverting; in which system, emotions are too early and too much excited, and tastes and feelings are considered as too exclusively making up the whole of the female character: in which the judgment is little exercised, the reasoning powers are seldom brought into action, and self-knowledge and self-denial scarcely included.

The propensity of mind which we are considering, if unchecked, lays its possessors open to unjust prepossessions and exposes them to all the danger of unfounded attachments. In early youth, not only love at first sight, but also friendship, of the same sudden growth, springs up from an ill-directed sensibility; and in after-life, women under the powerful influence of this temper, conscious that they have much to be borne with, are too readily inclined to select for their confidential connexions, flexible and flattering companions, who will indulge and perhaps admire their faults, rather than firm and honest friends, who will reprove and would assist in curing them. We may adopt it as a general maxim, that an obliging, weak, yielding complaisant friend, full of small attentions, with little religion, little judgment, and much natural acquiescence and civility, is a most dangerous, though generally a too much desired confidant: she soothes the indolence, and gratifies the vanity of her friend, by reconciling her to her faults, while she neither keeps the understanding nor the virtues of that friend in exercise; but withholds from her every useful truth, which by opening her eyes might give her pain. These obsequious qualities are the "soft green"* on which the soul loves to repose itself. But it is not refreshing or a wholesome repose: we should not select, for the sake of a present case, a soothing flatterer, who will lull us into a pleasing oblivion of our failings, but a friend, who, valuing our

---

*[Edmund] Burke's "Sublime and Beautiful"

soul's health above our immediate comfort, will rouse us from torpid indulgence to animation, vigilance and virtue.

An ill-directed sensibility also leads a woman to be injudicious and eccentric in her *charities*; she will be in danger of proportioning her bounty to the immediate effect which the distressed object produces on her senses: and she will be more liberal to a small distress presenting itself to her own eyes, than to the more pressing wants and better claims of those miseries, of which she only hears the relation. There is a sort of stage effect, which some people require for their charities; she will be apt also to desire, that the object of her compassion shall have something interesting and amiable in it, such as shall furnish pleasing images and lively pictures to her imagination, and engaging subjects for description; forgetting, that in her charities, as well as in every thing else, she is to be a "follower of Him who pleased not himself;" forgetting, that the most coarse and disgusting object is as much the representative of Him, who said "Inasmuch as ye do it to one of the least of these, ye do it unto me," as the most interesting: nay, the more uninviting and repulsive cases may be better tests of the principle on which we relieve, than those which abound in pathos and interest, as we can have less suspicion of our motive in the latter case then in the former. But, while we ought to neglect neither of these supposed cases, yet the less our feelings are caught by pleasing circumstances, the less will be the danger of our indulging self-complacency, and the more likely shall we be to do what we do for the sake of Him who has taught us, that no deeds but what are performed on that principle, "shall be recompensed at the resurrection of the just."

But through the want of that governing principle which should direct her sensibility, a tender-hearted woman, whose hand, if she be actually surrounded with scenes and circumstances to call it into action, is

> Open as day to melting charity;

nevertheless may utterly fail in the great and comprehensive duty of christian love, for she has feelings which are acted upon solely by local circumstances and present events. Only remove her into another scene, distant from the wants she has been relieving; place her in the lap of indulgence, so entrenched with ease and pleasure, so immersed in the softness of life, that distress no longer finds any access to her presence, but through the faint and dull medium of a distant representation; remove her from the sight and sound of that misery which, when present, so tenderly affected her — she now forgets that misery exists; as she hears but little, and sees nothing of want and sorrow, she is ready to fancy that the world is grown happier than it was: in the mean time, with a quiet conscience and a thoughtless vanity, she has been lavishing on superfluities that money which she would cheerfully have given to a charitable case, had she not forgotten that any such were in existence, because *pleasure* had locked up the avenues through which misery used to find its way to her heart; and now, when again such a case forces itself into her presence, she laments with real sincerity that the money is gone which should have relieved it.

In the mean time, perhaps, other women of less natural sympathy, but whose sympathies are under better regulations, or who act from a principle which requires little stimulus, have, by an habitual course of self-denial, by a constant determination to refuse themselves unnecessary indulgencies, and by guarding against that dissolving *pleasure* which melts down the firmest virtue that allows itself to bask in its beams, have been quietly furnishing a regular provision for miseries which their knowledge of the state of the world teaches them are every where to be found, and which their obedience to the will of God tells them it is their duty both to find out and relieve; a general expectation of being liable to be called upon for acts of charity, will lead the conscientiously charitable always to be prepared.

On such a mind as we have been describing, *novelty* also will operate with peculiar force, and in nothing more than in the article of charity. Old established institutions whose continued existence must depend on the continued bounty of that affluence to which they owed their origin, will be sometimes neglected, as presenting no variety to the imagination, as having by their uniformity ceased to be interesting, there is now a total failure of those springs of mere sensitive feeling which set the charity a-going, and those sudden emotions of tenderness and gusts of pity, which once were felt, must now be excited by newer forms of distress. — As age comes on, that charity which has been the effect of mere feeling, grows cold and rigid, on account also of its having been often disappointed in its high expectations of the gratitude and subsequent merit of those it has relieved; and by withdrawing its bounty, because some of its objects have been undeserving, it gives clear proof that what it bestowed was for its own gratification; and now finding that self-complacency at an end, it bestows no longer. Probably too the cause of so much disappointment may have been, that ill choice of the objects to which feeling, rather than a discriminating judgment has led. The summer flowers of mere sensibility soon dry up, while the living spring of christian charity flows a like in all seasons.

The impatience, levity, and fickleness, of which women have been somewhat too generally accused, are perhaps in no small degree aggravated by the littleness and frivolousness of female pursuits. The sort of education they commonly receive, teaches girls to set a great price on small things. Besides this, they do not always learn to keep a very correct scale of degrees for rating the value of the objects of their admiration and attachment; but by a kind of unconscious idolatry, they rather make a merit of loving supremely things and persons which ought to be loved with moderation, and in a subordinate degree the one to the other. Unluckily, they consider moderation as so necessarily indicating a cold heart and narrow soul, and they look upon a state of indifference with so much horror, that either to love or hate with energy is supposed by them to proceed from a higher state of mind than is possessed by more steady and equitable characters. — Whereas it is in fact the criterion of a warm but well-directed sensibility, that while it is capable of loving with energy, it must be enabled, by the judgment which governs it, to suit and adjust its degree of interest to the nature and excellence of the object about which it is interested; for unreasonable prepossession, disproportionate attachment, and capricious or precarious fondness, is not sensibility.

Excessive but unintentional *flattery* is another fault into which a strong sensibility is in danger of leading its possessor. A tender heart and a warm imagination conspire to throw a sort of radiance round the object of their love, till people are dazzled by a brightness of their own creating. The worldly and fashionable borrow the warm language of sensibility without having the really warm feeling; and young ladies get such a habit of saying, especially of writing, such over obliging and flattering things to each other, that this mutual politeness, aided by the self-love so natural to us all, and by an unwillingness to search into our own hearts, keeps up the illusion, and we get a habit of taking our character from the good we hear of ourselves, which others assume, but do not very well know, rather than from the evil we *feel* in ourselves, and which we therefore ought to be thoroughly acquainted with.

Ungoverned sensibility is apt to give a wrong direction to its anxieties; and its affection often falls short of the true end of friendship. If the object of its regard happens to be sick, what inquiries! what prescriptions! what an accumulation is made of cases in which the remedy its fondness suggests has been successful! What an unaffected tenderness for the perishing body! Yet is this sensibility equally alive to the immortal interests of the sufferer? Is it not silent and at ease when it contemplates the dearest friend persisting in opinions essentially dangerous; in practices unquestionably wrong? Does it not view all this not only without a generous ardor to point out the peril and refuse the friend; but if that friend be supposed to be dying, does it not even make it the *criterion* of kindness to let her die undeceived? What a want of true sensibility to feel for the pain, but not for the danger of those we love! Now see what sort of sensibility the Bible teaches! "Thou shalt not hate thy brother in thine heart, but thou shalt in any wise rebuke him, and shalt not suffer sin upon him."* But let that tenderness which shrinks from the idea of exposing what it loves to a momentary pang, figure to itself the bare possibility, that the object of its own fond affection may not be the object of the Divine favor! Let it shrink from the bare conjecture, that "the familiar friend with whom it has taken sweet counsel," is going down to the gates of death, unrepenting, unprepared, and yet unwarned.

But mere human sensibility goes a shorter way to work. Not being able to give its friend the pain of hearing her faults or knowing her danger, it works itself up into the quieting delusion that no danger exists, at least not for the objects of its own affection; it gratifies itself by inventing a salvation so comprehensive as shall take in all itself loves with all their faults; it creates to its own fond heart an ideal and exaggerated divine mercy, which shall pardon and receive all in whom this blind sensibility has an interest, whether they be good or whether they be evil.

In regard to its application to religious purposes, it is a test that sensibility has received its true direction when it is supremely turned to the love of God: for to possess an overflowing fondness for our fellow-creatures and fellow-sinners, and to be cold and insensible to the Essence of goodness and perfection, is an inconsistency to which the feeling heart is awfully liable. God has himself the first claim to the sensibility he bestowed. "He *first* loved us:" this is a *natural* cause of love. "He loved us while we were sinners:" this is a *supernatural* cause. He continues to love us though we neglect his favors, and slight His mercies: this would wear out any earthly kindness. He forgives us, not petty neglects, not occasional sights, but grievous sins, repeated offences, broken vows, and

---

*Leviticus 19.17

unrequited love. What human friendship performs offices so calculated to touch the soul of sensibility?

Those young women in whom feeling is indulged to the exclusion of reason and examination, are peculiarly liable to be the dupes of prejudice, rash decisions, and false judgment. The understanding having but little power over the will, their affections are not well poized, and their minds are kept in a state ready to be acted upon by the fluctuations of alternate impulses; by sudden and varying impressions; by casual and contradictory circumstances; and by emotions excited by every accident. Instead of being guided by the broad views of general truth, and having one fixed principle, they are driven by the impetuosity of the moment. And this impetuosity blinds the judgment as much as it misleads the conduct; so that for want of a habit of cool investigation and inquiry, they meet every event without any previously formed opinion or rule of action. And as they do not accustom themselves to appreciate the real value of things, their attention is as likely to be led away by the under parts of a subject, as to seize on the leading feature. The same eagerness of mind which hinders the operation of the discriminating faculty, leads also to the error of determining on the rectitude of an action by its success, and to that of making the event of an undertaking decide on its justice or propriety; it also leads to that superficial and erroneous way of judging which fastens on exceptions, if they make in one's own favor, as grounds of reasoning, while they lead us to overlook received and general rules which tend to establish a doctrine contrary to our wishes.

Open-hearted, indiscreet girls, often pick up a few strong notions, which are as false in themselves as they are popular among the class in question: such as, "that warm friends must make warm enemies;" — that "the generous love and hate with all their hearts;" — that "a reformed rake makes the best husband;" — that "there is no medium in marriage, but that it is a state of exquisite happiness or exquisite misery;" with many other doctrines of equal currency and equal soundness! These they consider as axioms, and adopt as rules of life. From the two first of these oracular sayings, girls are in no small danger of becoming unjust through the very warmth of their hearts: for they will get a habit of making their estimate of the good or ill qualities of others, merely in proportion to the greater or less degree of kindness which they themselves have received from them. Their estimation of general character is thus formed on insulated and partial grounds; on the accidental circumstance of personal predilection or personal pique. Kindness to themselves or their friends involves all possible excellence; neglect, all imaginable defects. Friendship and gratitude can and should go a great way; but as they cannot convert vice into virtue, so they ought never to convert truth into falsehood. And it may be the more necessary to be upon our guard in this instance, because the very idea of gratitude may mislead us, by converting injustice into the semblance of a virtue. Warm expressions should therefore be limited to the conveying a sense of our own individual obligations which are real, rather than employed to give an impression of general excellence in the person who has obliged us, which may be imaginary. A good man is still good, though it may not have fallen in his way to oblige or serve *us*, nay, though he may have neglected or even unintentionally hurt us: and sin is still sin, though committed by the person in the world to whom we are the most obliged and whom we most love.

We come next to that fatal and most indelicate, nay gross maxim, that "a reformed rake makes the best husband;" an aphorism to which the principles and the happiness of so many young women have been sacrificed. It goes upon the preposterous supposition, not only that effects do not follow causes, but that they oppose them; on the supposition, that habitual vice creates rectitude of character, and that sin produces happiness: thus flatly contradicting what the moral government of God uniformly exhibits in the course of human events, and what Revelation so evidently and universally teaches.

For it should be observed, that the reformation is generally, if not always supposed to be brought about by the all-conquering force of female charms. Let but a profligate young man have a point to carry by winning the affections of a vain and thoughtless girl; he will begin his attack upon her heart, by undermining her religious principles, and artfully removing every impediment which might have obstructed her receiving the addresses of a man without character. And while he will lead her not to hear without ridicule the mention of that change of heart, which scripture teaches and experience proves the power of Divine grace can work on a vicious character; while he will teach her to sneer at a change which he would treat with contempt, because he denies the possibility of so strange and miraculous a conversion; yet he will not scruple to swear, that the power of her beauty has worked a revolution in his own loose practices, which is equally complete and instantaneous.

But supposing it possible that his reformation were genuine, it would even then by no means involve the truth of her proposition, that past libertinism insures future felicity; yet many a weak girl, confirmed in this

palatable doctrine by examples she has frequently admired of those surprising reformations so conveniently effected in the last scene of most of
our comedies, has not scrupled to risk her earthly and eternal happiness
with a man, who is not ashamed to ascribe to the influence of her beauty
that power of changing the heart, which he impiously denies to Omnipo-
tence itself.

As to the last of these practical aphorisms, that "there is no medium in
marriage, but that it is a state of exquisite happiness or exquisite misery;"
this, though not equally sinful, is equally delusive: for marriage is only
one modification of human life, and human life is not commonly in itself
a state of exquisite extremes; but is for the most part that mixed and
moderate state, so naturally dreaded by those who set out with fancying
this world a state of rapture, and so naturally expected by those who know
it to be a state of probation and discipline. Marriage, therefore, is only
one condition, and often the best condition, of that imperfect state of
being, which, though seldom very exquisite, is often very tolerable; and
which may yield much comfort to those who do not look for constant
transport. But, unfortunately, those who find themselves disappointed of
the unceasing raptures they had anticipated in marriage, disdaining to sit
down with so poor a provision as comfort, and scorning the acceptance of
that moderate lot which Providence commonly bestows with a view to
check despondency and to repress presumption; give themselves up to the
other alternative; and, by abandoning their hearts to discontent, make to
themselves that misery with which their fervid imaginations had filled
the opposite scale.

The truth is, these young ladies are very apt to pick up their opinions,
less from the divines than the poets; and the poets, though it must be
confessed they are some of the best embellishers of life, are not *quite* the
safest conductors through it: for in travelling through a wilderness,
though we avail ourselves of the harmony of singing-birds to render the
grove delightful, yet we never think of following them as guides to
conduct us through its labyrinths.

Those women, in whom the natural defects of a warm temper have
been strengthened by an education which fosters their faults, are very
dexterous in availing themselves of a hint, when it favours a ruling
inclination, sooths vanity, indulges indolence, or gratifies their love of
power. They have heard so often from their favourite sentimental
authors, and their more flattering male friends, "that when Nature
denied them strength, she gave them fascinating graces in compensation;

that their strength consists in their weakness;" and that "they are endowed with arts of persuasion which supply the absence of force, and the place of reason;" that they learn, in time, to pride themselves on that very weakness, and to become vain of their imperfections; till at length they begin to claim for their defects, not only pardon, but admiration. Hence they get to cherish a species of feeling which, if not checked, terminates in excessive selfishness; they learn to produce their inability to bear contradiction as a proof of their tenderness; and to indulge in that sort of irritability in all that relates to themselves which inevitably leads to the utter exclusion of all interest in the sufferings of others. Instead of exercising their sensibility in the wholesome duty of relieving distress and visiting scenes of sorrow, that sensibility itself is pleaded as a reason for their not being able to endure sights of woe, and for shunning the distress it should be exerted in removing. That exquisite sense of feeling which God implanted in the heart as a stimulus to quicken us in relieving the miseries of others, is thus introverted, and learns to consider *self* not as the agent, but the object of compassion. Tenderness is made an excuse for being hard-hearted; and instead of drying the weeping eyes of others, this false delicacy reserves its selfish tears for the more elegant and less expensive sorrows of the melting novel or the pathetic tragedy.

When feeling stimulates only to self-indulgence; when the more exquisite affections of sympathy and pity evaporate in sentiment, instead of flowing out in active charity, and affording assistance, protection, or consolation to every species of distress; it is an evidence that the feeling is of a spurious kind; and instead of being nourished as an amiable tenderness, it should be subdued as a fond and base self-love.

That idleness, to whose cruel inroads many women of fortune are unhappily exposed, from so having been trained to consider wholesome occupation, vigorous exertion, and systematic employment, as making part of the indispensable duties of life, lays them open to a thousand evils of this kind, from which the useful and the busy are exempted: and, perhaps, it would not be easy to find a more pitiable object than a woman with a great deal of time and a great deal of money on her hands, who, never having been taught the conscientious use of either, squanders both at random, or rather moulders both away, without plan, without principle, and without pleasure; all whose projects begin and terminate in self: who considers the rest of the world only as they may be subservient to her gratification; and to whom it never occurred, that both her time and money were given for the gratification and good of others.

It is not much to the credit of the other sex, that they now and then lend themselves to the indulgence of this selfish spirit in their wives, and cherish by a kind of false fondness those faults which should be combated by good sense and a reasonable counteraction: slothfully preferring a little false peace, the purchase of precarious quiet, and the reputation of good nature, to the higher duty of forming the mind, fixing the princi- ples, and strengthening the character of her with whom they are con- nected. Perhaps too a little vanity in the husband helps out his good nature; he secretly rewards himself for his sacrifice by the consciousness of his superiority; he feels a self-complacency in his patient condescention to her weakness, which tacitly flatters his own strength: and he is, as it were, paid for stooping by the increased sense of his own tallness. Seeing also, perhaps, but little of other women, he gets to believe that they are all pretty much alike, and that as a man of sense, he must content himself with what he takes to be the common lot. Whereas, in truth, by his misplaced indulgence, he has rather *made* his own lot than *drawn* it; and thus through an indolent despair in the husband of being able to effect any improvement by opposition, it happens, that many a helpless, fret- ful, and daudling wife acquires a more powerful ascendency than the most discreet and amiable woman; and that the most absolute female tyranny is established by these sickly and capricious humors.

The poets again, who to do them justice, are always ready to lend a helping hand when any mischief is to be done, have contributed their full share towards confirming these feminine follies; they have strengthened by adulatory maxims, sung in seducing strains, those faults which their talents and their influence should have been employed in correcting. When fair and youthful females are complimented with being

Fine by defect and delicately weak!

is not a standard of feebleness held out to them to which vanity will gladly resort, and to which softness and indolence can easily act up, or rather *act down*, if I may be allowed the expression?

When ladies are told by the same misleading, but to them, high authority, that "smiles and tears are the irresistible arms with which nature has furnished them for conquering the strong," will they not eagerly fly to this cheap and ready artillery, instead of laboring to furnish themselves with a reasonable mind, and equable temper, and a meek and quiet spirit?

Every animal is endowed by Providence with the peculiar powers adapted to its nature and its wants; while none, except the human, by grafting art on natural sagacity, injures or mars the gift. Spoilt women, who fancy there is something more *picquant* and alluring in the mutable graces, than in the monotonous smoothness of an even temper, and who also having heard much, as was observed before, about their "amiable weakness," learn to look about them for the best succedanum to strength, the supposed absence of which they sometimes endeavor to supply by artifice. By this engine the weakest woman frequently furnishes the converse to the famous reply of the French Minister, who, when he was accused of governing the mind of that feeble Queen Mary de Medicis by sorcery, replied, "that the only sorcery he had used, was that influence which strong minds naturally have over weak ones."

But though it be fair so to study the tempers, defects, and weaknesses of others, as to convert our knowledge of them to the promotion of their benefit and our own; and though it be making a lawful use of our penetration to avail ourselves of the faults of others for "their good to edification;" yet all deviations from the straight line of truth and simplicity; every plot insidiously to turn influence to unfair account; all contrivances to extort from a bribed compliance what reason and justice would refuse to our wishes; these are some of the operations of that lowest and most despicable engine, selfish cunning, by which *little minds sometimes govern great ones.*

And unluckily, women, from their natural desire to please, and from their sometimes doubting by what means this grand end may be best effected, are in more danger of being led into dissimulation than men; for dissimulation is the result of weakness, and the refuge of doubt and distrust, rather than of conscious strength, the dangers of which lie another way. Frankness, truth and simplicity, therefore, as they are inexpressibly charming, so are they peculiarly commendable in women, and nobly evince that while the possessors of them wish to please, (and why should they not wish it) they disdain to have recourse to any thing but what is fair, and just, and honorable to effect it; that they scorn to attain the most desired end by any but the most lawful means. The beauty of simplicity is indeed so intimately felt and generally acknowledged by all who have a true taste for personal, moral, or intellectual beauty, that women of the deepest artifice often find their account in assuming an exterior the most foreign to their character, and by affecting the most studied *naiveté*. It is curious to see the quantity of *art* some people put in practice in order to appear *natural*; and the deep *design* which is set at work to exhibit *simplicity*. And indeed this feigned simplicity is the most mischievous, because the most engaging of all the Proteus forms which dissimulation can put on. For the most free and bold sentiments have been sometimes hazarded with fatal success under this unsuspected mask. And an innocent, quiet, indolent, artless manner, has been adopted as the most refined and successful accompaniment of sentiments, ideas and designs, neither artless nor innocent.

MARIA EDGEWORTH

(1767-1849)

Maria Edgeworth wrote works on education, children's tales, novels, and a few closet dramas. She was born in Black Bourton, the second of the twenty-one children of Richard Lovell Edgeworth, the brilliant but eccentric inventor and educator. Her mother, who was the first and apparently least treasured of his four wives, died when she was six, and Maria was raised by a succession of stepmothers. She received her early schooling in Derby and London, but when she was fifteen she moved to the family estate at Edgeworthstown, Ireland, where her father completed her education not just in books but in practical experience. He involved her in local politics, corrected her manuscripts, and collaborated with her on *Practical Education* (1798). Earlier, she had written *Letters for Literary Ladies* (1795) in which a liberal father (her own) and his conservative friend (Thomas Day, author of *Sandford and Merton*) debate the propriety of women writing books. In her lifetime, Edgeworth published a number of collections of children's tales, including *The Parent's Assistant* (1796), *Early Lessons* (1801), *Continuation of Early Lessons* (1814), and *Rosamond; A Sequel* (1821).

Edgeworth was also a productive novelist. Drawing on her observations of daily life in Ireland, she published *Castle Rackrent* (1800). It was a biting portrayal of absentee ownership, Irish poverty, and the decay of the faithful family retainer. Published anonymously and without her father's "corrections," it achieved such success that she put her name on the second edition. A number of the novels which followed— *Belinda* (1801), *The Absentee* (1812), *Patronage* (1814), *Ormond* (1817), *Helen* (1834)— contain much that is interesting and amusing, and they were generally well regarded in her lifetime.

Although much of her life was spent in Ireland, Maria Edgeworth traveled to London, Switzerland, and France, meeting many distinguished literary people. In 1802, she fell in love in Paris with a Swedish count who proposed marriage, but the match failed because she could not bring herself to live in Sweden. She grieved over this for a time and remained unmarried. After her father's death in 1817, she managed the Edgeworthstown estate and published only a few works. Near the end of her life, aged seventy, she worked to relieve many Irish people who suffered during the great Irish potato famine.

EDITIONS USED: *Practical Education*, 2 vols. (London, 1798); *Letters for Literary Ladies* (London, 1795).

ON SYMPATHY AND SENSIBILITY

THE ARTLESS expressions of sympathy and sensibility in children are peculiarly pleasing; people who, in their commerce with the world, have been disgusted and deceived by falsehood and affectation, listen with delight to the genuine language of nature. Those who have any interest in the education of children have yet a higher sense of pleasure in observing symptoms of their sensibility; they anticipate the future virtues which early sensibility seems certainly to promise; the future happiness which these virtues will diffuse. Nor are they unsupported by philosophy in these sanguine hopes. No theory was ever developed with more ingenious elegance, than that which deduces all our moral sentiments from sympathy. The direct influence of sympathy upon all social beings is sufficiently obvious, and we immediately perceive its necessary connexion with compassion, friendship, and benevolence; but the subject becomes more intricate when we are to analyse our sense of propriety and justice; of merit and demerit; of gratitude and resentment; self-complacency or remorse; ambition and shame.

We allow, without hesitation, that a being destitute of sympathy could never have any of these feelings, and must consequently be incapable of all intercourse with society; yet we must at the same time perceive, that a being endowed with the most exquisite sympathy must, without the assistance and education of reason, be, if not equally incapable of social intercourse, far more dangerous to the happiness of society. A person governed by sympathy alone must be influenced by the bad as well as by the good passions of others; he must feel resentment with the angry man; hatred with the malevolent; jealousy with the jealous; and avarice with the miser: the more lively his sympathy with these painful feelings, the greater must be his misery; the more forcibly he is impelled to action by this sympathetic influence, the greater, probably, must be his imprudence and his guilt. Let us even suppose a being capable of sympathy only with the best feelings of his fellow-creatures, still, without the direction of reason, he would be a nuisance in the world; his pity would stop the hand, and overturn the balance of justice; his love would be as dangerous as his pity; his gratitude would exalt his benefactor at the expence of the whole human race; his sympathy with the rich, the prosperous, the great, and the fortunate, would be so sudden, and so violent, as to leave him no time for reflection upon the consequences of tyranny, or the miseries occasioned by monopoly. No time for reflection, did we say? We forgot that we were speaking of a being destitute of the reasoning faculty! Such a being, no matter what his virtuous sympathies might be, must act either like a madman or a fool. On sympathy we cannot depend either for the correctness of a man's moral sentiments, or for the steadiness of his moral conduct. It is very common to talk of the excellence of a person's heart, of the natural goodness of his disposition; when these expressions distinctly mean any thing, they must refer to natural sympathy, or a superior degree of sensibility. Experience, however, does not teach us, that sensibility and virtue have any certain connexion with each other. No one can read the works of Sterne, or of Rousseau, without believing these men to have been endowed with extraordinary sensibility; yet who would propose their conduct in life as a model for imitation? That quickness of sympathy with present objects of distress, which constitutes compassion, is usually thought a virtue, but it is a virtue frequently found in persons of abandoned character. Mandeville*, in his essay upon Charity Schools, puts this in a strong light.

Should any one of us," says he, "be locked up in a ground room, where in a yard joining to it there was a thriving good-humoured child at play, of two or three years old, so near us that through the grates of the window we could almost touch it with our hands; and if, whilst we took delight in the harmless diversion, and imperfect prattle, of the innocent babe, a nasty overgrown sow should come in upon the child, set it a screaming, and frighten it out of its wits; it is natural to think that this would make us uneasy, and that with crying out, and making all the menacing noise we could, we should endeavour to drive the sow away. But if this should happen to be an half-starved creature, that, mad with hunger, went roaming about in quest of food, and we should behold the ravenous brute, in spite of our cries, and all the threatening gestures we could think of, actually lay hold of the helpless infant, destroy, and devour it; — to see her widely open her destructive jaws, and the poor lamb beat down with greedy haste; to look on the defenceless posture of tender limbs first trampled upon, then torn asunder; to see the filthy snout digging in the yet living entrails, suck up the smoking blood, and now and then to hear the crackling of the bones, and

*Bernard de Mandeville (1670–1733), author of *The Fable of the Bees* (1714), of which the essay on charity schools is a part.

the cruel animal grunt with savage pleasure over the horrid banquet; to hear and see all this what torture would it give the soul beyond expression! ***********Not only a man of humanity, of good morals, and commiseration, but likewise an highwayman, an housebreaker, or a murderer, could feel anxieties on such an occasion.

Amongst those monsters, who are pointed out by the historian to the just detestation of all mankind, we meet with instances of casual sympathy and sensibility; even their vices frequently prove to us, that they never became utterly indifferent to the opinion and feelings of their fellow-creatures. The dissimulation, jealousy, suspicion, and cruelty of Tiberius, originated perhaps more in his anxiety about the opinions which were formed of his character, than in his fears of any conspiricies against his life. The *"judge within," the habit of viewing his own conduct in the light in which it was beheld by the impartial spectator*, prompted him to new crimes; and thus his unextinguished sympathy, and his exasperated sensibility, drove him to excesses, from which a more torpid temperament might have preserved him*. When, upon his presenting the sons of Germanicus to the senate, Tiberius beheld the tenderness with which these young men were received, he was moved to such an agony of jealousy as instantly to beseech the senate that he might resign the empire. We cannot attribute either to policy, or fear, this strong emotion, because we know that the senate was at this time absolutely at the disposal of Tiberius, and the lives of the sons of Germanicus depended upon his pleasure.

The desire to excel, according to "Smith's Theory of Moral Sentiments," is to be resolved principally into our love of the sympathy of our fellow-creatures. We wish for their sympathy, either in our success, or in the pleasure we feel in superiority. The desire for this refined modification of sympathy may be the motive of good and great actions, but it cannot be trusted as a moral principle. Nero's love of sympathy made him anxious to be applauded on the stage as a fiddler and a buffoon. Tiberius banished one of his philosophic courtiers, and persecuted him till the unfortunate man laid violent hands upon himself, merely because he had discovered that the emperor read books in the morning to prepare him-

---

*Edgeworth is quoting here and elsewhere from Adam Smith's *Theory of Moral Sentiments* (1759).

self with questions for his literary society at night. Dionysius, the tyrant of Syracuse, sued in the most abject manner for an Olympic crown, and sent a critic to the gallies for finding fault with his verses. Had not these men a sufficient degree of sensibility to praise, and more than a sufficent desire for the sympathy of their fellow-creatures?

It is not from any perverse love of sophistry that the word sensibility has been used in these instances instead of *irritability*, which seems better to characterize the temper of a Dionysius, or a Tiberius; but in fact irritability, in common language, merely denotes an excessive or ill-governed degree of sensibility. The point of excess must be marked: sympathy must be regulated by education, and consequently the methods of directing sensibility to useful and amiable purposes must be anxiously studied, by all who wish either for the happiness or virtue of their pupils.

Long before children can understand reasoning, they can feel sympathy; during this early period of their education, example and habit, slight external circumstances, and the propensity to imitation, govern their thoughts and actions. Imitation is the involuntary effect of sympathy in children, hence those who have the most sympathy are most liable to be improved or injured by early examples. Examples of the malevolent passions should therefore be most carefully excluded from the sight of those who have yet no choice in their sympathy; expressions of kindness and affection in the countenance, the voice, the actions, of all who approach, and of all who have the care of infants, are not only immediately and evidently agreeable to the children, but ought also to be used as the best possible means of exciting benevolent sympathies in their mind. Children, who habitually meet with kindness, habitually feel complacency; that species of instinctive, or rather of associated affection, which always rises in the mind from the recollection of past pleasures, is immediately excited in such children by the sight of their parents. By an easy transition of ideas they expect the same benevolence, even from strangers, which they have experienced from their friends, and their sympathy naturally prepares them to wish for society; this wish is often improperly indulged.

At the age when children begin to unfold their ideas, and to express their thoughts in words, they are such interesting and entertaining companions, that they attract a large portion of our daily attention: we listen eagerly to their simple observations; we enter into their young astonishment at every new object; we are delighted to watch all their emotions; we help them with words to express their ideas; we anxiously endeavour to understand their imperfect reasonings, and are pleased to find, or put them in the right. This season of universal smiles and courtesy is delightful to children whilst it lasts, but it soon passes away; they soon speak without exciting any astonishment, and instead of meeting with admiration for every attempt to express an idea, they soon are repulsed for troublesome volubility; even when they talk sense, they are suffered to talk unheard, or else they are checked for unbecoming presumption. Children feel this change in public opinion and manners most severely; they are not sensible of any change in themselves, except, perhaps, they are conscious of having improved both in sense and language. This unmerited loss of their late gratuitous allowance of sympathy usually operates unfavourably upon the temper of the sufferers; they become shy and silent, and reserved, if not sullen; they withdraw from our capricious society, and they endeavour to console themselves with other pleafures. It is difficult to them to feel contented with their own little occupations and amusements, for want of the spectators and the audience which used to be at their command. Children of a timid temper, or of an indolent disposition, are quite dispirited and bereft of all energy in these circumstances; others, with greater vivacity, and more voluntary exertion, endeavour to supply the loss of universal sympathy by the invention of independent occupations; but they feel anger and indignation, when they are not rewarded with any smiles or any praise for their "virtuous toil." They naturally seek for new companions, either amongst children of their own age, or amongst complaisant servants. Immediately all the business of education is at a stand, for neither these servants, nor these playfellows, are capable of becoming their instructors; nor can tutors hope to succeed, who have transferred their power over the pleasures, and consequently over the affections, of their pupils. Sympathy now becomes the declared enemy of all the constituted authorities. What chance is there of obedience or of happiness, under such a government?

Would it not be more prudent to prevent, than to complain, of these evils? Sympathy is our first, best friend, in education, and by judicious management might long continue our faithful ally.

Instead of lavishing our smiles and our attention upon young children for a short period just at that age when they are amusing playthings, should not we do more wisely if we reserved some portion of our kindness a few years longer? By a proper *economy* our sympathy may last for many years, and may continually contribute to the most useful purposes. Instead of accustoming our pupils early to such a degree of our attention as cannot be supported long on our parts, we should rather suffer them to feel a little ennui at that age, when they can have but few independent or useful occupations. We should employ ourselves in our usual manner, and converse, without allowing children to interrupt us with frivolous prattle; but whenever they ask sensible questions, make just observations, or shew a disposition to acquire knowledge, we should assist and encourage them with praise and affection; gradually as they become capable of taking any part in conversation, they should be admitted into society, and they will learn of themselves, or we may teach them, that useful and agreeable qualities are those by which they must secure the pleasures of sympathy. Esteem, being associated with sympathy, will increase its value, and this connexion should be made as soon, and kept as sacred, in the mind as possible.

With respect to the sympathy which children feel for each other, it must be carefully managed, or it will counteract, instead of assisting us, in education. It is natural that those who are placed nearly in the same circumstances should feel alike, and sympathise with one another; but children feel only for the present, they have few ideas of the future, and consequently all that they can desire, either for themselves, or for their companions, is what will *immediately* please. Education looks to the future, and frequently we must ensure future advantage, even at the expence of present pain or restraint. The companion and the tutor then, supposing each to be equally good and equally kind, must command in a very different degree the sympathy of the child. It may, notwithstanding, be questioned whether those who are constant companions in their idle hours, when they are *very* young, are likely to be either as fond of one another when they grow up, or even as happy whilst they are children, as those are who spend less time together. Whenever the humours, interests, and passions, of others cross our own, there is an end of sympathy, and this happens almost every hour in the day with children; it is generally supposed that they learn to live in friendship with each other, and to bear with one another's little faults habitually, that they even reciprocally cure these faults, and learn, by early experience, those principles of honour and justice on which society depends. We may be deceived in this reasoning by a false analogy.

We call the society of children *society in miniature*; the proportions of the miniature are so much altered, that it is by no means an accurate resemblance of that which exists in the *civilized* world. Amongst children of different ages, strength, and talents, there must always be tyranny, injustice, and that worst species of inequality, which arises from superior force on the one side, and abject timidity on the other. Of this the spectators of juvenile disputes and quarrels are sometimes sensible, and they hastily interfere and endeavour to part the combatants, by pronouncing certain moral sentences, such as, "Good boys never quarrel; brothers must love and help one another." But these sentences seldom operate as a charm upon the angry passions; the parties concerned hearing it asserted that they must love one another, at the very instant when they happen to feel that they cannot, are still farther exasperated, and they stand at bay, sullen in hatred, or approach hypocritical in reconciliation. It is more easy to prevent occasions of dispute, than to remedy the bad consequences which petty altercations produce. Young children should be kept asunder at all times, and in all situations, in which it is necessary, or probable, that their appetites and passions should be in direct competition. Two hungry children, with their eager eyes fixed upon one and the same bason of bread and milk, do not sympathise with each other, though they have the same sensations; each perceives, that if the other eats the bread and milk, he cannot eat it. Hunger is more powerful than sympathy; but satisfy the hunger of one of the parties, and immediately he will begin to feel for his companion, and will wish that *his* hunger should also be satisfied. Even Mr. Barnet, the epicure, who is so well described in Moore's excellent novel, *after* he has crammed himself to the throat, asks his wife to "try to eat a bit." Intelligent preceptors will apply the instance of the bason of bread and milk in a variety of apparently dissimilar circumstances.

We may observe, that the more quickly children reason, the sooner they discover how far their interests are any ways incompatible with the interests of their companions. The more readily a boy calculates, the sooner he would perceive, that if he were to share his bason of bread and milk equally with a dozen of his companions, his own portion must be small. The accuracy of his mental division would prevent him from offering to part with that share which, perhaps, a more ignorant accountant would be ready to surrender at once, without being on that account more generous. Children, who are accurate observers of the countenance, and who have a superior degree of penetration, discover very early the symptoms of displeasure, or of affection, in their friends; they also perceive quickly the dangers of rivalship from their companions. If experience convinces them, that they must lose in proportion as their companions gain, either in fame, or in favour, they will necessarily dislike them as rivals; their hatred will be as vehement, as their love of praise and affection is ardent. Thus children, who have the most lively sympathy, are, unless they be judiciously educated, the most in danger of feeling early the malevolent passions of jealousy and envy. It is inhuman, and in every point of view unjustifiable in us, to excite these painful feelings in children, as we too often do, by the careless or partial distribution of affection and applause. Exact juftice will best prevent jealousy; each individual submits to justice, because each, in turn, feels the benefit of its protection. Some preceptors, with benevolent intentions, labour to preserve a perfect equality amongst their pupils, and from the fear of exciting envy in those who are inferior, avoid uttering any encomiums upon superior talents and merit. This management seldom succeeds; the truth cannot be concealed; those who feel their own superiority make painful reflections upon the injustice done to them by the policy of their tutors; those who are sensible of their own inferiority are not comforted, by the courtesy and humiliating forbearance with which they are treated. It is therefore best to speak the plain truth; to give to all their due share of affection and applause: at the same time we should avoid blaming one child at the moment when we praise another; we should never put our pupils in contrast with one another, or yet should we deceive them as to their respective excellencies and defects. Our comparison should rather be made between what the pupil *has been*, and what he *is*, than between what he *is*, and what any body else *is not*. By this style of praise we may induce children to become emulous of their former selves, instead of being envious of their competitors. Without deceit or affectation, we may also take care to associate general pleasure in a family with particular commendations; thus if one boy is remarkable for prudence, and another for generosity, we should not praise the generosity of the one at the expence of the prudence of the other, but we should give to each virtue its just measure of applause. If one girl sings, and another draws, remarkably well, we may show that we are pleased with both agreeable accomplishments, without bringing them into comparison. Nor is it necessary that we should be in a desperate hurry to balance the separate degrees of praise which we distribute exactly at the same moment, because if children are sure that the reward of their industry and ingenuity is secured by our justice, they will trust to us, though that reward may be for a few hours delayed. It is only where workmen have no confidence in the integrity or punctuality of their masters, that they are impatient of any accidental delay in the payment of their wages.

With the precautions which have been mentioned we may hope to see children grow up in real friendship together. The whole sum of their pleasure is much increased by mutual sympathy. This happy moral truth, upon which so many of our virtues depend, should be impressed upon the mind; it should be clearly demonstrated to the reason; it should not be repeated as an a priori, sentimental assertion.

Those who have observed the sudden, violent, and surprising effects of emulation in public schools, will regret the want of this *power* in the intellectual education of their pupils at home. Even the acquisition of talents and knowledge ought, however, to be but a secondary consideration, subordinate to the general happiness of our pupils. If we *could* have superior knowledge, upon condition that we should have a malevolent disposition, and an irritable temper, should we, setting every other moral consideration aside, be willing to make the purchase at such a price? Let any person, desirous to see a striking picture of the effects of scholastic competition upon the moral character, look at the life of that wonder of his age the celebrated Abeillard. As the taste and manners of the present times are so different from those of the age in which he lived, we see, without any species of deception, the real value of the learning in which he excelled, and we can judge both of his acquirements, and of his character, without prejudice. We see him goaded on by rivalship, and literary ambition, to astonishing exertions at one time, at another torpid in monkish indolence; at one time we see him intoxicated with adulation, at another listless, desponding, abject, incapable of maintaining his own self-approbation without the suffrages of those whom he despised. If his biographer does him justice, a more selfish, irritable, contemptible, miserable being, than the learned Abeillard could scarcely exift.

A philosopher, who, if we might judge of him by the benignity of his writings, was surely of a most amiable and happy temper, has yet left us a melancholy and discouraging history of the unsociable condition of men of superior knowledge and abilities. He supposes that those who have devoted much time to the cultivation of their understandings, have habitually less sympathy, or less exercise for their sympathy, than those who live less abstracted from the world; that consequently "all their social, and all their public affections, loss their natural warmth and vigour," whilst their selfish passions are cherished and strengthened, being kept in constant play by literary rivalship. It is to be hoped that there are men of the most extensive learning and genius, now living, who could, from their own experience, assure us that those are obsolete observations, no longer applicable to modern human nature. At all events we, who refer so much to education, are hopefully of opinion, that education can prevent these evils, in common with *almost* all the other evils of life. It would be an error, fatal to all improvement, to believe that the cultivation of the understanding impedes the exercise of the social affections. Obviously a man, who secludes himself from the world, and whose whole life is occupied with abstract studies, cannot enjoy any pleasure from his social affections; his admiration of the dead is so constant, that he has no time to feel any sympathy with the living. An individual of this ruminating species is humorously delineated in Mrs. D'Arblay's Camilla. Men, who are compelled to unrelenting labour, whether by avarice, or by literary ambition, are equally to be pitied. They are not models for imitation: they sacrifice their happiness to some strong passion or interest. Without this ascetic abstinence from the domestic and social pleasures of life, surely persons may cultivate their understandings, and acquire, even by mixing with their fellow-creatures, a variety of useful knowledge.

* * *

Without repeating here what has been said in many other places, it may be necessary to remind all who are concerned in *female* education, that peculiar caution is necessary to manage female sensibility; to make, what is called the heart, a source of permanent pleasure, we must cultivate the reasoning powers at the same time that we repress the enthusiasm of *fine feeling*. Women, from their situation and duties in society, are called upon rather for the daily exercise of quiet domestic virtues, than for those splendid acts of generosity, or those exaggerated expressions of tenderness, which are the characteristics of heroines in romance. Sentimental authors, who paint with enchanting colours all the graces and all the virtues in happy union, teach us to expect that this union should be indissoluble. Afterwards, from the natural influence of association, we expect in real life to meet with virtue when we see grace, and we are disappointed, almost disgusted, when we find virtue unadorned. This false association has a double effect upon the conduct of women; it prepares them to be pleased, and it excites them to endeavour to please by adventitious charms, rather than by those qualities which merit esteem. Women, who have been much addicted to common novel-reading, are always acting in imitation of some Jemima, or Almeria, who never existed, and they perpetually mistake plain William and Thomas for "*My Beverly!*" They have another peculiar misfortune; they require continual great emotions to keep them in tolerable humour with themselves; they must have tears in their eyes, or they are apprehensive that their hearts are growing hard. They have accustomed themselves to such violent stimulus, that they cannot endure the languor to which they are subject in the intervals of delirium. Pink appears pale to the eye that is used to scarlet, and common food is insipid to the taste which has been vitiated by the high seasonings of art.

A celebrated French actress, in the wane of her charms, and who, for that reason, began to feel weary of the world, exclaimed, whilst she was recounting what she had suffered from a faithless lover, "Ah c'étoit le bon temps, j'étois bien malheureuse!" ["ah it was a good time, I was very unhappy!"]

The happy age in which women can, with any grace or effect, be romantically wretched, is, even with the beautiful, but a short season of felicity. The sentimental sorrows of any female mourner, of more than thirty years standing, command but little sympathy, and less admiration; and what other consolations are suited to sentimental sorrows?

Women, who cultivate their reasoning powers, and who acquire tastes for science and literature, find sufficient variety in life, and do not require the *stimulus* of dissipation, or of romance. Their sympathy and sensibility are engrossed by proper objects, and connected with habits of useful exertion: they usually feel the affection which others profess, and actually enjoy the happiness which others describe.

AN ESSAY ON THE NOBLE SCIENCE OF
SELF-JUSTIFICATION

"For which an eloquence that aims to *vex*,
"With native tropes of anger arms the sex."

PARNEL.

ENDOWED, as the fair sex indisputably are, with a natural genius for the invaluable art of self-justification, it may not be displeasing to them to see its rising perfection evinced by an attempt to reduce it to a science. Possessed, as are all the fair daughters of Eve, of an hereditary propensity, transmitted to them undiminished through succeeding generations, to be "Soon moved with the slightest touch of blame;" very little precept and practice will confirm them in the habit, and instruct them in all the maxims of self-justification.

Candid pupil, you will readily accede to my first and fundamental axiom—

That a lady can do no wrong. But simple as this maxim may appear, and suited to the level of the meanest capacity, the talent of applying it on all the important, but more especially on all the most trivial, occurrences of domestic life, so as to secure private peace and public dominion, has hitherto been monopolized by the female adepts in the art.

Excuse me for insinuating by this expression, that there may yet be amongst you some novices. To these, if there be any such, I principally address myself.

And now, lest fired with ambition you lose all by aiming at too much, let me explain and limit my first principle, "That you can do no wrong." You must be aware that real perfection is beyond the reach of mortals; nor would I have you aim at it; indeed it is not in any degree necessary to our purpose. You have heard of the established belief in human infallibility which prevailed not many centuries ago, but since that happy period is past, leave the opinions of men to their natural perversity; their actions are the best test of their faith. Instead then of a belief in your infallibility, endeavour to enforce implicit submission to your authority. This will give you infinitely less trouble, and will answer your purpose as well.

Right and wrong, if we go to the foundation of things, are, as casuists tell us, really words of very dubious signification, perpetually varying with custom and fashion, and to be referred to, and adjusted ultimately by no other standards but opinion and force. Obtain power then by all means; power is the law of man; it is his law and yours.

But to return from a frivolous disquisition about right, let me teach you the art of defending the wrong. After having thus pointed out to you the "glorious end" of your labors, I must now instruct you in the equally "glorious means."

For the advantage of my subject I beg to consider you all, ladies, as married; but those who have not as yet the good fortune to have that common enemy, a husband, to combat, may in the mean time practise my precepts upon their fathers, brothers, and female friends; with caution, however, lest by discovering their arms too soon, they preclude themselves from the power of using them to the fullest advantage hereafter. I therefore recommend it to them to prefer, with a philosophical moderation, the future to the present.

Timid brides, you have, probably, hitherto been addressed as angels—Prepare for the time when you shall again become mortal. Take the alarm at the first approach of blame, at the first hint of a discovery that you are any thing less than infallible. Contradict, debate, justify, recriminate, rage, weep, swoon, do any thing but yield to conviction.

I take it for granted that you have already acquired sufficient command of voice; you need not study its compass; going beyond its pitch has a peculiarly happy effect upon some occasions. But are you voluble enough to drown all sense in a torrent of words? Can you be loud enough to overpower the voice of all who shall attempt to interrupt or contradict you? Are you mistress of the petulant, the peevish, and the sullen tones? Have you practised the sharpness which provokes reply, and the continual monotony which effectually precludes it, by setting your adversary to sleep? an event which is always to be considered as decisive of the victory, or at least as reducing it to a drawn battle—You and Morpheus divide the prize.

Thus prepared for an engagement, you will next, if you have not already done it, study the weak part of the character of your enemy—your husband I mean: if he be a man of high spirit, jealous of command, and impatient of controul; one who decides for himself, and is little troubled with the insanity of minding what the world says of him, you must proceed with extreme circumspection; you must not dare to provoke the combined forces of the enemy to a regular engagement, but harrass him with perpetual petty skirmishes; in these, though you gain little at a time, you will gradually weary the patience, and break the spirit of your opponent. If he be a man of spirit, he must also be generous; and what man of generosity will contend so trifles with a woman who submits to him in all affairs of consequence; who is in his power; who is weak, and who loves him.

"Can superior with inferior power contend?" No, the spirit of a lion is not to be roused by the teazing of an insect.

But such a man as I have described, besides being as generous as he is brave, will probably be of an active temper; then you have an inestimable advantage; for he will set a high value upon a thing for which you have none, time; he will acknowledge the force of your arguments merely from a dread of their length; he will yield to you in trifles, particularly in trifles which do not militate against his authority, not out of regard for you, but for his time; for what man can prevail upon himself to debate three hours about what could be as well decided in three minutes.

Left amongst infinite variety, the difficulty of immediate selection should at first perplex you, let me point out that matters of *taste* will afford you, of all others, the most ample and incessant subjects of debate. Here you have no criterion to appeal to. Upon the same principle, next to matters of taste, points of opinion will afford the most constant exercise to your talents. Here you will have an opportunity of citing the opinions of all the living and dead you have ever known, besides the dear privilege of repeating continually: "Nay, you never must allow that." Or, "You can't deny this, for it's the universal opinion — every body says so! every body thinks so! I wonder to hear you express such an opinion! Nobody but yourself is of that way of thinking." With innumerable other phrases with which a slight attention to polite conversation will furnish you. This mode of opposing authority to argument, and assertion to proof, is of such universal utility, that I pray you to practise it.

If the point in dispute especially be some opinion relative to your character or disposition, allow in general that "You are sure you have a great many faults," but to every specific charge, reply, "Well, I am sure I don't know, but I did not think that was one of my faults! nobody ever accused me of that before! Nay, I was always remarkable for the contrary; at least before I was acquainted with you — Sir; In my own family — ask any of my own friends; ask any of them; they must know me best."

But if instead of attacking the material parts of your character, your husband should merely presume to advert to your manners, to some slight personal habit which might be made more agreeable to him; prove in the first place, that it is his fault that it is not agreeable to him. — His eyes are changed, or opened; but it may perhaps have been a matter almost of indifference to him, till you undertook its defence — then make it of consequence by rising in eagerness, in proportion to the insignificance of your object; if he can draw consequences, this will be an excellent lesson — if you are so tender of blame in the veriest trifle, how unimpeachable must you be in matters of importance. As to personal habits, begin by denying that you have any; as all personal habits if they have been of any long standing must have become involuntary, the unconscious culprit may assert her innocence without hazarding her veracity.

However, if you happen to be detected in the very fact, and a person cries, "Now, now, you are doing it!" submit, but declare at the same moment "That it is the very first time in your whole life, you were ever known to be guilty of it; that therefore it can be no habit, and of course no ways reprehensible."

Extend also the rage for vindication to all the objects which the most remotely concern you; take even inanimate objects under your protection. Your dress, your furniture, your property, every thing which is, or has been yours defend, and this upon the principles of the soundest philosophy; these things all compose a part of your personal merit*; all that connected the most distantly with your idea gives pleasure or pain to others, becomes an object of blame or praise, and consequently claims your support or vindication.

In the course of the management of your house, children, family, and affairs, probably some few errors of omission or commission may strike your husband's pervading eye; but these errors, admitting them to be errors, you will never if you please allow to be charged to any deficiency in memory, judgment, or activity, on your part.

There are surely people enough around you to divide and share the blame — send it from one to another, till at last, by universal rejection, it is proved to belong to nobody. You will say however that facts remain unalterable; and that in some unlucky instance, in the changes and chances of human affairs, you may be proved to have been to blame. Some stubborn evidence may appear against you; an eye-witness perhaps; still you may prove an alibi, or balance the evidence. There is nothing equal to balancing evidence; doubt is you know the most philosophic state of the human mind, and it will be kind of you to preserve it in the breast of your husband.

Indeed the short method of denying absolutely all blameable facts, I should recommend to pupils as the best; and if in the beginning of their career as justification, they may startle at this mode, let them depend upon it that in their future practice it must become perfectly familiar. The nice distinction of simulation and dissimulation depends but on the trick of a syllable — palliation and extenuation are universally allowable in self-defence; prevarication inevitably follows, and falsehood "is but in the next degree."

Yet I would not destroy his nicety of conscience too soon, it may be of use. In your first setting out, you must establish credit; in proportion to your credit, will be the value of your future asseverations.

In the mean time, however, argument and debate are allowable to the most rigid moralist. You can never perjure yourself by swearing to a false opinion.

I come now to the art of reasoning: don't be alarmed at the name of reasoning, fair pupils, I will explain to you its meaning.

If instead of the fiery tempered being, I formerly described, you should fortunately be connected with a man, who, having formed a justly high opinion of your sex, should propose to treat you as his equal, and who in any little dispute which might arise between you, should desire no other arbiter than reason; triumph in his mistaken candor, regularly appeal to the decision of reason at the beginning of every contest, and deny its jurisdiction at the conclusion. I take it for granted that you will be on the wrong side of every question, and indeed, in general, I advise you to chuse the wrong side of an argument to defend; whilst you are young in the science, it will afford the best exercise, and as you improve, the best display of your talents.

If then, reasonable pupils, you would succeed in argument, follow pretty nearly these instructions.

Begin by preventing, if possible, the specific statement of any position, or if reduced to it, use the most *general terms*.

Use the happy ambiguity which all languages, and which most philosophers allow. Above all things, shun definitions; they will prove fatal to you; for two persons of sense and candor, who define their terms, cannot argue long without either convincing, or being convinced, or parting in equal good humour; to prevent which, go over and over the same ground, wander as wide as possible from the point, but always with a view to return at last precifely to the same spot from which you set out. I should remark to you that the choice of your weapons is a circumstance much to be attended to: chuse always those which your adversary cannot use. If your husband is a man of wit, you will of course undervalue a talent which is never connected with judgment: for your part, you do not pretend to contend with him in wit.

But if he be a sober minded man, who will go link by link along the chain of an argument, follow him at first, till he grows so intent that he does not perceive whether you follow him or not; then slide back to your own station, and when with perverse patience he has at last reached the last link of the chain, with one electric shock of wit, make him quit his hold, and strike him to the ground in an instant. Depend upon the sympathy of the spectators, for to one who can understand *reason*, you will find ten who admire *wit*.

But if you should not be blessed with "a ready wit," if demonstration should in the mean time stare you in the face, do not be in the least alarmed; anticipate the blow which you could neither foresee, nor prevent. Whilst you have it yet in your power, rise with becoming magnanimity, and cry, "I give it up! I give it up! La! let us say no more about it; I do so hate disputing about trifles. I give it up!" Before an explanation on the word trifle can take place, quit the room with flying colours.

If you are a woman of sentiment and eloquence, you have advantages of which I scarcely need apprise you. From the understanding of a man, you have always an appeal to his heart; or if not, to his *affection*, to his *weakness*. If you have the good fortune to be married to a weak man, always chuse the moment to argue with him when you have a full audience. Trust to the sublime power of numbers; it will be of use even to excite your own enthusiasm in debate; then as the scene advances, talk of his cruelty, and your sensibility, and sink with "becoming woe," into the pathos of *injured innocence*.

Besides the heart and the weakness of your opponent, you have still another chance, in ruffling his *temper*; which, in the course of a long conversation, you will have a fair opportunity of trying; and if, for philosophers will sometimes grow warm in the defence of truth, if he should grow absolutely *angry*, you will in an inverse proportion grow calm, and wonder at his rage, though you well know it has been created by your own provocation. The by-standers, seeing anger without any adequate cause, will all be of your side. Nothing provokes an irascible man, interested in debate, and possessed of an opinion of his own eloquence, so much as to see the attention of his hearers go from him: you will then, when he flatters himself that he has just fixed your eye with his *very best* argument, suddenly grow absent: — "Your house affairs must call you hence — or you have directions to give to your children — or the room is too hot, or too cold — the window must be opened — or door shut — or the candle wants snuffing." — Nay, without these interruptions, the simple motion of your eye may provoke a speaker; a butterfly, or the figure in a carpet may engage your attention in preference to him; or if these objects be absent, the simply averting your eye, looking through the window in quest of outward objects, will shew that your mind has not been abstracted, and will display to him at least your wish of not attending; he may however possibly have lost the habit of watching your eye for approbation; then you may assault his ear. If all other resources fail, beat with your foot that dead march to the spirits, that incessant tattoo, which so well deserves its name. Marvellous must be the patience of the much enduring man, whom some or other of these devices do not provoke; slight causes often produce great effects; the simple scratching of a pick-axe, properly applied to certain veins in a mine, will cause the most dreadful explosions.

Hitherto we have only professed to teach the defensive; let me now recommend to you the offensive part of the art of justification. As a supplement to reasoning, comes recrimination; the pleasure of proving that you are right is surely incomplete, till you have proved that your adversary is wrong; this might have been a secondary, let it now become a primary object with you; rest your own defence on it for farther security; you are no longer to confider yourself as obliged, either to deny, palliate, argue, or declaim, but simply justify yourself by criminating another; all merit, you know, is judged of by comparison. In the art of recrimination, your memory will be of the highest service to you; for you are to pen and keep an account current, of all the faults, mistakes, neglects, unkindnesses of those you live with; these you are to state against your own: I need not tell you that the balance will always be in your favor. In stating matters of opinion, produce the words of the very same person which passed days, months, years before, in contradiction to what he is then saying. By displacing, disjointing words and sentences, by misunderstanding the whole, or quoting only a part of what has been said, you may convict any man of inconsistency; particularly if he be a man of genius and feeling, for he speaks generally from the impulse of the moment, and of all others can the least bear to be charged with paradoxes. So far for a husband. Recriminating is also of sovereign use in the quarrels of friends; no friend is so perfectly equable, so ardent in affection, so nice in punctilio, as never to offend; then "Note his faults and con them by rote." Say you can forgive, but you can never forget; and surely it is much more generous to forgive and remember, than to forgive and forget. On every new alarm, call the unburied ghosts from former fields of battle; range them in tremendous array, call them one by one to witness against the conscience of your enemy, and ere the battle is begun, take from them all courage to engage.

There is one case I must observe to you, in which recrimination has peculiar poignancy. If you have had it in your power to confer obligations on any one, never cease reminding them of it; and let them feel that you have acquired an indefeasible right to reproach them without a possibility of their retorting. It is a maxim with some sentimental people, "To treat their servants as if they were their friends in distress. I have observed that people of this cast make themselves amends, by treating their friends in distress as if they were their servants."

Apply this maxim—you may do it a thousand ways, especially in company. In general conversation, where every one is supposed to be on a footing, if any of your humble companions should presume to hazard an opinion contrary to yours, and should begin with, "I think—" look as the man did when he said to his servant, "You think! Sir—what business have you to think?"

Never fear to lose a friend by the habits which I recommend; reconciliations, as you have often heard it said—reconciliations are the cement of friendship; therefore friends should quarrel to strengthen their attachment, and offend each other for the pleasure of being reconciled.

I beg pardon for digressing—I was, I believe, talking of your husband, not of your friends—I have gone far out of the way.

If in your debates with your husband, you should want "Eloquence to vex him," the dull prolixity of narration, joined to the complaining monotony of voice which I formerly recommended, will supply its place, and have the desired effect; Morpheus will prove propitious; then, ever and anon as the soporific charm begins to work, rouse him with interrogatories, such as, "Did not you say so? Don't you remember? Only answer me that!"

By the bye, interrogatories artfully put may lead an unsuspicious reasoner, you know, always to your own conclusion.

In addition to the patience, philosophy, and other good things which Socrates learned from his wife, perhaps she taught him this mode of reasoning.

But after all, the precepts of art, and even the natural susceptibility of your tempers, will avail you little in the sublime of our science, if you cannot command that ready enthusiasm which will make you enter into the part you are acting; that happy imagination which shall make you believe all you fear and all you invent.

Who is there amongst you who cannot or who will not justify when they are accused. Vulgar talent! the sublime of our science, is to justify before we are accused. There is no reptile so vile but what will turn when it is trodden on; but of a nicer sense and nobler species are those whom nature has endowed with antennæ, which perceive and withdraw at the distant approach of danger. Allow me another allusion; similies cannot be crowded too close for a female taste; and analogy, I have heard, my fair pupils, is your favourite mode of reasoning.

The sensitive plant is too vulgar an allusion; but if the truth of modern naturalists may be depended upon, there is a plant which instead of receding timidly, like the sensitive plant, from the intrusive touch, angrily protrudes its venomous juices upon all who presume to meddle with it: don't you think this plant would be your fittest emblem.

Let me, however, recommend it to you, nice souls, who of the Mimosa kind, "Fear the dark cloud, and feel the coming storm," to take the utmost precaution, lest the same susceptibility which you cherish as the dear means to torment others, should insensibly become a torment to yourselves.

Distinguish then between sensibility and susceptibility; between the anxious solicitude not to give offence, and the captious eagerness of vanity to prove that it ought not to have been taken; distinguish between the desire of praise and the horror of blame; can any two things be more different than the wish to improve, and the wish to demonstrate that you have never been to blame?

Observe, I only wish you to distinguish these things in your own minds; I would by no means advise you to discontinue the laudable practice of confounding them perpetually in speaking to others.

When you have nearly exhausted human patience in explaining, justifying, vindicating,—when in spite of all the pains you have taken, you have more than half betrayed your own vanity, you have a never-failing resource, in paying tribute to that of your opponent, as thus—

> I am sure you must be sensible that I should never take so much pains to justify myself if I were indifferent to your opinion—I know that I ought not to disturb myself with such trifles, but nothing is a trifle to me which concerns you—I confess I am too anxious to please, I know it's a fault, but I can't cure myself of it now—Too quick sensibility, I am conscious, is the defect of my disposition; it would be happier for me if I could be more indifferent I know.

Who could be so brutal as to blame so amiable, so candid a creature? Who would not submit to be tormented with kindness?

When once then your captive condescends to be flattered by such arguments as these, your power is fixed; your future triumphs can be bounded only by your own moderation; they are at once secured and justified.

Forbear not then, happy pupils:—but, arrived at the summit of power, give a full scope to your genius, nor trust to genius alone; to exercise in all its extent your privileged dominion, you must acquire, or rather you must pretend to have acquired, infallible skill in the noble art of physiognomy;

immediately the thoughts as well as the words of your subjects are exposed to your inquisition.

Words may flatter you, but the countenance never can deceive you; the eyes are the windows of the soul, and through them you are to watch what passes in the inmost recesses of the heart. There if you discern the slightest ideas of doubt, blame, or displeasure; if you discover the slightest symptoms of revolt, take the alarm instantly. Conquerors must maintain their conquests, and how easily can they do this, who hold a secret correspondence with the minds of the vanquished? Be your own spies then; from the looks, gestures, slightest motions of your enemies, you are to form an alphabet, a language, intelligible only to yourselves; yet by which you shall condemn them; always remembering that in sound policy, suspicion justifies punishment. In vain, when you accuse your friends of the high treason of blaming you, in vain let them plead their innocence, even of the intention. "They did not say a word which could be tortured into such a meaning." No, but "they looked daggers, though they used none."*

And of this you are to be the sole judge, though there were fifty witnesses to the contrary.

How should indifferent spectators pretend to know the countenance of your friend, as well as you do? You that have a nearer, a dearer interest in attending to it? So accurate have been your observations, that no thought of their soul escapes you; nay, you often can tell even what they are going to think of.

The science of divination, certainly claims your attention; beyond the past and the present, it shall extend your dominion over the future; from slight words, half finished sentences, from silence itself you shall draw your omens, and auguries.

"I am sure you were going to say," or, "I know such a thing was a sign you were inclined to be displeased with me."

In the ardor of innocence, the culprit to clear himself from such imputations, incurs the imputation of a greater offence. Suppose to prove that you were mistaken, to prove that he could not have meant to blame you, he should declare, that at the moment you mention, "You were quite foreign to his thoughts, he was not thinking at all about you."

---

*See Figure 5 (the epigraph on the title page of Collier's *Art of Ingeniously Tormenting*).

Then in truth you have a right to be angry. To one of your class of justificators, this is the highest offence; possessed as you are of the firm opinion, that all persons, at all times, on all occasions, are intent upon you alone. Is it not less mortifying to discover that you were thought ill of, than that you were not thought of at all? "Indifference you know, sentimental pupils, is more fatal to love than even hatred."

Thus my dear pupils, I have endeavoured to provide precepts, adapted to the display of your several talents, but if there should be any amongst you, who have no talents, who can neither argue nor persuade, who have neither, sentiment nor enthusiasm, I must indeed, congratulate them; they alone are the true adepts in the science of Self Justification; indulgent nature, often even in the weakness, provides for the protection of her creatures; just Providence, as the guard of stupidity, has enveloped it with the impenetrable armour of obstinacy.

Fair ideots! let women of sense, wit, feeling, triumph in their various arts, yours are superior. Their empire, absolute as it sometimes may be, is perpetually subject to sudden revolutions. With them, a man has some chance of equal sway, with a fool he has none. Have they hearts and understandings? — then the one may be touched, or the other in some unlucky moment convinced; even in their very power lies their greatest danger — not so with you — In Vain let the most candid of his sex attempt to reason with you; let him begin with, "Now, my dear, only listen to reason—" You stop him at once with "No, my dear, you know I don't pretend to reason; I only say that's my opinion."

Let him go on to prove that yours is a mistaken opinion — you are ready to acknowledge it, long before he desires it. "You acknowledge it may be a wrong opinion; but still it is your opinion." You do not maintain it in the least, either because you believe it to be wrong or right, but merely because it is yours. Exposed as you might have been to the perpetual humiliation of being convinced, nature seems kindly to have denied you all perception of truth, or at least all sentiment of pleasure from the perception.

With an admirable humility, you are as well contented to be in the wrong as in the right; you answer all that can be said to you, with a provoking humility of aspect.

"Yes, I don't doubt but what you say may be very true, but I can't tell; don't think myself capable of judging on these subjects; I am sure you must know much better than I do. I don't pretend to say but what your opinion is very just; but I own I am of a contrary way of thinking; I always thought so and I always shall."

Should a man with persevering temper tell you, that he is ready to adopt your sentiments if you will only explain them; should he beg only to have a reason for your opinion—No, you can give no reason. Let him urge you to say something in its defence—No; like Queen Anne, you will only repeat the same thing over again, or be silent. Silence is the ornament of your sex; and in silence, if there be not wisdom, there is safety. You will then, if you please, according to your custom, sit listening to all entreaties to explain, and speak—with a fixed immutability of posture, and a pre-determined deafness of the eye, which shall put your opponent utterly out of patience; yet still by persevering with the same complacent importance of countenance, you shall half persuade people you could speak if you would; you shall keep them in doubt by that true want of meaning, "which puzzles more than wit;" even because they cannot conceive the excess of your stupidity, they shall actually begin to believe that they themfelves are stupid. Ignorance and doubt are the great parents of the sublime.

Your adversary finding you impenetrable to argument, perhaps would try wit—but, "On the impassive ice, the lightnings play." His eloquence or his kindness will avail less; when in yielding to you after a long debate he expects to please you, you will answer undoubtedly with the utmost propriety, "That you should be very sorry he yielded his judgment to you; that he is very good; that you are much obliged to him; but, that as to the point in dispute, it is a matter of perfect indifference to you; for your part you have no choice at all about it; you beg that he will do just what he pleases; you know that it is the duty of a wife to submit; but you hope however, you may have an opinion of your own."

Remember all such speeches as these will lose above half their effect, if you cannot accompany them with the vacant stare, the insipid smile, the passive aspect of the humbly perverse.

Whilst I write, new precepts rush upon my recollection; but the subject is inexhaustible. I quit it with regret, fully sensible of my presumption in having attempted to instruct those, who whilst they read, will smile in the consciousness of superior powers. Adieu then my fair readers!—Long may you prosper in the practice of an art peculiar to your sex. Long may you maintain unrivalled dominion at home and abroad; and long may your husbands rue the hour when first they made you promise "*to obey.*"

ANNA LAETITIA BARBAULD

(1743–1825)

A poet, essayist, and editor of great versatility and energy, Anna Barbauld was the eldest and only daughter of the nonconformist clergyman and educator Dr. John Aikin and his wife Jane Jennings. She was born in Kibworth, Leicestershire, where her father ran a school for boys. Her brother John, who became a well-known physician and author, encouraged her writing throughout her life. She was precocious as a child, reportedly being able to read at three and going on to read many of the renowned English authors, and learning French and Italian. Her unusual abilities and industriousness finally convinced her father to allow her to learn Latin and Greek, studies usually reserved exclusively for males. Throughout her life, she was extremely shy, a quality she attributed to her early life in the country where she was surrounded almost entirely by boys.

When she was fifteen, her father became a tutor at the Warrington Academy for Dissenters, a well-known center for liberal intellectual thought. There she met Dr. Joseph Priestley, who was then a tutor at the school and who later became famous not only as a scientist but also as a writer of theological and political tracts. Priestley encouraged her to write poetry. Her brother included some of her poems in his *Essay on Song-Writing* (1772) and urged her to publish her own first volume of *Poems* (1773). *Poems* was greatly admired and was reissued four times during its first year. The same year, she exhibited a talent for prose in *Miscellaneous Pieces in Prose*, published with her brother and containing one of her finest essays, "Against Inconsistency in Our Expectations."

At thirty-one, Anna married Rochemont Barbauld, a clergyman of French ancestry, who had been educated at the Warrington Academy. They settled at Palgrave, Suffolk, where Barbauld started a boys' school, which Anna's talents for teaching and management helped to make a success. Unable to have children of their own, the Barbaulds adopted Anna's nephew Charles Rochemont Aikin. Her husband's unstable temperament suffered under the strain of running the school, however, so the Barbaulds closed it and settled in Hampstead where Anna became a friend of Joanna Baillie and her sister, as well as Maria Edgeworth and her father.

During the eleven years at Palgrave, the Barbaulds regularly visited London, where Anna's early admirer Elizabeth Montagu and her publisher Joseph Johnson introduced her to many of the day's literary celebrities, including Hester Chapone and Hannah More. She continued writing, publishing devotional works, hymns, and essays on the education of children. In the early 1790s, she published several political tracts. She also began publishing verse again, including a poem against the slave trade, as well as some of her most amusing verse, which appeared in the *Monthly Magazine*. She contributed fourteen papers to her brother's popular book *Evenings at Home* (1792–95); she also edited the poems of Mark Akenside and William Collins and the letters of Samuel Richardson.

Despite the move to Hampstead, her husband's mental health declined so severely that he had to be shut up in a madhouse. In 1808 he drowned while trying to escape. His death was the great grief of her life, but it also freed her for sustained literary work. She edited a fifty-volume set of *The British Novelists* (1810), complete with critical prefaces and a commentary that represents the first systematic attempt to establish a canon of the eighteenth-century novel. Included in *The British Novelists* are the works of eight women authors. Her literary acquaintance now numbered some of the new "Romantic" writers such as Wordsworth, Coleridge, and Walter Scott. She published her last two works in 1811, an anthology for girls, *The Female Speaker*, and the poem *Eighteen Hundred and Eleven* which was savaged in the *Quarterly Review*. Despite this hostile review, Barbauld did continue to publish (anonymously) as a reviewer for *The Monthly Review*. From 1809 to 1815 (the last year for which *The Monthly Review* kept records of its reviewers), Barbauld published over three hundred notices and reviews of poetry, novels, and educational works. It seems reasonable to assume that she may have published additional reviews in the intervening years between 1815 and her death on March 9, 1825.

EDITION USED: *The Works of Anna Laetitia Barbauld*, ed. Lucy Aikin, 2 vols. (London, 1825).

AGAINST INCONSISTENCY IN OUR EXPECTATIONS

What is more reasonable, than that they who take pains for any thing, should get most in that particular for which they take pains? They have taken pains for power, you for right principles; they for riches, you for a proper use of the appearances of things: see whether they have the advantage of you in that for which you have taken pains, and which they neglect: If they are in power, and you not, why will not you speak the truth to yourself, that you do nothing for the sake of power, but that they do every thing? No, but since I take care to have right principles, it is more reasonable that I should have power. Yes, in respect to what you take care about, your principles. But give up to others the things in which they have taken more care than you. Else it is just as if, because you have right principles, you should think it fit that when you shoot an arrow, you should hit the mark better than an archer, or that you should forge better than a smith.

[Elizabeth] Carter's Epictetus.

AS MOST of the unhappiness in the world arises rather from disappointed desires, than from positive evil, it is of the utmost consequence to attain just notions of the laws and order of the universe, that we may not vex ourselves with fruitless wishes, or give way to groundless and unreasonable discontent. The laws of natural philosophy, indeed, are tolerably understood and attended to; and though we may suffer inconveniences, we are seldom disappointed in consequence of them. No man expects to preserve orange-trees in the open air through an English winter; or when he has planted an acorn, to see it become a large oak in a few months. The mind of man naturally yields to necessity; and our wishes soon subside when we see the impossibility of their being gratified. Now, upon an accurate inspection, we shall find, in the moral government of the world, and the order of the intellectual system, laws as determinate fixed and invariable as any in Newton's Principia. The progress of vegetation is not more certain than the growth of habit; nor is the power of attraction more clearly proved than the force of affection or the influence of example. The man therefore who has well studied the operations of nature in mind as well as matter, will acquire a certain moderation and equity in his claims upon Providence. He never will be disappointed either in himself or others. He will act with precision; and expect that effect and that alone from his efforts, which they are naturally adapted to produce. For want of this, men of merit and integrity often censure the dispositions of Providence for suffering characters they despise to run away with advantages which, they yet know, are purchased by such means as a high and noble spirit could never submit to. If you refuse to pay the price, why expect the purchase? We should consider this world as a great mart of commerce, where fortune exposes to our view various commodities, riches, ease, tranquillity, fame, integrity, knowledge. Every thing is marked at a settled price. Our time, our labour, our ingenuity, is so much ready money which we are to lay out to the best advantage. Examine, compare, choose, reject; but stand to your own judgement; and do not, like children, when you have purchased one thing, repine that you do not possess another which you did not purchase. Such is the force of well-regulated industry, that a steady and vigorous exertion of our faculties, directed to one end, will generally insure success. Would you, for instance, be rich? Do you think that single point worth the sacrificing every thing else to? You may then be rich. Thousands have become so from the lowest beginnings by toil, and patient diligence, and attention to the minutest articles of expense and profit. But you must give up the pleasures of leisure, of a vacant mind, of a free unsuspicious temper. If you preserve your integrity, it must be a coarse-spun and vulgar honesty. Those high and lofty notions of morals which you brought with you from the schools, must be considerably lowered, and mixed with the baser alloy of a jealous and worldly-minded prudence. You must learn to do hard, if not unjust things; and for the nice embarrassments of a delicate and ingenuous spirit, it is necessary for you to get rid of them as fast as possible. You must shut your heart against the Muses, and be content to feed your understanding with plain, household truths. In short, you must not attempt to enlarge your ideas, or polish your taste, or refine your sentiments; but must keep on in one beaten track, without turning aside either to the right hand or to the left. "But I cannot submit to drudgery like this—I feel a spirit above it." 'Tis well: be above it then; only do not repine that you are not rich.

Is knowledge the pearl of price? That too may be purchased—by steady application, and long solitary hours of study and reflection. Bestow these, and you shall be wise. "But (says the man of letters) what hardship is it that many an illiterate fellow who cannot construe the motto of the arms on his coach, shall raise a fortune and make a figure, while I have little more than the common conveniences of life." *Et tibi magna satis!*—Was it in order to raise a fortune that you consumed the sprightly hours of youth in study and retirement? Was it to be rich that you grew pale over the midnight lamp, and distilled the sweetness from the Greek and Roman spring? You have then mistaken your path, and ill employed your industry. "What reward have I then for all my labours?" What reward! A large comprehensive soul, well purged from vulgar fears, and perturbations, and prejudices; able to comprehend and interpret the works of man—of God. A rich, flourishing, cultivated mind, pregnant with inexhaustible stores of entertainment and reflection. A perpetual spring of fresh ideas; and the conscious dignity of superior intelligence. Good heaven! and what reward can you ask besides?

"But is it not some reproach upon the economy of Providence that such a one, who is a mean dirty fellow, should have amassed wealth enough to buy half a nation?" Not in the least. He made himself a mean dirty fellow for that very end. He has paid his health, his conscience, his liberty for it; and will you envy him his bargain? Will you hang your head and blush in his presence because he outshines you in equipage and show? Lift up your brow with a noble confidence, and say to yourself, I have not these things, it is true; but it is because I have not sought, because I have not desired them; it is because I possess something better. I have chosen my lot. I am content and satisfied.

You are a modest man — You love quiet and independence, and have a delicacy and reserve in your temper which renders it impossible for you to elbow your way in the world, and be the herald of your own merits. Be content then with a modest retirement, with the esteem of your intimate friends, with the praises of a blameless heart, and a delicate ingenuous spirit; but resign the splendid distinctions of the world to those who can better scramble for them.

The man whose tender sensibility of conscience and strict regard to the rules of morality makes him scrupulous and fearful of offending, is often heard to complain of the disadvantages he lies under in every path of honour and profit. "Could I but get over some nice points, and conform to the practice and opinion of those about me, I might stand as fair a chance as others for dignities and preferment." And why can you not? What hinders you from discarding this troublesome scrupulosity of yours which stands so grievously in your way? If it be a small thing to enjoy a healthful mind, sound at the very core, that does not shrink from the keenest inspection; inward freedom from remorse and perturbation; unsullied whiteness and simplicity of manners; a genuine integrity

"Pure in the last recesses of the mind;"

if you think these advantages an inadequate recompense for what you resign, dismiss your scruples this instant, and be a slave-merchant, a parasite, or — what you please.

"If these be motives weak, break off betimes;"

and as you have not spirit to assert the dignity of virtue, be wise enough not to forgo the emoluments of vice.

I much admire the spirit of the ancient philosophers, in that they never attempted, as our moralists often do, to lower the tone of philosophy, and make it consistent with all the indulgences of indolence and sensuality. They never thought of having the bulk of mankind for their disciples; but kept themselves as distinct as possible from a worldly life. They plainly told men what sacrifices were required, and what advantages they were which might be expected.

"Si virtus hoc una potest dare, fortis omissis
Hoc age deliciis. . . . ."
["If your object is proper living — whose isn't — and virtue alone can
provide it, be strong in giving up pleasures"]

Horace Ep. 1.6.30

If you would be a philosopher these are the terms. You must do thus and
thus: there is no other way. If not, go and be one of the vulgar.

There is no one quality gives so much dignity to a character as
consistency of conduct. Even if a man's pursuits be wrong and
unjustifiable, yet if they are prosecuted with steadiness and vigour, we
cannot withhold our admiration. The most characteristic mark of a great
mind is to choose some one important object, and pursue it through life.
It was this made Cæsar a great man. His object was ambition; he pursued
it steadily, and was always ready to sacrifice to it every interfering passion
or inclination.

There is a pretty passage in one of Lucian's dialogues, where Jupiter
complains to Cupid that though he has had so many intrigues, he was
never sincerely beloved. In order to be loved, says Cupid, you must lay
aside your ægis and your thunder-bolts, and you must curl and perfume
your hair, and place a garland on your head, and walk with a soft step,
and assume a winning obsequious deportment. But, replied Jupiter, I am
not willing to resign so much of my dignity. Then, returns Cupid, leave
off desiring to be loved — He wanted to be Jupiter and Adonis at the same
time.

It must be confessed, that men of genius are of all others most inclined
to make these unreasonable claims. As their relish for enjoyment is
strong, their views large and comprehensive, and they feel themselves
lifted above the common bulk of mankind, they are apt to slight that
natural reward of praise and admiration which is ever largely paid to
distinguished abilities; and to expect to be called forth to public notice
and favour: without considering that their talents are commonly very
unfit for active life; that their eccentricity and turn for speculation
disqualifies them for the business of the world, which is best carried on
by men of moderate genius; and that society is not obliged to reward any
one who is not useful to it. The poets have been a very unreasonable race,
and have often complained loudly of the neglect of genius and the
ingratitude of the age. The tender and pensive Cowley, and the elegant
Shenstone, had their minds tinctured by this discontent; and even the

sublime melancholy of Young was too much owing to the stings of disappointed ambition.

The moderation we have been endeavouring to inculcate will likewise prevent much mortification and disgust in our commerce with mankind. As we ought not to wish in ourselves, so neither should we expect in our friends contrary qualifications. Young and sanguine, when we enter the world, and feel our affections drawn forth by any particular excellence in a character, we immediately give it credit for all others; and are beyond measure disgusted when we come to discover, as we soon must discover, the defects in the other side of the balance. But nature is much more frugal than to heap together all manner of shining qualities in one glaring mass. Like a judicious painter she endeavours to preserve a certain unity of style and colouring in her pieces. Models of absolute perfection are only to be met with in romance; where exquisite beauty, and brilliant wit, and profound judgement, and immaculate virtue, are all blended together to adorn some favourite character. As an anatomist knows that the racer cannot have the strength and muscles of the draught-horse; and that winged men, griffins, and mermaids must be mere creatures of the imagination; so the philosopher is sensible that there are combinations of moral qualities which never can take place but in idea. There is a different air and complexion in characters as well as in faces, though perhaps each equally beautiful; and the excellencies of one cannot be transferred to the other. Thus if one man possesses a stoical apathy of soul, acts independent of the opinion of the world, and fulfills every duty with mathematical exactness, you must not expect that man to be greatly influenced by the weakness of pity, or the partialities of friendship: you must not be offended that he does not fly to meet you after a short absence; or require from him the convivial spirit and honest effusions of a warm, open, susceptible heart. If another is remarkable for a lively active zeal, inflexible integrity, a strong indignation against vice, and freedom in reproving it, he will probably have some little bluntness in his address not altogether suitable to polished life; he will want the winning arts of conversation, he will disgust by a kind of haughtiness and negligence in his manner, and often hurt the delicacy of his acquaintance with harsh and disagreeable truths.

We usually say—that man is a genius, *but* he has some whims and oddities—such a one has a very general knowledge, *but* he is superficial; &c. Now in all such cases we should speak more rationally did we substitute *therefore* for *but*. He is a genius, *therefore* he is whimsical; and the like.

It is the fault of the present age, owing to the freer commerce that different ranks and professions now enjoy with each other, that characters are not marked with sufficient strength: the several classes run too much into one another. We have fewer pedants, it is true, but we have fewer striking originals. Every one is expected to have such a tincture of general knowledge as is incompatible with going deep into any science; and such a conformity to fashionable manners as checks the free workings of the ruling passion, and gives an insipid sameness to the face of society, under the idea of polish and regularity.

There is a cast of manners peculiar and becoming to each age, sex, and profession; one, therefore, should not throw out illiberal and commonplace censures against another. Each is perfect in its kind. A woman as a woman: a tradesman as a tradesman. We are often hurt by the brutality and sluggish conceptions of the vulgar; not considering that some there must be to be hewers of wood and drawers of water, and that cultivated genius, or even any great refinement and delicacy in their moral feelings, would be a real misfortune to them.

Let us then study the philosophy of the human mind. The man who is master of this science, will know what to expect from every one. From this man, wise advice; from that, cordial sympathy; from another, casual entertainment. The passions and inclinations of others are his tools, which he can use with as much precision as he would the mechanical powers; and he can as readily make allowance for the workings of vanity, or the bias of self-interest in his friends, as for the power of friction, or the irregularities of the needle.

ON PREJUDICE

IT IS to speculative people, fond of novel doctrines, and who, by accustoming themselves to make the most fundamental truths the subject of discussion, have divested their minds of that reverence which is generally felt for opinions and practices of long standing, that the world is ever to look for its improvement or reformation. But it is also these speculatists who introduce into it absurdities and errors, more gross than any which have been established by that common consent of numerous individuals, which opinions long acted upon must have required for their basis. For systems of the latter class must at least possess one property, — that of being practicable; and there is likewise a presumption that they are, or at least originally were, useful; whereas the opinions of the speculatist may turn out to be utterly incongruous and eccentric. The speculatist may invent machines which it is impossible to put in action, or which, when put in action, may possess the tremendous power of tearing up society by the roots. Like the chemist, he is not sure in the moment of projection whether he shall blow up his own dwelling and that of his neighbour, or whether he shall be rewarded with a discovery which will secure the health and prolong the existence of future generations. It becomes us, therefore, to examine with peculiar care those maxims which, under the appearance of following a closer train of reasoning, militate against the usual practices or genuine feelings of mankind. No subject has been more canvassed than education. With regard to that important object, there is a maxim avowed by many sensible people, which seems to me to deserve particular investigation. "Give your child," it is said, "no *prejudices*: let reason be the only foundation of his opinions; where he cannot reason, let him suspend his belief. Let your great care be, that as he grows up he has nothing to unlearn; and never make use of authority in matters of opinion, for authority is no test of truth." The maxim sounds well, and flatters perhaps the secret pride of man, in supposing him more the creature of reason than he really is; but, I suspect, on examination we shall find it exceedingly fallacious. We must first consider what a *prejudice* is. A prejudice is a sentiment in favour or disfavour of any person, practice, or opinion, previous to and independent of examining their merits by reason and investigation. Prejudice is pre-judging; that is, judging previously to evidence. It is therefore sufficiently apparent, that no *philosophical belief* can be founded on mere prejudice; because it is the business of philosophy to go deep into the nature and properties of things: nor can it be allowable for those to indulge prejudice who aspire to lead the public opinion; those to whom the high office is appointed of sifting truth from error, of canvassing the claims of different systems, of exploding old and introducing new tenets. These must investigate with a kind of audacious boldness every subject that comes before them; these, neither imprest with awe for all that mankind have been taught to reverence, nor swayed by affection for whatever the sympathies of our nature incline us to love, must hold the balance with a severe and steady hand, while they are weighing the doubtful scale of probabilities; and with a stoical apathy of mind, yield their assent to nothing but a preponderancy

of evidence. But is this an office for a child? Is it an office for more than
one or two men in a century? And is it desirable that a child should grow
up without opinions to regulate his conduct, till he is able to form them
fairly by the exercise of his own abilities? Such an exercise requires at least
the sober period of matured reason: reason not only sharpened by argu-
mentative discussion, but informed by experience. The most sprightly
child can only possess the former; for let it be remembered, that though
the reasoning powers put forth pretty early in life, the faculty of using
them to effect does not come till much later. The first efforts of a child in
reasoning resemble those quick and desultory motions by which he gains
the play of his limbs; they show agility and grace, they are pleasing to
look at, and necessary for the gradual acquirement of his bodily powers;
but his joints must be knit into more firmness, and his movements
regulated with more precision, before he is capable of useful labour and
manly exertion. A reasoning child is not yet a reasonable being. There is
great propriety in the legal phraseology which expresses maturity, not by
having arrived at the possession of reason, but of that power, the late
result of information, thought, and experience—discretion, which alone
teaches, with regard to reason, its powers, its limits, and its use. This the
child of the most sprightly parts cannot have; and therefore his attempts
at reasoning, whatever acuteness they may show, and how much soever
they may please a parent with the early promise of future excellence, are
of no account whatever in the sober search after truth. Besides, taking it
for granted (which however is utterly impossible) that a youth could be
brought up to the age of fifteen or sixteen without prejudice in favour of
any opinions whatever, and that he is then set to examine for himself
some important proposition,—how is he to set about it? Who is to
recommend books to him? Who is to give him the previous information
necessary to comprehend the question? Who is to tell him whether or no
it is important? Whoever does these will infallibly lay a bias upon his
mind according to the ideas he himself has received upon the subject. Let
us suppose the point in debate was the preference between the Roman
catholic and protestant modes of religion. Can a youth in a protestant
country, born of protestant parents, with access, probably, to hardly a
single controversial book on the Roman catholic side of the question,—
can such a one study the subject without prejudice? His knowledge of
history, if he has such knowledge, must, according to the books he has
read, have already given him a prejudice on the one side or the other; so
must the occasional conversation he has been witness to, the appellations

he has heard used, the tone of voice with which he has heard the words monk or priest pronounced, and a thousand other evanescent circumstances. It is likewise to be observed, that every question of any weight and importance has numerous dependencies and points of connexion with other subjects, which make it impossible to enter upon the consideration of it without a great variety of previous knowledge. There is no object of investigation perfectly insulated; — we must not conceive therefore of a man's sitting down to it with a mind perfectly new and untutored: he must have passed more or less through a course of studies; and, according to the colour of those studies, his mind will have received a tineture, — that is, a prejudice. — But it is, in truth, the most absurd of all suppositions, that a human being can be educated, or even nourished and brought up, without imbibing numberless prejudices from every thing which passes around him. A child cannot learn the signification of words without receiving ideas along with them; he cannot be impressed with affection to his parents and those about him, without conceiving a predilection for their tastes, opinions, and practices. He forms numberless associations of pain or pleasure, and every association begets a prejudice; he sees objects from a particular spot, and his views of things are contracted or extended according to his position in society: as no two individuals can have the same horizon, so neither can any two have the same associations, and different associations will produce different opinions, as necessarily as, by the laws of perspective, different distances will produce different appearances of visible objects. Let us confess a truth, humiliating perhaps to human pride; — a very small part only of the opinions of the coolest philosopher are the result of fair reasoning; the rest are formed by his education, his temperament, by the age in which he lives, by trains of thought directed to a particular track through some accidental association — in short, by *prejudice*. But why, after all, should we wish to bring up children without prejudices? A child has occasion to act, long before he can reason. Shall we leave him destitute of all the principles that should regulate his conduct, till he can discover them by the strength of his own genius? If it were possible that one whole generation could be brought up without prejudices, the world must return to the infancy of knowledge, and all the beautiful fabric which has been built up by successive generations must be begun again from the very foundation. Your child has a claim to the advantage of your experience, which it would be cruel and unjust to deprive him of. Will any father say to his son,

"My dear child, you are entering upon a world full of intricate and perplexed paths, in which many miss their way, to their final misery and ruin. Amidst many false systems, and much vain sciences, there is also some true knowledge; there is a right path: I believe I know it, for I have the advantage of years and experience, but I will instil no prejudices into your mind; I shall therefore leave you to find it out as you can; whether your abilities are great or small, you must take the chance of them. There are various systems in morals; I have examined and found some of a good, others of a bad tendency. There is such a thing as religion; many people think it the most important concern of life: perhaps I am one of them: perhaps I have chosen from amidst the various systems of belief, — many of which are extremely absurd, and some even pernicious, — that which I cherish as the guide of my life, my comfort in all my sorrows, and the foundation of my dearest hopes: but far be it from me to influence you in any manner to receive it; when you are grown up, you must read all the books upon these subjects which you can lay your hands on, for neither in the choice of these would I presume to prejudice your mind: converse with all who pretend to any opinions upon the subject; and whatever happens to be the result, you must abide by it. In the mean time, concerning these important objects you must keep your mind in a perfect equilibrium. It is true you want these principles more now than you can do at any other period of your life; but I had rather you never had them at all, than that you should not come fairly by them."

Should we commend the wisdom or the kindness of such a parent? The parent will perhaps plead in his behalf, that it is by no means his intention to leave the mind of his child in the uncultivated state I have supposed. As soon as his understanding begins to open, he means to discuss with him those propositions on which he wishes him to form an opinion. He will make him read the best books on the subject, and by free conversation and explaining the arguments on both sides, he does not doubt but the youth will soon be enabled to judge satisfactorily for himself. I have no objection to make against this mode of proceeding: as a mode of *instruction*, it is certainly a very good one: but he must know little of human nature, who thinks that after this process the youth will be really in a capacity of judging for himself, or that he is less under the dominion of prejudice than if he had received the same truths from the mere authority of his parent; for most assuredly the arguments on either side will not have been set before him with equal strength or with equal warmth. The persuasive tone, the glowing language, the triumphant retort, will all be reserved for the side on which the parent has formed his own conclusions. It cannot be otherwise; he cannot be convinced himself of what he thinks a truth without wishing to convey that conviction, nor without thinking all that can be urged on the other side weak and futile. He cannot in a matter of importance neutralize his feelings: perfect impartiality can be the result only of indifference. He does not perhaps seem to dictate, but he wishes gently to guide his pupil; and that wish is seldom disappointed. The child adopts the opinion of his parent, and seems to himself to have adopted it from the decisions of his own judgement; but all these reasonings must be gone over again, and these opinions undergo a fiery ordeal, if ever he comes really to think and determine for himself.

The fact is, that no man, whatever his system may be, refrains from instilling prejudices into his child in any matter he has much at heart. Take a disciple of Rousseau, who contends that it would be very pernicious to give his son any ideas of a Deity till he is of an age to read Clarke or Leibnitz, and ask him if he waits so long to impress on his mind the sentiments of patriotism—the civic affection. O no! you will find his little heart is early taught to beat at the very name of liberty, and that, long before he is capable of forming a single political idea, he has entered with warmth into all the party sentiments and connexions of his parent. He learns to love and hate, to venerate or despise, by rote; and he soon acquires decided opinions, of the real ground of which he can know absolutely nothing. Are not ideas of female honour and decorum imprest first as prejudices; and would any parent wish they should be so much as canvassed till the most settled habits of propriety have rendered it safe to do it? In teaching first by prejudice that which is afterwards to be proved, we do but follow Nature. Instincts are the prejudices she gives us: we follow them implicitly, and they lead us right; but it is not till long afterwards that reason comes and justifies them. Why should we scruple to lead a child to right opinions in the same way by which Nature leads him to right practices!

Still it will be urged that man is a rational being, and therefore reason is the only true ground of belief, and authority is not reason. This point requires a little discussion. That he who receives a truth upon authority has not a reasonable belief, is in one sense true, since he has not drawn it from the result of his own inquiries; but in another it is certainly false, since the authority itself may be to him the best of all reasons for believing it. There are few men who, from the exercise of the best powers of their minds, could derive so good a reason for believing a mathematical truth as the authority of Sir Isaac Newton. There are two principles deeply implanted in the mind of man, without which he could never attain knowledge, — curiosity, and credulity; the former to lead him to make discoveries himself, the latter to dispose him to receive knowledge from others. The credulity of a child to those who cherish him is in early life unbounded. This is one of the most useful instincts he has, and is in fact a precious advantage put into the hands of the parent for storing his mind with ideas of all kinds. Without this principle of assent he could never gain even the rudiments of knowledge. He receives it, it is true, in the shape of prejudice; but the prejudice itself is founded upon sound reasoning, and conclusive though imperfect experiment. He finds himself weak, helpless, and ignorant; he sees in his parent a being of knowledge and powers more than his utmost capacity can fathom; almost a god to him. He has often done him good, therefore he believes he loves him; he finds him capable of giving him information upon all the subjects he has applied to him about; his knowledge seems unbounded, and his information has led him right whenever he has had occasion to try it by actual experiment: the child does not draw out his little reasonings into a logical form, but this is to him a ground of belief, that his parent knows every thing, and is infallible. Though the proposition is not exactly true, it is sufficiently so for him to act upon: and when he believes in his parent with implicit faith, he believes upon grounds as truly rational as when, in after life, he follows the deductions of his own reason.

But you will say, I wish my son may have nothing to unlearn, and therefore I would have him wait to form an opinion till he is able to do it on solid grounds. And why do you suppose he will have less to unlearn if he follows his own reason than if he followed yours? If he thinks, if he inquires, he will no doubt have a great deal to unlearn, whichever course you take with him; but it is better to have some things to unlearn, than to have nothing learnt. Do you hold your own opinions so loosely, so hesitatingly, as not to think them safer to abide by than the first results of his stammering reason? Are there no truths to learn so indubitable as to be without fear of their not approving themselves to his mature and well-directed judgment? Are there none you esteem so useful as to feel anxious that he be put in possession of them? We are solicitous not only to put our children in a capacity of acquiring their daily bread, but to bequeath to them riches which they may receive as an inheritance. Have you no mental wealth you wish to transmit, no stock of ideas he may begin with, instead of drawing them all from the labor of his own brain? If, moreover, your son should not adopt your prejudices, he will certainly adopt those of other people; or, if on subjects of high interest he *could* be kept totally indifferent, the consequence would be, that he would conceive either that such matters were not worth the trouble of inquiry, or that nothing satisfactory was to be learnt about them: for there are negative prejudices as well as positive.

Let parents, therefore, not scruple to use the power God and Nature have put into their hands for the advantage of their offspring. Let them not fear to impress them with prejudices for whatever is fair and honourable in action—whatever is useful and important in systematic truth. Let such prejudices be wrought into the very texture of the soul. Such truths let them appear to know by intuition. Let the child never remember the period when he did not know them. Instead of sending him to that cold and hesitating belief which is founded on the painful and uncertain consequences of late investigation, let his conviction of all the truths you deem important be mixed up with every warm affection of his nature, and identified with his most cherished recollections—the time will come soon enough when his confidence in you will have received a check. The growth of his own reason and the development of his powers will lead him with a sudden impetus to examine every thing, to canvass every thing, to suspect every thing. If he finds, as he certainly will find, the results of his reasoning different in some respects from those you have given him, far from being now disposed to receive your assertions as proofs, he will rather feel disinclined to any opinion you profess, and struggle to free himself from the net you have woven about him.

The calm repose of his mind is broken, the placid lake is become turbid, and reflects distorted and broken images of things; but be not you alarmed at the new workings of his thoughts,—it is the angel of reason which descends and troubles the waters. To endeavour to influence by authority would be as useless now as it was salutary before. Lie by in silence, and wait the result. Do not expect the mind of your son is to resemble yours, as your figure is reflected by the image in the glass; he was formed, like you, to use his own judgement, and he claims the high privilege of his nature. His reason is mature, his mind must now form itself. Happy must you esteem yourself, if amidst all lesser differences of opinion, and the wreck of many of your favourite ideas, he still preserves those radical and primary truths which are essential to his happiness, and which different trains of thought and opposite modes of investigation will very often equally lead to.

Let it be well remembered that we have only been recommending those prejudices which go before reason, not those which are contrary to it. To endeavour to make children, or others over whom we have influence, receive systems which we do not believe, merely because it is convenient to ourselves that they should believe them, though a very fashionable practice, makes no part of the discipline we plead for. These are not prejudices, but impositions. We may also grant that nothing should be received as a prejudice which can be easily made the subject of experiment. A child may be allowed to find out for himself that boiling water will scald his fingers, and mustard bite his tongue; but he must be *prejudiced* against ratsbane, because the experiment would be too costly. In like manner it may do him good to have experienced that little instances of inattention or perverseness draw upon him the displeasure of his parent; but that profligacy is attended with loss of character, is a truth one would rather wish him to take upon trust.

There is no occasion to inculcate by prejudices those truths which it is of no importance for us to know till our powers are able to investigate them. Thus the metaphysical questions of space and time, necessity and free-will, and a thousand others, may safely be left for that age which delights in such discussions. They have no connexion with conduct; and none have any business with them at all but those who are able by such studies to exercise and sharpen their mental powers: but it is not so with those truths on which our well-being depends; these must be taught to all, not only before they can reason upon them, but independently of the consideration whether they will ever be able to reason upon them as long as they live. What has hitherto been said relates only to instilling prejudices into *others*; how far a man is to allow them in himself, or, as a celebrated writer expresses it, to *cherish* them, is a different question, on which perhaps I may some time offer my thoughts*. In the mean time I cannot help concluding, that to reject the influence of prejudice in education is itself one of the most unreasonable of prejudices.

---

*The reference is to Edmund Burke's defense of prejudice in *Reflections on the Revolution in France* (1790).

Song 1

Come here, fond youth, whoe'er thou be,
That boasts to love as well as me;
And if thy breast have felt so wide a wound,
Come hither, and thy flame approve;
I'll teach thee what it is to love,   5
And by what marks true passion may be found.

It is to be all bathed in tears;
To live upon a smile for years;
To lie whole ages at a beauty's feet:
To kneel, to languish, and implore;   10
And still, though she disdain, adore: —
It is to do all this, and think thy sufferings sweet.

It is to gaze upon her eyes
With eager joy and fond surprise;
Yet tempered with such chaste and awful fear   15
As wretches feel who wait their doom;
Nor must one ruder thought presume,
Though but in whispers breathed, to meet her ear.

It is to hope, though hope were lost;
Though heaven and earth thy passion crossed;   20
Though she were bright as sainted queens above,
And thou the least and meanest swain
That folds his flock upon the plain, —
Yet if thou darest not hope, thou dost not love.

It is to quench thy joy in tears;   25
To nurse strange doubts and groundless fears:
If pangs of jealousy thou hast not proved, —
Though she were fonder and more true
Than any nymph old poets drew, —
O never dream again that thou hast loved!   30

If when the darling maid is gone,
 Thou dost not seek to be alone,
Wrapt in a pleasing trance of tender woe,
  And muse, and fold thy languid arms,
  Feeding thy fancy on her charms,   35
Thou dost not love,—for love is nourished so.

If any hopes thy bosom share
 But those which Love has planted there,
Or any cares but his thy breast enthrall,—
  Thou never yet his power hast known;   40
  Love sits on a despotic throne,
And reigns a tyrant, if he reigns at all.

Now if thou art so lost a thing,
 Here all thy tender sorrows bring,
And prove whose patience longest can endure: 45
  We'll strive whose fancy shall be lost
  In dreams of fondest passion most;
For if thou thus hast loved, O never hope a cure!

Verses on Mrs. Rowe

Such were the notes our chaster Sappho sung,
And every Muse dropped honey on her tongue.
Blest shade! how pure a breath of praise was thine,
Whose spotless life was faultless as thy line;
In whom each worth and every grace conspire,— 5
The Christian's meekness, and the poet's fire.
Learn'd without pride, a woman without art;
The sweetest manners, and the gentlest heart.
Smooth like her verse her passions learned to move,
And her whole soul was harmony and love. 10
Virtue that breast without a conflict gained,
And easy, like a native monarch, reigned.
On earth still favoured as by Heaven approved,
The world applauded, and Alexis loved.
With love, with health, with fame and friendship blest, 15

And of a cheerful heart the constant feast,
What more of bliss sincere could earth bestow?
What purer heaven could angels taste below?
But bliss from earth's vain scenes too quickly flies;
The golden cord is broke; — Alexis dies!   20
Now in the leafy shade and widowed grove
Sad Philomela mourns her absent love;
Now deep retired in Frome's enchanting vale,
She pours her tuneful sorrows on the gale;
Without one fond reserve the world disclaims,   25
And gives up all her soul to heavenly flames.
Yet in no useless gloom she wore her days;
She loved the work, and only shunned the praise:
Her pious hand the poor, the mourner blest;
Her image lived in every kindred breast.   30
Thynn, Carteret, Blackmore, Orrery approved,
And Prior praised, and noble Hertford loved;
Seraphic Kenn, and tuneful Watts were thine,
And virtue's noblest champions filled the line.
Blest in thy friendships! in thy death, too, blest!   35
Received without a pang to endless rest.
Heaven called the saint matured by length of days,
And her pure spirit was exhaled in praise.
Bright pattern of thy sex, be thou my Muse;
Thy gentle sweetness through my soul diffuse: 40
Let me thy palm, though not thy laurel share,
And copy thee in charity and prayer: —
Though for the bard my lines are far too faint,
Yet in my life let me transcribe the saint.

An Address to the Deity

God of my life! and author of my days!
Permit my feeble voice to lisp thy praise;
And trembling, take upon a mortal tongue
That hallowed name to harps of seraphs sung.
Yet here the brightest seraphs could no more   5

Than veil their faces, tremble, and adore.
Worms, angels, men, in every different sphere
Are equal all, — for all are nothing here.
All nature faints beneath the mighty name,
Which nature's works through all their parts proclaim.   10
I feel that name my inmost thoughts controul,
And breathe an awful stillness through my soul;
As by a charm, the waves of grief subside;
Impetuous Passion stops her headlong tide:
At thy felt presence all emotions cease,   15
And my hushed spirit finds a sudden peace,
Till every worldly thought within me dies,
And earth's gay pageants vanish from my eyes;
Till all my sense is lost in infinite,
And one vast object fills my aching sight.   20

But soon, alas! this holy calm is broke;
My soul submits to wear her wonted yoke;
With shackled pinions strives to soar in vain,
And mingles with the dross of earth again.
But he, our gracious Master, kind as just,   25
Knowing our frame, remembers man is dust.
His spirit, ever brooding o'er our mind,
Sees the first wish to better hopes inclined;
Marks the young dawn of every virtuous aim,
And fans the smoking flax into a flame.   30
His ears are open to the softest cry,
His grace descends to meet the lifted eye;
He reads the language of a silent tear,
And sighs are incense from a heart sincere.
Such are the vows, the sacrifice I give;   35
Accept the vow, and bid the suppliant live:
From each terrestrial bondage set me free;
Still every wish that centres not in thee;
Bid my fond hopes, my vain disquiets cease,
And point my path to everlasting peace.   40

If the soft hand of winning Pleasure leads
By living waters, and through flowery meads,

When all is smiling, tranquil, and serene,
And vernal beauty paints the flattering scene,
O teach me to elude each latent snare,   45
And whisper to my sliding heart—Beware!
With caution let me hear the syren's voice,
And doubtful, with a trembling heart, rejoice.
If friendless, in a vale of tears I stray,
Where briars wound, and thorns perplex my way.   50
Still let my steady soul thy goodness see,
And with strong confidence lay hold on thee;
With equal eye my various lot receive,
Resigned to die, or resolute to live;
Prepared to kiss the sceptre or the rod,   55
While God is seen in all, and all in God.

I read his awful name, emblazoned high
With golden letters on the illumined sky;
Nor less the mystic characters I see
Wrought in each flower, inscribed in every tree;   60
In every leaf that trembles to the breeze
I hear the voice of God among the trees;
With thee in shady solitudes I walk,
With thee in busy crowded cities talk;
In every creature own thy forming power,   65
In each event thy providence adore.
Thy hopes shall animate my drooping soul,
Thy precepts guide me, and thy fears controul:
Thus shall I rest, unmoved by all alarms,
Secure within the temple of thine arms;   70
From anxious cares, from gloomy terrors free,
And feel myself omnipotent in thee.

Then when the last, the closing hour draws nigh,
And earth recedes before my swimming eye;
When trembling on the doubtful edge of fate   75
I stand, and stretch my view to either state:
Teach me to quit this transitory scene
With decent triumph and a look serene;
Teach me to fix my ardent hopes on high,
And having lived to thee, in thee to die.   80

To Mr. Barbauld
NOVEMBER, 14, 1778.

Come, clear thy studious looks awhile,
    'T is arrant treason now
    To wear that moping brow,
When I, thy empress, bid thee smile.

    What though the fading year   5
    One wreath will not afford
    To grace the poet's hair,
    Or deck the festal board;

A thousand pretty ways we'll find
To mock old Winter's starving reign;   10
We'll bid the violets spring again,
Bid rich poetic roses blow,
Peeping above his heaps of snow;
We'll dress his withered cheeks in flowers,
    And on his smooth bald head   15
    Fantastic garlands bind:
    Garlands, which we will get
From the gay blooms of that immortal year,
    Above the turning seasons set,
Where young ideas shoot in Fancy's sunny bowers.   20

    A thousand pleasant arts we'll have
To add new feathers to the wings of Time,
    And make him smoothly haste away:
    We'll use him as our slave,
    And when we please we'll bid him stay,   25
And clip his wings, and make him stop to view
    Our studies, and our follies too;
How sweet our follies are, how high our fancies climb.

    We'll little care what others do,
    And where they go, and what they say;   30

Our bliss, all inward and our own,
Would only tarnished be, by being shown.
   The talking restless world shall see,
   Spite of the world we'll happy be;
         But none shall know   35
         How much we're so,
      Save only Love, and we.

Washing-Day

.................and their voice,
Turning again towards childish treble, pipes
And whistles in its sound. —

The Muses are turned gossips; they have lost
The buskined step, and clear high-sounding phrase,
Language of gods. Come then, domestic Muse,
In slipshod measure loosely prattling on
Of farm or orchard, pleasant curds and cream,   5
Or drowning flies, or shoe lost in the mire
By little whimpering boy, with rueful face;
Come, Muse, and sing the dreaded Washing-Day.
Ye who beneath the yoke of wedlock bend,
With bowed soul, full well ye ken the day   10
Which week, smooth sliding after week, brings on
Too soon; — for to that day nor peace belongs
Nor comfort; — ere the first gray streak of dawn,
The red-armed washers come and chase repose.
Nor pleasant smile, nor quaint device of mirth,   15
E'er visited that day: the very cat,
From the wet kitchen scared and reeking hearth,
Visits the parlour, — an unwonted guest.
The silent breakfast-meal is soon dispatched;
Uninterrupted, save by anxious looks   20

Cast at the lowering sky, if sky should lower.
From that last evil, O preserve us, heavens!
For should the skies pour down, adieu to all
Remains of quiet: then expect to hear
Of sad disasters, — dirt and gravel stains   25
Hard to efface, and loaded lines at once
Snapped short, — and linen-horse by dog thrown down,
And all the petty miseries of life.
Saints have been calm while stretched upon the rack,
And Guatimozin smiled on burning coals;   30
But never yet did housewife notable
Greet with a smile a rainy washing-day.
— But grant the welkin fair, require not thou
Who call'st thyself perchance the master there,
Or study swept, or nicely dusted coat,   35
Or usual 'tendance; — ask not, indiscreet,
Thy stockings mended, though the yawning rents
Gape wide as Erebus; nor hope to find
Some snug recess impervious: shouldst thou try
The 'customed garden walks, thine eye shall rue   40
The budding fragrance of thy tender shrubs,
Myrtle or rose, all crushed beneath the weight
Of coarse checked apron, — with impatient hand
Twitched off when showers impend: or crossing lines
Shall mar thy musings, as the wet cold sheet   45
Flaps in thy face abrupt. Woe to the friend
Whose evil stars have urged him forth to claim
On such a day the hospitable rites!
Looks, blank at best, and stinted courtesy,
Shall he receive. Vainly he feeds his hopes   50
With dinner of roast chicken, savoury pie,
Or tart or pudding: — pudding he nor tart
That day shall eat; nor, though the husband try,
Mending what can't be helped, to kindle mirth
From cheer deficient, shall his consort's brow   55
Clear up propitious: — the unlucky guest
In silence dines, and early slinks away.
I well remember, when a child, the awe
This day struck into me; for then the maids,

I scarce knew why, looked cross, and drove me from them: 60
Nor soft caress could I obtain, nor hope
Usual indulgencies; jelly or creams,
Relic of costly suppers, and set by
For me their petted one; or buttered toast,
When butter was forbid; or thrilling tale   65
Of ghost or witch, or murder—so I went
And sheltered me beside the parlour fire:
There my dear grandmother, eldest of forms,
Tended the little ones, and watched from harm,
Anxiously fond, though oft her spectacles   70
With elfin cunning hid, and oft the pins
Drawn from her ravelled stocking, might have soured
One less indulgent. —
At intervals my mother's voice was heard,
Urging dispatch: briskly the work went on,   75
All hands employed to wash, to rinse, to wring,
To fold, and starch, and clap, and iron, and plait.
Then would I sit me down, and ponder much
Why washings were. Sometimes through hollow bowl
Of pipe amused we blew, and sent aloft   80
The floating bubbles; little dreaming then
To see, Mongolfier, thy silken ball
Ride buoyant through the clouds—so near approach
The sports of children and the toils of men.
Earth, air, and sky, and ocean, hath its bubbles,   85
And verse is one of them—this most of all.

Octogenary Reflections

Say, ye who through this round of eighty years
Have proved its joys and sorrows, hopes and fears, —
Say, what is life, ye veterans, who have trod,
Step following step, its flowery, thorny road?
Enough of good to kindle strong desire,   5
Enough of ill to damp the rising fire,

Enough of love and fancy, joy and hope,
To fan desire and give the passions scope.
Enough of disappointment, sorrow, pain,
To seal the wise man's sentence, All is vain,—   10
And quench the wish to live those years again.
Science for man unlocks her various store,
And gives enough to urge the wish for more;
Systems and suns lie open to his gaze,
Nature invites his love, and God his praise;   15
Yet doubt and ignorance with his feelings sport,
And Jacob's ladder is some rounds too short.
Yet still to humble hope enough is given
Of light from reason's lamp, and light from heaven,
To teach us what to follow, what to shun,   20
To bow the head and say "Thy will be done!"

APPENDIX

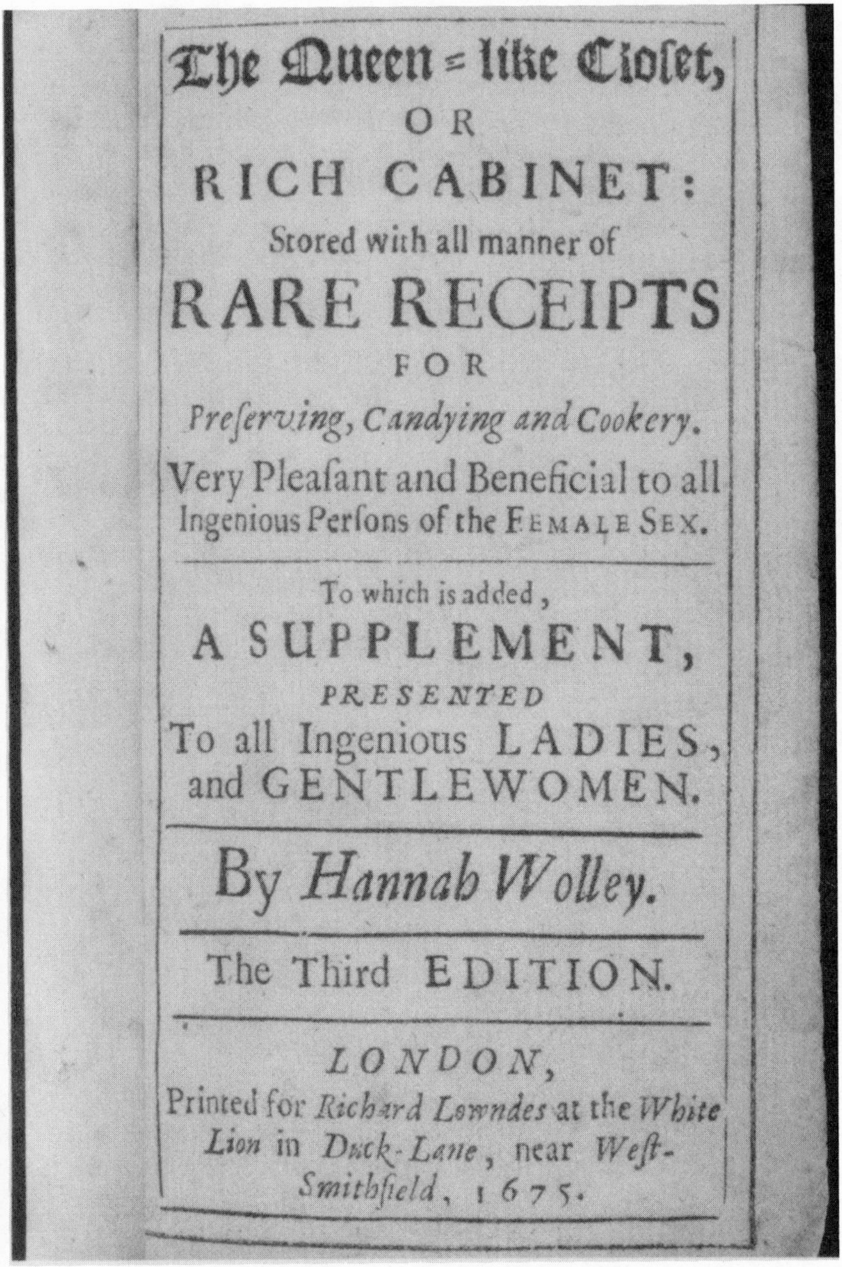

𝕿𝖍𝖊 𝕼𝖚𝖊𝖊𝖓 = 𝖑𝖎𝖐𝖊 𝕮𝖑𝖔𝖘𝖊𝖙,

OR

RICH CABINET:

Stored with all manner of

RARE RECEIPTS

FOR

Preserving, Candying and Cookery.

Very Pleasant and Beneficial to all
Ingenious Persons of the FEMALE SEX.

To which is added,

A SUPPLEMENT,

PRESENTED

To all Ingenious LADIES,
and GENTLEWOMEN.

By *Hannah Wolley.*

The Third EDITION.

LONDON,
Printed for *Richard Lowndes* at the *White
Lion* in *Duck-Lane*, near *West-
Smithfield*, 1 6 7 5.

Figure 1: Title page, Hannah Wooley, *The Queen-like Closet.*

Figure 2: Frontispiece (The Compleat Beau), *An Essay In Defence of the Female Sex* (London, 1696).

Figure 3: Frontispiece, *The Ladies Calling* (Oxford, 1677). This work has been attributed to both Richard Allestree and Lady Dorothy Pakington.

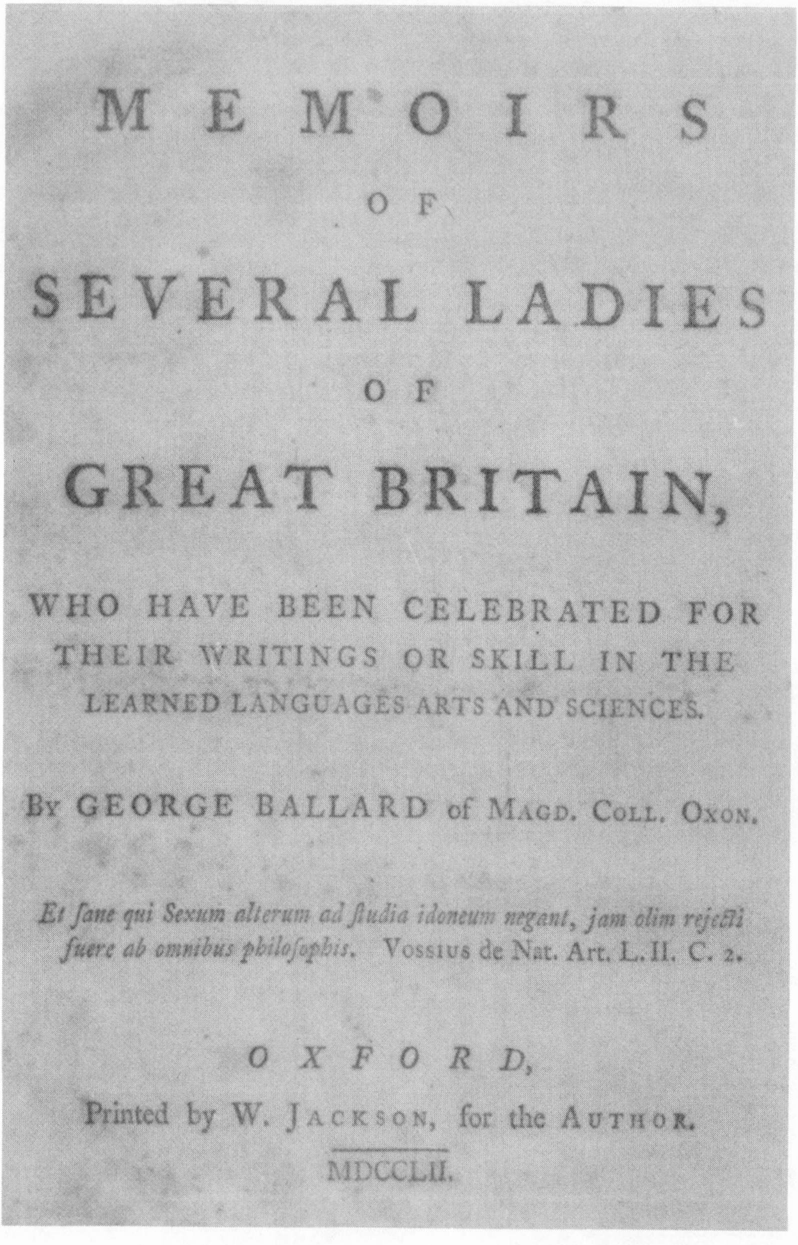

MEMOIRS

OF

SEVERAL LADIES

OF

GREAT BRITAIN,

WHO HAVE BEEN CELEBRATED FOR
THEIR WRITINGS OR SKILL IN THE
LEARNED LANGUAGES ARTS AND SCIENCES.

By GEORGE BALLARD of MAGD. COLL. OXON.

Et fane qui Sexum alterum ad ftudia idoneum negant, jam olim rejecti
fuere ab omnibus philofophis. VOSSIUS de Nat. Art. L. II. C. 2.

OXFORD,

Printed by W. JACKSON, for the AUTHOR.

MDCCLII.

Figure 4: Title page, George Ballard, *Memoirs of Several Ladies of Great Britain* (1752).

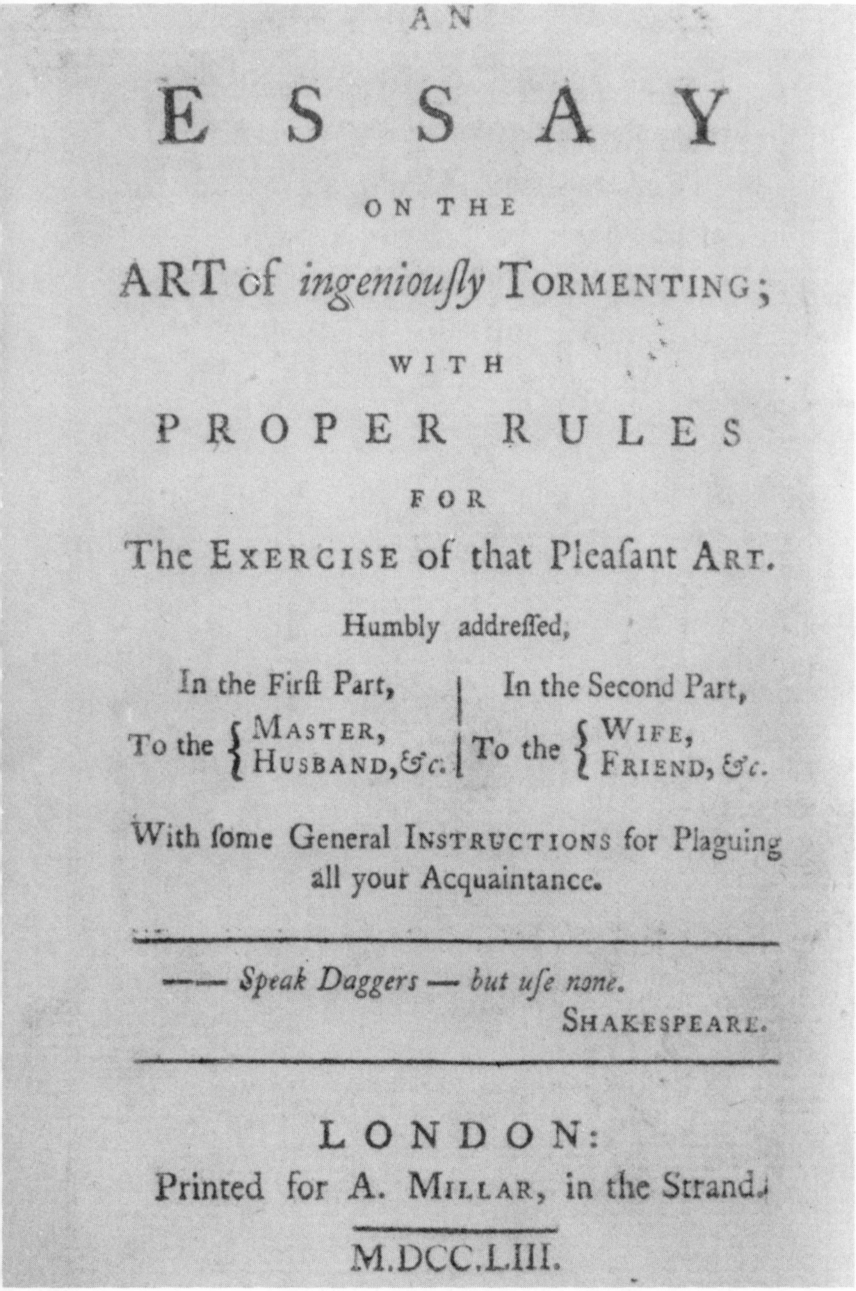

A N

E S S A Y

ON THE

ART of *ingeniously* TORMENTING;

WITH

P R O P E R R U L E S

FOR

The EXERCISE of that Pleafant ART.

Humbly addreffed,

In the Firſt Part,	In the Second Part,
To the { MASTER, HUSBAND, &c.	To the { WIFE, FRIEND, &c.

With fome General INSTRUCTIONS for Plaguing all your Acquaintance.

―――― *Speak Daggers* ― *but ufe none.*
SHAKESPEARE.

L O N D O N:

Printed for A. MILLAR, in the Strand.

M.DCC.LIII.

Figure 5: Title page, Jane Collier, *An Essay on The Art of Ingeniously Tormenting* (London, 1753).

Figure 6: Aphra Behn, Frontispiece, *The Works of Aphra Behn*, ed. Montague Summers (London, 1915).

Figure 7: Katherine Philips. Frontispiece, *Poems By the most deservedly Admired Mrs. Catherine Philips* (London, 1710).

Figure 8: Lady Rachel Russell. Frontispiece. *Letters of Lady Rachel Russell* (London, 1792).

Figure 9: Catherine Talbot. Frontispiece, *The Works of the Late Miss Catharine Talbot* London, 1812).

Engraved by Mackenzie

Eliz. Carter.

Born Dec. 10th 1717.

Died Feby 19th 1806.

From an original Cameo in the possession
of Lady Charlotte Finch.

Figure 10: Elizabeth Carter. Frontispiece, *Memoirs of the Life of Mrs. Elizabeth Carter*, ed. Montagu Pennington (London, 1807).

Lady Mary Wortley Montagu.

1720.

Engraved by Caroline Watson
engraver to her Majesty,
from a picture by Sr Godfrey Kneller in
the collection of the Marquis of Bute.

Published June 1, 1803, by Richard Phillips N°71 St Pauls Church Yard, London.

gure 11: Lady Mary Wortley Montagu. Frontispiece, *The Works of the Right Honoura-*
e *Lady Mary Wortley Montagu* (London, 1803).

Figure 12: Mary Wollstonecraft. Frontispiece, William Godwin, *Memoirs of The Auth* *of A Vindication of The Rights of Woman* (London, 1798).

Figure 13: This beautiful illustration is made from a drawing by Susanna Highmore; it appears in Anna Barbauld's edition of *The Correspondence of Samuel Richardson* (London, 1804). From left to right the figures are: Samuel Richardson (reading from the manuscript of his novel, *Sir Charles Grandison*), Mr. Mulso, Mr. Edward Mulso, Miss Mulso (later Hester Chapone, essayist and poet), Miss Prescott, Reverend John Duncombe (author of *The Feminead*), and Susanna Highmore (later Mrs. Duncombe).